The Big Book of
ADVENTURE TRAVEL

Fourth Edition

ABOUT THE AUTHOR

James C. Simmons is the author of 13 books, more than 500 magazine articles, and hundreds of newspaper articles on travel, history, and wildlife. Raised in Cincinnati, he received his bachelor's degree from Miami University, Ohio, and a doctorate in nineteenth-century British literature from the University of California at Berkeley. Before becoming a freelance writer, he taught courses on British and American literature at Boston University and San Diego State University. His sixth book, *Americans: The View from Abroad*, won first prize as Best Travel Book of 1990 in the Lowell Thomas Competition of Travel Journalism. He has been a member of the Society of American Travel Writers since 1983. His travels over the past three decades have taken him to more than 100 countries. He makes his home in San Diego

Jim also writes privately commissioned life, family, and corporate histories. Please visit his website at www.yourbiography.com.

Also by James C. Simmons

The Novelist as Historian: Essays on the Victorian Historical Novel

Truman Capote: The Story of His Bizarre and Exotic Boyhood (with Marie Rudisill)

The Secrets Men Keep (with Ken Druck)

Passionate Pilgrims: English Travelers to the World of the Desert Arabs

Americans: The View from Abroad

Castaway in Paradise: The Incredible Adventures of True-Life Robinson Crusoes

Star-Spangled Eden: Nineteenth-Century America through the Eyes of Dickens, Wilde, Frances Trollope, and Other British Travelers

The Southern Haunting of Truman Capote (with Marie Rudisill)

The Big Book of
ADVENTURE TRAVEL

Fourth Edition

James C. Simmons

AVALON
TRAVEL
publishing

For Jack Reardon

Big Book of Adventure Travel
Fourth Edition

James C. Simmons

Published by
Avalon Travel Publishing
5855 Beaudry St.
Emeryville, CA 94608, USA

Fourth edition— January 2001
5 4 3 2 1

Please send all comments,
corrections, additions,
amendments, and critiques to:

**Big Book of
Adventure Travel**
AVALON TRAVEL PUBLISHING
5855 BEAUDRY ST.
EMERYVILLE, CA 94608, USA
email: info@travelmatters.com
www.travelmatters.com

Copyright © 2001, 1997, 1995, 1994 by James C. Simmons
Cover © 2001 by Avalon Travel Publishing
© Illustrations, photos, and maps copyright Avalon Travel Publishing, 2001.
All rights reserved.
Some photos and illustrations are used by permission
and are the property of the original copyright owners.

Library of Congress Cataloging-in-Publication Data:
Simmons, James C.
  The big book of adventure travel / James C. Simmons.—4th ed.
     p. cm.
Includes index
  ISBN 1-56691-251-2 (pbk.)
  1. Outdoor recreation—Directories. 2. Safaris—Directories. I.
Title.
  GV191.35 .S56 2001
  796.5'025—dc21
                              00-058280

Editor: Nancy Gillan
Production: Melissa Sherowski
Design: Janine Lehmann
Cover Design: Kari Gim
Illustrations & Typesetting: Diane Rigoli
Front Cover Photo: White Water Rafting/ Karl Weatherly
Back Cover Photos: Bicycling in Alaska/Alaska Bicycle Adventures; Peru's Inca Trail/Bill
Abott, Wilderness Travel; Kayaking in Belize/Lucy Wallingford, SlickRock Adventures

Distributed in the United States and Canada by Publishers Group West
Printed in the United States by Publishers Press

CONTENTS

INTRODUCTION TO ADVENTURE TRAVEL

THE ADVENTURE APPEAL

More and more Americans are agreeing with Helen Keller that "Life is either a daring adventure or nothing at all," and seeking something different from the traditional margarita-by-the-poolside vacation. There has been, in short, a profound revolution in the travel habits of many Americans. People are now more interested in participatory vacation experiences. They want to get involved, not just go along with a group and tour director. They seek change, an alien environment, and, most of all, challenge.

The world has never been more accessible. From the highest mountains to the deepest caverns we can get there, and we do, in ever-increasing numbers. Susan Marg, a photographer from Del Mar, California, recalls a recent adventure-travel trip: "I travel to learn, to meet people, and see new cultures. I try not to have a boring sightseeing trip. My last trip was a two-week cultural expedition through Morocco. We visited numerous areas where outsiders rarely go. And I took a wonderful selection of photographs of the local people and their markets."

All those years of watching *National Geographic* documentaries and "Nova" programs on television have whetted the appetites of many people to see those special places themselves. Organized adventure-travel expeditions represent one of the fastest growing areas in the travel industry. They are marvelous opportunities to learn about diverse habitats, see and photograph rare forms of animal and plant life, and experience some of the most exotic parts of our world. Accompanying naturalists turn such trips into learning experiences through slide shows, lectures, and films that pave the way for a greater understanding of our world's wild places.

For many travelers the major advantages of signing on to an organized adventure-travel trip through an operator are the stimulating companions and great dinner-table conversations they can expect to enjoy. The typical participant possesses a college degree, a keen interest in the outdoors, and a strong commitment to environmentalism. "We offer our clients an opportunity to explore the earth in a supportive environment with compatible trip members and a caring, knowledgeable leader," insists Will Weber, the founder of Journeys International.

But there are other important benefits to traveling with a group on an organized adventure-travel trip. Planning a trip on your own to a remote part of the Third World can often be a frustrating and stressful experience for the individual unfamiliar with the intricacies of distant government bureaucracies. By letting a knowledgeable operator handle all such details, the traveler is then free to focus on the experience itself without the host of distractions the solitary adventurer must endure.

The general public may naively think of adventure travel as the exclusive preserve of the younger generation. But adventure travel has nothing to do with age and everything to do with spirit. Most adventure-travel trip operators know that seniors frequently constitute a majority of their clientele and often put their younger counterparts to shame when it comes to patience and good spirits if events take an unexpected turn for the worse. "I have often noticed that older people have an extra reserve of energy," observes Sven-Olof Lindblad, the president of Special Expeditions.

On the other hand, the field has become so popular that many of the larger operators now offer trips designed for families with small children. For years, Journeys International of Ann Arbor, Michigan, has offered special family trekking expeditions in Nepal. When a youngster gets too tired to walk, he or she can ride in style in a special basket on the back of a Sherpa porter.

Adventure travel will always appeal as long as there is a Walter Mitty buried within us or a Tom Sawyer, struggling to be set free and eager to explore the wonders of McDonougal's Cave.

ADVICE FOR THE NOVICE ADVENTURER

Adventure travel is for people in good health who have open minds, enjoy the outdoors, and want to explore remote and exotic parts of our planet. If that describes you, then you should consider an adventure-travel vacation. The basic ingredient necessary is an inquisitive, adventuresome mind. Having this, prospective adventurers should consider the following advice:

- Start off with an overnight camping experience, perhaps with a local chapter of the Sierra Club.
- Remember that adventure trips are not deluxe tours and often lack certain creature comforts, especially if camping is involved.
- Book your trips through reputable outfitters, who will provide experienced guides with special expertise.
- Investigate the challenges you will face on the trip. Some operators rate adventures on a scale of I through V in terms of difficulty. Properly evaluating the fitness requirements—and making certain you meet them—can make the difference between the adventure or the fiasco of a lifetime. If in doubt, describe your physical condition to the operator and ask his/her advice. If you are not in great shape, then consider starting with something less physically challenging, such as an expeditionary cruise or a barge trip along a French canal. Most operators insist that people do a pretty good job of evaluating their own condition and few get in over their heads.
- Be safety-conscious and prudent at all times. Adventure travel can be as safe or as dangerous as you want to make it. The surest way to cut the risk to a minimum is not to do it on your own but rather to go with a reputable operator. Major operators will handle hundreds of clients every year and not have one serious injury. They have excellent safety records because with each group they send competent guides who know the areas and the risks involved and work to minimize them. Of course, some kinds of adventure travel (white-water kayaking, for instance) inherently involve more risk than others (such as tall-ship cruising in the Caribbean). If you have any questions about the risks involved, talk to the operator and ask for the names of previous participants whom you could call.
- And finally, always strive to maintain a flexible attitude when traveling through wilderness areas and Third World countries. Understand that no operator can guarantee you real adventure and accept the fact that the farther off the beaten path you go, the less predictable your journey will be.

HOW TO USE THIS BOOK

The Big Book of Adventure Travel is divided into two sections, Land Adventures and Water Adventures. Each section is divided further into activities offered within that category. In turn, each activity is divided into major geographic regions. All seven continents are used for these divisions, as well as the major oceans and seas, such as the Pacific and the Caribbean. Trips are listed alphabetically by country. The United States and Canada are treated as distinct geographic areas and are subdivided into states or provinces.

PRICE: All trips are rated as inexpensive, moderate, or expensive, depending upon their cost per day. The breakdown is as follows:

Inexpensive: under $100/day
Moderate: between $100 and $200/day
Expensive: over $200/day

COUPONS: Most of the operators listed here offer readers of *The Big Book of Adventure Travel* a five or ten percent discount. Many have extended this discount to include all the trips in their catalogs. In order to qualify for this reduction, readers must submit the original operator's coupon (found in the back of the book) when they reserve space on a trip. In most cases, the operator will then give them a credit toward their final payment. Each coupon can be used only once and for only one person. Couples will have to purchase two copies of the book. Readers should contact the individual operators to see what restrictions, if any, apply to their coupons.

IMPORTANT NOTICE

Readers must understand that many forms of adventure travel involve a certain amount of risk. Neither James C. Simmons nor Avalon Travel Publishing has a financial interest in any of the operators whose trips are described in this book. Therefore, neither the author nor the publisher can assume any responsibility whatsoever for the operators and the quality of their trips, nor for any injury, death, loss, or property damage brought about by any reader's participation in the trips described in The Big Book of Adventure Travel. *Readers take these trips at their own risk.*

LAND ADVENTURES

"The adventurer is within us, and he contests for our favor with the social man we are obliged to be."

WILLIAM BOLITHO,
Twelve Against the Gods

1
BACKPACKING, TREKKING, AND HIKING EXPEDITIONS

Religious artifacts line the trail sides in Nepal
Steve Conlon/Above the Clouds Trekking

"Know how to tramp and you know how to live," insisted Stephen Graham in his classic 1926 book, *The Gentle Art of Tramping.* "Know how to meet your fellow wanderer, how to be passive to the beauty of nature and how to be active to its wildness and its rigor. Tramping brings one to reality."

Walking is the first thing a child learns and the last thing an older person wants to give up. Few forms of exercise provide greater enjoyment or more benefits. Hiking and walking today are more popular than ever before. In America, the opportunities for exploring wilderness by foot are virtually unlimited. Our national park system boasts over 12,000 miles of scenic trails, while the U.S. Forest Service maintains another 100,000 miles. The most ancient form of travel known to man, hiking offers the most intimate means by which one can explore new cultures and environments.

Today in the organized adventure travel industry, hiking refers primarily to a walk between inns or huts, in which the participants carry only light packs or none at all. For longer trips, treks are now the most popular form of travel; porters or pack animals carry all the expedition's baggage and supplies, leaving participants free of heavy burdens to enjoy the trail and scenery. Independent hikers usually prefer backpacking, carrying on their backs everything they need to make themselves self-sufficient in the wilderness.

AFRICA

TANZANIA

The Kilimanjaro Trek

Operator: Mountain Travel-Sobek, 6420 Fairmount Ave., El Cerrito, Calif. 94530; (888) 687-6235 or (510) 527-8100; www.mtsobek.com. *Price:* Expensive. *Season:* Throughout the year. *Length:* 18 days. *Accommodations:* Tented camps and mountain huts. Five percent discount with BBAT coupon.

Few of the world's mountains enjoy the majesty and mystique of Kilimanjaro, at 19,340 feet the highest mountain in Africa. The grueling, nontechnical climb to its summit tests minds as well as bodies. This expedition includes a seven-day climb along the popular Marangu route, staying nights in mountain huts. Porters carry all the gear. Participants are not required to have any technical climbing skills. One day is spent on the enormous summit, which is crowned with no fewer than 15 glaciers flowing off three ice fields. Before the trek, the group spends several days visiting Manyara and Ngorongoro Crater National Parks, remarkable places to see the full realm of East African wildlife. Trekkers also make a warm-up hike to the top of Mt. Meru Crater.

ZAMBIA

Walking Safari

Operator: Wilderness Travel, 1102 Ninth St., Berkeley, Calif. 94710; (800) 368-2794 or (510) 558-2488; www.wildernesstravel.com. *Price:* Expensive. *Season:* June–mid-September. *Length:* 13 days. *Accommodations:* Thatch huts, tent camps, and lodges. Five percent discount with BBAT coupon.

Travelers on this safari literally walk in the footsteps of elephants, hippos, and lions, leopards, and their prey as they experience Africa in a much more primal way than those visitors who view their game from inside vehicles. Five days are spent on a foot safari through the "Valley of the Elephants" in South Luanga National Park, a 5,000-square-mile chunk of unspoiled Africa. Trekkers are accompanied by highly skilled, armed wildlife guides. The first two days are spent exploring from Luwi Bush Camp, a remote and unusual woodland area rich in hartebeests, roans, and reedbucks. For the next three days participants walk along the Mupamadzi River, which supports an abundance of wildlife.

A walking safari offers great potential for the close observation of some of Africa's biggest game

James Sano/Geographic Expeditions

ZIMBABWE

The Hunters and the Hunted: A Foot Safari Through the African Bush

For those travelers tired of landscapes flooded with garishly painted vans converging on hapless wildlife, this is a chance to experience Africa as the early British explorers did, by an expeditionary foot safari through the bush. Groups on these adventures are strictly limited to six people plus the guides, men who once worked as professional hunters and know the animals and countryside intimately. Trekkers carry their own backpacks and walk in the cool hours of the morning. The heat of the day is spent at watering holes to observe the wildlife there. Five days are spent in Matobo National Park, tracking rhinos, visiting Bushman caves with their colorful wall paintings, and climbing to remote black-eagle breeding sites. Another five days are then spent trekking through Hwange National Park, home to 40,000 elephants and large numbers of cape buffalo and lions along with 400 species of birds. Nights are spent sleeping in the open.

Operator: Geographic Expeditions, 2627 Lombard St., San Francisco, Calif. 94123; (800) 777-8183 or (415) 922-0448; www.geoex.com.
Price: **Expensive.**
Season: June–September.
Length: 14 days.
Accommodations: Lodges and tent camps. Five percent discount with BBAT coupon.

ANTARCTICA

In the Footsteps of Ernest Shackleton Across South Georgia Island

Operator: Geographic Expeditions, 2627 Lombard St., San Francisco, Calif. 94123; (800) 777-8183 or (415) 922-0448; www.geoex.com. *Price:* Expensive. *Season:* November. *Length:* 23 days. *Accommodations:* Shipboard cabins and wilderness camps. Five percent discount with BBAT coupon.

About the size of Long Island, South Georgia is an inhospitable but beautiful world of craggy and precipitous mountains of alpine proportions. Great tongues of glacial ice and snow spill down from the cloud-covered heights to the frigid sea below. Around its fringes the pebble beaches and grassy slopes teem with one of the richest concentrations of wildlife to be found anywhere—fur and elephant seals, gentoo and king penguins, and thousands of seabirds. In 1914 Ernest Shackleton set sail from here on the ill-fated expedition which was to win him a permanent place in the annals of courage and survival. This rigorous and demanding expedition retraces the route of Shackleton's heroic crossing of the island's glaciers and mountains, the final leg in his epic effort to save his shipmates stranded on Elephant Island 800 miles to the west. A visit will also be made to Grytviken, a well-preserved whaling station where Shackleton's body is buried in the small cemetery.

ASIA

BHUTAN

The Complete Bhutan: West to East

Of the handful of kingdoms still existing today, only one is genuinely medieval. In Bhutan, the last true Buddhist kingdom in the Himalayas, both the king and his subjects wear the same simple robes. Here, in a country so isolated that even nails are still a novelty, the visitor finds preserved the most traditional Buddhist lifestyle in Asia. This trek is

Trekkers through the Bhutanese high country find both spectacular mountain scenery and an abundance of local culture

Steve Conlon/Above the Clouds Trekking

designed to give participants an authentic taste of each of Bhutan's distinct regions, while at the same time allowing time for a five-day trek in the remote heart of the kingdom. Trekkers begin their walk at the end of the road in Chakhar, the central valley of Bumthang, and soon visit several Buddhist monasteries and temples, all reachable only by foot. Crossing a high pass, the group descends into the Tang Valley. On the final two days they hike over a ridge into the remote valley of Ura and camp in the heart of a pine forest. The trekking portion of the trip ends in the rarely visited village of Shingkar.

Operator: Above the Clouds Trekking, 115 Spencer Hill Rd., Hinesburg, Vt. 05461; (800) 233-4499 or (802) 482-4848; www.aboveclouds.com. **Price:** Expensive. **Season:** April, May, October, and November. **Length:** 15 days. **Accommodations:** Tent camps and guest houses. Five percent discount with BBAT coupon.

"Little boys love machines; girls adore horses. Grown men and women like to walk."

EDWARD ABBEY
A VOICE CRYING IN THE WILDERNESS

CHINA

Tibetan Walking Adventure

Operator:
Worldwide Adventures,
1170 Sheppard Ave. West,
#45, Toronto, Ont., Canada
M3K 2A3; (800) 387-1483
or (416) 633-5666;
www.worldwidequest.com.
Price: Moderate.
Season: May, June,
and October.
Length: 15 days.
Accommodations: Hotels with
two nights of tent camp.
Five percent discount with
BBAT coupon.

Tibet, the ancient "Roof of the World" and the mystical "Kingdom of the Snows," has for the last century evoked images of a lost Shangri-la. The operator has built this popular trip around a series of day hikes designed to enhance the participants' understanding of the country's rich cultural history. Visits to famous Dzongs (forts) and monasteries in Lhasa, Shigatse, and Gyantse allow travelers to experience ancient Tibet, while a side trip to Rongphu Monastery provides a fabulous view of the sheer North Face of Mt. Everest.

MALAYSIA

Trekking, Caving, Rafting, and Kayaking on Borneo

Operator:
Outer Edge Expeditions,
4830 Mason Rd., Howell,
Mich. 48843; (800) 322-
5235 or (517) 552-5300;
www.outer-edge.com.
Price: Moderate.
Season: April and
September.
Length: 16 days.
Accommodations: Hotels
and lodges. Five percent
discount with BBAT
coupon.

Once famous for its fierce headhunters, Borneo is an almost-mythical island with a richness of natural and cultural treasures few other Asian regions can match. Participants on these expeditions can expect to have their arduous traveling rewarded with sights and experiences few travelers have known. They begin with a two-day climb of 13,455-foot Mt. Kinabalu, the highest peak in Southeast Asia. Later adventures include an exploration of the rain-forest canopy by means of a walkway high above the jungle floor below; white-water rafting the Padas River's Class IV rapids; two days of underground exploration in the Clearwater Cave, the largest system in Southeast Asia; kayaking another stretch of the Padas River rich in wildlife; and two days in a jungle longhouse with Iban tribespeople, once notorious for their headhunting.

Monasteries and mountains are two of the main attractions drawing trekkers to Nepal

Steve Conlon/Above the Clouds Trekking

NEPAL

The Forbidden Kingdom of Mustang

Tightly sealed off from the outside world until 1992, the tiny kingdom of Mustang preserves within its boundaries a culture and a way of life little changed over the centuries. Culturally, it is a part of Tibet that escaped the corrosive impact of the Chinese occupation, more Tibetan than Tibet itself, with Tibetan Buddhist monasteries that predate any monasteries in Tibet and a well-preserved Tibetan Buddhism. This moderate trek offers perhaps the best way to explore the culture and sights of Mustang, where only a handful of foreigners have penetrated. The first several days are spent hiking along the bottom of the Kali Gandaki River gorge, one of the deepest in Asia, an area inhabited by Thakali locals, before entering a region populated by the Gurung people, visiting towns along the way. Lunch will be taken one day at Lo Gyekar monastery, which is older than the oldest monastery in Tibet. A highlight is an overnight visit to the large medieval village of Lo Manthang, one of the last walled cities in the world in which the wall is intact and functional.

Operator: Above the Clouds Trekking, 115 Spencer Hill Rd., Hinesburg, Vt. 05461; (800) 233-4499 or (802) 482-4848; www.aboveclouds.com. *Price:* Expensive. *Season:* April, May, and September. *Length:* 15 days. *Accommodations:* Tent camps. Five percent discount with BBAT coupon.

Classic Trek Around Annapurna

Operator:
Mountain Travel-Sobek,
6420 Fairmount Ave., El
Cerrito, Calif. 94530;
(888) 687-6235 or
(510) 527-8100;
www.mtsobek.com.
Price: Moderate.
Season: April and October.
Length: 31 days.
Accommodations: Hotels and
tent camps. Five percent
discount with BBAT
coupon.

The 10th-highest mountain in the world, Annapurna-I (26,540 feet) is actually just one of several awesome monuments bearing the same name scattered along a 64-mile-long massif. This lengthy expedition, which includes 24 days of strenuous hiking, begins in the lush valley of the Marsyandi River (first opened to foreigners in 1977) and follows ancient Tibetan-Nepalese trade routes through Hindu and Buddhist hill villages. In the Manang Valley, trekkers encounter gypsy traders of Tibetan origins whose villages are picturesque clusters of medieval stone huts. The women wear their wealth in chunks of turquoise or lumps of coal. From Manang, the trail climbs abruptly from dense forests to alpine pastures. The expedition crosses north of the Annapurna massif at Thorong La pass (17,771 feet) and descends past many Hindu and Buddhist shrines. Sherpa porters and pack animals carry all personal baggage.

The Adventure Travel Hall of Fame:
JOE NARDONE

Nearly 4.5 million foot-steps, 15 blisters, five rat-tlesnake encounters, and 153 days after he started, Joe Nardone, on September 3, 1994, became the first person to walk the Pony Express trail in its entirety. The 52-year-old retired real-estate agent from Laguna Hills, California, started his adventure on April 3 at the former Pony Express head-quarters in St. Joseph, Missouri, where the trail and the short-lived business had started 134 years ago that day. From there he walked the length of the 2,000-mile trail that riders on horseback used from April of 1860 to November of 1861 to transport mail to California.

Backed up by a friend in a van, he walked an average of 20 miles a day through rain and snow. Along the way he put monuments at six station sites and gave 28 lectures on the trail's history. When he finished, he did not take a break from his obsession. Instead he sat down at his computer and wrote a book about the trail and his hike.

Mt. Everest from Gokyo

Because more than 10,000 trekkers a year were crowding the trail to the Mt. Everest Base Camp, an alternative route to the world's most famous mountain was developed. Trekkers on this route walk through the serene and scenic Gokyo Lakes district along a trail that offers superb views of Everest and several other 8,000-meter peaks, including Lhotse, Makalu, and Cho Oyu. Highlights include the lovely villages in the Khumbu where, in 1974, the last sighting of a yeti occurred; a climb of Goky Ri (17,990 feet) for what many regard as the finest view of Everest; and a visit to the fabled Thyangboche monastery, situated in what many regard as the most beautiful spot in Nepal. This popular trek fills up quickly, so make your reservations early.

Operator:
Above the Clouds Trekking, 115 Spencer Hill Rd., Hinesburg, Vt. 05461; (800) 233-4499 or (802) 482-4848; www.aboveclouds.com.
Price: Expensive.
Season: April and October.
Length: 19 days.
Accommodations: Tent camps. Five percent discount with BBAT coupon.

The Jaljale Himal High Ridge Trek

The operator pioneered this trek back in 1987, and it is now on the way to becoming a classic. The route offers a pristine Himalayan wilderness with numerous views of four of the world's five tallest peaks (including Mt. Everest), friendly people, and an absence of other trekkers along the trail—just yak-herders and pilgrims! The villagers in this part of Nepal have rarely seen other trekkers, and continue in their dress and customs an uncorrupted tradition of medieval Nepal. Some highlights of the trek are the town of Chainpur, where families put their wealth into bronze castings produced by the lost-wax casting method, which is much prized throughout the Himalayan region; Kangchenjunga Pathibhara, a pilgrims' destination where Hindus from all over eastern Nepal congregate to climb a steep, rocky stairway to make animal sacrifices; and the colorful bazaar in the market town of Taplejung.

Operator:
Above the Clouds Trekking, 115 Spencer Hill Rd., Hinesburg, Vt. 05461; (800) 233-4499 or (802) 482-4848; www.aboveclouds.com.
Price: Expensive.
Season: October.
Length: 24 days.
Accommodations: Tent camps. Five percent discount with BBAT coupon.

VIETNAM

Vietnam Trails

Operator: Himalayan Travel/Peregrine, 110 Prospect St., Stamford, Conn. 06901; (800) 225-2380; (203) 359-3711; www.gorp.com/ himtravel.htm. **Price:** Inexpensive. **Season:** Throughout the year. **Length:** 22 days. **Accommodations:** Hotels, longhouses, and village huts. Five percent discount with BBAT coupon.

This journey for the adventurous traveler visits the relatively unexplored remote and beautiful Central Highlands before continuing on to northern Vietnam and the scenic Halong Bay and Hanoi. The centerpieces are challenging hikes: first, through the Central Highlands, passing through traditional Montagnard villages with one night spent in a remote and traditional Bahnar village; and then a second trek through remote Hoa Binh Province in northern Vietnam among its traditional hill people. Trekkers can expect considerable cultural contacts with a variety of ethnic groups, including the Muong, Hmong, and Thai, as they walk through a landscape of rice paddies, bamboo groves, clusters of farm buildings, and isolated villages. At other times participants travel by bus, elephant-back, riverboat, and bus to visit a variety of special destinations, including floating markets, the imperial city of Hue, and the 3,000 spectacular limestone islands of Halong Bay.

AUSTRALASIA

AUSTRALIA

Inn-to-Inn Hiking Through Tasmania

Operator: Wilderness Travel, 1102 Ninth St., Berkeley, Calif. 94710; (800) 368-2794 or (510) 558-2488; www.wildernesstravel.com. **Price:** Expensive. **Season:** February, March, and November.

Proclaimed a World Heritage site, Tasmania offers dramatic peaks and mirror-like lakes, incomparable beaches and seascapes, rare temperate rain forests, and a spectacular wild river, the Franklin. The fact that it lies 150 miles off the southern coast of Australia has kept Tasmania uncongested, tidy, and fresh. It is, as Australians say, a "two-lane island," which makes it the perfect place for bush-hiking. The highlights include the coastal Abestos

Range National Park with its Forester kangaroos, wallabies, and wombats; a night search for the elusive Tasmanian devil; and a walk through the ancient forests of Franklin-Gordon Wild Rivers National Park.

Length: 13 days.
Accommodations: Lodges, hotels, and cabins. Five percent discount with BBAT coupon.

NEW ZEALAND

Lodge-to-Lodge Trek Along the Milford Track

One of the world's greatest treks, the Milford Track is 34 miles of well-maintained trail through beech rain forests and moss-covered fern forests, across swinging bridges that span thundering rivers, and over the McKinnon Pass (3,800 feet). The walk terminates at Milford Sound, New Zealand's most spectacular fjord. There hikers can rest their feet on a cruise across the sound, where they can expect to see dolphins, penguins, and fur seals.

Operator:
Adventure Center,
1311 63rd St., Suite 200,
Emeryville, Calif. 94608;
(800) 227-8747 or
(510) 654-1879;
www.adventure-center.com.
Price: Moderate.
Season: November–March.
Length: 5 days.
Accommodations: Lodges in dormitory-style sleeping rooms. Five percent discount with BBAT coupon.

PAPUA NEW GUINEA

Kokoda Trail Trek

One of Asia's classic walks, the Kokoda Trail winds over the knife-edged ridges and through the jungle-covered valleys of southern New Guinea. In 1942, Australian and Japanese forces fought a bloody campaign here for the control of Port Moresby; 12,000 Japanese and 6,000 Australian soldiers died in the seven months of bitter fighting. The Kokoda Trail runs through the heart of this battlefield. Trekkers still find rusting helmets, Bren guns, and unexploded ammunition scattered throughout the bush, and occasional piles of human bones that bear mute testimony to the violence of the conflict.

Operator:
Himalayan Travel/Peregrine,
110 Prospect St.,
Stamford, Conn. 06901;
(800) 225-2380;
(203) 359-3711;
www.gorp.com/himtravel.htm
Price: Moderate.
Season: June and September.
Length: 15 days.
Accommodations: Jungle camps. Five percent discount with BBAT coupon.

"My idea of hell is having to stay in one place for a long time. My idea of a holiday is going home."
PAUL THEROUX
NATIONAL GEOGRAPHIC MAGAZINE, SEPTEMBER 1989

CANADA

NEW BRUNSWICK

Hiking the Maritime Coast of the Bay of Fundy

Operator: New England Hiking Holidays, P.O. Box 1648, North Conway, N.H. 03860; (800) 869-0949 or (603) 356-9696; www.nehikingholidays.com. *Price:* Moderate. *Season:* July–September. *Length:* 5 days. *Accommodations:* Hotels. Ten percent discount with BBAT coupon.

Located just over the border from Maine, the enormous Bay of Fundy stretches for 94 miles and is 32 miles wide at its mouth. The bay is famous for its swift tidal currents, with 70-foot tides occasionally recorded. Settled in the 1660s, the coast offers hikers unmatched scenery and huge flocks of migrating shorebirds. Participants on these trips visit Fundy National Park; hike a portion of the Canadian Coastal Trail; and explore the beach at St. Mary's Point, a resting spot for hundreds of thousands of the migrating shorebirds.

NOVA SCOTIA

Hiking the Cabot Trail

Operator: North Wind Guided Hiking & Walking Tours, P.O. Box 46, Waitsfield, Vt. 05673; (800) 496-5771 or (802) 496-5771; www.northwindtouring.com *Price:* Moderate. *Season:* September. *Length:* 7 days. *Accommodations:* Country inns. Five percent discount with BBAT coupon.

The resource binding together the Maritime Provinces of New Brunswick, Nova Scotia, and Prince Edward Island has historically been fishing, especially for the cod which were found in vast schools in the western Atlantic. Traditional livelihoods such as fishing and farming continue to thrive along these coasts, unfettered by the kind of commercialism that abounds along the coast of Maine and much of the eastern seaboard to the south. The operator has selected a series of day hikes through some of the area's most photogenic scenery, often along ridges overlooking the sea. In the distance hikers will frequently see whales swimming by. The Cape Smokey trail includes time for snacking on wild blueberries, picked fresh from the bush.

QUEBEC
Hiking the Gaspé Peninsula

Over 600 miles east of Montreal, the Gaspé Peninsula offers visitors a landscape of rugged mountains, dramatic islands, and small fishing villages inhabited mainly by people of French descent. The land is dominated by the mighty St. Lawrence Seaway. Hikers on this tour explore the Forillion Federal Park for a hike up Mont St. Alban with its impressive views of the sea and cliffs; the Parc de la Gaspésie with its 4,000-foot peaks, where they explore a subarctic environment that supports numerous moose, deer, and woodland caribou; and Bonaventure Island with its abundance of birdlife for a lovely walk along a path that runs atop the high cliffs. A van carries all personal luggage.

Operator: New England Hiking Holidays, P.O. Box 1648, North Conway, N.H. 03860; (800) 869-0949 or (603) 356-9696; www.nehikingholidays.com. *Price:* Moderate. *Season:* September. *Length:* 6 days. *Accommodations:* Hotels. Ten percent discount with BBAT coupon.

EUROPE
AUSTRIA
Inn-to-Inn Hiking in the Austrian and Swiss Alps

Participants on these popular trips spend their nights at inns in scenic towns, while their days are given over to hikes along the excellent network of trails in the eastern ramparts of the Alps. The route travels from the Appenzellerland in Switzerland between the Bordensee and the Alpstein mountains, to the Rhine Valley on the Swiss–Austrian border, and then to the lovely Bregenzerwald Mountains of Vorarlberg and Austria's high alpine peaks of Montafon. A highlight is the Bregenzerwald, where the charming houses in the villages sport colorful shutters and windows trimmed with handmade lace. The women in this region still wear the handsome,

Operator: New England Hiking Holidays, P.O. Box 1648, North Conway, N.H. 03860; (800) 869-0949 or (603) 356-9696; www.nehikingholidays.com. *Price:* Expensive. *Season:* July and August. *Length:* 8 days. *Accommodations:* Traditional inns. Ten percent discount with BBAT coupon.

stiffly starched folk dresses of their ancestors. On their final day, hikers walk through the spectacular gorge of Rappenlochschlucht to an idyllic alpine village and then up to a peak that offers views of the Rhine Valley.

BRITAIN

Classic Coast-to-Coast Trek Across England

Operator: Wilderness Travel, 1102 Ninth St., Berkeley, Calif. 94710; (800) 368-2794 or (510) 558-2488; www.wildernesstravel.com. *Price:* Moderate. *Season:* May–September. *Length:* 15 days. *Accommodations:* Hotels and guesthouses. Five percent discount with BBAT coupon.

"The Coast-to-Coast Walk is simply the finest long-distance, cross-country walk in the British Isles," Bill Birkett insists in his *Classic Walks in Great Britain.* This trip passes through three of Britain's most celebrated National Parks: the Lake District, the Yorkshire Dales, and the North York Moors. Hikers begin at the St. Bees Head lighthouse overlooking the Irish Sea, then head inland along a well-marked trail into the Lake District National Park, through countryside celebrated by such great Romantic poets as Wordsworth and Coleridge. In Westmoreland, they travel along an ancient Roman road and easy paths formed by generations of sheep. The 12th day takes hikers through the valley of Swaledale, better known as "Herriot Country" after the writings of British veterinarian James Herriot, who lived here. On the 15th day trekkers pass through the mythical countryside of the Yorkshire Moors, made famous by the novels of the Bronte sisters. The trek concludes at the quaint fishing village of Robin Hood's Bay on the North Sea. Hikers also make full-day excursions to the medieval cities of Durham and York.

"There is in the nature of every man . . . a longing to see and know the strange places of the world. Life imprisons us all in its coil of circumstances, and the dreams of romance that color boyhood are forgotten, but they do not die."

FREDERICK O'BRIEN
WHITE SHADOWS IN THE SOUTH SEAS

Inn-Based Walking Tours of the Lake District

The Lake District contains some of the best-loved scenery in England. For almost two centuries its combination of craggy mountains, serene lakes, and green valleys has attracted more visitors than any other part of the country. The Romantic poets William Wordsworth and Samuel Taylor Coleridge both lived here and found the area an inspiration for some of their most famous poems. Many of the treks are within the Lake District National Park, which offers a wonderful variety of hikes, from gentle lakeside rambles to challenging, remote mountainous terrain, including England's highest mountain, Scafell Pike.

Operator: New England Hiking Holidays, P.O. Box 1648, North Conway, N.H. 03860; (800) 869-0949 or (603) 356-9696; www.nehikingholidays.com. *Price:* Expensive. *Season:* July. *Length:* 8 days. *Accommodations:* Inns. Five percent discount with BBAT coupon.

Trekking England's Enchanted Cotswolds

Ever since the Middle Ages the Cotswolds have been noted for sheep; the export of woolen cloth formed the basis of England's economy until the start of the Industrial Revolution. Participants enjoy a leisurely hike through a countryside of rolling hills studded with historical artifacts, ranging from Neolithic long-barrow graves to the great Gothic abbey at Hailes. They pass through charming storybook villages of honey-colored Cotswold stone, including Painswick, Stanway, and Winchcombe. A van carries all luggage.

Operator: Above the Clouds Trekking, 115 Spencer Hill Rd., Hinesburg, Vt. 05461; (800) 233-4499 or (802) 482-4848; www.aboveclouds.com. *Price:* Expensive. *Season:* May, July, and September. *Length:* 9 days. *Accommodations:* Country hotels. Five percent discount with BBAT coupon.

FRANCE

The Lot Valley and the Pyrenees

Day-hikers explore a part of southern France rarely seen by tourists. They follow ancient footpaths, connecting villages scarcely changed since the Middle Ages, traveling in the footsteps of medieval pilgrims who often used those same paths for their journey to Santiago de Compostela. Hikers pass through a rugged landscape where ancient castles

Operator: New England Hiking Holidays, P.O. Box 1648, North Conway, N.H. 03860; (800) 869-0949 or (603) 356-9696; www.nehikingholidays.com.

Price: Expensive.
Season: June.
Length: 8 days.
Accommodations: Historic
châteaus and inns. Ten
percent discount with
BBAT coupon.

Operator.
REI Adventures,
P.O. Box 1938,
Sumner, Wash. 98390;
(800) 622-2236 or
(253) 4437-1100;
www.rei.com/travel.
Price: Moderate.
Season: May, June, and
September.
Length: 9 days.
Accommodations: Small
hotels. Five percent dis-
count with BBAT coupon.

still dominate the landscape. Three days are spent hiking along the dramatic Lot River valley. Two nights are spent in Conques, a well-preserved medieval village, which was once an important stopping place for pilgrims on their way into Spain.

Hiking Inn-to-Inn Provence

Hiking through the south of France is a sybarite's dream of châteaus, chardonnay, and friendly smiles. The clear, dazzling light and Mediterranean landscapes of the region inspired the finest paintings of van Gogh and Cézanne. The hiking route follows the popular Grand Randonee Trail, which crosses France from the Cote d'Azur to the Atlantic. A major focus is the rugged Verdon River Gorge, whose towering limestone cliffs have earned it the reputation as the "Grand Canyon of France." Visits are also made in the hamlets of Moustiers Sainte Marie, a historic pottery town overlooking the Verdon River; and Chasteuil, home to numerous craftspeople. Daily hiking distances average 10 miles. A van carries all luggage.

The Adventure Travel Hall of Fame: ALEXANDRA DAVID-NEEL

Until the early 20th century, cumbersome cultural restrictions prevented most Western women from participating in the exploration of the world beyond. Yet in the late 19th century a small band of astonishing women explorers burst forth on the scene, drawn by the magnet of remote Tibet, then virtually unvisited by outsiders. Perhaps the most remarkable of these women was Alexandra David-Neel, for whom Tibet became the consuming passion of her adventurous life. Her obsession began in 1912 when the Frenchwoman, as a journalist, traveled to the Himalayan foothills in Nepal and became the first Western woman ever granted a private interview with the Dalai Lama. Her knowledge of Buddhist doctrine so impressed her host that he advised her to learn the Tibetan language. This she did and then made her first journey into Tibet, crossing illegally into the forbidden kingdom to spend time at a monastery. There she met several Buddhist nuns and

Backpacking Through Corsica

The whole of Corsica sometimes seems like one enormous mountain, 114 miles long, rising to 8,943 feet from the blue waters of the Mediterranean. Running the length of the island's interior is the Grand Rondonee, a maintained 177-mile-long hiking path that follows ancient shepherds' trails. The route crosses only three roads and passes through just one village. The operator offers two different treks, one covering the southern portion of the Grand Rondonee and the other the upper portion. On both trips trekkers walk through impressive wilderness scenery of fir and beech forests, jagged peaks, and rushing mountain rivers. Both are vehicle-supported, although participants can expect to carry backpacks for about four days. Operator:

Operator:
Himalayan Travel/Sherpa,
110 Prospect St.,
Stamford, Conn. 06901;
(800) 225-2380;
(203) 359-3711;
www.gorp.com/himtravel.htm
Price: Inexpensive.
Season: July and August.
Length: 15 days.
Accommodations: Hotels and tent camps. Five percent discount with BBAT coupon.

Périgord Noir Trek

Straddling the Dordogne River, Périgord consists of four separate regions—White, Green, Purple,

learned that for most of the year they lived in the higher altitudes of the Himalayas, either in tiny communities or as hermits in snowbound caves. On her next trip to Tibet she disguised herself as an anchorite (a person who has retired to a solitary place for a life of religious seclusion) and lived through the winter in a tiny rock hut at the foot of a mountain, beside a cave where a famous Tibetan mystic dwelled. He became her religious mentor. In 1923, at the age of 56, she set out from China disguised as a beggar woman on her most dangerous journey of exploration into Tibet, trekking for eight months through the snowbound high country and valleys with only a backpack, a begging bowl, and a revolver strapped to her waist beneath her clothing. She became the first Westerner to penetrate the holy city of Lhasa, the seat of Tibetan Buddhism, where she investigated the practice and philosophy of the country's religion. That trip yielded the material for her classic book My Journey to Lhasa, and established her as one of the world's leading authorities on Tibetan Buddhism. Traveling, she once insisted, was the way to stay truly young, for "travel not only stirs the blood, it gives strength to the spirit." She finally died on September 8, 1969, just before her 101st birthday.

Operator:
Above the Clouds Trekking,
115 Spencer Hill Rd.,
Hinesburg, Vt. 05461;
(800) 233-4499 or
(802) 482-4848;
www.aboveclouds.com.
Price: Expensive.
Season: May, June, and
October.
Length: 7 days.
Accommodations: Hotels.
Five percent discount with
BBAT coupon.

and Black. Each has its own charms, but Périgord Noir (Black) exceeds the others for beauty, history, and the variety of its attractions, ranging from prehistoric Cro-Magnon cave paintings to magnificent châteaus from the Middle Ages. This trek begins and ends in Sarlat-la-Canéda and does a clockwise loop through the region, bordered by the Vézère River to the northwest and the Dordogne to the south. The varied nature of the itinerary is suggested early on after the trekkers depart the village of Les Eyzies: they walk along the bank of the Vézère River in the morning and then shift to canoes in the afternoon for a leisurely paddle downstream, followed the next morning by a visit to Font du Gaume, a cave which boasts several fine paintings of bison on its wall, art left by Cro-Magnon man tens of thousands of years ago. A van carries all luggage.

GERMANY

Bavarian Walk

Operator:
Euro-Bike & Walking Tours,
P.O. Box 990, DeKalb, Ill.
60115; (800) 321-6060 or
(815) 758-8851;
www.eurowalk.com.
Price: Expensive.
Season: July and September.
Length: 8 days.
Accommodations: Hotels.
Five percent discount with
BBAT coupon.

Perhaps no other region in Germany exhibits such a distinct regionalism as Bavaria, which existed for centuries as a separate kingdom. Even today the people here are more inclined toward traditional costumes and cultural ways than their northern cousins are. Participants on these walks pass through an alpine landscape of meadows, waterfalls, and towering peaks. The attractions along the way include Garmisch-Partenkirchen, a picturesque town enlivened by frescoes and window boxes ablaze with geraniums; the picturesque village of Oberammergau, the European center for woodworking crafts, famous for its annual passion play that boasts a cast of 2,000 performers; and Linderhof, one of "Mad" King Ludwig II's exorbitant castles. A support van carries all luggage.

IRELAND

Hiking the Southwestern Coast

This popular trip focuses on the celebrated counties of Clare and Kerry, where travelers can easily experience the quintessential Ireland of unspoiled coastlines, farmlands bordered by stone walls and hedgerows, picturesque villages, and lush forests. The trip begins in County Clare with a trek through the heart of the Burren, a wild glacio-karstic limestone plateau, and then a five-mile walk along the edge of the Cliffs of Moher, a sheer precipice towering 700 feet above the Atlantic. Several days are then spent in the lovely Dingle Peninsula, where David Lean's movie Ryan's Daughter was filmed. The final three days are taken up with day hikes in Killarney in the footsteps of such greats of British literature as Alfred Tennyson, William Thackeray, and Sir Walter Scott.

Operator:
New England Hiking Holidays, P.O. Box 1648, North Conway, N.H. 03860; (800) 869-0949 or (603) 356-9696; www.nehikingholidays.com.
Price: Expensive.
Season: August.
Length: 7 days.
Accommodations: Historic hotels. Ten percent discount with BBAT coupon.

A Walk Through Ireland's Emerald Countryside

Connemara has long enjoyed a reputation for having Ireland's best walking country—dramatic mountains presenting a sweep of crag and valley that reaches to the sea. The region is also the heartland of Gaeltacht, where English is understood but the ancient Gaelic language is still spoken in everyday speech. Participants on this inn-to-inn trek explore the wonders of Connemara and South Mayo Counties, where residents still live in thatch-roofed cottages and cook over open peat fires in central hearths. One day is spent walking along the Western Way, one of Ireland's finest long-distance trails, ending at the shores of the country's second-largest lake. Ample time is allowed for visits to important cultural sites along the way, such as the 19th-century Kylemore Abbey, originally built as a magnificent Gothic-style castle for a wealthy English surgeon and now a Benedictine convent. A support van carries all luggage.

Operator:
Mountain Travel-Sobek, 6420 Fairmount Ave., El Cerrito, Calif. 94530; (888) 687-6235 or (510) 527-8105; www.mtsobek.com.
Price: Expensive.
Season: June to September.
Length: 8 days.
Accommodations:
Farmhouses and inns. Five percent discount with BBAT coupon.

Hikers follow paths laid down by medieval monks through a sun-drenched landscape in Tuscany

Lauren Hefferon/Ciclismo Classico

ITALY

Hike Through Tuscany

Operator:
Ciclismo Classico,
30 Marathon St.,
Arlington, Mass. 02474
(800) 866-7314 or
(781) 646-3377;
www.ciclismoclassico.com.
Price: Expensive.
Season: May–early October.
Length: 8 days.
Accommodations: Hotels.
Five percent discount with
BBAT coupon.

This hike follows paths established by Vallombrosan monks in the 11th century, through a Tuscan countryside saturated in history and dotted with castles and vineyards. Tuscans regard themselves as the most civilized of all Italians, insisting that their culture is the oldest and their Italian the purest. Participants start their hike from a 17th-century farmhouse in Greve, in the heart of Chianti country. Hikers follow trails that lead past many delights, including the birthplace of Giovanni da Verrazano, the discoverer of New York Harbor. They then proceed at a leisurely pace through Gaiole to Siena. A full day is devoted to a walking tour of Siena's burnt-colored, narrow medieval streets. Time is allowed for visits to the most important artistic, architectural, and historical sites, such as the Palazzo Pubblico with its 14th-century frescos by Simone Martini. The trip ends in the town of Volterra, a perfect example of a medieval Italian fortress city, which also boasts important Etruscan and Roman ruins. A van carries all personal luggage.

Hiking Through the Italian Alps

Although not high by Swiss standards, the Italian Dolomites are among the most dramatic mountains in Europe—sheer spires sculptured into fantastic shapes. For decades they have been a major European center for rock climbing. But they are also one of great places for day hikers, who walk along excellent trails across alpine meadows ablaze with wildflowers against a backdrop of stark peaks. Most ascents and descents are of 2,000 feet or less. A support van carries all luggage.

Operator:
Mountain Travel-Sobek,
6420 Fairmount Ave.,
El Cerrito, Calif. 94530;
(888) 687-6235 or
(510) 527-8105;
www.mtsobek.com.
Price: Expensive.
Season: June, August,
and September.
Length: 10 days.
Accommodations: Hotels.
Five percent discount
with BBAT coupon.

PORTUGAL

Walking the Azores

After years of mounting successful cycling tours of Portugal's famed Atlantic Islands, the operator decided to place his Azores expertise at the service of day hikers. This unique trip focuses on exotic São Miguel Island with its dramatic seacoasts and emerald valleys, cascading waterfalls, and villages untouched by time. Hikers walk along forest tracks and quiet lanes, enjoy spectacular views from high ridges, tour Europe's only tea plantation, climb to the rims of the two crater lakes of Sete Cidades, and relax with a rewarding soak under a hot waterfall. Daily walks average four to 10 miles.

Operator:
Easy Rider Tours,
P.O. Box 228,
Newburyport, Mass. 01950;
(800) 488-8332 or
(978) 463-6955;
www.easyridertours.com.
Price: Expensive.
Season: August.
Length: 7 days.
Accommodations: Small
hotels. Five percent discount with BBAT coupon.

"Adventure is just a state of mind, and a very pleasant one, and no harm to any body, and a great asset if you use it right."
ARCHIE CARR
THE WINDWARD ROAD

A small group of day-trippers walks along the backroads of Portugal's Azores Islands

Jim Goldberg/Easy Rider Tours

SPAIN

Walking the Way of the Moors

Operator:
Easy Rider Tours, P.O. Box 228, Newburyport, Mass. 01950; (800) 488-8332 or (978) 463-6955; www.easyridertours.com.
Price: Moderate.
Season: March and October.
Length: 10 days.
Accommodations: Range from an 18th-century palacio to a spa straight out of the Arabian Nights. Five percent discount with BBAT coupon.

Settled by the Berbers and occupied by the Moors until the late 16th century, southern Spain is a land saturated in history, reflecting both North African and Mediterranean cultures in its architecture, cuisine, and handicrafts. Day-hikers begin with a seaside walk through the cliffs and dunes of Cabo de Gata Natural Park, pass palm trees, domed Arab cisterns, and African flamingos feeding at the salt flats. Next they transfer to Laujar de Andarax, famous for its hearty wines and Renaissance fountains, for an easy day hike through pine forests along the Andarax River. Other stops include Laroles, where traditional craftspeople make colorful woven rugs and wicker baskets; the cliff-hanging villages of the Poqueira Valley; and Granada, the famed City of the Moors famous for its imposing mosque, so large that its interior now houses a cathedral, and its hundreds of patios with fountains. Daily walks average four to 10 miles. A support van carries all luggage.

Basque Country Hikes

This inn-to-inn trek provides a mixture of great walking with an immersion in Basque culture in the Pyrenees Mountains along the border between Spain and France. The range is notable for its many streams, waterfalls, and distinctive deep, steep-walled amphitheatric cirques at the upper ends of its valleys. Hikers find themselves walking through an alpine landscape of forested slopes, high meadows, streams, and jagged limestone peaks. Each departure features a visit to a different local festival, such as Pamplona's famous Running of the Bulls during the Fiesta of San Fermin in July. A support van carries all luggage.

Operator:
Wilderness Travel,
1102 Ninth St.,
Berkeley, Calif. 94710;
(800) 368-2794 or
(510) 558-2488;
www.wildernesstravel.com.
Price: Expensive.
Season: June and
September.
Length: 10 days.
Accommodations: Small inns,
hotels, and paradors. Five
percent discount with
BBAT coupon.

SWITZERLAND

Berner Oberland Trek

The Berner Oberland range bisects Switzerland east to west and includes some of Europe's most celebrated mountains. Hikers on this trek go inn-to-inn from Interlaken through the fabled mountain villages of Grindelwald, Wengen, Murren, the Kiental, and Kandersteg, wending their way among a dazzling array of peaks, passes, glaciers, lakes, and waterfalls. A highlight is Lauterbrunnental, arguably the most beautiful valley in Switzerland, where waterfalls plunge over sheer 3,000-foot cliffs. Trekkers have plenty of time along the way to admire the wildflowers, appreciate folkways in the more remote villages, and snap pictures fit for a calendar. Hiking distances average less than 12 miles a day. A support vehicle carries all luggage.

Operator:
Ryder-Walker Alpine
Adventures, P.O. Box 947,
Telluride, Colo. 81435;
(888) 586-8365 or
(970) 728-6481;
www.ryderwalker.com.
Price: Expensive.
Season: August.
Length: 7 days.
Accommodations: Hotels and
inns. Five percent discount
with BBAT coupon.

"Don't fret [when you travel] about attaining The Inner Quest. Make your goal a geographic one—the spiritual stuff will take care of itself."

DAVID ROBERTS
OUTSIDE, FEBRUARY 1990

The Engadine Trek

Operator:
Ryder-Walker Alpine
Adventures, P.O. Box 947,
Telluride, Colo. 81435;
(888) 586-8365 or
(970) 728-6481.
Price: Expensive.
Season: September.
Length: 7 days.
Accommodations: Hotels and
inns. Five percent discount
with BBAT coupon.

This inn-to-inn trek covers the length of the Inn River Valley, almost from the Austrian to the Italian border. This is a moderately strenuous hike which passes from the gentler terrain of the lower Engadine; through the upper Engadine with its majestic, glaciated peaks; and into Val Bregaglia and its wild and dramatic granite spires. The villages along the way range from tiny antique Guarda and Soglio to pristine Sils Maria and the pleasant resort town of Pontresina. Participants hike along ancient footpaths that link tiny villages, ruins, and lively towns; climb to passes and summits; and traverse the valley above sparkling lakes before plunging into Val Bregaglia with its spectacular Sciora range. A support van transports all luggage.

The Mont Blanc Circuit

Operator:
Mountain Travel–Sobek,
6420 Fairmount Ave.,
El Cerrito, Calif. 94530;
(888) 687-6235 or
(510) 527-8105;
www.mtsobek.com.
Price: Moderate.
Season: June–September.
Length: 13 days (with a 9-
day "express" version of
the tour also available).
Accommodations: Mountain
inns and dorm-style
refuges. Five percent discount with BBAT coupon.

For centuries people have been drawn, almost as if on a pilgrimage, to Mont Blanc, the highest mountain in Europe. One of the world's greatest walks, this trek makes a complete circuit of this legendary massif. Participants hike through alpine France, Italy, and Switzerland against an ever-changing panorama of tumbling glaciers, famous peaks, glorious wildflowers, and lovely meadows. Starting in Chamonix, hikers cross a succession of cols and descend into each of the seven valleys in three countries that radiate from Mont Blanc. A support vehicle carries all luggage.

"I want to be thoroughly used up when I die, for the harder I work the more I live. Life . . . is sort of a splendid torch which I have got hold of for a moment, and I want to make it burn as brightly as possible before I hand it off to future generations."

GEORGE BERNARD SHAW

LATIN AMERICA

ARGENTINA

Trekking Patagonia

A land of vast distances and few people, Patagonia also boasts some of the finest alpine scenery and most pristine wilderness in all South America. This trek begins with a three-day crossing through a hanging valley along the eastern flanks of the Andes to El Chalten and Monte FitzRoy. (Packhorses carry all gear.) Four days in the Chalten area are highlighted by a hike on Torre Glacier to the foot of Cerro Torre, a peak of striking beauty. The group then moves to Estancia Helsingfors, a ranch situated on the southwest corner of Lake Viedma, for day hikes into the surrounding mountains. The trip ends with a one-hour walk (using crampons) across the top of the Perito Moreno Glacier, a vast ribbon of ice stretching several miles wide and scores of miles long.

Operator: Above the Clouds Trekking, 115 Spencer Hill Rd., Hinesburg, Vt. 05461; (800) 233-4499 or (802) 482-4848; www.aboveclouds.com.
Price: Expensive.
Season: January, March, November, and December.
Length: 15 days.
Accommodations: Hotels, ranch house, and tent camps. Five percent discount with BBAT coupon.

MEXICO

Trekking with the Tarahumara Indians in Copper Canyon

Mexico's Barranca del Cobre, the largest and deepest canyon complex in North America, is still largely undiscovered by the world's visitors. Of the 50,000 travelers who visit the rim each year, only a handful make it to the Tarahumara Indians' home at the bottom of the canyon. The most traditional of the North American Indian tribes, some 60,000 Tarahumaras inhabit the canyons, insulated from the modern world by isolation and the intractability of the landscape and leading a late–Stone Age lifestyle that has not changed in centuries. Hikers see ancient mines, cave-dwelling Tarahumaras, exotic birdlife, and some of the most spectacular

Operator: Remarkable Journeys, P.O. Box 31855, Houston, Tex. 77231; (800) 856-1993 or (713) 721-2517; www.remjourneys.com.
Price: Moderate.
Season: November.
Length: 5 days.
Accommodations: Tent camps. Five percent discount with BBAT coupon.

Hikers through the central desert of Baja California experience a rich variety of desert plants and spectacular vistas

Lynn Mitchell/Baja Discovery

scenery in Mexico. A layover day is spent at a beautiful swimming hole and beach in the heart of the canyon. Stock animals carry all camping gear.

Walking Tours of Baja California

Operator: Baja Discovery, P.O. Box 152527, San Diego, Calif. 92195; (800) 829-2252 or (619) 262-0700; www.bajadiscovery.com.
Price: Moderate.
Season: May and November.
Length: 4 days.
Accommodations: Hotels. Five percent discount with BBAT coupon.

This "Walk Baja" botanical adventure provides small groups of walkers with breathtaking scenery, from the wide, sandy beaches along the Pacific Ocean to the Central Desert, a wonderland of cactus and boulders. The area supports more than 120 kinds of cacti, 70 of them endemic (occurring nowhere else). Hundreds of giant cardon cacti stud the desert floor, great masses of fluted columns towering 40 feet and higher. These are among the longest-lived plants in the world, some individuals reaching the ripe old age of 200 years. Also common are the bizarre boojum cacti, looking for all the world like giant upside-down carrots, rising to heights of 70 feet from a base of two feet, the individual branches twisting themselves into all sorts of whimsical shapes. Hikers also explore canyons and arroyos, see cave paintings left by ancient Indians, and visit an old onyx mine at El Marmol. These are easy walks of five or six miles each.

PERU

Classic Trek Along the Inca Trail to Machu Picchu

This 35-mile trek follows a centuries-old highway once used by Incan royalty for their pilgrimages. Hikers take five days to reach the fabled "Lost City of the Incas," allowing ample opportunity to explore the remnants of the New World's greatest Indian civilization. The trek begins at the small village of Chilca on the banks of the Urubamba River. Climbing steadily to 13,776 feet, the trail passes the ruins of ancient terraces, aqueducts, frontier outposts, stone baths, and tombs. Porters carry all baggage. Two days are spent at Machu Picchu exploring the finest complex of Indian ruins in the Western Hemisphere. On the day before the start of the trek, visitors raft the Urubamba.

Operator: Wilderness Travel, 1102 Ninth St., Berkeley, Calif. 94710; (800) 368-2794 or (510) 558-2488; www.wildernesstravel.com.
Price: Expensive.
Season: Throughout the year.
Length: 12 days.
Accommodations: Hotels and tent camps. Five percent discount with BBAT coupon.

Hikers along the famous Inca Trail have numerous opportunities to experience the colorful culture of the local Indians
Bill Abbott/Wilderness Travel

MIDDLE EAST

TURKEY

Trekking Taurus and Cappadocia

Operator: Himalayan Travel/Sherpa, 110 Prospect St., Stamford, Conn. 06901; (800) 225-2380; (203) 359-3711; www.gorp.com/himtravel.htm. *Price:* Inexpensive. *Season:* June, July, and September. *Length:* 15 days. *Accommodations:* Hotels and tent camps. Five percent discount with BBAT coupon.

Trekkers on this tour explore two parts of Turkey by foot, far from the tourist crowds, where they can expect to find beautiful scenery, high mountains, unspoiled countryside, and a traditional rural hospitality. Cappadocia in central Turkey is an astonishing landscape of dramatic natural beauty. Erosion by water and wind have produced a haunting, surrealist region of cones, columns, and canyons. For 1,000 years, local Christians cut monasteries and churches into the Cappadocian rock. Hikers walk along ancient paths to visit rock churches, cave dwellings, and rock formations. The trek through the Taurus Mountains in southern Turkey takes walkers through peaceful pine forests and past numerous waterfalls. Highlights include an ascent to the summit of Mt. Embler (11,169 feet) and visits with Yoruk nomads who live in black goat-hair tents. Pack animals carry all luggage.

UNITED STATES

CALIFORNIA

The High Sierra Trail to Mt. Whitney

Operator: Southern Yosemite Mountain Guides, P.O. Box 301, Bass Lake, Calif. 93604; (800) 231-4575 or (559) 658-8735; www.symg.com. *Price:* Inexpensive.

Backpackers walk along one of the most spectacular trails in the western United States, through Sequoia National Park with its towering sequoia trees and across high plateaus. Few of the park's visitors make it much beyond the parking lots, so trekkers will have the trails largely to themselves. A midpoint stop is made at a natural hot springs certain to rejuvenate tired muscles. Mount Whitney, at

Hikers through Death Valley in the spring can enjoy both the dramatic scenery and a blooming of desert flowers

Andrew Kronen/REI Adventures

14,494 feet the highest peak in the United States south of Alaska, rises at the border. The climax is a climb to the summit.

Backpacking in the Ansel Adams Wilderness

The Ansel Adams Wilderness may be one of the best-kept secrets of the high Sierra. Located on the southern border of Yosemite National Park, it has mile upon mile of sweeping granite ridges, spectacular vistas, and excellent trout-fishing in the many sparkling high-mountain lakes. Meadows are blanketed in subalpine flora such as aster, cow parsnip, lupine, and mule ears. These trips begin and end at Bass Lake. All food and camp supplies are packed in on mules, leaving trekkers free to carry only day packs. A base camp is set up in the middle of the high Sierra, from which day trips are made to surrounding areas. Warning: These trips are popular, so book early!

Lake Tahoe Lodge-Based Hiking

Lake Tahoe's deep, blue, clear waters are nestled in a splendid mountain wilderness made accessible by hundreds of miles of well-maintained

Season: August and September.
Length: 10 days.
Accommodations: Tent camps. Ten percent discount with BBAT coupon.

Operator: Southern Yosemite Mountain Guides, P.O. Box 301, Bass Lake, Calif. 93604;
(800) 231-4575 or
(559) 658-8735;
www.symg.com.
Price: Moderate.
Season: July–September.
Length: 7 days.
Accommodations: Tent camps. Ten percent discount with BBAT coupon.

Operator:
Tahoe Trips & Trails,
Box 6952, Tahoe City, Calif.
96145; (800) 581-4453 or
(530) 583-4506;
www.tahoetrips.com.
Price: Expensive.
Season: July, August, October.
Length: 5 days.
Accommodations: Lodge.
Five percent discount with
BBAT coupon.

Operator:
Tahoe Trips & Trails, Box
6952, Tahoe City, Calif.
96145; (800) 581-4453 or
(530) 583-4506;
www.tahoetrips.com.
Price: Expensive.
Season: May and November.
Length: 3 and 5 days.
Accommodations: Fine inns.
Five percent discount with
BBAT coupon.

trails. The operator has devised a series of day hikes to introduce hikers to some of the area's most celebrated scenic wonders. The walks include the Rubicon Trail in Bliss State Park through a fir forest with panoramic views of the lake's bays; a short stretch of the celebrated Pacific Crest Trail, which runs from Canada to Mexico; and an easy climb of Mt. Tallac (elevation 9,735 feet) for the fine view from the summit over the entire Lake Tahoe area.

Wine Country Hiking

California's Napa Valley enjoys a world-famous reputation for light-bodied wines, gastronomic adventure, and magnificent lodgings. Hidden among the celebrated vineyards are dozens of miles of fine walking trails, virtually unknown except to the local residents. This popular trip begins in Sonoma Valley at Beauty Ranch, where novelist Jack London once lived, with a hike through lovely eucalyptus groves to London's private lake and the charred ruins of his beloved Wolf House. Another day is spent hiking the headwaters of Sonoma Creek at what was once the Wappo Indian village of Wilikos for ridge-top views of six counties, including portions of San Francisco Bay. The itinerary also allows plenty of time for visits to the tasting rooms of local wineries.

Hiking Death Valley's Backcountry

Death Valley National Park is a big-picture affair—half again the size of the state of Delaware and more than 100 miles long. The valley is also a blast-furnace example of nature at its outer limits—with a record high summer temperature of 134 degrees (set in 1913) and an average annual rainfall of less than two inches. The valley is in the record books as the lowest (280 feet below sea level), hottest, and driest place in North America. The region's seldom-traveled backcountry offers hikers fascinating geological features and a unique ecosystem. The operator sets up two base camps in different environments of the park; hikers make day trips of six to 10 miles from these sites, thus eliminating the need for burdensome backpacks. (A van transports hikers and their personal belongings from one campsite to the next.) Highlights include a hike through the Titus Canyon narrows, a deep, impressive slot canyon, and a hike down another canyon to two remote oases, one boasting a 60-foot waterfall. The spring departures are timed to catch Death Valley's cacti and wildflowers in bloom.

Climbing Seminar and Summitting of Mt. Shasta

Mountain climbing, both the technical and the uphill hiking varieties, has mushroomed in popularity in recent years. At 14,161 feet, Mt. Shasta is the second highest volcano in the United States. Seminar enrollment is open to both beginning and intermediate climbers. Participants receive personalized instruction in a wide variety of climbing techniques and equipment usage on snow and ice, including ice-axe arrests, the proper use of crampons and ice axes, knots and the use of rope, belays, crevasse rescue, and route finding. For the climax, students put their newly acquired skills to the test in a 12-hour round-trip climb to the sum-

Operator:
REI Adventures,
P.O. Box 1938,
Sumner, Wash. 98390;
(800) 622-2236 or
(253) 4437-1100;
www.rei.com/travel.
Price: Moderate.
Season: March.
Length: 6 days.
Accommodations: Tent camps. Five percent discount with BBAT coupon.

Operator:
REI Adventures,
P.O. Box 1938,
Sumner, Wash. 98390;
(800) 622-2236 or
(253) 4437-1100;
www.rei.com/travel.
Price: Moderate.
Season: June–September.
Length: 5 days.
Accommodations: Tent camps. Five percent discount with BBAT coupon.

Students in the REI Adventures' climbing seminar practice their new skills in the high country of Mt. Shasta

Rusty Brennan/REI Adventures

mit of Mt. Shasta. The operator offers one climbing seminar for women only.

COLORADO

Rocky Mountain National Park Rambler

Operator:
The World Outside,
2840 Wilderness Pl., #F,
Boulder, Colo. 80501;
(800) 488-8493 or
(303) 413-0938;
www.theworldoutside.com.
Price: Moderate.
Season: July–September.
Length: 6 days.
Accommodations: Inns. Ten
percent discount with
BBAT coupon.

Colorado's most popular park presents visitors with a dazzling array of snowy peaks, rugged ridges, and massive cirques. Its famous Trail Ridge Road enjoys a reputation as America's highest highway, topping 12,000 feet as it crosses the Continental Divide. The park has more than 355 miles of trails. Hikers on this trip explore far off the beaten track, enjoying the park's remote corners. One day is spent hiking past echoing waterfalls to enter the barren landscape of Glacier Gorge, a stunning testimony to the mighty forces of nature. On another day hikers above the treeline in the tundra country above Trail Ridge Road pass through what looks like an acreswide bonsai garden. With a growing season measured in weeks, stunted trees and plants have struggled for centuries to attain their Lilliputian size.

The Adventure Travel Hall of Fame: DISABLED ADVENTURERS

On August 9, 1996, a blind mountain climber completed his climb up El Capitan, a granite monolith towering 3,200 feet above Yosemite Valley that has challenged generations of adventurers. Erik Weihenmayer, 28, a Phoenix schoolteacher, reached the top to cheers from 20 observers, including three sighted climbing companions who crested the top ahead of him. He made the four-day climb "to show

potential rather than limitations." Weihenmayer insisted, "If you can climb El Capitan, you can do anything. Blind people, visually impaired people, and disabled people have huge potential. That's one of the messages of the climb." The year before, he had hiked through the ice and snow on Mount McKinley for 19 days.

Other disabled adventurers have also demonstrated that a handicap should be no barrier to challenging outdoor experiences.

MAINE

Hiking Through Acadia National Park

The Maine coast through Acadia is a place where mountains tumble to the Atlantic and end in battered cliffs, where breakers claw into coves and inlets, and where hikers can fish with one hand and sample blueberries from a wind-stunted bush with the other. These popular trips focus on Mount Desert Island, exploring every corner by means of well-maintained trails. Some wind their way along the shore line to sandy beaches, hug the many lakeshores, or follow the more gentle carriage paths that John D. Rockefeller, Jr., constructed in the 1920s. A van carries all personal luggage.

Operator: New England Hiking Holidays, P.O. Box 1648, North Conway, N.H. 03860; (800) 869-0949 or (603) 356-9696; www.nehikingholidays.com.
Price: Expensive.
Season: June–mid-October.
Length: 4 days.
Accommodations: Historic inns at Northeast Harbor and Bar Harbor. Ten percent discount with BBAT coupon.

MICHIGAN

Hike and Bike the Porcupine Mountains

Located in the extreme western portion of the Upper Peninsula, Porcupine Mountains State

---

Mark Wellman, a paraplegic park ranger, climbed El Capitan in 1989 and later ascended Half Dome on the other side of Yosemite Valley. He literally hauled himself up the mountains by his arms. He gained only inches at a time, using ropes placed by his companion, Mike Corbett. During his nine-day ascent of El Capitan he was buffeted by winds and pitiless heat. At times he dangled with nothing but air between him and the valley floor 2,000 feet down. And every night he slept precariously strapped into a sleeping bag. But inch by inch, despite pain and frustration, he struggled toward his goal. The climbs proved his philosophy about what it takes to make a dream come true. "Just do it," he said later, "even if it's six inches at a time."

And in 1995 Todd Huston, 33, on one good leg and one $8,000 prosthesis climbed the highest mountain peak in each state in 67 days, setting a world record. Back home in Newport Beach, California, he told journalists that he wants to make a career of inspiring others. "Everybody has a challenge, but God gives us the power to overcome it," he said. "I practice what I preach. The mountain climbs were my way of showing it."

Operator: Michigan Bicycle Touring, 3512 Red School Rd., Kingsley, Mich. 49649; (231) 263-5885; www.bikembt.com. *Price:* Moderate. *Season:* June through early September. *Length:* 5 days. *Accommodations:* Lodges. Five percent discount with BBAT coupon.

Park is Michigan's largest and least-civilized park, a place so remote that even the merciless lumber barons of the 19th century left it untouched. Its 58,000 acres offer some of the wildest and most spectacular landscape in the Midwest and are home to a rich selection of wildlife, including deer, black bear, and bald eagles. Participants on this tour explore the park's backcountry by both foot and bicycle. Special attractions include the waterfalls in the Black River Canyon, old mining towns, and the largest stand of virgin pine and hemlock east of the Mississippi. Two days are for hikes, three for biking.

Backpacking Through Isle Royale National Park

Operator: The Northwest Passage, 1130 Greenleaf Ave., Wilmette, Ill. 60091; (800) RECREATE or (847) 256-4409; www.nwpassage.com. *Price:* Moderate. *Season:* September. *Length:* 7 days. *Accommodations:* Tents at campgrounds. Five percent discount with BBAT coupon.

This isolated wilderness park, the least-visited national park in the country, lies in the western reaches of Lake Superior and is famous as a habitat for wolf and moose. On Isle Royale everybody hikes, for there are no cars or horses. But hiking here is a joy. Trails springy with moss wind past beaver ponds and glades ablaze with wild iris. On this backpacking adventure hikers traverse the island lengthwise, crossing 45 miles from Rock Harbor to Windigo, along one of the most remote trails east of the Rocky Mountains.

"Of the gladdest moments in human life, methinks, is the departure upon a distant journey to unknown lands. Shaking off with one mighty effort the fetters of Habit, the leaden weight of Routine, the cloak of many Cares, and the slavery of Home, man feels once more happy. The blood flows with the fast circulation of childhood . . . afresh dawns the morn of life."

EXPLORER SIR RICHARD BURTON
JOURNAL ENTRY FOR DECEMBER 2, 1856

MONTANA

Hiking Glacier and Waterton National Parks

The ancient ice sheets are long gone; only a few dozen small glaciers remain. Yet the broad, bathtub-shaped valleys of western Montana's Glacier National Park offer hikers more than 700 miles of trails. With day pack on back, in a few hours a hiker can be alone in some of the most dramatic, unspoiled wilderness in the country. Participants on these trips do a series of day hikes through the backcountry wilderness of Glacier National Park, viewing alpine meadows, turquoise lakes, ice caves, and waterfalls. The last day is spent hiking in Waterton National Park just across the Canadian border.

Operator: Backcountry, P.O. Box 4029, Bozeman, Mont. 59772; (800) 575-1540 or (406) 586-3556; www.backcountrytours.com. *Price:* Expensive. *Season:* July and August. *Length:* 6 days. *Accommodations:* Lodges. Five percent discount with BBAT coupon.

Backpacking Among the Peaks and Lakes of the Selway–Bitterroot Wilderness

Backpackers on this fairly strenuous trip explore the spectacular alpine world of the eastern half of the vast Selway–Bitterroot Wilderness along the boundary between Montana and Idaho. Here they will find dense forests, rugged canyons, sparkling glacial lakes, and towering peaks. This is a particularly good area to see wolves. Fishermen will want to pack in their rods for some fine fishing in the clear streams and lakes. Not including day hikes, the trip is about 30 miles.

Operator: Big Wild Adventures, 5663 West Fork Rd., Darby, Mont. 59829; (406) 821-3747. *Price:* Moderate to expensive, depending upon the number of people. *Season:* July. *Length:* 6 days. *Accommodations:* Tents. Five percent discount with BBAT coupon.

NEW HAMPSHIRE

White Mountains Weekend Hiking Trips

New Hampshire's White Mountains are a major tourist destination. Yet travelers willing to do a little day hiking can easily lose the crowds in the splendid wilderness of one of New England's most scenic areas. Participants on these weekend escapes discover the waterfalls, lakes, cliffs, and mountain

Operator: New England Hiking Holidays, P.O. Box 1648, North Conway, N.H. 03860; (800) 869-0949 or (603) 356-9696; www.nehikinghol-idays.com.

Hikers through New England's Lake District find numerous pretty vistas to give them an excuse to pause

New England Hiking Holidays

Price: Expensive.
Season: May–mid-October.
Length: 2 and 3 days.
Accommodations: Nights are spent at the gracious Inn at Thorn Hill, which dates back to 1895. Ten percent discount with BBAT coupon.

peaks of Crawford Notch, Pinkham Notch, and other spots within the Mount Washington Valley, and also visit an Appalachian Mountain Club Hut. Hikers on the three-day trips will range a little farther afield and explore the scenic splendor of Franconia Notch. A van carries all personal luggage. The operator also offers five-day trips.

NEW MEXICO

In the Footsteps of the Anasazi

Operator: North Wind Guided Hiking & Walking Tours, P.O. Box 46, Waitsfield, Vt. 05673; (800) 496-5771 or (802) 496-5771; www.northwindtouring.com
Price: Moderate.
Season: April.
Length: 5 days.
Accommodations: Hotel. Five percent discount with BBAT coupon.

A people whose domain once spread over an area larger than the state of California, the Anasazi were compulsive builders who, without the benefit of the wheel or beasts of burden, raised great structures unequaled until the centuries-later introduction of structural steel. In Chaco Canyon National Park, in New Mexico's northeastern corner, the Anasazi civilization reached its highest peak of development. Between the years of A.D. 1000 and 1200, the Chacoans evolved the largest and most important economic, religious, cultural, and political center north of Mexico. Thirteen large towns once sprawled across the canyon floor, home to perhaps 7,000 Indians. Participants on this trip explore by day hikes the many impressive ruins and the spectacular scenery of Chaco Canyon, often walking along paths the Indians once used.

NORTH CAROLINA

Inn-to-Inn Trekking in the Blue Ridge Mountains

The operator offers a variety of popular day hikes, exploring the beautiful trails lying just off the famous Blue Ridge Parkway. Options include a hike up Grandfather Mountain, which offers the walker some of the most spectacular vistas in the area; Linville Gorge, one of the East's most spectacular wild canyons; and the Boone Fork Trail, a five-mile loop that takes walkers past numerous waterfalls. Departures are timed to coincide with the spring wildflower displays and the colorful fall foliage. A van carries all personal luggage.

Operator: New England Hiking Holidays, P.O. Box 1648, North Conway, N.H. 03860; (800) 869-0949 or (603) 356-9696; www.nehikingholidays.com.
Price: Expensive.
Season: Late-April–October.
Length: 5 days.
Accommodations: Historic inns. Ten percent discount with BBAT coupon.

OREGON

Llama Trekking in Northeastern Oregon

Llama treks have increased in popularity since people have discovered the advantages of these gentle ruminants as pack animals over the more traditional horses and mules. Llamas are easier to handle, require almost no care, step lightly on the trails, and are great for people over 50 who still enjoy camping in remote wilderness areas but no longer want the burden of 60-pound backpacks. These popular trips visit the Eagle Cap Wilderness area, Oregon's largest. Uncrowded and unspoiled, the region was carved by glaciers and features rugged granite peaks that reach 10,000 feet. The area's forests are home to mule deer, elk, bighorn sheep, and mountain goats. These are great trips for children.

Operator: Hurricane Creek Llama Treks, 63366 Pine Tree Rd., Enterprise, Ore. 97828; (800) 528-9609 or (541) 432-4455; www.hcltrek.com.
Price: Moderate.
Season: June–August.
Length: 5 days.
Accommodations: Tent camp. Five percent discount with BBAT coupon.

UTAH

Backpacking Through the Escalante Wilderness

Operator: Big Wild Adventures, 5663 West Fork Rd., Darby, Mont. 59829; (406) 821-3747. *Price:* Moderate. *Season:* May; other departures by special arrangement. *Length:* 7 days. *Accommodations:* Tent camps. Five percent discount with BBAT coupon.

The lower canyons of the Escalante River form the heart of one of the West's most remote areas. This is a landscape of colorful sandstone cliffs, arches, and alcoves; water trickling into inviting pools; and the greenery of cottonwood trees. In the company of a naturalist/guide, backpackers on this trip explore the natural wonders of this rarely visited region of the Glen Canyon National Recreation Area. Average daily hiking distance is seven miles. The schedule includes two rest days to allow participants an opportunity to explore the Escalante's hidden side canyons, hanging gardens, and rock arches. Special attractions are the cliff dwellings, storage wells, ceremonial kivas, and pictographs created by the Anasazi Indians more than 600 years ago. The operator supplies all camping equipment.

VERMONT

Day Hikes, Fall Foliage, and Country Inns

Operator: North Wind Guided Hiking & Walking Tours, P.O. Box 46, Waitsfield, Vt. 05673; (800) 496-5771 or (802) 496-5771; www.northwindtouring.com *Price:* Moderate. *Season:* August, September, and October. *Length:* 6 days. *Accommodations:* Country inns. Five percent discount with BBAT coupon.

These tours offer hikers the chance to see a Vermont reminiscent of a Norman Rockwell painting. Hikers walk through an unspoiled, bucolic countryside dotted with apple orchards, dairy farms, covered bridges, and log cabins. And fall has its special bonuses—fields of orange pumpkins, V-formations of geese flying south, and farm stands piled high with the autumnal harvest. The tour ends with a hike to the famous Trapp Family Lodge.

VIRGINIA

Hiking the Blue Ridge Mountains

Once America's western frontier, the Blue Ridge Mountains still cradle the weathered log cabins and split-rail fences of mountain folk whose forefathers left the settled valleys to wrest a living from the highlands and secluded hollows. Here for the day hiker await gleaming waterfalls, fascinating rock formations sporting such names as Devil's Courthouse and Wildcat Rocks, and ridge after ridge of rolling, forested mountains. Hikes are made along the legendary Appalachian Trail. The operator times departures to coincide with each spring's annual wildflower display.

Operator:
North Wind Guided Hiking & Walking Tours, P.O. Box 46, Waitsfield, Vt. 05673; (800) 496-5771 or (802) 496-5771; www.northwindtouring.com
Price: Moderate.
Season: May.
Length: 5 days.
Accommodations: Country inn. Five percent discount with BBAT coupon.

WASHINGTON

Backpacking Mount Rainier

Mount Rainier National Park's 378 square miles have something for everybody. Located just a short drive from Seattle, the park draws almost 2 million visitors each summer. At 14,410 feet, Mount Rainier is the crown jewel in the Cascade Range and boasts the largest glacier system in the lower 48 states. More than 300 miles of trails probe the wilderness haunts of deer, bear, elk, bobcat, and mountain goat. Backpackers on these trips hike among alpine meadows, lush forests, and glacier-fed lakes in the shadow of Mt. Rainier. Their route includes the Northern Loop Trail and portions of the famous Wonderland Trail that circles Washington's highest peak.

Operator:
REI Adventures, P.O. Box 1938, Sumner, Wash. 98390; (800) 622-2236 or (253) 437-1100; www.rei.com/travel.
Price: Moderate.
Season: July–September.
Length: 7 days.
Accommodations: Tent camps. Five percent discount with BBAT coupon.

Hiking Lodge-to-Lodge in Olympic National Park

Three different ecosystems—central mountains, rain-forested valleys, and detached ocean shore—unite in Olympic National Park's 900,000 acres. Over 90 percent of the park is roadless. Hikers on this adventure explore all three realms, spending evenings in historic lodges. Highlights include the Hoh Rain Forest, an emerald-green primeval world and home to some of the world's tallest trees; the sea stacks of Rialto Beach; and Hurricane Ridge,

Operator:
REI Adventures, P.O. Box 1938, Sumner, Wash. 98390; (800) 622-2236 or (253) 437-1100; www.rei.com/travel.
Price: Moderate.
Season: July and August.

Length: 7 days.
Accommodations: Lodges.
Five percent discount with
BBAT coupon.

for a fantastic view of the San Juan Islands. One
free day allows hikers the option of taking the ferry
ride to Victoria, British Columbia.

WYOMING

Llama Trek Through Yellowstone National Park

Operator: Yellowstone
Llamas, Box 5042,
Bozeman, Mont. 59717;
(406) 586-6872.
Price: Moderate.
Season: July to mid-
September.
Length: 3, 4, and 5 days.
Accommodations: Tent
camps. Five percent dis-
count with BBAT coupon.

The patriarch of our national parks, Yellowstone is
the oldest and, outside of Alaska, the largest
American park. These treks avoid all the usual
tourist spots in favor of backcountry wilderness
areas rarely visited by outsiders. Accompanied by
their llamas, which carry all the gear and supplies,
hikers average five miles a day along game trails,
traveling into the heart of the park among herds of
elk, across meadows ablaze with wildflowers, and
past thermal areas. A llama trek is the perfect way
to experience the natural wonders of this great
park. Avid fisherfolk will think they have died and
gone to heaven.

Over the past decade llamas
have gained in popularity
for use as pack animals,
allowing hikers to enjoy isolated wilderness areas in
greater comfort

Yellowstone Llamas

PROFILE
STEVE CONLON
ABOVE THE CLOUDS TREKKING

A reflective Steve Conlon, the founder and director of Above the Clouds Trekking, relaxes in his office and contemplates a subject which has been in his thoughts a great deal in recent weeks: the high passes of the Himalayan Mountains.

"Looking through thousands of slides during the preparation of my company's catalog, I became aware that I was drawn repeatedly to images of trekkers crossing passes," he observes. "I began to realize how richly laden with significance passes are, both geographically and symbolically. Geographically, passes separate two worlds that are often total opposites. Passes between Himalayan summits separate the lush green valleys of the south from the arid Tibetan plateau to the north. To anyone who has ever hiked in the mountains and crossed a pass, memories of the trek are frequently anchored around pass crossings along the way.

"To the people who live at the feet of the Himalayas—Buddhist, Hindu, and animist alike—there is another level of significance to passes. They have a positive aspect in that they provide access through an otherwise impenetrable barrier, facilitating travel and trade. But equally important passes are places where good spirits reside. Most Buddhists will pick up one or more rocks, preferably white, on their way up to a pass, and deposit this rock on the cairn that they know they'll find there. Often they'll carry prayer flags to place at the pass, the constant wind there sending those prayers in all directions.

"For me, passes have always symbolized passage, a transition from one stage of life to the next. Like all good things they require effort, sometimes great effort. One often begins the ascent to the pass focused on the goal ahead, only to learn along the way the lesson of the pass: the journey, and the spirit in which we undertake it, mean more at the end than the attainment itself."

Conlon's marriage to a Nepalese woman, his fluency in the language, and thorough grasp of the subtleties of Nepalese culture have made him unique in the annals of organized trekking to that country. Above the Clouds Trekking is today the largest operator of treks in Nepal. The company's itineraries eschew the popular trekking routes, such as the Annapurna Circuit, in favor of those in remote areas where a pristine culture and landscape still prevail and few outsiders penetrate.

"Our specialty is taking people to those parts of Nepal where trekking is not well established, where you'll meet lots of local people going about their lives the way they always have," Conlon insists. "We normally meet fewer than five other trekkers the whole time we're out on many of our treks, in contrast to the 500 a day you can meet in some areas. Not that we have anything against other trekkers—it's simply that we don't imagine our clients have traveled 9,000 miles to encounter some folks they might have met the previous summer in Yosemite."

Conlon was born and raised in Worchester, Massachusetts, where, he insists, his upbringing was rather conventional, with no hint of the adventures which lay ahead. He never ventured off the East Coast until he attended graduate school in Chicago at Northwestern University, where he took an MBA with an eye toward a job on Wall Street. But that all changed in 1970 when a stint in the Army landed him at a language school in El Paso, Texas, studying the Vietnamese language. He discovered he possessed an extraordinary ability to learn difficult languages quickly and accurately. But the experience also awakened him in other ways. He spent most of his days off with friends hiking through the wilderness of nearby New Mexico. "This was my first exposure to the wilderness," he recalls today. "Those experiences awakened a love of wild areas in me and a need to search them out."

As soon as he got out of the Army, Conlon bought a one-way air ticket to Europe where he traveled leisurely from country to country, learning new cultures and eventually mastering nine languages, ranging from German and Turkish to Hindi and Farsi. "The more I traveled, the more addicted I became," he admits. "I just couldn't get enough."

In late 1972 Conlon took a train from Istanbul to Delhi, India, and then caught a small bus to Kathmandu. The arrival in Nepal and his first night within sight of the Himalayas changed him forever. As he recalls: "We arrived at our lodgings just before sundown, when the Himalayan range was all ablaze with the colors of the setting sun while a full moon rose pink and orange and gold right out of the mountains. I knew then there was something important in Nepal for me."

The tourist industry in Nepal at the time was virtually undeveloped. Kathmandu boasted only a half-dozen hotels and a handful of operators providing treks for foreigners. Conlon spent two months there, much of the time on solo treks through the backcountry, and then returned to the States. He recalls:

"I came back but I couldn't stop thinking about Nepal. I had to go back. It became an obsession with me. There was such a contrast between that world and the world I'd been aiming for. My original goal had been to go to Wall Street and make lots of money in the stock market. By contrast, the people in Nepal had very little by our standards. But they have this positive energy, no matter how hard the work is. They turn sorrow into something positive."

In 1975 Conlon returned to Kathmandu and lived there for three years. He opened a language school teaching English to local Nepalese, studied Nepali and quickly developed a fluency in that language, and trekked through the mountains on his breaks. What was the biggest cultural adjustment he had to make to his new country? "It was psychological," he says. "In Nepal time isn't measured by the clock, but by the sun and the seasons. Everything is *bholi*—that means 'tomorrow.' And bholi never comes. Things get done when they get done. Life is at a slow pace because the purpose of life is enjoyment."

In 1978 eager to learn photography, Conlon moved to New York City where he learned the trade from a photographer in a studio. In 1980 he returned to Kathmandu and opened a photography studio there. He continued to spend many weeks of the year trekking through remote parts of Nepal, eventually visiting 65 of the country's 75 districts. On one of his treks, in a small village, he met Muna, the young woman who would soon become his wife.

"Marriages in Nepal at that time were almost always arranged between families," Conlon explains. "Ours was a love match which has become more common now. What we had in common was a similar world-view and a love of all things Nepalese."

The pair married and settled in Kathmandu. Then Muna became pregnant, and the couple moved back to Worchester for the birth of a son in March 1982. "Now that I had a family I needed a better-paying career," Conlon remembers. "Just before we left Kathmandu, three Sherpas had approached me and asked me to set up a trekking company in America to bring clients to Nepal. I thought about their suggestions all the way home on the airplane. After my son's birth, I knew that was what I wanted to do. And so Above the Clouds Trekking was born. That first year we had just five clients."

When Above the Clouds started, trekking was already well established in Nepal. Trips were generally organized with an emphasis on the mountains, with the local people pushed into the background. "American trekking operators at that time paid little attention to the culture of Nepal," Conlon insists. "I saw too much of what I came to label as 'telephoto treks.' Local villagers, sometimes including the owner of the land on which the trekking party would be camped, were kept on the perimeter of the camp. You could almost hear the Western leader saying to his clients, 'Yes, these people are exotic, quaint, and colorful, but they may also have diseases that are exotic, quaint, and colorful, so don't get too close. Get out your telephoto lenses, and we'll get some nice, tight portraits of the natives.' To me, this style of trekking was robbing both the locals and the trekkers of an experience that I knew to be not only very rewarding but the essence of the trekking experience in Nepal."

This led Conlon to focus on the culture, particularly in those areas being penetrated for the first time by outsiders from the Western world, making the locals active partners in the developing tourism. He also insisted that a proportionate share of the revenue generated by his treks should remain in local communities, providing the people there with material benefits.

Most operators had been using Sherpas for porters and guides. But, as Conlon points out, Sherpas are regarded as foreigners in many parts of Nepal. He began recruiting his staff from the non-Sherpa regions, first hiring them as porters, then training them as cooks and promoting them to head guides. "That means that when we now bring one of our groups into their district, they are received as family rather than as intruders," Conlon observes. "Our staff often have a personal connection with the people there that the Sherpas do not. This noticeably changes the kinds of experiences our clients have in those districts. This also gives the local people a sense they have a personal investment in the business of trekking."

Conlon works closely with the American Himalayan Foundation on their projects in the Himalayan enclave of Mustang, raising money for the construction of schools where the children of the region can be instructed in their native language, setting up health-care facilities, and bringing electricity to remote villages.

Conlon also decided early on to keep his group size small, averaging nine clients per group and never more than 15. He also decided to avoid the more popular trekking routes which are often overwhelmed by the crowds of trekkers. For example, the Nepalese government issues over 40,000 trekking permits annually for the classic Annapurna Circuit route, but only 400 for the route around Manaslu, the world's eighth-tallest mountain. "The 40,000-plus trekkers on the Annapurna Circuit are causing enough erosion—of both soil and culture—that adding further to that by the presence of our clients is neither beneficial nor necessary," Conlon insists.

In 1985 Conlon began offering his clients treks in both Europe and South America. Again the emphasis has been on cultural interaction. On his

Patagonia treks, for example, he puts his clients up whenever possible at estancias, or sheep ranches, which may span 100,000 acres and are run by fourth- and fifth-generation Europeans. These treks provide great opportunities to meet the famous gauchos, those South American cowboys who still wear their distinctive costumes.

Has Conlon found his Shangri-la in Nepal? "If you go looking for Shangri-la, you won't find it," he insists. " But if you just sit and take in what's there, it will find you."

2

BICYCLE TOURING

The bicycle is the most civilised conveyance known to man," British novelist Iris Murdoch once insisted. "Other forms of transport grow daily more nightmarish. Only the bicycle remains pure in heart."

Many Americans agree. A Gallup poll several years ago found that bicycling is the second most popular recreational sport in America. Some 10 million serious cyclists ride regularly, keeping their muscles, hearts, and lungs in top form.

More and more people have discovered in the bicycle the perfect vehicle for long-distance traveling: swift enough to satisfy their urge to "get somewhere" and slow enough to let them enjoy the countryside in the process. In the past decade, bicycle touring has mushroomed into a big business. Two-wheeled vacations are one of the fastest growing areas within the adventure travel field. Their appeal is obvious: bike tours promise an invigorating mixture of adventure, scenic beauty, camaraderie, and hard work—plus all the advantages of the packaged tour in which the operator handles arrangements for accommodations and meals.

There are other benefits as well. Operators can generally provide a selection of rental bikes, which means no hassles at airports. A van with special bike racks accompanies the group, carrying all luggage, picking up weary cyclists, and making instant road repairs when a bicycle breaks down. Groups are small, usually fewer than 20 members. Cyclists ride at their own pace and often have a choice of routes from easy to challenging, to suit their physical abilities. And they can always look forward to a fine meal in a comfortable country inn at the end of each day.

The Bicycle Travel Association estimates that mountain bikes comprise more than half of all bikes now sold in the United States. The new popularity of these rugged off-road bikes indicates that many cyclists are seeking a much more adventuresome biking experience. With these machines they can strike out from paved roads along primitive, rarely used logging roads and park trails into their favorite wilderness areas.

"Bike riders are close to all of nature," 62-year-old William Quinn observed during his 1979 solo bike journey across the United States. "They know what a mountain really is, or what a 30-knot wind means, or how far 50 miles stretches out."

Amen to that, William.

Cyclists pedal through a
small village in the
countryside of Mali
David Mozer/Bicycle Africa

AFRICA

MALI

Sahel Journey

The uniqueness of the bicycle as a mode of travel in Africa often serves as an icebreaker, generating cross-cultural opportunities missed by travelers using more conventional means of transportation. The West African country of Mali is rich in both culture and history. Cyclists explore the Sahel, a broad savanna running along the southern edge of the Sahara Desert. For centuries the region has been a crossroads of trade, bringing together people from a variety of cultures. Highlights of the trip are visits to the legendary cities of Timbuktu, Mopti, and Djenne, the fascinating enclave of the Dogon people, and a truly extraordinary riverboat trip on the Niger River.

Operator:
Bicycle Africa,
4887 Columbia Dr. South,
Seattle, Wash. 98108;
(206) 767-0848;
www.ibike.org/bikeafrica.
Price: Inexpensive.
Season: October-November.
Length: 15 days.
Accommodations: Small
hotels and village housing.
Five percent discount with
BBAT coupon.

*"Two roads diverged in a wood, and I— I took the one less traveled by,
And that has made all the difference."*

ROBERT FROST
"THE ROAD NOT TAKEN"

ZIMBABWE

Zimbabwe by Bicycle

Operator:
Bicycle Africa,
4887 Columbia Dr. South,
Seattle, Wash. 98108;
(206) 767-0848;
www.ibike.org/bikeafrica.
Price: Inexpensive.
Season: July–August.
Length: 16 days.
Accommodations: Small
hotels and village housing.
Five percent discount with
BBAT coupon.

Cyclists on these popular biking expeditions pedal over paved roads and experience the many moods of the Zambezi River, the breathtaking splendor of Victoria Falls, castle rocks, flourishing wildlife, traditional rock art, and excellent museums. A special feature of the operator's tours is the opportunity for extensive interaction with the local people in all walks of life on visits to schools and farms. "Rural Zimbabwe is a model of peace and cooperation and has inspiring demonstrations of grassroots-initiated social and economic progress," the operator insists. Highlights are one-day canoe and rafting adventures on the celebrated Zambezi River.

ASIA

INDIA

North India Cycle

Operator:
Worldwide Adventures,
1170 Sheppard Ave. West,
#45, Toronto, Ont., Canada
M3K 2A3; (800) 387-1483
or (416) 633-5666;
www.worldwidequest.com.
Price: Moderate.
Season: January, March, and
November.
Length: 15 days.
Accommodations: Hotels and
tent camps. Five percent
discount with BBAT
coupon.

The operator has been running this highly popular trip since 1979. Perhaps there is no better way to discover the richness of Indian village life than from the seat of a bicycle. Participants on this tour pedal from Delhi to Agra (with a visit to the Taj Mahal) and then on to the cities of Udaipur and Jaipur. Routes run along quieter country roads well away from the main highways. The focus throughout is on experiencing village life, with ample opportunity to meet village elders and join in local festivities. Cyclists also visit the famous bird sanctuary at Bharatpur and the Ranthambhore National Park, where the jungle supports a small population of tigers. A support bus accompanies the group.

THAILAND

Mountain Biking in Northern Thailand

For the Thais the province of Chiang Mai has long been their Shangri-la, a land of ancient temples, beautiful women, and stunning scenery. Cyclists on this mountain-bike tour pedal along seldom traveled trails through remote villages to visit ethnic tribes in traditional attire, going about their daily lives little changed in modern times. Participants meet the Karen, Shan, Lisu, Akha, Black, Red Lahu, and Gahliang (Long Neck) tribes. Much of the ride is along strenuous single track with steep hills and challenging downhill runs.

Operator: Asian Pacific Adventures, 9010 Reseda Blvd., #227, Northridge, Calif. 91324; (800) 825-1680 or (818) 886-5190; www.asianpacificadventures.com. *Price:* Moderate. *Season:* February, November, and December. *Length:* 14 days. *Accommodations:* Hotels and guesthouses. Five percent discount with BBAT coupon.

VIETNAM

A Mountain-Bike Tour of the Vietnamese Countryside

Perhaps no better way exists for foreign visitors to meet the people of Vietnam than from the seat of a bicycle— after all, bicycles are the preferred means of travel by most rural Vietnamese. Participants on these tours explore many of the scenic, cultural, and historic sights of this country, where the people are among the friendliest toward Americans in all Asia. The itinerary includes Ho Chi Minh City (formerly Saigon), where bike-tourers pedal along wide boulevards designed by the French; Cu Chi, the amazing tunnel complex built during the Vietnam War; a ride along the South China Sea coast past pagodas, beaches, old French villas, and quaint fishing villages; Hoi An, a 16th-century town preserved just as the early European traders found it; and Hanoi, far more traditional than its southern sister city, Ho Chi Minh City.

Operator: Asian Pacific Adventures, 9010 Reseda Blvd., #227, Northridge, Calif. 91324; (800) 825-1680 or (818) 886-5190; www.asianpacificadventures.com. *Price:* Moderate. *Season:* February, July, October, and December. *Length:* 18 days. *Accommodations:* Hotels. Five percent discount with BBAT coupon.

"The world . . . is a curious sight, and very much unlike what people write."

LORD BYRON

AUSTRALASIA

NEW ZEALAND

South Island Odyssey

Operator: Backroads, 801 Cedar St., Berkeley, Calif. 94710; (800) 462-2848 or (510) 527-1555; www.backroads.com. *Price:* Expensive. *Season:* November–March. *Length:* 15 days. *Accommodations:* Hotels, lodges, and private homes. Five percent discount with BBAT coupon.

This tour has been carefully tailored to include some of New Zealand's most celebrated wilderness attractions, including the spectacular Southern Alps. Participants cycle along beautiful Marlborough Sound, through fertile wine and apple country, and into the magnificent Buller Gorge. For six days they follow the wild western coast past numerous deserted gold-mining towns, an area reminiscent of America's Old West. Several days are spent in Westland National Park exploring the Fox and Franz Josef Glaciers. In Wanaka, riders take a break from cycling for a ski-plane ride over nearby glaciers and a boat cruise on Milford Sound. Total cycling distance is 700 miles. A support van accompanies the group.

The Adventure Travel Hall of Fame: LARRY AND BARBARA SAVAGE

The idea of a 23,000-mile, round-the-world bicycle odyssey came suddenly in early 1977 to Larry and Barbara Savage, both just a few years out of college and living in Santa Barbara, California. It began as a fantasy to relieve the tedium of a daily routine of careers that had hit plateaus. But two years and 25 countries later they had done it. Their route took them up the Pacific coast to Prince Rupert, Canada, across the continent to Washington, D.C., and then down the southeastern coast to Miami. From there they flew to Luxembourg and cycled around Europe with side trips to Morocco and Egypt before flying to New Delhi, India. The couple pedaled across northern India to Katmandu, Nepal, and flew to Bangkok for another leg of cycling to Singapore. They finished up in

CANADA

ALBERTA

Inn-to-Inn Tour Through the Canadian Rockies

Along the western edge of Alberta lies one of North America's greatest bicycling roads: the spectacular Icefields Parkway. Cyclists on this tour ride wide-shouldered roads, along relatively flat country between two magnificent mountain ranges, into the heart of the Canadian Rockies. They travel from Banff to Jasper, stopping along the way to explore such major attractions as Moraine Lake, Lake Louise, and the massive Columbia Icefield. This is a wilderness rich in black bear, elk, and moose. A support van accompanies each group.

Operator: Backroads, 801 Cedar St., Berkeley, Calif. 94710; (800) 462-2848 or (510) 527-1555; www.backroads.com.
Price: Expensive.
Season: June to mid-September.
Length: 5 days.
Accommodations: Hotels and lodges. Five percent discount with BBAT coupon.

New Zealand and French Polynesia.

When the Savages finally arrived back at Los Angeles International Airport, they had survived broken frames, a blizzard in the Alps, various wild animals, rock-throwing Egyptians, teeming Indians, and monsoon-like rains. Their biggest worry before starting had been whether their marriage would survive the intense togetherness and challenges of the adventure they had laid out for themselves. But at the end Barbara could write in her book, Miles from Nowhere: A Round-the-World Bicycle Adventure: "After two solid years of constantly being with one another, of sharing and working together, of weathering the disasters and savoring the triumphs, we were now more a part of each other than I had ever before dreamed possible. Our journey had helped us to come to know each other almost completely, and out of that knowledge had blossomed a special love and respect." Two years later, as her book was going to press, Barbara died from head injuries suffered in a cycling accident near her home in Santa Barbara.

PRINCE EDWARD ISLAND

Prince Edward Island by Bicycle

Operator:
Classic Adventures,
P.O. Box 153,
Hamlin, N.Y. 14464;
(800) 777-8090 or
(716) 964-8488;
www.classicadventures.com.
Price: Moderate.
Season: July and August.
Length: 7 days.
Accommodations: Country
inns. Five percent discount
with BBAT coupon.

Participants on these tours pedal around this scenic southeastern Canadian island on uncrowded roads through a gentle terrain perfect for bicycling. PEI also has seaside cliffs, long stretches of white-sand beaches, and colorful fishing villages. Other attractions include Green Gables, the house that inspired Lucy Maud Montgomery's classic Anne of Green Gables; Prince County, where the descendants of the hardy Arcadian settlers from 200 years ago still maintain their French language and traditions; and the Micmac Indians of Lennox Island. A support van accompanies each group.

QUEBEC

Cycling Historic Quebec

Operator:
Classic Adventures,
P.O. Box 153,
Hamlin, N.Y. 14464;
(800) 777-8090 or
(716) 964-8488;
www.classicadventures.com.
Price: Expensive.
Season: July to mid-
September.
Length: 7 days.
Accommodations: Fine
hotels. Five percent dis-
count with BBAT coupon.

This popular tour focuses on the countryside and major historic sites around the great city of Quebec. Cyclists begin east of Montreal and pedal along the scenic banks of the Richlieu River to its juncture with the St. Lawrence Seaway and then through flat farmland. Once in Quebec participants enjoy a historical tour of the city and then make a leisurely bike ride around Orleans Island, visiting several villages with fine examples of 18th-century architecture. A support van accompanies each group.

YUKON TERRITORY

Cycling in the Footsteps of the Klondikers

In 1898, over 30,000 gold-seekers made their way down the river to the gold fields near Dawson City.

A cyclist pauses at a sign post outside Quebec

Classic Adventures

The countryside is still littered with abandoned relics from that exciting period—Indian camps, trappers' cabins, old Northwest Mounted Police posts, and steamboat wrecks. Cyclists on this trip follow in their footsteps from Skagway to Dawson City. The first stage is a ride on the White Pass & Yukon Railroad, one of the continent's most spectacular rail journeys, to Frasier. From there cyclists pedal past a string of scenic alpine lakes and across the border into Canada. Their route takes them along the shore of Lake LeBarge (made famous in Robert Service's poem, "The Cremation of Sam Magee"), through a landscape of numerous lakes and dense forests, along the banks of the mighty Yukon River, and finally into Dawson City, once called the Paris of the North and home to 30,000 people, but now largely abandoned. A support van accompanies all groups.

Operator:
Alaskan Bicycle Adventures, 907 E. Dowling Rd., #29, Anchorage, Alaska 99518; (800) 770-7242 or (907) 243-2329; www.alaskabike.com.
Price: Expensive.
Season: June and August.
Length: 8 days.
Accommodations: Lodges and hotels. Five percent discount with BBAT coupon.

EUROPE

BRITAIN

Bike Tour of Southern England

Operator: Euro-Bike & Walking Tours, P.O. Box 990, DeKalb, Ill. 60115; (800) 321-6060 or (815) 758-8851; www.eurowalk.com. *Price:* Expensive. *Season:* July and September. *Length:* 8 days. *Accommodations:* Hotels. Five percent discount with BBAT coupon.

Participants on this tour cycle through a world of soaring cathedrals, villages of thatch-roofed houses, royal castles, and stately homes brimming with arts and antiques. They pedal through some of the most celebrated destinations in England, following a route through British history that takes them from the mysteries of Stonehenge through the literary-rich Isle of Wight (adopted by the Victorians as a summer retreat), to Winchester, the capital of King Alfred's England. A support van accompanies all groups.

CZECH REPUBLIC

Vienna-to-Prague Cycle Tour

Operator: REI Adventures, P.O. Box 1938, Sumner, Wash. 98390; (800) 622-2236 or (253) 4437-1100; www.rei.com/travel. *Price:* Moderate. *Season:* Late May–early September. *Length:* 10 days. *Accommodations:* Pensions and medieval mansions. Five percent discount with BBAT coupon.

Participants on this tour experience a well-rounded taste of European culture, from worldly capital cities to exquisite Moravian towns dating back to Baroque and Renaissance times. Travel is along quiet country back roads over rolling and hilly terrain. Once in the Czech Republic, cyclists pedal across a region of neatly harvested vineyards, beautiful lakes, and imposing limestone cliffs. Stops are made at Lednice Park and Lednice Castle; the picturesque Bohemian villages of Bitov, Slavonice, and Dacice; the 13th-century fortified town of Jindrichuv Hradec; and the Czech lake district.

Renaissance Treasures

This cycling expedition begins and ends in Prague, but participants spend their days pedaling through Southern Bohemia along deserted country lanes through a bountiful agricultural region, an area of well-manicured farms and gently rolling, wooded hills. Ample opportunity is allowed for leisurely visits to the enchanting villages, castles, and cathedrals along the way. At Jindrichuv Hradec, a historic town founded in the 13th century, they tour a magnificent 16th-century Renaissance château. Other stops include the crystal manufacturing works in Chlum u Trebone and the beautiful town of Cesky Krumlov, which has been called "the crown jewel of southern Bohemian towns." A support van accompanies each group.

Operator:
Kolotour Bicycle Holidays, P.O. Box 1493, Boulder Creek, Calif. 95006; (800) 524-7099 or (831) 338-3101; www. kolotour.com.
Price: Expensive.
Season: July and August.
Length: 7 days.
Accommodations: Hotels and pensions. Five percent discount with BBAT coupon.

FRANCE

A Food-and-Wine-Lover's Tour of Provence

Cycling through the south of France is a sybarite's dream of châteaus, chardonnay, and friendly smiles. This tour of Provence's most celebrated vineyards, restaurants, and hotels is well worth pumping for. The clear, dazzling light and Mediterranean landscapes of the region inspired the finest paintings of van Gogh and Cézanne. The tour begins with a ride through the valley of the Gardon River and the bustling medieval village of Uzes. The second day starts with a private walking tour of the exquisitely preserved Pont-du-Gard, part of a three-tiered, 31-mile aqueduct built by the Romans in the year 19 B.C. The road to Rasteau passes several vineyards and medieval villages clinging precariously to the rocky outcroppings. A support van accompanies all groups.

Operator:
Vermont Bicycle Touring, Box 711, Bristol, Vt. 05443; (800) 245-3838 or (802) 453-4811; www.vbt.com.
Price: Expensive.
Season: May–mid-October.
Length: 7 days.
Accommodations: Hotels, ranging from elegant rural retreats to small village hotels. Five percent discount with BBAT coupon.

"Nature, strong and wild, is like a Saga chiseled into snow and ice, that at times has moods as fine and gentle as a poem. But nature is also like cold steel, reflecting the play of colors in the bright sun." FRIDTJOF NANSEN
ARCTIC EXPLORER

A group of cyclists takes a lunch break at a fine restaurant in Burgundy

Euro-Bike and Hiking Tours

Deluxe Bicycle Tour of Burgundy

Operator: Euro-Bike & Walking Tours, P.O. Box 990, DeKalb, Ill. 60115; (800) 321-6060 or (815) 758-8851; www.eurobike.com.
Price: Expensive.
Season: July and September.
Length: 6 days.
Accommodations: Upscale hotels. Five percent discount with BBAT coupon.

Choice wines, superb savory cuisine, and exceptional lodging set apart this tour through an exquisite region the French call "Paradis de la Gastronomie." Burgundy is, quite simply, the grande dame of French wine-making. A highlight is organized wine-tasting sessions at several of the region's most celebrated vineyards, including the Château de Meursault with its famous 15th-century cellars. A cultural highlight is the ancient abbey St. Valérien, considered a masterpiece of medieval architecture. A support van accompanies all groups.

"A good traveler does not, I think, much mind the uninteresting places. He is there to be inside them, as a thread is inside the necklace it strings. The world, with unknown and unexpected variety, is a part of his own leisure; and this living participation is, I think, what separates the traveler and the tourist, who remains separate, as if he were at a theater, and not himself a part of whatever the show may be."

FREYA STARK
ALEXANDER'S PATH

Tour Along the Dordogne River Valley

Between the world-famous wine regions of Burgundy and Bordeaux lies the Dordogne River Valley, perhaps France's most beautiful rural landscape. Participants on these tours cycle from the medieval town of Roumegouse to Les Eyzies-de-Tayac, the capital of French prehistory. Along the way they visit the picturesque amphitheater overlooking the Autoire River; Rocamadour, a medieval pilgrimage site; and Chateau Beynac, a castle once captured by Richard the Lionhearted. In the caverns of Font-de-Gaume near Les Eyzies, cyclists tour a 35,000-year-old Cro-Magnon art gallery where magnificent murals depict prehistoric mammoths and great bisons. A support van accompanies the group.

Operator: Europeds, 761 Lighthouse Ave., Monterey, Calif. 93940; (800) 321-9552 or (831) 646-4920; www.europeds.com. *Price:* Expensive. *Season:* May–October. *Length:* 7 days. *Accommodations:* First-class hotels. Five percent discount with BBAT coupon.

Classic Bicycle Tour of the Loire

Long known as the "Garden of France," the Loire Valley is synonymous with magnificent châteaus, gastronomic adventure, and light-bodied wines. Francois I, Leonardo da Vinci, and Joan of Arc are three who made their home here. Cyclists on these tours pedal along flat roads through a peaceful countryside, among lavish palaces and stately manor houses mirrored in the waters of the France's longest river. The historical stops include Amboise, where da Vinci lies buried; the Château de Chenonceaux, a famous castle constructed across the Cher River; and Chambord, with its great château built by Francois I. A support vehicle accompanies each group.

Operator: Europeds, 761 Lighthouse Ave., Monterey, Calif. 93940; (800) 321-9552 or (408) 372-1173; www.europeds.com. *Price:* Expensive. *Season:* June–September. *Length:* 7 days. *Accommodations:* Hotels. Five percent discount with BBAT coupon.

GREECE

Coastal Tour of Classical Greece

This popular tour is the perfect match for lovers of history and antiquities. It is also an excellent opportunity to meet the friendly and hospitable Greek

Operator:
Classic Adventures,
P.O. Box 153, Hamlin, N.Y.
14464; (800) 777-8090 or
(716) 964-8488;
www.classicadventures.com.
Price: Moderate.
Season: May and September.
Length: 12 days.
Accommodations: Small
hotels. Five percent discount with BBAT coupon.

people who live in small villages along the route. Although Greece is largely a mountainous country, this tour follows a flat coastal route. Several days are spent cycling the western island of Zakinthos, with ample free time to explore the sights or just lounge on the beaches. Other highlights include Olympia, the site of the ancient Olympic games, and a cog-rail train ride to the imposing gorge of Kalavrita. A support van accompanies groups.

Monks from the Greek Orthodox Church greet cyclists on a Classic Adventures tour of coastal Greece
Classic Adventures

Inn-to-Inn Cycling Adventure in Crete

Operator: The Northwest
Passage, 1130 Greenleaf
Ave., Wilmette, Ill. 60091;
(800) RECREATE or
(847) 256-4409;
www.nwpassage.com.
Price: Moderate.
Season: May.
Length: 8 days.
Accommodations: Local pensions, hotels, and inns. Five percent discount with BBAT coupon.

Crete has long been popular with travelers. But few have had the opportunity to explore by bicycle the island's magnificent mountains, stunning Mediterranean sea coast, deep wooded gorges, and picturesque villages by bicycle. The tour begins in Heraklion, the largest city on the island. The first day participants pedal through the Lasithi Plateau, famous for its hundreds of windmills, to the village of Agios Nikolaos. Cyclists also visit the seaside resort of Plakias, the castle of Frangokastello, and Matala, famous back in the 1970s for its hippie population. On one day the group hikes for a 10-mile stretch through the Samarian Gorge. There are also plenty of opportunities to visit important archaeological sites reaching back to 2,000 B.C. A support van follows each group.

IRELAND

Yeats Country and Donegal

For cyclists tired of the crowds of tourists they often find in many parts of Ireland, this trip offers a ready escape to the far northwestern corner of the Republic. The counties of Sligo and Donegal remain among Ireland's best-kept secrets. Here cyclists will find themselves pedaling through some of the country's finest scenery and friendliest people. Sligo's tranquil lanes pass through a fairy-tale landscape, which inspired the poet William B. Yeats. The route continues from the tweed shops of Donegal Town to the rugged peninsulas of the Gaeltacht, the western fringe of Eire's Gaelic-speaking community. The remote village of Glencolumbcille overlooks a wealth of archaeological sites and a magnificent beach pounded by wild surf. A layover day in Dunfanaghy lets participants visit two inspiring inland settings: Glenveagh

Operator: Easy Rider Tours, P.O. Box 228, Newburyport, Mass. 01950; (800) 488-8332 or (978) 463-6955; www.easyridertours.com. *Price:* Moderate. *Length:* 10 days. *Season:* July–September. *Accommodations:* Country inns and B&Bs. Five percent discount with BBAT coupon.

A cyclist pedaling through the Irish countryside takes a roadside rest.

Jim Goldberg/Easy Rider Tours

National Park, where native red deer still roam freely, and the Glebe House, home to artist Derek Hill's eclectic art collection where Picasso paintings hang side-by-side with folk art produced by local fishermen-turned-painters. A support van accompanies each group.

ITALY

Giro D'Italia, the Ultimate Italian Cycling Experience

Operator:
Ciclismo Classico,
30 Marathon St.,
Arlington, Mass. 02474;
(800) 866-7314 or
(781) 646-3377;
www.ciclismoclassico.com.
Price: Expensive.
Season: June–early
September.
Length: 15 days.
Accommodations: Hotels.
Five percent discount with
BBAT coupon.

Cyclists on this popular trip pedal along some of Italy's most beautiful roads and through seven of her most fascinating regions. From the canals of storybook Venice to the roughly hewn mountain towns of Abruzzo, this itinerary provides participants with an amazing variety of Italy's scenery, gastronomy, culture, and history. Stops are made at such celebrated Italian treasures as Ravenna, Florence, Arezzio (a well-preserved medieval city which once boasted great wealth), Spoleto (set amidst a countryside rich with Roman antiquities), and Popoli, where a visit is made to the ghostly, abandoned Rocca Calasio, a medieval castle. At the trip's end cyclists can unwind and relax on the Island of Ischia in the Bay of Naples, famous for its spas and natural springs. A support vehicle accompanies each group.

Cycling and Snorkeling on Sardinia and Corsica

Operator:
Ciclismo Classico,
13 Marathon St.,
Arlington, Mass. 02474;
(800) 866-7314 or
(781) 646-3377;
www.ciclismoclassico.com.
Price: Expensive.
Season: May, June, and
September.

Separated by only 18 miles of sea, the islands of Sardinia and Corsica offer cycling visitors landscapes saturated in prehistoric monuments; empty, winding roads; and dramatic coastlines. Participants on these tours begin in northern Sardinia with a ride along the splendid Costa Smeralda, a retreat for the Italian rich and famous. Then they travel by ferry to Bonifacio, a magnificent port town in southern Corsica. The group then spends four days pedaling along the island's beautiful coastal road with numerous breaks to swim in the blue waters. A stop is also made at Filitosa, Corsica's most important historic site, to see stone monuments dating back 5,000 years. The trip ends in Bastia, a charming port town with narrow streets and ancient churches.

Length: 6 or 11 days.
Accommodations: Hotels. Five percent discount with BBAT coupon.

PORTUGAL

Spring in the Alentejo

With its brilliant fields of poppies, medieval hilltop castles, and gleaming, whitewashed villages, one might think of the Alentejo as the Provence of Portugal! The operator schedules all departures during spring, when wildflowers carpet the hillsides and produce an explosion of color. Cyclists will share the country lanes with ox-drawn carts and

Operator: Easy Rider Tours, P.O. Box 228, Newburyport, Mass. 01950; (800) 488-8332 or (978) 463-6955; www.easyridertours.com.
Price: Moderate.
Season: March and May.
Length: 8 days.
Accommodations: Inns and pousadas. Five percent discount with BBAT coupon.

The warm waters off Portugal's coast offer cyclists a refreshing break
Jim Goldberg/Easy Rider Tour

women in traditional black dress, often with enormous loads balanced upon their heads. The route takes riders through the walled city of Monsaraz; Vila Viçosa, where the ruined medieval castle of King Dinis overlooks the town; Estremoz, a town of white marble crowned by a castle and flanked by scenic vineyards; and Castelo de Vide, famous for its medieval castle and Renaissance-era fountains. A support van accompanies all groups.

Minho Grape Escape

Operator:
Easy Rider Tours, P.O. Box 228, Newburyport, Mass. 01950; (800) 488-8332 or (978) 463-6955; www.easyridertours.com.
Price: Moderate.
Season: June and September.
Length: 9 days.
Accommodations: Manor houses and paradors. Five percent discount with BBAT coupon.

This is an adventure for wine-lovers seeking new tastes from Minho, one of Portugal's premier wine-producing regions. Cyclists pedal through timeless villages along the banks of the Rio Lima, Rio Minho, and Rio Coura, and up the Atlantic coast into Spanish Galicia. Attractions along the way include Peneda-Gerês National Park with its spectacular granite peaks; the village of Soajo, its houses and streets hewn from rough granite slabs; the sidewalk cafés and nearby beaches of the seaside village of Caminha; Bayonna, where Columbus's Pinta first docked upon its return from the New World; and Oporto, world-renowned for its vintage wines. A support van accompanies all groups.

SPAIN

Cycling Through Andalucia

Operator:
Easy Rider Tours, P.O. Box 228, Newburyport, Mass. 01950; (800) 488-8332 or (978) 463-6955; www.easyridertours.com.
Price: Expensive.
Season: May–July.
Length: 10 days.

Nowhere in the Iberian peninsula is the Moorish influence more pronounced than in "Al-Andalus," the last stronghold of the Arabs before they were banished by Spanish King Ferdinand and Queen Isabella in 1492. Participants on these trips pedal from Seville to Grenada through a region noted for its excellent wines and local cuisine. A highlight is the Córdoba, famous for the Mezquita (Spain's most beautiful mosque) and a magnificent 16-arched Roman bridge. The tour ends in Grenada,

A cyclist rides along a quiet road in the backcountry of southern Spain

Jim Goldberg/Easy Rider Tour

where cyclists will tour the Alhambra (a vast structure straight out of The Arabian Nights) and enjoy some of the finest flamenco dancing in all Spain. A support van accompanies all groups.

Accommodations: Hotels and a graciously restored 16th-century monastery. Five percent discount with BBAT coupon.

LATIN AMERICA

COSTA RICA

Costa Rica by Bike

This cycling adventure includes rain forests, rivers, jungles, volcanoes, and beaches, each with its own unique flora and fauna. The itinerary allows for plenty of opportunity for the cyclists to experience not only the local people and culture of this unique

Operator:
Worldwide Adventures,
1170 Sheppard Ave. West,
#45, Toronto, Ont., Canada
M3K 2A3; (800) 387-1483
or (416) 633-5666;
www.worldwidequest.com.
Price: Moderate.
Season: January, February,
and March.
Length: 8 days.
Accommodations: Hotels.
Five percent discount with
BBAT coupon.

Central American country but also its wealth of natural beauty and abundant wildlife. Highlights include the Caño Negro Wildlife Refuge, where the cyclists board a riverboat for a trip down the Rio Frio through dense jungle that supports an abundance of tropical birds, iguanas, and monkeys; Arenal, one of the world's most active volcanoes, where one can always count on seeing rivers of lava spilling down its sides; and the lovely beaches and excellent swimming of Playa Hermosa. A support van accompanies all groups.

CUBA

Cuba by Bike

Operator:
Worldwide Adventures,
1170 Sheppard Ave. West,
#45, Toronto, Ont., Canada
M3K 2A3; (800) 387-1483
or (416) 633-5666;
www.worldwidequest.com.
Price: Moderate.
Season: Throughout the
year.

Just in the past year or so Cuba has opened up to organized adventure travel groups. Visit now before the trickle of North American travelers becomes a wave! The operator has put together an itinerary that includes Old Havana (which has been designated a World Heritage Site), rural Cuba (a land of lush green tobacco fields and farmers who still harvest their crops with oxen and cart), and the superb beaches with their warm seas.

Great Achievements in Adventure Travel

In June of 1989 a group of three Americans and four Soviets, four men and three women, embarked from a beach on the Sea of Japan for the first-ever bicycle crossing of Siberia, what participant Mark Jenkins called "the last great ride." Five months and 7,500 miles later four of the group completed the epic ride from Vladivostok to Leningrad. They traveled through eight time zones and covered twice the distance from New York to Los Angeles. Their route took them from the Pacific Ocean to Lake Baikal to the Ural Mountains and finally to the Baltic Sea. Within three weeks, just north of Manchuria, the one road that crosses Siberia vanished. The cyclists labored an entire

Highlights include the Piñar del Rio province, a region famed for the diversity of its natural beauty; Cayo Levisa, a small coral key off the north coast, a wonderland of white coral beaches, thick mangroves, and abundant seabirds; and the Cuevas de los Indios, caves of the pre-Columbian Indians who once inhabited the region. A support van accompanies each group.

Length: 8 days.
Accommodations: Hotels. Five percent discount with BBAT coupon.

UNITED STATES

ALASKA

Alaskan Adventure

This popular trip combines half-days of bicycling with canoeing, hiking, and sea-kayaking adventures, topped off with a visit to Denali National Park and a glacier cruise across Prince William Sound. The itinerary begins with a combination van-ride and cycle trip along the Denali Highway, while ahead looms Mt. McKinley, at 20,320 feet the highest mountain in North America. Canoes are used to explore the Tangle Lakes, a collection of

Operator: Alaskan Bicycle Adventures, 907 E. Dowling Rd., #29, Anchorage, Alaska 99518; (800) 770-7242 or (907) 243-2329; www.alaskabike.com.
Price: Expensive.
Season: June to early September.

month getting through an 800-mile swamp, riding game trails and going village to village. Beyond the swamp lay Lake Baikal, the world's deepest, and on the other side rutted dirt roads for thousands of miles. The cyclists lived on potatoes, milk, and bread for much of their ride and camped in remote wilderness areas. Finally, on October 25, 1989, the three Americans and one Russian bicycled into Leningrad and rode to the Winter Palace, a bottle of champagne in hand. As Jenkins wrote later in his book, Off the Map: Bicycling Across Siberia: "We stood there straddling our bikes and somewhere far, far inside we wanted to howl crazy with glory and triumph, but we didn't. . . . We were tired. We were numb. We hugged each other and dumped the bottle of champagne over our heads and began to shiver because it was starting to snow

The lightly traveled highways of Alaska are a perfect way for cyclists to view up close some of the state's scenic wonders

Alaska Bicycle Adventures

Length: 7 days. *Accommodations:* Cabins, inns, and hotels. Five percent discount with BBAT coupon.

beautiful glacial lakes strung out along the Tangle River. Cyclists then pedal down the Edgerton Highway into Wrangell–St. Elias National Park, dominated by the massive volcano Mt. Wrangell. Next stop is the Chugach Mountains for a pedal

The Adventure Travel Hall of Fame: KEVIN FOSTER

On May 11, 1990, Kevin Foster, 30, a part-time actor from Ojai, California, set out to become the first person to bicycle on top of the Great Wall of China from one end to the other. He started at the wall's westernmost pass, Jiayuguan in Gansu province, but had to skip a long stretch that traverses a closed military area. He walked alongside portions of the wall that are in ruins, bicycling 1,175 miles of the 3,700-mile-long wall. He became the first person to bicycle any substantial distance on the monument, which China's emperors built more than 2,000 years ago to keep out foreigners. The 12 days he spent bicycling from

along the Tsaina River toward Thompson Pass and past the Worthington Glacier. The sea-kayaking portion takes place on Shoup Bay off Prince William Sound where the abundant wildlife includes seals, otters, bald eagles, and humpback whales. A support van accompanies all groups.

Alcan Highway Expedition

Bikers on this expedition pedal from Juneau to Anchorage, a distance of 700 miles over some of the most remote paved highways in the world. The U.S. Army built the Alcan Highway in 1942 in a crash program, and while the road has been upgraded many times since, the wilderness along the road remains untouched. The biking portion begins in Haines on the Inside Passage, and cyclists spend the first night near a river which boasts the largest concentration of bald eagles in the world. After crossing into Canada, cyclists pedal past Kluane Lake (the largest in the Yukon Territory), through St. Elias National Park, and across several large rivers. Four days are spent circling the mighty Wrangell Mountains, the largest volcanoes in North America. Other highlights include a stop in the ghost town of Chitina, abandoned in 1938; the Worthington Glacier located just yards away from the highway; and at the

Operator: Alaskan Bicycle Adventures, 907 E. Dowling Rd., #29, Anchorage, Alaska 99518; (800) 770-7242 or (907) 243-2329; www.alaskabike.com. *Price:* Expensive. *Season:* June–August. *Length:* 12 days. *Accommodations:* Lodges and hotels. Five percent discount with BBAT coupon.

Beijing east to the ocean were the toughest because the wall snakes through mountainous terrain. In places it simply stops and yields to sheer cliffs. "I carried the bike more than rode over this stretch," he admitted later. "There were a couple of times I went to take a step and there was a 20-foot drop. I was able to grab the bushes and hold on." He also encountered the worst bureaucratic barriers of the trip when local police began demanding he obtain a separate travel permit for each county he passed through. Then on June 30, dodging startled guards who wanted to arrest him, he whizzed down the last stretch of the Great Wall to reach the ocean, completing his end-to-end journey on the ancient monument. "I didn't enjoy the authority part," he said later. "Meeting the people along the wall—those were the best times."

trip's conclusion, a cruise across Prince William Sound to see the large numbers of whales, sea lions, seals, and otters as well as the mighty Columbia Glacier. A support van accompanies all groups.

ARIZONA

A Mountain-Bike Tour Along the North Rim of the Grand Canyon

Operator:
Rim Tours, 1233 S. Hwy. 191, Moab, Utah 84532; (800) 626-7335 or (435) 259-5223; www.rimtours.com. *Price:* Moderate. *Season:* June and July. *Length:* 4 and 5 days. *Accommodations:* Tent camps. Five percent discount with BBAT coupon.

Averaging 1,000 feet higher than the South Rim, the North Rim's alpine vegetation and more varied vistas offer cyclists one of the most exciting rides to be found in the West and an easy way to escape from the crowds of tourists on the other side. Following trails across the Kaibab Plateau through forests of ponderosa pine and aspen forests, riders pedal across rolling terrain at altitudes between 7,500 and 9,000 feet. Cyclists will have numerous opportunities to enjoy views of the Grand Canyon.

Mountain bikes are a perfect way to explore the wonders of the Sonoran Desert in Arizona
The World Outside

Sonora Desert Singletracker

Southern Arizona has an environment supporting three distinct desert ecosystems where some 30 cactus species flourish, ranging from the giant saguaro to the minuscule fishhook. Visitors to the remote wildernesses may also see bighorn sheep, mule deer, and the elusive peccary roaming the stark, sun-blistered mountains, rocky canyons, and sweeping outwash plains. The operator offers mountain biking trips through some of the most pristine of the wilderness areas. Bikers pedal through the heart of the Santa Catalina Mountains and along the Arizona Trail on one of the steepest single-track rides around, at one point dropping over 5,100 feet.

Operator:
The World Outside,
2840 Wilderness Pl., #F,
Boulder, Colo. 80501;
(800) 488-8493 or
(303) 413-0938;
www.theworldoutside.com.
Price: Moderate.
Season: April, October, and November.
Length: 5 days.
Accommodations: Tent camps. Ten percent discount coupon with BBAT coupon.

CALIFORNIA

Weekend Mountain-Bike Trip in Yosemite National Park

This adventure has proven enormously popular with residents from the nearby San Francisco Bay area, eager to explore the wealth of seldom-traveled mountain bike trails in the Sierra National Forest. Cyclists pedal through thickly carpeted forests of pine and fir; down a thrilling, 4,000-foot descent; over clear, tumbling alpine streams; and across granite slickrock ridgelines with spectacular views of the High Sierra. The trails are a combination of scenic fire road and rugged four-wheel-drive trails. On the second day the group lunches at "The Amphitheater," a granite phenomenon with 100-mile views of the high country. From this 7,000-foot level cyclists then head downhill for the 4,000-foot, 25-mile descent to beautiful Bass Lake.

Operator:
Southern Yosemite
Mountain Guides,
P.O. Box 301, Bass Lake,
Calif. 93604;
(800) 231-4575 or
(559) 658-8735;
www.symg.com.
Price: Inexpensive.
Season: May–October.
Length: 3 days.
Accommodations: Chalet on Bass Lake. Ten percent discount with BBAT coupon.

"With beauty all around me, I walk."
NAVAJO PRAYER

A four-wheel-drive support vehicle accompanies all groups and carries all necessary repair tools.

Inn-to-Inn Ride Through the California Wine Country

Operator: Backroads, 801 Cedar St., Berkeley, Calif. 94710; (800) 245-3874 or (510) 527-1555; www.backroads.com.
Price: Expensive.
Season: Throughout the year.
Length: 6 days.
Accommodations: Five-star inns and health spas. Five percent discount with BBAT coupon.

The operator bills this as "the most luxurious bicycle inn tour in America." The popular trip through the Napa Valley wine country is as much a connoisseur's tour of country inns as it is of California wineries. Cyclists spend their first night at Madrona Manor, a Victorian mansion that gives Falcon Crest a run for its money. A 26-mile ride the next day ends at the historic Mount View Hotel, where riders enjoy a mud bath or soothing massage before sampling the nouvelle cuisine in the hotel's famous restaurant. Participants have plenty of time for wine-tasting at the many celebrated wineries which make Napa Valley America's premier wine-producing region. Cyclists then travel the Sonoma Valley, stopping at its historic Spanish mission, to the Sonoma Mission Inn, northern California's finest health spa. The trip concludes at the Inn at the Tides, where the rooms look out over the blue Pacific.

Lake Tahoe Lodge-Based Mountain Biking

Operator: Tahoe Trips & Trails, Box 6952, Tahoe City, Calif. 96145; (800) 581-4453 or (530) 583-4506; www.tahoetrips.com.
Price: Expensive.
Season: August and September.
Length: 3 and 5 days.
Accommodations: Lodge. Five percent discount with BBAT coupon.

For mountain-bike enthusiasts the Lake Tahoe area has become a favorite destination, offering both splendid scenery and challenging trails. The operator has put together a lodge-based adventure that introduces cyclists to some of the most rewarding backcountry rides in northern California. Highlights include a ride aboard a cable car up the mountain in Squaw Valley for a cycling adventure at the 8,200 foot level; a ride to Sardine Peak along an abandoned logging road to an old fire-lookout station with magnifi-

"One attribute of a high civilization is a development of the spirit of adventure, of the will to experiment."
VILHJALMUR STEFANSSON
AMERICAN ARCTIC EXPLORER OF THE EARLY 1900s

The famed Colorado Trail offers some of the most challenging mountain biking in the country

Todd Campbell: Rim Tours

cent views of unspoiled forest; and the famous Flume Trail, cut into granite 1,200 feet above Lake Tahoe, with stunning views of the entire lake.

COLORADO

Durango's Colorado Trail

The area around Durango offers some of the state's most challenging mountain biking experiences. The focus of this mountain biking adventure is the western section of the famed Colorado Trail, which runs 470 miles from Denver to Durango. This stretch offers some of the most spectacular mountain scenery of the entire trail. A highlight is the Cascade Creek drainage with its abundance of wildflowers and the views of Engineer Mountain. The operator warns that this challenging trip is only for advanced cyclists with technical experience. They ride narrow trails at high altitudes between 10,000 and 12,000 feet with a probability of thundershowers every day.

Hut-to-Hut Mountain Biking Through the Rockies

Named after a U.S. Army ski troop that trained in

Operator:
Rim Tours, 1233 S. Hwy. 191, Moab, Utah 84532; (800) 626-7335 or (435) 259-5223; www.rimtours.com.
Price: Moderate.
Season: July.
Length: 4 and 5 days.
Accommodations: Tent camps. Five percent discount with BBAT coupon.

Operator:
The World Outside,
2840 Wilderness Pl., #F,
Boulder, Colo. 80501;
(800) 488-8493 or
(303) 413-0938;
www.theworldoutside.com.
Price: Moderate.
Season: July and August.
Length: 6 days.
Accommodations:
Comfortable trail huts. Ten
percent discount with
BBAT coupon.

Colorado during the Second World War, the Tenth Mountain Division Trail connects Aspen to Vail, passing through a spectacular wilderness setting remote from the usual summer crowds. The 300 miles of single-track and forest trails constitute this country's most extensive hut-served trail network. The huts are actually spacious, two-story log cabins in the style of French chalets, featuring vaulted ceilings, varnished pine furniture, woodstoves, large sundecks, and photovoltaic lighting. Bikers on these adventures follow a circuitous route through the rugged Holy Cross Wilderness, pedaling a mix of old mining roads, abandoned railway grades, forest trails, and single tracks. Along the way they explore remote ghost towns and hike to secluded alpine lakes and summits.

Operator:
Vermont Bicycle Touring,
Box 711, Bristol, Vt. 05443;
(800) 245-3868 or
(802) 453-4811;
www.vbt.com.
Price: Expensive.
Season: July–September.
Length: 5 days.
Accommodations: Historic
inns, such as the Jed Prouty
Inn (1793), which is on the
National Historic Register.
Five percent discount with
BBAT coupon.

MAINE

Penobscot Bay

The Maine coast offers well-maintained, quiet roads ideal for bike touring, along with an excellent mix of scenery. The itinerary of this tour allows cyclists to visit small fishing villages, craft shops, antiques stores, art galleries, lighthouses, and museums while cycling the scenic shoreline. The picturesque towns of Blue Hill and Castine anchor the itinerary, as cyclists explore the surrounding countryside. The road connecting the two passes through a collage of white clapboard houses, saltwater marshes, farms, and blueberry fields. The first day is given over to a cycling excursion around the island of Isleboro. A support van accompanies all groups.

MARYLAND

Exploring the Shoreline of Chesapeake Bay

"Heaven and earth never agreed better to frame a

place for men's habitation," Captain John Smith wrote enthusiastically about this area in 1607. One of the great natural resources of the eastern United States, Chesapeake Bay is perhaps most celebrated for its unrivaled boating opportunities. But the mixture of historic sites, beautiful scenery, and well-maintained flat roads make the region a paradise for cyclists. Riders on these relaxing trips pedal through numerous picturesque villages set in a verdant countryside. One highlight is the fishing village of Rock Hall, where the group boards a skipjack bound for St. Michaels, home of the Chesapeake Bay Maritime Museum.

Operator: Vermont Bicycle Touring, Box 711, Bristol, Vt. 05443; (800) 245-3868 or (802) 453-4811; www.vbt.com.
Price: Moderate.
Season: May–October.
Length: 6 days.
Accommodations: Historic inns. Five percent discount with BBAT coupon.

MASSACHUSETTS

Bike Tour of Martha's Vineyard and Nantucket Islands

Cyclists on this tour divide their time between the two most famous islands in New England, both of which offer ideal bicycling conditions because of limited traffic, excellent roads, and gentle terrain. On Martha's Vineyard, riders stay at a 17th-century inn and explore at leisure the secluded beaches and the Victorian villages of Edgartown, Chappaquiddick, and Oak Bluffs. Evening

Operator: Vermont Bicycle Touring, Box 711, Bristol, Vt. 05443; (800) 245-3868 or (802) 453-4811; www.vbt.com.
Price: Expensive.
Season: May–October.
Length: 6 days.
Accommodations: Local inns. Five percent discount with BBAT coupon.

"Now that I was in shape, cycle touring seemed like a great way to travel. We moved slowly enough to see and hear things that to passing motorists were only blurs of color and sound. We took in the textures and odors of the soil and the vegetation. And because bicycling is such a quiet mode of travel, wild animals weren't frightened away when we came up on the road toward them. Deer, accustomed to seeing and hearing huge, noisy boxes of accelerated steel on the roads, often loped to the edge of the pavement to find out what we were. And, too, touring by bicycling made it easy for us to meet people."

BARBARA SAVAGE
MILES FROM NOWHERE: A ROUND-THE-WORLD BICYCLE ADVENTURE

options include a production at one of the excellent local theaters or perhaps dancing at a trendy nightspot. Next stop is Nantucket, for 200 years the home port of a great whaling fleet. Cyclists explore the island's quiet moors and cranberry bogs, numerous wildlife refuges, and the tiny village of 'Sconset, which looks like a set for the musical Brigadoon.

MICHIGAN

Mackinac Wayfarer

Operator: Michigan Bicycle Touring, 3512 Red School Rd., Kingsley, Mich. 49649; (231) 263-5885; www.bikembt.com. *Price:* Expensive. *Season:* June, August, and September. *Length:* 5 days. *Accommodations:* Inns. Five percent discount with BBAT coupon.

Michigan boasts some of the most beautiful, lightly traveled yet well-kept back roads in the country. Participants on this tour explore the northern portions of the state's lower peninsula, skirting the scenic coast of Lake Michigan from Charlevoix through hilly countryside toward Petoskey on Little Traverse Bay. Much of the cycling is through lightly settled farmland. At Mackinaw City, riders take a ferry to Mackinac Island, a bicyclist's dream, where horse-drawn buggies and bikes are the only traffic. (Automobiles are prohibited.) Two nights are spent on Mackinac, Michigan's most popular tourist attraction and a location for the 1979 film Somewhere in Time. A support van accompanies the group.

Biking Through the Upper Peninsula

Operator: Michigan Bicycle Touring, 3512 Red School Rd., Kingsley, Mich. 49649; (231) 263-5885; www.bikembt.com. *Price:* Moderate. *Season:* June–mid-September. *Length:* 5 days. *Accommodations:* Inns and cabins. Five percent discount with BBAT coupon.

Across the majestic Mackinac Bridge is Michigan's Upper Peninsula, a world apart. This tour explores the unspoiled wilderness of the Keweenaw Peninsula, the 1843 scene of one of America's first mining booms. Cyclists ride along miles of rugged Lake Superior shoreline, past ghost towns, abandoned mines, and many waterfalls. Other highlights include Fort Wilkins (1844), the last remain-

A large part of the appeal of Classic
Adventures' Southern trips is the opportunity for cyclists to see firsthand some of the
important historic sites of the Old South

Classic Adventures

ing original wooden fort east of the Mississippi
River, and the picturesque Copper Harbor
Lighthouse (1866). A support van accompanies the
group.

MISSISSIPPI

Cycling Through the Antebellum Souths

"We are a ghost-ridden people," novelist William
Faulkner once observed about Southerners.
Cyclists on these popular trips experience a ghost-
ridden landscape as they pedal from Nashville,
Tennessee, to Natchez, Mississippi, past sprawling
cotton plantations, Civil War battlefields, and
stately mansions straight out of Gone with the
Wind. The route is the Natchez Trace, which dates
back several hundred years to its first use by Indians

Operator:
Classic Adventures,
P.O. Box 153,
Hamlin, N.Y. 14464;
(800) 777-8090 or
(716) 964-8488;
www.classicadventures.com.
Price: Moderate.
Season: April and October.
Length: 7 days.
Accommodations: Inns. Five
percent discount with
BBAT coupon.

and later by pioneers as a shortcut to the Ohio Valley. In 1806, Congress made it a National Road. The northern section of the route tends to be cooler and hillier, while the southern section is flatter and warmer. The tour ends at the historic city of Natchez, which boasts over 500 antebellum buildings still standing, including scores of stately mansions and plantation homes. A support vehicle accompanies all groups.

MONTANA

Pedaling Through Glacier National Park

Operator: Timberline Bicycle Tours, 7975 E. Harvard, #J, Denver, Colo. 80231; (800) 417-2453 or (303) 759-3804; timberline.com/tours. *Price:* Expensive. *Season:* July and August. *Length:* 8 days. *Accommodations:* Lodges. Five percent discount with BBAT coupon.

This northern Montana park boasts a superb glacier-carved mountain wilderness that is quite similar in climate, flora, and fauna to central Alaska, along with 50 glaciers and 200 lakes. Cyclists on this popular trip pedal the grand loop of both Glacier and Waterton Lakes National Parks. A highlight is the ride along the spectacular Going-to-the-Sun Highway and over Logan Pass (6,046 feet) past glacial snowfields, waterfalls, and spectacular vistas at every switchback. On the third day the group cycles across the border into Canada for a visit to Waterton Park, spending the night at the famous Prince of Wales Hotel overlooking the lake. The return is along the sparsely traveled eastern perimeter of Glacier National Park for two evenings at the grand Glacier Park Lodge. On their day of rest, cyclists have the option of a half-day of white-water rafting on the Flathead River or numerous fine hiking excursions. A support vehicle follows the group.

NORTH CAROLINA

Coastal Odyssey

Take towering waves, whipped to a boil by frequent Atlantic gales, against a fragile barrier of lonely islands. Add the ghosts of pirates and the hulks of hundreds of decaying shipwrecks. Season with wheeling seabirds, scrappy game fish, dunes sculpted by the winds, shells, and sunsets in rainbow hues. What you have is Cape Hatteras and the other barrier islands that make the North Carolina coast one of the most spectacular in the nation. These tours explore the best parts of this magical area. Of special interest are elegant Tryon Palace, the home of North Carolina's colonial governor; historic Ocracoke Island, which boasts some of the finest beaches on the Eastern Seaboard; and the Cedar Island Wildlife Refuge, where over 300 bird species have been spotted. A support van accompanies all groups.

Operator: Vermont Bicycle Touring, Box 711, Bristol, Vt. 05443; (800) 245-3868 or (802) 453-4811; www.vbt.com.
Price: Expensive.
Season: May, September, and October.
Length: 6 days.
Accommodations: Country inns. Five percent discount with BBAT coupon.

OREGON

Rogue River Rambler

The itinerary on this popular road adventure takes bikers through some of the Pacific Northwest's most spectacular scenery as they pedal from the Pacific coast along the lovely Rogue River Valley into the rugged alpine setting of the Cascades. Beginning in Eugene, the cyclists travel through the Siuslaw National Forest and along the Smith River until they reach the coast. They then head north to the mouth of the Rogue River, where they turn inland. From the town of Agness they climb 4,600 feet in 16 miles and cross over Bearcamp Pass to be rewarded with an incredible downhill ride to once again find themselves pedaling along the

Operator: Timberline Bicycle Tours, 7975 E. Harvard, #J, Denver, Colo. 80231; (800) 417-2453 or (303) 759-3804; www.timberline.com/tours.
Price: Moderate.
Season: August.
Length: 9 days.
Accommodations: Inns and lodges. Five percent discount with BBAT coupon.

"I knew that the universe was wider than my view of it, and would always be, and I learned that if the mass of men lived lives of quiet desperation, too often they were, for want of confidence or courage, the authors of that desperation."

AUGUST DERLETH
WALDEN WEST

Rogue River Valley. They spend the final two nights at Crater Lake National Park. A support van follows all groups.

Cycling Around Crater Lake

Operator:
Backcountry,
P.O. Box 4029, Bozeman,
Mont. 59772;
(800) 575-1540 or
(406) 586-3556;
www.backcountrytours.com.
Price: Expensive.
Season: August.
Length: 6 days.
Accommodations: Lodges.
Five percent discount with
BBAT coupon.

Six thousand five hundred years ago, 12,000-foot-high Mt. Mazama erupted with a titanic roar and then collapsed into a crater 1,932 feet deep. Over the centuries this filled to form Crater Lake, the deepest (and bluest!) lake in the United States and the seventh-deepest in the world. Cyclists on these adventures pedal on well-maintained paved roads through old-growth forests on a leisurely ride around the 33-mile caldera rim. This is one of the most scenic bike rides in North America, with impressive views of volcanic peaks in every direction. One day is spent hiking along the Rogue River to view deep canyons and lava tubes.

UTAH

Cycling Canyonlands National Park

Operator:
Rim Tours, 1233 S. Hwy.
191, Moab, Utah 84532;
(800) 626-7335 or
(435) 259-5223;
www.rimtours.com.
Price: Moderate.
Season: April, May,
September, and October.
Length: 3, 4, 5, and 6 days.
Accommodations: Hotel and
tent camps. Five percent
discount with BBAT
coupon.

The White Rim Trail, located in the heart of Canyonlands National Park, is one of the finest mountain bike trails in the nation. This trip offers a perfect combination of great riding and spectacular scenery. Cyclists pedal along the "White Rim" layer of sandstone, with dramatic canyons below and majestic red rock cliffs above, through a landscape studded with rock spires, pillars, and arches. Visits will be made to Anasazi Indian ruins tucked away in remote corners of the park. The operator also offers separate tours focusing on The Maze, a remote region of sinuous canyons, distorted buttes, top-heavy hoodoos, and some of the most bizarre, gravity-defying rock formations found anywhere.

The Best of Bryce to Zion Tour

This mountain-bike tour focuses on two of the crown jewels in the National Park system. Bryce is really not a canyon but the cracked and eroded eastern face of southern Utah's Paunsaugunt Plateau, sporting a wilderness of phantom-like rock spires. Shaped mainly by water's incessant toil, Zion's deep canyons cleave through faulted sandstone plateaus formed of sediments left by ancient seas and lakes. Cyclists pedal along single- and double-track trails through red rock canyons and along picturesque desert streams. The trip ends at the bottom of Zion Canyon with a hike up the celebrated Narrows, where the walls rise 2,000 feet overhead but can be only 15 feet apart.

Operator: Rim Tours, 1233 S. Hwy. 191, Moab, Utah 84532; (800) 626-7335 or (435) 259-5223; www.rimtours.com. *Price:* Moderate. *Season:* June–September. *Length:* 6 days. *Accommodations:* Tent camps. Five percent discount with BBAT coupon.

Mountain Biking the Kokopelli Trail

Linking Grand Junction, Colorado, and the fat-tire mecca of Moab, Utah, the legendary Kokopelli Trail is a tough but rewarding adventure that traverses dramatic canyon country and high-mountain scenery. The route is a 140-mile roller coaster of jeep roads and trails that include some 8,000 vertical feet of climbing in the snowcapped La Sal Mountains. Few who ride the Kokopelli will forget the trail's finale—a 4,000-foot, heart-pounding descent that winds through high-country pine and aspen, then juniper and piñon, and finally the sandstone domes of Moab's renowned Slickrock Trail. An off-road vehicle carries all supplies.

Operator: The World Outside, 2840 Wilderness Pl., #F, Boulder, Colo. 80501; (800) 488-8493 or (303) 413-0938; www.theworldoutside.com. *Price:* Moderate. *Season:* May and September. *Length:* 5 days. *Accommodations:* Tent camps. Ten percent discount coupon with BBAT coupon.

VERMONT

Champlain Valley

The locals jokingly refer to their Lake Champlain Valley as "New England's West Coast." And in a sense it is—a west coast composed of the sixth-largest body of fresh water in the United States. Long and slender, it stretches 110 miles along two-thirds of the Vermont–New York border. Cyclists pedal through

Operator: Vermont Bicycle Touring, Box 711, Bristol, Vt. 05443; (800) 245-3868 or (802) 453-4811; www.vbt.com.

Price: Moderate.
Season: May–September.
Length: 5 days.
Accommodations: Historic country inns. Five percent discount with BBAT coupon.

the Champlain Valley between the Green Mountains and the Adirondacks on one of the most scenic rides in New England. Starting in the small town of Danby and riding north through farmland and orchards and across covered bridges, cyclists visit the Morgan Horse Farm and take a cable-drawn ferry ride across Lake Champlain to Fort Ticonderoga, where Vermont's Revolutionary War hero Ethan Allen outfoxed the British in 1777. The trip ends in Middlebury, a picturesque college town. A support van accompanies all groups.

Operator:
Backroads, 801 Cedar St., Berkeley, Calif. 94710; (800) 245-3874 or (510) 527-1555; www.backroads.com.
Price: Moderate.
Season: June–September.
Length: 6 days.
Accommodations: Country inn and health resort. Five percent discount with BBAT coupon.

WASHINGTON

Biking the Islands of Puget Sound

Some 768 jade-green islands lie scattered across Puget Sound, sheltered by the magnificent Olympic Mountains. This popular tour travels by ferryboat to savor some of the best sights that the Pacific Northwest offers. Cyclists spend several days each on two of the most popular and scenic islands. On big San Juan Island they cycle along quiet roads past hidden bays and secluded beaches. Next they travel to Orcas Island's peaceful villages, lovely Cascade Lake, and lush forests. They also make a day trip to nearby Lopez Island for some leisurely cycling and swimming. Cycling distances are short.

Operator:
Backcountry, P.O. Box 4029, Bozeman, Mont. 59772; (800) 575-1540 or (406) 586-3556; www.backcountrytours.com.
Price: Expensive.
Season: July to early September.
Length: 6 days.
Accommodations: Park lodges. Five percent discount with BBAT coupon.

WYOMING

Multi-Sport Grand Teton Adventure

The special appeal of the Tetons lies in the way they rise so precipitously from the lake-studded valley of Jackson Hole, the tallest peak clawing the sky at nearly 14,000 feet. One of the largest herds of elk in North America migrates from the valley floor each summer to the high country. Participants on this popular trip—perfect for families—bike, canoe, horseback-ride, and raft

Bicycles are a popular way to experience the wonders of Yellowstone National Park

Timberline

through Grand Teton National Park's many attractions.

Cycling the Yellowstone Country

This popular trip focuses on two of our most celebrated national parks, Yellowstone and Grand Teton. Cyclists assemble in Jackson Hole and the next morning start pedaling along the Lewis River. Their route takes them over the Continental Divide and down into the geyser basins, past Old Faithful, and on toward Grand Teton National Park. Daily mileage is modest, and a support wagon follows the group.

Operator: Timberline Bicycle Tours, 7975 E. Harvard, #J, Denver, Colo. 80231; (800) 417-2453 or (303) 759-3804; www.timberline.com/tours. *Price:* Expensive. *Season:* June–August. *Length:* 7 days. *Accommodations:* Park lodges. Five percent discount with BBAT coupon.

PROFILE
LAUREN HEFFERON
CICLISMO CLASSICO

"I t was during the farmhouse lunch when all culinary control was lost," writer Carolyn Rice reflected on her Ciclismo Classico bicycle tour of southern Italy. "It was there that I realized that this trip would be as much about food as anything else. As pizza baked in the wood-fired oven, we sat at a long table while the local wine was poured. Then the antipasto started coming. And coming. Among the dishes were *cicoria e fava*, sautéed chicory and pureed fava beans; marinated squid, anchovies and mussels; baked olives; spicy sausage and orecchiette ('little ears') pasta with broccoli rabe. There was a potted, fermented ricotta cheese that was a big hit. Claudio, our guide, explained that this was cheese that had 'slept.'"

This is exactly the sort of experience that Lauren Hefferon, the red-haired founder of Ciclismo Classico, emphasizes in her tours, which are designed as immersions in Italian culture. Her own life history—including an Italian-American heritage, fluency in the Italian language, a strong educational background in Italian culture, marriage to an Italian man, and over 100,000 miles of bike touring, chiefly in Italy—helps ensure this.

"I try to give my clients the experience I've had in Italy—which was very family-oriented," Hefferon insists. "What people like about our tours is the local color. We really get involved with local people. I don't want to sell a tour. I want people to feel like they're learning a different culture."

Ciclismo Classico is the only tour company to specialize exclusively in Italian bicycling and walking vacations. Hefferon has developed over 20 different itineraries, each one rich in authentic Italian experiences. "Cycling is a simple pleasure," she says. "When you pedal through the Italian countryside, it's almost like you're churning out the scenery as you bike. You really can't experience the sounds and smells of Italy when you're stuck in a train or a car."

Hefferon first heard the sounds of cycling at a young age, growing up in the small city of Keene, New Hampshire. She was an active, competitive, sports-oriented youth. After she injured her knee skiing, she took up cycling in earnest. She remembers: "Throughout my high-school years, I spent my weekends biking. I mapped out an itinerary and then pedaled by myself to visit friends and family in nearby towns. I loved to hang out in the local bike shop, discussing with the people there when bike touring would become a big business in America. I knew back then that it was a perfect recreational sport for Americans. At that time, bicycling was really was not popular, at least for longer trips."

To celebrate her graduation from high school in 1979, Hefferon planned a lengthy bike tour along the coast of Maine and around Nova Scotia. A couple of her buddies from school accompanied her. "This was all new at the time," she insists. "No operator offered organized tours in this area back then. That experience got me hooked on bicycle touring. I became a committed cycle-tourist and bought the best equipment available."

Hefferon then went to college, selecting Cornell University largely because of the cycling opportunities it offered in the nearby countryside. She majored in anthropology. In 1982 she spent a year in Peru on an Earthwatch scholarship, surveying archaeological sites in the mountains near Lima. The next year a California publishing company brought out her senior thesis as a book titled, Cycle Food.

Hefferon's focus on Italy was a natural outgrowth of the fact that she had grown up in an Italian-American family. After graduation from Cornell, she was awarded a Rotary Scholarship for a year in Italy. "I had no idea of what I wanted to do for a living, but knew that I would probably go into business for myself and focus on one of my major interests," she recalls. "That first summer in Europe I cycled over 3,000 miles all over Europe on just $10 a day before finally settling down in Perugia, Italy. One of my first adventures was to check out my Italian roots. I cycled across Italy to the small town where my grandmother had been born. That was an amazing experience. The village proved more rugged, primitive, and beautiful than I had ever imagined."

Hefferon soon discovered the Italian culture had embraced serious cycling far beyond anything she had known in America. She became the first woman to be admitted into the exclusive male membership of several prestigious cycling clubs. She notes:

"Cycling has a long tradition in Italy that Italians like to brag about. Although they are impressed with America's high-tech cycling boom, Italians will quickly remind you that they are still number one. Being number one, however, means that those who participate in the sport follow certain conventions in dress, training, and even how to have fun on a bicycle."

Hefferon moved to Florence and spent three years there. During her summers in Italy, she designed and led bicycle tours of Italy for an American operator to supplement her income. That experience convinced her there was a healthy market for well-designed bicycle tours focused on Italy. "There was nobody specializing in Italian cycling tours," she reflects today, "and I saw the need for an Italian expert."

Shortly before she left Italy in 1986, Hefferon met Mauro Rugiero, destined to become her husband. "He is a recreational biker, not the fanatical cyclist I am," she freely admits.

Hefferon started Ciclismo Classico in 1988, taking $3,000 out of her savings account to finance her new business. That first year she offered three itineraries, all in the Tuscany area, and had 18 clients. From that first season, she knew she had chosen the correct career move. "I love Italy, but it's really the clients who get me excited," she says today. "By the second year, I was pretty sure we'd do well. I'd seen enough people seize my enthusiasm and heard enough clients say, 'We're having a great time.'"

Hefferon soon found her potent formula of challenging cycling and Italian know-how a hit in the competitive bike-touring market. Like many other operators, she supplies her clients with top-quality bicycles for rent and provides each group with a support van that carries all the luggage between hotels. Those cyclists who prefer to ride rather than pedal through the hilly regions can do so. Distances vary from 20 to 50 miles per day, with each tour covering several hundred miles in total.

While biking is central to each trip, Hefferon also offers her clients a broad range of other options designed to immerse them in Italian culture. These include optional Italian language lessons; special festivals such as medieval pageants, Renaissance jousts, religious processions, and harvest festivals; cultural activities such as Italian folk dancing, music, and art; and Italian cooking lessons.

All of Ciclismo Classico's tours are itinerary-driven. Hefferon sets up an itinerary first, seeking out those areas which offer a variety of experiences. Then she looks for three- and four-star hotels to accommodate her clients. "The more charm they have, the better," she says.

Hefferon is constantly searching for new guides to lead her trips. Her two dozen guides are evenly split between American and Italian nationalities. "Good guides aren't easy to come by," she insists. "My guides have to be able to establish themselves as experts within the first two days of a tour. The minute a guide loses the clients' confidence, it's hard to regain it."

Ciclismo Classico's clients range in age from 30 to 70. The older clients have repeatedly demonstrated they are more than a match for their younger counterparts. "Cycling always brings out the teenager in people," Hefferon insists. "Everyone on a bicycle is not the same age—the spirit is what it's all about."

What about those stories of crazy Italian drivers? "The Italian roads are really quite safe for bicyclists," Hefferon insists. "Italian drivers actually have great respect for bicyclists and are quite considerate of them when they encounter them on the roads."

In 1994 Hefferon expanded her tours to include a selected number of walking tours. These have proven popular and she plans to make this a major growth area for her company in coming years. Other changes include a move to a Victorian house in Arlington which overlooks the Minute Man Bike Path, Boston's busiest bike path.

In 1997 Hefferon and her husband, Mauro, a bespectacled lawyer, had a son they named Lorenzo after Lorenzo de' Medici, the great Florentine humanist. To celebrate his birth and introduce him to Ciclismo Classico, the couple hosted a 13-day "Bambino Baptismal Tour" that pedaled around southern Sicily, the Aeolian Islands, and finally ended at Cittadella del Capo, Mauro's tiny seaside village in northern Calabria.

"My son has changed my perspective on the business," Hefferon admits. "I will be making a major push in the future for family-oriented bike tours. We will work out of a base, do bike rides in the morning, and have an Italian day-care center for the younger children in the afternoons to free up the parents and their older children for family activities. Our first such family trip happened in the summer of 1998. We operated out of a villa in Tuscany. It was a big success."

3
WILDLIFE AND NATURAL HISTORY EXPEDITIONS

"There is something about safari life that makes you forget your troubles and feel the whole time as if you had drunk half a bottle of champagne—bubbling over with heartfelt gratitude for being alive," Isak Dinesen wrote in *Out of Africa*.

Wildlife and natural history expeditions offer marvelous opportunities to learn about diverse habitats, see and photograph rare forms of animal and plant life, climb unusual geological formations, and travel through exotic worlds. Naturalists often accompany these trips, turning them into learning experiences that pave the way for a greater understanding of the world's wild places.

East Africa is the world's premier destination for wildlife safaris. Every year the game-thronged plains of Kenya and Tanzania draw record numbers of visitors who book safaris by Land Cruiser, hot-air balloon, camel or horseback, foot, and raft. Each offers its own unique advantages. A park such as Masai Mara takes on an entirely different perspective when viewed by foot instead of from the inside of a vehicle.

The Galapagos Islands and Antarctica are two other major areas with superb wildlife. But the options are virtually unlimited. The world offers countless Edens waiting to be explored. Adventure travelers can kayak with orcas off British Columbia, observe active volcanoes and geysers in Iceland, boat through the great Amazonian rain forest, watch tigers from atop an elephant in India's Kanha National Park, pet a gray whale in Baja California, and canoe through the Okefenokee National Wildlife Refuge.

An elephant approaches a vehicle for closer inspection in a Botswana park

Mountain Travel-Sobek

AFRICA

BOTSWANA

Botswana Camping Safari

Botswana is roughly the size of Kenya but with only 1 million inhabitants. Its Okavango Delta region offers a magnificent profusion of wildlife, with some of the finest game-viewing in all Africa. This expedition starts in Zimbabwe with a visit to Victoria Falls, then crosses the border into Botswana for stays in Moremi and Chobe National Parks, which have some of the largest concentrations of elephants still left in Africa. The days here are taken up with game drives and bush hikes. Several days are spent in the legendary Okavango Delta, a 9,000-square-mile network of lagoons and waterways similar to Florida's Everglades. One of the most unique and pristine wildlife areas in Africa, it supports a veritable garden of exotic and colorful flora and fauna.

Operator: Mountain Travel-Sobek, 6420 Fairmount Ave., El Cerrito, Calif. 94530; (888) 687-6235 or (415) 527-8100; www.mtsobek.com.
Price: Expensive.
Season: Throughout the year.
Length: 18 days.
Accommodations: Tented camps. Five percent discount with BBAT coupon.

KENYA

Deluxe Safari for Disabled Travelers

The operator has experience escorting groups of disabled travelers on safari in Kenya. One seat is removed from a nine-passenger minibus to accommodate four people and their wheelchairs comfortably. A professional assistant for the disabled also accompanies the group. The safari itinerary includes the Masai Mara, Lake Nakuru, and Amboseli National Parks, with stops at the Karen Blixen Homestead and Museum and the Mt. Kenya Safari Club.

Operator: Directions Unlimited, 123 Green Lane, Bedford Hills, N.Y. 10507; (800) 533-5343 or (914) 241-1700.
Price: Moderate.
Season: Year-round.
Length: 13 days.
Accommodations: Lodges and hotels.

MALAWI

Safari Through Africa's Least-Visited Wilderness

Operator:
Custom African Travel
Services, 31 Gray St.,
Cambridge, Mass. 02138;
(617) 491-1678;
www.gwcats.com.
Price: Expensive.
Season: June or by special
arrangement.
Length: 14 days.
Accommodations: Lodges,
cottages, and hotels.

Malawi is a small, politically stable country, which is still unspoiled and practically untouched by tourism. Surrounded by Mozambique, Zambia, and Tanzania, it has a lake which occupies 20 percent of the country. On this unusual safari small groups of 10 people experience a variety of habitats, including the Shire River, home to large populations of elephants and hippos; Lake Malawi, home to the world's largest number of cichlid fish species and a profusion of birdlife; the montane plateau of the Nyika, home to roan antelopes and several species of birds endemic to the area; and the Luangwa Valley in Zambia, a world-class wilderness area with an abundance of lions and leopards. Wildlife-viewing is done by foot, horseback, boat, and vehicles. Travelers can also snorkel or scuba-dive among hundreds of brilliant-colored cichlid fish in Lake Malawi.

MOROCCO

Camel Trek Through the Sahara

Operator:
Wilderness Travel,
1102 Ninth St.,
Berkeley, Calif. 94710;
(800) 368-2794 or
(510) 558-2488;
www.wildernesstravel.com.
Price: Expensive.
Season: June–mid-
September.
Length: 15 days.
Accommodations: Tent camps
and hotels. Five percent discount with BBAT coupon.

Stretching 3,000 miles across the northern third of Africa and 1,000 miles deep, the Sahara is one of those exotic destinations suffused with mystery and mystique. Participants on this adventure spend four days exploring this exotic landscape, Bedouin-style, from high atop a camel, crossing dry lake beds in the shadows of beautiful red sand dunes. Hospitality among the nomads is legendary, so trekkers can expect to take tea in the tents of the desert dwellers. Additional activities include a trek through the High Atlas Mountains, populated with white-robed Berbers; and a visit to the old city of Fez, which has remained virtually unchanged for centuries.

A highlight in rarely visited Namibia is the vast collection of red sand dunes in the Central Namib Desert

Journeys International

NAMIBIA

Namibia Explorer

This amazing corner of southern Africa is one of the continent's last frontiers and is virtually unvisited by American travelers. Namibia is a vast, sparsely inhabited land, dry and silent, which nonetheless supports a rich variety of wildlife. Members of this safari travel by minivan to the major wilderness areas. Highlights include visits to the enormous sand dunes of the Central Namib Desert; the Damaraland Wilderness Reserve, famous for its desert-dwelling elephants; Etosha National Park, home to one of the richest and most diverse collections of wildlife in Africa; and Mudumu National Park, where three days are spent exploring this fragile wetland system by boat and foot. The safari ends with visits to Chobe National Park in Botswana and Victoria Falls in Zimbabwe.

Operator: Journeys International, 107 Aprill Dr., #3., Ann Arbor, Mich. 48103; (800) 255-8735 or (734) 665-4407; www.journeys-intl.com.

Price: Moderate.

Season: Throughout the year.

Length: 15 days.

Accommodations: Tent camps and lodges. Five percent discount with BBAT coupon.

"To a person uninstructed in natural history, a country or seaside stroll is a walk through a gallery filled with wondrous works of art, nine tenths of which have their faces turned to the wall." THOMAS HENRY HUXLEY

The high hills around
Serengheti offer unparalleled
views across the distant
plains

Anton Lemmy/Wilderness Travel

TANZANIA

Serengeti Wildlife Safari

Operator:
Wilderness Travel,
1102 Ninth St.,
Berkeley, Calif. 94710;
(800) 368-2794 or
(510) 558-2488;
www.wildernesstravel.com.
Price: Expensive.
Season: Throughout the
year.
Length: 17 days.
Accommodations: Tent camps
and lodges. Five percent
discount with BBAT
coupon.

Northern Tanzania is home to the most impressive wildlife spectacle in the world, the annual migration of millions of wildebeests, zebras, and gazelles, stalked along the way by their predators—lions, leopards, cheetahs, and hyenas. Participants on this safari not only spend four days experiencing the wonders of Serengeti National Park but also visit other legendary East African parks, such as Lake Manyara, which boasts over 350 species of birds and large numbers of elephants; Ngorongoro Crater, a 105-square-mile caldera, home to one of Africa's largest concentrations of wildlife, some 35,000 animals; and Olduvai Gorge, where Mary Leakey discovered "Lucy," the 1.75-million-year-old Australopithecine skull.

"Ex Africa semper aliquid novi."
[There is always something new from Africa.]

PLINY THE YOUNGER
LETTERS

ASIA

EASTERN RUSSIA

Kamchatka Peninsula and the Rim of Fire

This slice of Russian Far East lies nine time zones east of Moscow. The peninsula holds a 500-mile-stretch of volcanoes, a wilderness of fuming peaks, ancient lakes, and end-of-the-world lava flows. The cities are almost all urban purgatories, but the wilderness beyond is home to upwards of 20,000 bears. Until the end of the Cold War, the Soviet military closed the peninsula to all outsiders. Highlights of this adventure are a hike to the summit of Avacha, an active volcano; a float trip down the trout-laden waters of the Bystraya River; and a cultural immersion in the traditional lifestyles of the Koryak and Even indigenous peoples.

Operator:
Mir Corp., 85 S. Washington St., #210, Seattle, Wash. 98104; (800) 424-7289 or (206) 624-7289; www.mircorp.com.
Price: Expensive.
Season: July.
Length: 16 days.
Accommodations: Hotels and lodges. Five percent discount with BBAT coupon.

AUSTRALASIA

AUSTRALIA

Snorkeling with Dwarf Minke Whales on the Great Barrier Reef

Minke whales are among the smallest of the great cetaceans, and the dwarf minke whales are the smallest of this species. Averaging a respectable 20 feet in length, the dwarf minke was first recognized in 1986 as a different form than the common minke. Congregating off the northern portion of the Great Barrier Reef, this population of dwarf minke whales has gained a reputation for friendliness, often approaching watchers in nearby boats. These whales are still hunted; so by supporting the Australian whale-watching industry, participants help make the future for these whales more secure. En route to the minke whale site, visitors have the

Operator:
Oceanic Society Expeditions, Fort Mason Center, Bldg. E, San Francisco, Calif. 94123; (800) 326-7491 or (415) 441-1106; www.oceanic-society.org.
Price: Expensive.
Length: 7 days.
Season: June.
Accommodations: Cabins on an 85-foot boat. Five percent discount with BBAT coupon.

opportunity to snorkel over the shallow-water coral gardens and bommies of Ribbon Reefs and make a stop at the world-famous Cod Hole.

Heron Island

Operator: Adventure Center, 1311 63rd St., Suite 200, Emeryville, Calif. 94608; (800) 227-8747 or (510) 654-1879; www.adventure-center.com. *Price:* Moderate. *Season:* Throughout the year. *Length:* 7 days. *Accommodations:* Island bungalows. Five percent discount with BBAT coupon.

One of only two resort islands located directly on the Great Barrier Reef, Heron enjoys an international reputation among divers and snorkelers. Poised atop the southern end of the reef, the island provides an unrivaled ease of access to the marine wonderland beyond. The reefs around Heron are part of a national marine park and support over 1,500 species of fish and 500 species of coral. Boats take divers and snorkelers out for half-day dives. Heron offers other attractions, including the only green-turtle rookery on the Great Barrier Reef that's accessible to the public, and large numbers of exotic nesting birds.

A snorkeler explores the natural wonders of the Great Barrier Reef

James C. Simmons

A kayak becomes the best viewing platform from which to observe the activities of orcas off Canada's western coast

David Arcese/Northern Lights Expeditions

CANADA

BRITISH COLUMBIA

Eye-to-Eye with Orcas

Off the west coast of Canada, in the Inside Passage, is found the largest and most accessible concentration of orcas in the world. Each summer more than 200 of the big black-and-white killer whales gather, drawn by millions of salmon on the way to their spawning grounds. These expeditions use extremely stable 20-foot sea kayaks to paddle quietly among the pods of orcas, often coming within a few feet of their six-foot-high dorsal fins. Hydrophones in the water capture orca vocalizations from as far as five miles away. The area abounds in sea lions, black bear, eagles, minke whales, deer, and porpoises. No previous kayaking experience is required. The operator provides all camping equipment.

Operator: Northern Lights Expeditions, P.O. Box 4289, Bellingham, Wash. 98227; (800) 754-7402 or (360) 734-6334; www.seakayaking.com.
Price: Moderate.
Season: Weekly departures June–September.
Length: 6 days.
Accommodations: Tent camps on uninhabited islands. Five percent discount with BBAT coupon.

"A man needs a little madness; otherwise, he never cuts the rope to become free."

FROM THE FILM ZORBA THE GREEK, 1964

MANITOBA

Polar Bear Expedition

Operator: Natural Habitat Adventures, 2945 Center Green Ct. South, Boulder, Colo. 80301; (800) 543-8917 or (303) 449-3711; www.nathab.com. *Price:* Expensive. *Season:* October and November. *Length:* 6 to 9 days. *Accommodations:* Hotels. Five percent discount with BBAT coupon.

To the Eskimo people, the polar bear symbolizes wisdom and strength. But to early European explorers, the big bears were fearsome white ghosts that could easily kill a man or ravage his food caches. Participants on these expeditions travel to Churchill, the northernmost town in Manitoba, where large numbers of polar bears congregate each winter. Members ride across the frozen tundra in specially constructed vehicles to observe and photograph the behavior of these magnificent bears, and may also see Arctic foxes, rock and willow ptarmigans, and snowy owls.

NORTHWEST TERRITORIES

A Congregation of 1,000 Beluga Whales in the High Arctic

One of the last remote and unexplored areas of the globe is that of the far north. Members of these expeditions spend nights at a comfortable lodge on Somerset Island, 480 miles north of the Arctic Circle and only 900 miles south of the geographic North Pole. During the long Arctic days they

The Adventure Travel Hall of Fame: RORY NUGENT

"Never travel in the rain. Giant fish and crocodiles attack during the storms. Pray to Ram when you see a whirlpool. He may hear you and save you. When the moon is up, sleep with your knives." This was the advice an Indian shipbuilder gave

American adventurer Rory Nugent before he set off in a 12-foot skiff to become the first Westerner to paddle down the Brahmaputra River from Burma to Bangladesh. The ostensible goal of his travels was to search for the pink-headed duck, last seen in the wild in India in 1935. To this end Nugent deter-

explore the spectacular Arctic landscape, home to numerous mammals and bird species specially adapted to survive the harsh environment. The highlight is the congregation of 1,000 beluga whales at the mouth of a river just 15 minutes' walk from the lodge. The whales are in the height of their nursing season and can be observed rolling in the gravel at the mouth of the river in an effort to remove their molting skin. Polar bears are also common in the area, as are the "unicorns of the sea," the famed narwhals. Participants also visit the grave sites of the ill-fated Franklin expedition and the famed seabird island of Prince Leopold.

Operator:
Natural Habitat Adventures, 2945 Center Green Ct. South, Boulder, Colo. 80301; (800) 543-8917 or (303) 449-3711; www.nathab.com.
Price: Expensive.
Season: June–August.
Length: 9 days.
Accommodations: Lodge.
Five percent discount with BBAT coupon.

Aurora Borealis Odyssey

"Who but God can conceive such infinite scenes of glory?" asked Charles F. Hall, a 19th-century polar explorer after observing a display of the aurora borealis. "Who but God could execute them, painting the heavens in such gorgeous display?" Few natural phenomena have exerted a greater pull over the imaginations of men as the aurora borealis. Most of the Eskimo groups from Siberia to Greenland visualized the aurora as spirits of the dead playing ball with a walrus' skull. This natural-history adventure is specially designed for those who want to see and photograph these curtains of color. Participants travel to a remote part of the

Operator:
Arctic Odysseys, 2000 McGilvra Blvd. East, Seattle, Wash. 98112; (800) 574-3021 or (206) 325-1977; www.arcticodysseys.com.
Price: Expensive.
Season: March.
Length: 7 days.
Accommodations: Lodge.
Five percent discount with BBAT coupon.

---

mined to explore two wilderness areas that had been unvisited by foreigners since 1947—one a narrow section in northeastern Sikkim and the other in the upper Brahmaputra River Valley. His travels soon became a pilgrimage for the rare and elusive duck. Before embarking on the river he fell in with Gurkha guerrillas fighting with homemade weapons for a free Gurkhaland, even joining them on a raid against Indian occupational troops. Finally, on the river he and an Indian companion survived whirlpools, giant leeches, and river pirates but found no pink-headed duck. However, he did see several white-winged wood ducks, India's second-rarest species. And his adventure yielded an improbable and stylish travel narrative, The Search for the Pink-Headed Duck.

An Inuit Eskimo examines the landscape at the North Pole on an Arctic Odysseys expedition

George Holton/Arctic Odysseys

Northwest Territory just north of the Great Slav Lake. At night they study the auroral displays, while during the day they explore the nearby Arctic wilderness by dogsled, cross-country ski, snowshoe, and snowmobile.

ONTARIO

Algonquin Dogsledding

Operator:
Worldwide Adventures, 1170 Sheppard Ave. West, #45, Toronto, Ont., Canada M3K 2A3; (800) 387-1483 or (416) 633-5666; www.worldwidequest.com.

This weekend dogsled adventure has been a perennial favorite since 1987 when the operator first offered it. Dogsledding was perfected a century ago in the Yukon frontier by prospectors and homesteaders who needed a reliable means of transportation across the frozen landscape. Participants drive their own sled and team of dogs the entire trip through the snow-covered wilderness of Canada's popular Algonquin Park. Alaskan huskies are used exclusively. The dogs are powerful and accustomed to traveling many miles in a day. No previous mushing experience is necessary; the dogs and their keeper will train you.

Price: Moderate.
Season: January–March.
Length: 3 days.
Accommodations: Lodge and heated tent camp. Five percent discount with BBAT coupon.

QUEBEC

The Harp Seals of St. Lawrence

Every March some 250,000 harp seals enter the Gulf of St. Lawrence to bear their young on the vast floating ice fields just west of the picturesque Magdalene Islands. Known as "whitecoats," these adorable newborn pups shed their snowy-white fur and turn grey within three weeks. In 1987 Canada banned commercial hunting of whitecoats, and today is working toward the creation of a tourist industry to boost the local economy. Participants on these adventures travel by helicopter from their hotel to the nearby ice floes and walk among thousands of mother seals and their pups. The nature photography is superb.

Operator: Natural Habitat Adventures, 2945 Center Green Ct. South, Boulder, Colo. 80301; (800) 543-8917 or (303) 449-3711; www.nathab.com.
Price: Expensive.
Season: March.
Length: 6 days.
Accommodations: Hotels. Five percent discount with BBAT coupon.

CARIBBEAN

DOMINICAN REPUBLIC

The Humpback Whales of the Silver Bank

In late winter and early spring hundreds of humpback whales congregate between the Grand Turk and the Dominican Republic, an area considered to be the primary mating and calving ground for the North Atlantic humpback whale. Over 1,000 of these big whales migrate to the shallow Silver Bank from their northern feeding grounds off Canada and Western Europe, providing divers with perhaps the finest whale-diving in the world. Some of these

Operator: Natural Habitat Adventures, 2945 Center Green Ct. South, Boulder, Colo. 80301; (800) 543-8917 or (303) 449-3711; www.nathab.com.
Price: Expensive.

Season: March.
Length: 8 days.
Accommodations: Shipboard cabins on a motor yacht.
Five percent discount with BBAT coupon.

60-foot-long animals weigh more than 50 tons. Large groups of males, called "rowdy groups," compete aggressively for receptive females. The result is a ceaseless line of challengers, almost constantly breaching, ramming, slamming, lob-tailing, or fin-slapping. Particularly captivating are the famed humpbacks' songs. Passengers will also have considerable opportunity to snorkel among these big whales, observing their behavior at close range.

EUROPE

ICELAND

Whale-Watching and Natural History

Operator:
Oceanic Society Expeditions,
Fort Mason Center, Bldg. E,
San Francisco, Calif. 94123;
(800) 326-7491 or
(415) 441-1106;
www.oceanic-society.org.
Price: Expensive.
Length: 11 days.
Season: May–June.
Accommodations: Hotels.
Five percent discount with BBAT coupon.

A major opportunity of this expedition is the chance to observe Keiko, the killer whale that starred in the popular film *Free Willy*. In the spring of 2001 he became the first captive killer whale to be returned to the wild. Iceland also offers cetacean-lovers perhaps the ultimate experience. The cold waters nearby support abundant populations of killer, humpback, blue, and sperm whales; white-beaked dolphins; and harbor porpoises. Surprisingly friendly minke and fin whales are also found in the protected waters. Iceland is also a bird-watcher's paradise because of the abundance of seabirds, including 8 million puffins. Participants will visit the Westman Islands, home to large colonies of nesting razorbills, kittiwakes, fulmars, guillemots, and storm petrels, and will stop at the lunar landscape around Lake Myvatn, where American astronauts trained for their moon walks.

"A good traveling companion must be equal parts mediator, entertainer, father confessor, educator, and psychologist."
RANDY WAYNE WHITE
OUTSIDE, AUGUST 1996

LATIN AMERICA

ARGENTINA

Wildlife Observation by Sea Kayak Along the Coast of Patagonia

The remote Valdés Peninsula with its 1 million Magellanic penguins, thousands of elephant seals and sea lions, right whales, and countless seabirds, boasts one of South America's greatest profusions of wildlife. The sea kayak offers visitors a marvelous viewing platform from which to observe these magnificent sea creatures at close quarters. A full range of right-whale behavior can be observed, including breaching and tail-lobbing. Orcas are also common in the area. The expedition concludes with several days of overland travel, with good opportunities to see the ostrich-like rhea, armadillos, and the llama-related trademark of Patagonia, the intriguing guanaco.

Operator: Whitney & Smith Legendary Expeditions, P.O. Box 2097, Banff, Alb., Canada T0L 0C0; (403) 678-3052; www.legendaryex.com. *Price:* Expensive. *Season:* October. *Length:* 14 days. *Accommodations:* Hotels and tent camps. Five percent discount with BBAT coupon.

"I learned early that the richness of life is adventure."

SUPREME COURT JUSTICE WILLIAM O. DOUGLAS

A sea kayak is a perfect platform for the observation of wildlife off the Argentina's remote Valdés Peninsula

Steve Smith/Whitney & Smith

BELIZE

A Naturalist's Odyssey into the Mayan Heartland

Operator: Journeys International, 107 Aprill Dr., #3., Ann Arbor, Mich. 48103; (800) 255-8735 or (734) 665-4407; www.journeys-intl.com. *Price:* Expensive. *Season:* January–April. *Length:* 8 days. *Accommodations:* Hotels and lodges. Five percent discount with BBAT coupon.

Largely overlooked by travelers to Latin America, Belize boasts an extraordinary diversity of flora and fauna—more than 500 species of birds, 250 varieties of orchids, and many of the last wild jaguars. This expedition visits rain forests, pine-covered mountains, Mayan ruins, waterfalls, caves, and the world's second-largest barrier reef. Participants explore the Mountain Pine Ridge Forest Reserve, which boasts both Mayan ruins and the Rio Frio Cave in the Chiquibul rain forest, a site of ancient Mayan rituals; visit Tikal National Park across the border in Guatemala, which contains 3,000 separate Mayan ruins; see the Che Chem Ha Cave with its cache of large pots dating back 1,500 years; take a boat trip down the Macal River for the excellent birding; and finally, spend two days at Southwater Cay on the Barrier Reef, snorkeling over the spectacular coral reef formations.

Belize Whale Sharks and Dolphins

Whale sharks are the largest fish in the world, measuring up to 30 feet in length. These elusive crea-

The Adventure Travel Hall of Fame: MARK SHAND

Looking around for a new adventure in the late 1980s, British travel writer Mark Shand decided on a whim to ride across India for 800 miles on the back of an elephant, from the Bay of Bengal to the world's largest elephant bazaar at Sonepur on the Ganges. He flew to Bhubaneshwar, south-west of Calcutta, where he spent £4,000 on a 30-year-old female elephant. He named her Tara, the Hindu word for "star." Rescued from a life of begging, the scrawny and mistreated Tara was transformed through Shand's tender attention and care on their journey into a star attraction. He soon learned that elephants are revered in most parts of India. The animal

tures congregate annually off Belize's coast to feed on fish spawn (masses of fish eggs). These gentle giants are generally found within 20 feet of the water's surface, an ideal depth for snorkelers to observe the behavior of these magnificent animals. There are also excellent opportunities to swim with bottlenose and spotted dolphins. A naturalist accompanies the snorkelers on these and other dives to explore Laughing Bird Marine Reserve and its fringing reef studded with hard and soft corals. The area offers snorkelers an opportunity to observe a rich profusion of brilliant sponges, rich corals, and colorful tropical fish.

Operator:
Oceanic Society
Expeditions, Fort Mason
Center, Bldg. E, San
Francisco, Calif. 94123;
(800) 326-7491 or
(415) 441-1106;
www.oceanic-society.org.
Price: Moderate.
Length: 7 days.
Season: May–June.
Accommodations: Beachfront cabanas. Five percent discount with BBAT coupon.

BRAZIL

Amazon Expedition

There is no place like the Amazon, with its network of waterways sprawling across an area two-thirds the size of the United States. One-fifth of all the river water in the world spills from the Amazon's mouth into the Atlantic Ocean. The river supports some 2,000 species of fish, 1,800 species of birds, and 200 species of land mammals, including the world's largest ant (1.4 inches), longest snake (38 feet), and biggest rodent (4 feet from head to tail). Its

Operator:
Nature Expeditions
International, 7860 Peters
Rd., #F-103,
Plantation, Fla. 33324;
(800) 869-0639 or
(954) 693-8852;
www.naturexp.com.
Price: Expensive.

represents the elephant-headed deity Ganesh, the Hindu God of Protection. Blessed by priests, entertained by princes, Tara and Shand shuffled happily through towns and villages, Tara sucking up rice and bananas from roadside stands and Shand scattering rupees in compensation. Everywhere they went, the adventurer, his unusual steed, and his five eccentric Indian companions drew an inquisitive crowd of admirers. Merely arriving at Sonepur on the Ganges was not the end of the story. Finding a good home for Tara became the greatest challenge of the entire trip. Their parting, as Shand describes it in his book, Travels on My Elephant, is appropriate to a love story—they share a whiskey together, he kisses Tara on the eyelid, and she drops a fat tear on his cheek. He then embarked on a crusade to save the endangered Indian elephant, urging the creation of fenced corridors along the wild elephants' old migratory routes.

Season: Throughout the year.
Length: 8 days.
Accommodations: Hotels and jungle lodges. Five percent discount with BBAT coupon.

vast jungle also harbors approximately 50,000 Indians who are increasingly threatened by civilization. Members of this expedition travel by plane, riverboat, and dugout canoe to experience the upper Amazon.

COSTA RICA

Tropical Wilderness Explorer

Operator: Journeys International, 107 Aprill Dr., #3., Ann Arbor, Mich. 48103; (800) 255-8735 or (734) 665-4407; www.journeys-intl.com.
Price: Expensive.
Season: January–March.
Length: 10 days.
Accommodations: Comfortable lodges. Five percent discount with BBAT coupon.

The small country of Costa Rica boasts a world-class national park system with exceptional birdlife and flora that includes over 1,000 species of orchids alone, world-class rivers, white-sand beaches, lush mountain rain forests, and active volcanoes. Participants on this popular trip cover the full range of the country's natural attractions, from pristine beaches to tropical rain forests, visiting Arenal Volcano on Lake Arenal, a prime area for bird-watching; Monteverde Cloud Forest Reserve, perhaps the best place to view the resplendent quetzal, widely regarded as the most beautiful bird in the Americas; and Tiskita, a rain-forest reserve in the remote region of Golfito on the southern Pacific coast overlooking a deserted tropical beach.

ECUADOR

In the Footsteps of Charles Darwin on the Galapagos Islands

Operator: Mountain Travel-Sobek, 6420 Fairmount Ave., El Cerrito, Calif. 94530; (888) 687-6235 or (510) 527-8105; www.mtsobek.com.
Price: Expensive.
Season: Throughout the year.

"A separate center of creation," Charles Darwin marveled at the Galapagos Islands, the inspiration for much of his thesis on evolution. An archipelago of active volcanoes and arid, rocky terrain, long celebrated as home to some of the strangest and most wonderful wildlife imaginable, these islands are one of the world's greatest natural treasures. Participants on these expeditions travel aboard comfortable yachts to explore all the important islands in this exotic Eden. This is an environment devoid of natural predators, in which the mammal, bird, and reptile species exist peacefully side by side. Participants also have numerous opportunities to snorkel and dive.

Length: 11 and 14 days.
Accommodations: Shipboard cabins. Five percent discount with BBAT coupon.

MEXICO

Whale-Watching from a Shore-Based Camp in Baja California

Located on the Pacific side of the Baja California peninsula, San Ignacio Lagoon offers the visitor nothing less than the finest whale-watching in the world. More than 2,000 gray whales are in residence here each winter. This is also the home of the "friendly," or "petting," whales. Whale cows, often with calves in tow, present themselves to the small boats filled with observers, patiently lie alongside, and expect to have their heads, backs, and sides massaged. Nowhere else can one see such a range of whale behavior, including courtship, copulation, birth, sleeping, spy-hopping, and breaching. There is also excellent birding in the nearby saltwater mangrove swamps. Local fishermen from a nearby village are used as boatmen to take guests around the lagoon.

Operator:
Baja Discovery,
P.O. Box 152527,
San Diego, Calif. 92195;
(800) 829-2252 or
(619) 262-0700;
www.bajadiscovery.com.
Price: Expensive.
Season: January–March.
Length: 5, 7, and 8 days.
Accommodations: Tent camp. Five percent discount with BBAT coupon.

San Ignacio Lagoon on the Pacific coast of Baja California is home to the friendly, or petting, whale phenomenon
Baja Discovery

Wildlife of the Sea of Cortez

Operator: Baja Discovery, P.O. Box 152527, San Diego, Calif. 92195; (800) 829-2252 or (619) 262-0700; www.bajadiscovery.com. *Price:* Expensive. *Season:* May. *Length:* 7 days. *Accommodations:* Hotels and beach huts. Five percent discount with BBAT coupon.

Small groups of travelers locate at a nature camp on an isolated cove 15 miles south of Bahia de los Angelos just off the Sea of Cortez in a region often called the Mexican Galapagos. The area supports a large resident population of finback whales as well as numerous giant plankton-eating whales, sharks, and manta rays. Nights are spent in simple thatch-roofed huts with concrete floors, windows, and attached bathrooms located on a white-sand beach off a cove that offers excellent snorkeling. Local fishermen take clients farther out in their fishing boats to explore some of the uninhabited large islands that are rich in birdlife. There visitors can spy ash-throated flycatchers displaying courtship behavior, ladder-back woodpeckers at work on the giant cardon cacti, house finches that look as though they have been dipped in strawberry juice, and a dozen other species.

PERU

Manu Rain Forest Expedition

The World Wildlife Fund has called Peru's Manu National Park "the most important rain forest park

---

The Adventure Travel Hall of Fame: GEOFFREY MOORHOUSE

Stretching 3,000 miles across the northern third of Africa and 1,000 miles deep, the Sahara Desert is one of those exotic destinations suffused with mystery and mystique. In November of 1972, just before his 41st birthday, British journalist Geoffrey Moorhouse set out to become the first man in modern history to make an east-west crossing by camel from the Atlantic Ocean to the Nile River, a journey of 3,600 miles. "My primary aim in going to the desert was not to establish a record, much as I might enjoy doing so, but to explore an extremity of human experience," he reflected later in a fine book about his travels, *The Fearful*

in the world." In 1977 UNESCO declared the region a biosphere reserve, thus emphasizing its international importance as one of the few reserves in the world that protects entire unhunted and unlogged watersheds. It is the only park in the world with over 1,000 species of birds and 15,000 species of plants confirmed. (In 1982 two naturalists set a world record when they sighted 331 species of birds in a single 24-hour period.) The park's 4.5 million acres are home to many of the rarest and most endangered species in South America, including the black caiman, giant otter, ocelot, jaguar, spectacled bear, and five species of eagles. Participants on this trip experience a total immersion in Manu National Park by means of numerous day hikes through the forest, canoe excursions on forest lakes, and motorized dugout canoes on the rivers.

Operator: Journeys International, 107 Aprill Dr., #3, Ann Arbor, Mich. 48103; (800) 255-8735 or (734) 665-4407; www.journeys-intl.com.
Price: Expensive.
Season: May–December.
Length: 10 days.
Accommodations: Lodges and safari camps. Five percent discount with BBAT coupon.

SURINAM

Rain Forest, Wildlife, and Sea Turtles

Bordering Brazil, Surinam has one of the highest percentages of tropical rain forest of any country. This expedition visits a variety of world-famous natural sites. The Brownsberg Nature Park boasts the

Void. He entered the desert at the edge of El Djouf, the Empty Quarter of the Western Sahara, where great dunes of sand rolled away for several hundred miles to the north and east, a region almost entirely devoid of any vegetation. In the desert, he soon learned, everything is the enemy. The noontime temperature sometimes hit 130 degrees, while the nights were bitterly cold. Even hotter than the air, the sand scalded his feet and legs. During storms sand coated his eyes, throat, and food with layers of grit. In the infrequent oases he found the well water seasoned with mud, urine, and camel dung. Along the way he confronted thirst, dysentery, hunger, and the treachery of Arab companions. The arrival of the summer heat forced Moorhouse to end his journey after 2,000 miles on March 5, 1973, at the oasis village of Tamanrasset in southern Algeria. He and his Tuareg guide had walked the last 373 miles.

Operator:
Oceanic Society
Expeditions, Fort Mason
Center, Bldg. E,
San Francisco, Calif. 94123;
(800) 326-7491 or
(415) 441-1106;
www.oceanic-society.org.
Price: Moderate.
Season: March.
Length: 13 days.
Accommodations: Small
lodges. Five percent dis-
count with BBAT coupon.

finest rain-forest trails in South America, from which the walker can see a rich profusion of bromeliads, epiphytes, and orchids as well as toucans, macaws, jacamars, and seven species of monkeys. Raleigh Falls Nature Reserve, beautifully situated along the Coppename River, is home to a rich selection of mammals and birds, including the dramatic cock-of-the-rock, macaws, giant river otters, and primates. The Galibi Sea Turtle Nature Reserve offers excellent opportunities to observe the nesting behavior of leatherback and green sea turtles. (The leatherbacks reach a length of six feet and weigh 1,000 pounds.)

NORTH POLE

Dogsled and Ski Expedition to the Magnetic North Pole

Operator:
The Northwest Passage,
1130 Greenleaf Ave.,
Wilmette, Ill. 60091; (800)
RECREATE or (847) 256-
4409; www.nwpassage.com.
Price: Expensive.
Season: April–May.
Length: 16 days.
Accommodations: Snow
camps. Five percent dis-
count with BBAT coupon.

The North Pole has long held a curious fascination as the ultimate travel destination. This rugged expedition is just the thing for adventurers eager to do the "Great Pole Vault." Using dogsleds and skis, participants follow the same route used by Admiral Robert Peary in his historic dash from 88 degrees North to the North Pole. The expedition returns from the North Pole on board a chartered aircraft. This is a tough, dangerous, but ultimately rewarding trip. Interested parties must have had or be willing to acquire dogsled experience and must attend a five-night team-building "shakedown" journey in Iqaluit. The operator also offers an all-women dogsledding expedition to the North Pole.

By Chartered Aircraft to the North Pole

For those adventurers who want the North Pole without the agony of exertion that an overland dogsled expedition requires, then a dash to the Far North on a chartered aircraft is just the thing. Participants fly to Eureka, a Canadian weather station located at 80 degrees North latitude on the west coast of Ellesmere Island. Here they experience the life of an isolated research station while observing packs of Arctic wolves at close range. Weather permitting, they then depart on their chartered turboprop Twin Otter for the flight to the top of the world. A stop is made at Lake Hazen, the northernmost lake in the world, to take on fuel from a cache. The plane then lands at the North Pole for a visit of several hours. Three days are also spent at Grise Fjord, where members and their Inuit guides board snowmobiles to visit nearby glaciers and Eskimo villages.

Operator: Arctic Odysseys, 2000 McGilvra Blvd. East, Seattle, Wash. 98112; (800) 574-3021 or (206) 325-1977; www.arcticodysseys.com. *Price:* Expensive. *Season:* April–May. *Length:* 7 days. *Accommodations:* Research station and hotels. Five percent discount with BBAT coupon.

THE PACIFIC

MIDWAY

Midway Atoll: Natural and Maritime History

Midway is a remote coral atoll located 1,250 miles west-northwest of Hawaii. Best known as the staging area for one of the fiercest battles of World War II, it supports one of the most spectacular concentrations of seabirds in the Pacific, including a half-million nesting pairs of the Laysan albatrosses (better known as gooney birds) and the second largest black-footed albatross colony. Thirteen other species of migratory seabirds also nest here, along with four species of migratory shorebirds. The endangered Hawaiian monk seal also utilizes the atoll. Off limits to civilians for over 50 years, Midway welcomed its first tourists in 1997. The U.S. Fish & Wildlife Service has established strict guidelines to minimize visitors' impact on the ecosystem. Activities include snorkeling, scuba diving, birdwatching, historical tours, swimming, and beachcombing.

Operator: Oceanic Society Expeditions, Fort Mason Center, Bldg. E, San Francisco, Calif. 94123; (800) 326-7491 or (415) 441-1106; www.oceanic-society.org. *Price:* Expensive. *Season:* Throughout the year. *Length:* 8 days. *Accommodations:* Rooms in restored military barracks. Five percent discount with BBAT coupon.

UNITED STATES
ALASKA

Alaskan Air Safari

Operator: Sky Trekking Alaska, 485 Pioneer Dr., Wasilla, Alaska 99654; (800) 770-4966 or (907) 373-4966; www.skytrekkingalaska.com.
Price: Expensive.
Season: Throughout the year.
Length: Client's preference.
Accommodations: Lodges, fishing camps, and cabins. Five percent discount with BBAT coupon.

Larger than Texas, Alaska with its 580,000 square miles requires the traveler to have a regard for both time and distance in order to see much of the state. For those travelers for whom time is of greater concern than money, the best way to see the backcountry wilderness is by plane. With two planes able to land on water or ground, the operator offers a variety of customized-flying adventures with activities that include glacier climbs, dogsled rides, world-class fishing, bear-watching, and nature walks throughout the state. On one popular three-day aerial adventure passengers sky-trek over Lliamna, Alaska's largest lake and a spawning ground for the largest sockeye salmon run in the world; fly over Katmai National Park (the 1912 site of North America's largest volcanic eruption in recent centuries) and enjoy a picnic lunch in nearby Geographic Harbor; move on to Kodiak Island for some bear-watching; and finally visit the remote Barren Islands to observe one of the state's largest concentrations of sea mammals and seabirds.

Admiralty Island boasts perhaps the largest population of grizzly bears in North America
Alaska Discovery

The Bears of Admiralty Island

The grizzly bear is the largest and most dangerous carnivore in the world, reaching up to 9 feet when standing on its hind legs and weighing more than 1,200 pounds in old age. Generally, the big bears are viewed only from a remote distance. However, participants on these one-day sea-kayaking adventures get up close and personal, observing the bears at the Stan Price Bear Sanctuary at Pack Creek, one of the country's premier spots for observing the big bears. Departures are timed to coincide with the annual salmon run, when the bears are out in great numbers. Participants travel by floatplane from Juneau to Admiralty Island.

Operator:
Alaska Discovery,
5310 Glacier Hwy.,
Juneau, Alaska 99801;
(800) 586-1911 or
(907) 780-6226;
www.akdiscovery.com.
Price: Expensive.
Season: July and August.
Length: 1 day. Five percent discount with BBAT coupon.

CALIFORNIA

Jeep Tours of the Desert Wilderness near Palm Springs

Most of the Palm Springs area's 3 million annual visitors come for its splendid golf courses, swimming pools, tennis courts, and palm-shaded avenues. However, nature-lovers seeking high adventure need not despair. Desert Adventures, an ecotour jeep company, enjoys exclusive tour rights to certain wilderness areas nearby. Naturalists turn each trip into a learning experience and pave the way to a greater understanding of the region's wild places. One popular tour, the "Mystery Canyon Adventure," takes visitors in jeeps past the shoreline of ancient Lake Cahuilla near the Salton Sea before continuing to the Painted Hills near the San Andreas Fault.

Operator:
Desert Adventures, 67-555
E. Palm Canyon Dr.,
Suite A-104,
Cathedral City, Calif. 92234;
(888) 440-JEEP or
(760) 324-JEEP;
www.red-jeep.com.
Price: Moderate.
Season: Year-round.
Length: 4 hours. Ten percent discount with BBAT coupon.

"To the Arab the desert is a place of privation, pain, and death. For the Westerner the desert is a challenge, a flight into weightlessness, an escape from tedium."

WILLIAM POLK AND WILLIAM MARES
PASSING BRAVE

An Out-of-Africa Experience in Southern California

Operator:
San Diego Wild Animal Park, 15500 San Pasqual Valley Rd., Escondido, Calif. 92027; (800) 934-2267 or (760) 738-5022.
Price: Inexpensive.
Season: Several days a week throughout the year.
Length: 3 and 4 hours.

Owned and operated by the world-famous San Diego Zoo, the Wild Animal Park is the only American facility of its kind—a rural preserve where different species mingle much as they do in the wild, and where rare and exotic animals on the edge of extinction are bred and studied in an incomparably inviting laboratory. Some 3,000 animals, representing 450 species, inhabit 2,200 acres. For years, animal-lovers and photographers had to be satisfied with viewing the park's animals from the confines of a silent electric monorail that glides around its perimeter. Now, groups of 10 people each are permitted into the park on flatbed trucks. Accompanied by keeper-guides, visitors spend up to four hours enjoying one of the greatest opportunities anywhere in the world for observing and photographing wildlife. Although still wild, the park's animals are accustomed to the trucks' presence; they go about their business of courting, breeding, feeding, and playing, unmindful of nearby photographers snapping off dozens of rolls of film.

COLORADO

Hut-to-Hut Skiing Through the Mountains

Named after a U.S. Army ski troop that trained in Colorado during the Second World War, the Tenth Mountain Division Trail stretches from Aspen to Vail, passing through a spectacular winter wonderland remote from the lift lines and crowded chic

"I went to the woods because I wished to live deliberately, to front only the essential facts of life, and to see if I could not learn what it had to teach, and not, when I came to die, discover that I had not lived."

HENRY DAVID THOREAU
WALDEN

downhill-ski resorts. Over 100 miles of trails connect four huts and two private lodges. Each hut sleeps 16 people and includes amenities such as mattresses, wood-burning stoves and gas burners, photovoltaic lighting, and kitchen supplies. The trail has been designed for the intermediate skier. However, certain sections are more difficult and require more advanced skiing skills. This is serious backcountry skiing for individuals in excellent physical condition. Skiers carry full backpacks and travel at elevations between 8,000 and 11,000 feet.

Operator:
Paragon Guides, P.O. Box 130, Vail, Colo. 81658; (877) 926-5299 or (970) 926-5299; www.paragonguides.com.
Price: Expensive.
Season: December to mid-April.
Length: 3, 4, and 5 days.
Accommodations: Mountain huts. Five percent discount coupon with BBAT coupon.

TEXAS

Tornado-Chasing Across the Western Plains

Participants race across a checkerboard of blowing wheat and cornfields through that region where the Gulf of Mexico's sultry air collides with the moisture-laden winds from the Arctic generating massive thunderstorms in a search for their offspring, tornadoes. Each morning the guide logs onto his computer to get the latest meteorological data in the hopes of pinpointing where conditions are most favorable for the formation of large thunderstorms in the Texas, Oklahoma, Nebraska, and Kansas area. (Be prepared for lots of driving!) Tornado-chasing is an inherently high-risk activity. Chasers can expect golf ball–size hailstones, drenching rains, high winds, and, if successful, tornadoes, one of the most violent weather phenomena in the world.

Operator:
Silver Lining Tours, 2701 Longmire Dr., #1016, College Station, Tex. 77845; (409) 764-8505; www.silverliningtours.com.
Price: Expensive.
Season: May and June.
Length: 10 days.
Accommodations: Roadside motels. Five percent discount with BBAT coupon.

WYOMING

A Half-Day Wildlife Safari into the Yellowstone Backcountry

The richest wildlife preserve in the "Lower 48," Yellowstone National Park finds its most popular attractions overwhelmed by mobs of tourists each

Yellowstone National Park offers visitors perhaps the finest wildlife viewing in the United States

Great Plains Wildlife Institute

Operator:
Great Plains Wildlife Institute, P.O. Box 7580, Jackson Hole, Wyo. 83001; (307) 733-2623.
Price: Inexpensive.
Season: Throughout the year.
Length: 4 hours.

summer. Now visitors seeking some sanity far from the madding crowds can do so easily, thanks to the Great Plains Wildlife Institute. It provides both early morning and late afternoon expeditions to the backcountry for some of the finest wildlife viewing available anywhere. Clients can expect to see a wide variety of species, including moose, bison, bighorn sheep, elk, coyotes, bald eagles, trumpeter swans, beavers, and mule deer. Transportation is a comfortable safari vehicle equipped with opening roof-hatches and spotting scopes. A naturalist/driver accompanies all groups. (The operator also offers a full-day expedition.)

Weeklong Wildlife Safari Through Yellowstone and Grand Teton National Parks

Operator:
Great Plains Wildlife Institute, P.O. Box 7580, Jackson Hole, Wyo. 83002; (307) 733-2623; www.wildlifesafari.com.
Price: Expensive.

For visitors seeking an in-depth study of the ecology and wildlife of these two parks and beyond, the operator runs what just may be the finest safari of its kind in North America. Traveling in a four-wheel-drive vehicle and accompanied by a professional wildlife biologist, participants venture beyond the crowds to experience a wild America as it was when Lewis and Clark traveled through this area almost two centuries before. The safari tracks reintroduced wolves in Yellowstone; scouts for bighorn sheep, grizzly bears, coyotes, and pronghorn antelopes; visits moose and elk feeding grounds in the Tetons; and observes one of the nation's few remaining herds of wild horses. A highlight is an evening rafting trip down the peaceful Snake River in the Tetons. The operator provides binoculars and spotting scopes.

Length: 7 days.
Season: June–September.
Accommodations: Inns and lodges.

Wolf and Bear Weekend Safaris in Yellowstone

The operator promises wildlife-lovers on these trips the chance to experience "the best springtime bear and wolf viewing in the country." The small groups travel in custom safari vehicles in the company of professional wildlife biologists. Often bears and wolves will be sighted together as both hunt for newborn elk calves. Early morning and twilight hours are the most rewarding times to view these two imposing species as they engage in their hunts. The biologists know exactly where the bears and wolves den and so greatly increase the chances of observing these animals. The operator provides binoculars and spotting scopes.

Operator:
Great Plains Wildlife Institute, P.O. Box 7580, Jackson Hole, Wyo. 83002; (307) 733-2623; www.wildlifesafari.com.
Price: Expensive.
Length: 2 days.
Season: May and June.
Accommodations: Lodge.

"Although it can be a forbidding moonscape, the Arctic is also varied, majestic, serene, memorably beautiful and occasionally gentle. The far North is not only a prowling polar bear, a battering storm, and vicious cold, but also a fat bumblebee buzzing among the delicate yellow Arctic poppies."

DR. WILLIAM E. TAYLOR, JR.
FOREWORD TO FRED BRUEMMER'S THE ARCTIC WORLD

PROFILE

TOM SEGERSTROM
GREAT PLAINS WILDLIFE INSTITUTE

"T here is something about safari life that makes you forget your troubles and feel the whole time as if you had drunk half a bottle of champagne—bubbling over with heartfelt gratitude for being alive," Isak Dinesen observed in her famous memoir, *Out of Africa*.

For decades an African safari has reigned as Americans' most popular travel fantasy, the ultimate trip to see wildlife in its natural habitat. But many travelers today have learned that North America also boasts spectacular concentrations of wildlife that can be every bit as impressive as those found on the distant plains of Kenya and Tanzania. These wildlife safaris offer participants exciting field experiences at a fraction of the cost of an African safari, and are often more conducive to family travel.

These domestic safaris also provide marvelous opportunities to learn about diverse habitats, see and photograph unusual forms of animal life, and travel through exotic environments. Accompanying naturalists turn these trips into learning experiences that pave the way for a greater understanding of our country's wild places.

Northwestern Wyoming, encompassing Grand Teton and Yellowstone National Parks, is home to a greater variety and profusion of wildlife than anywhere else in the continental United States. This includes a major portion of North America's population of pronghorn antelopes, one-fifth of its grizzly bears, the last remaining free-ranging buffalo herds, and large numbers of elk, moose, and bighorn sheep. Some 270 bird species have been spotted in the area, including such rare species as trumpeter swans, great gray owls, water ouzels, and Swainson's hawks.

"What we have here in the Yellowstone National Park area is a remnant of the diversity and abundance of wildlife we once enjoyed as a country 150 years ago on the Great Plains but lost with the arrival of civilization," insists Tom Segerstrom, the wildlife biologist who heads up Great Plains Wildlife Institute in Jackson Hole, Wyoming. "The greater Yellowstone region is the largest intact ecosystem in the lower 48 states. It's dense with moose, bison, eagles, deer, and ducks. And I believe visitors can actually contribute to conserving it, not simply aim their binoculars at it."

Segerstrom founded Great Plains Wildlife Institute to provide the public with unique wildlife experiences which allow them to engage in an active participation through a variety of research projects. "Participation in GPWI expeditions requires involvement," according to the company's ambitious mission statement. "This personal interaction with wild, free-ranging animals cannot be obtained from zoos, TV, or publications. Participants witness the value of the resource and the joys of stewarding it while learning the complexities of balancing conflicting resource demands. This exposure and personal involvement increases political support for wildlife and wilderness areas while contributing to the economic demands of actual wildlife stewardship projects."

Last year GPWI handled over 3,000 clients (60 percent of whom were women) who booked into a variety of half-day, one-day, weekend, and seven-day safaris that explored the wilderness areas in and around Grand Teton and Yellowstone. It is the only safari company with state permits to travel off the main roads in these areas, in part because the biologist guides and their clients contribute fieldwork to the various agencies that administer Wyoming's wildlife.

Segerstrom's clients travel in customized Chevy Suburbans equipped with slide-back roofs and high-powered spotting scopes. Group size is limited to six people (as compared to the 16-member groups common to other operators). The company biologists are carefully selected for both their professional expertise and their social skills. ("Unfortunately, too many field biologists prefer animals to people and so are not well suited for the position of a wildlife guide," says Segerstrom.) Nights are spent at comfortable lodgings, such as Jackson Hole's Painted Buffalo Lodge and Yellowstone's Roosevelt Lodge.

"Wildlife is the primary product we offer, not a secondary product, as with a rafting company," Segerstrom insists. "People go out with us to see wildlife. That's why we exist. Our clients on our seven-day trips can expect to see upwards of 65 species. On the one-day trips they can see 25 species in summer and 15 to 18 in winter. Late May and early June is the best time of the year for wildlife viewing in northwestern Wyoming. The baby animals are abundant, and this brings out the large predators. The winter season, on the other hand, is especially good for viewing the large hoofed-animal species—the buffalo, elk, moose, mule deer, bighorn sheep, pronghorn antelope, white-tail deer, and mountain goats. These all get concentrated in certain predictable areas. Because of the heavy snowfall the animals are not free to move around, as they are in the summer months. On our winter trips into the National Elk Reserve, for example, our clients will see upwards of 7,500 elk in a single day of viewing."

One popular GPWI trip is its Wolf and Bear Weekend Safaris offered each May. Clients have a 70 percent chance of seeing wolves and a 100 percent chance of seeing both black and grizzly bears. "The daytime temperatures are still cool, so the animals have not yet switched to a more nocturnal behavior," explains Segerstrom. "The wolves have pups, which start to emerge from their dens in May. Denning restricts the areas where the wolves will roam, so the chances of our clients viewing interesting behavior is greatly increased. Also this is the time when the elk start to calve. Both the wolves and bears have a much greater demand for food in May and they are out in the open meadows hunting the newborn elk calves, which makes them easier to see, too.

"The highlights come when the animals seemingly 'perform' for us, as if on cue," Segerstrom reports. "One morning we went out early to photograph some moose. We snapped them up close, then returned to the ranch for breakfast. Just as we sat down, moose started parading past our picture window, one after another. We couldn't eat. Every time we picked up our forks, there was another great photo opportunity at the window."

Born in Minnesota in 1955, Segerstrom earned his bachelors and masters degrees in fish and wildlife management at the University of Montana in Bozeman. He wrote his masters thesis on the impact of human activity on pronghorn antelopes and later published the results in an article for a scholarly journal. From 1981 to 1987 he worked as a field biologist for the Wyoming Fish and Game Department, monitoring wildlife populations.

Segerstrom founded GPWI in 1986 and ran it for two years out of Casper before moving to Jackson Hole, where a larger market for his kinds of trips existed. At the beginning he offered just seven-day safaris and usually customized these to his clients' interests. For example, if they expressed a major interest in mountain lions, then he took them to a ranch which had reported a heavy loss of livestock, putting his people up in the bunkhouse and spending the days searching for mountain lions. He spent much of his time with his clients educating them in the principles of field biology.

"All this was quite new back in 1986 when the traditional ways of getting involved with wildlife in this country were through hunting and fishing," Segerstrom reflects. "I wanted to offer people the opportunity to interact with wildlife, much as I had done as a field biologist for the state. I concluded that all those years of watching National Geographic specials and "Nova" programs on PBS had made people much more interested in having a more active, participatory wildlife-viewing experience. When I looked around the United States for companies offering this kind of experience, I saw none. That's when I decided to found GPWI."

Segerstrom knew there were many federal and state agencies interested in gathering data on wildlife but they lacked the funding for research projects. He decided to fill this niche by offering his clients an opportunity to participate in wildlife research. The clients pay for the experience, the wildlife agencies get valuable data, and GPWI makes a profit. The company's research projects have ranged from a study of how forest fires affect porcupines, tracking the movement of elk herds (with the use of radio transmitters), and making a population count of bald eagles and trumpeter swans. On recent seven-day trips, clients and their biologist guide spent two-hour stretches in a 14-foot raft on the Snake River taking a census of the otters living along the banks.

"What we are promoting is citizen science," Segerstrom says proudly. "These animals are held in common ownership in the United States. They belong to all of us. We have learned that our clients, after they have returned home from one of our safaris, often get involved in the stewardship of wildlife in their own regions as volunteers with their own local agencies."

The great forest fire of 1988 which burned a large chunk of the wilderness in Yellowstone National Park actually proved a boon for GPWI. As Segerstrom is quick to tell his clients, the park had not experienced a major fire for over a century and as a result the diversity of vegetation was being lost in an encroaching pine forest. "Now when we go into the parts of the park which were burned, we find a carpet of young aspen trees growing," he explains. "Wildlife viewing has improved dramatically. The animals are no longer hidden away in dense forests but stand out in the newer meadows and scrub lands. We spend a lot of time on our longer trips visiting the burned areas and explaining to our clients the enormous benefits to the ecosystem of periodic burns."

As for the future, Segerstrom is content to keep GPWI small and focused on northwestern Wyoming. "We do not plan to expand our operations to other parts of the country," he says. "We want to remain specialists in the Yellowstone ecosystem."

4

CULTURAL EXPEDITIONS

"If you reject the food, ignore the customs, fear the religions and avoid the people, you might better stay home," novelist James Michener once warned. "You are like a pebble thrown into water; you become wet on the surface but you are never a part of the water."

For the traveler lured by the giant heads of Easter Island, the crafts of Bali, the cave art of France, or the ways of the Masai people in Kenya, the great cultures of the world, both past and present, have never before been so accessible. Cultural expeditions are journeys of discovery with a strong emphasis on education. Many are led by authorities in the culture, history, and art of the regions being visited. Lectures, both formal and informal, are often a part of the daily schedules. Participants on these trips will find themselves immersed in a foreign

The people of the Mursi tribe along the Omo River Valley of southern Ethiopia are one of the most isolated groups in Africa
Irma Turtle/Turtle Tours

culture, eating the local food, drinking the local beverages, meeting the local people, and visiting local homes.

"No man is an island entire of itself," wrote poet John Donne 300 years ago. The same is true of cultures. By breaking down our linguistic and cultural myopia, these trips reaffirm for us that valuable lesson.

"The right good book is always a book of travel. It is about life's journey."

H. M. TOMLINSON
THE SEA AND THE JUNGLE

AFRICA

Africa All the Way from Morocco to South Africa

Participants on these lengthy expeditions cross Africa the hard way, in custom-built vehicles specially designed to drive through every kind of road condition from sand to swamp. The trip begins in London, passes through 22 countries, and ends in Cape Town, South Africa, 13,000 miles later—after crossing the Sahara Desert, the Central African jungles, and the savannas of East Africa. Adventures along the way include a two-day trek in the High Atlas Mountains, a dugout canoe trip in Zaire, a two-day trek to a Pygmy village, a trek to view mountain gorillas at Kahuzi-Biega Park, six days of game-viewing in East African parks, a stop at Victoria Falls, and an expedition by canoe through the famous Okavango Delta. The operator supplies all camping equipment. Participants are expected to help with camp chores.

Operator: Adventure Center/Dragoman, 1311 63rd St., Suite 200, Emeryville, Calif. 94608; (800) 227-8747 or (510) 654-1879; www.adventure-center.com.
Price: Inexpensive.
Season: Throughout the year.
Length: 29 and 33 weeks.
Accommodations: Tent camps. Five percent discount with BBAT coupon.

CENTRAL AFRICAN REPUBLIC

Expedition to the Bayaka Pygmies

Participants on these 16-day expeditions travel by boat and foot to the home of the Bayaka Pygmies, still living as hunters and gatherers in the Lobaye Forest. Considered the first inhabitants of Africa, these "little people of the forest" find refuge in this immense jungle and consider the forest their mother protector and provider. They have remained nomadic throughout the centuries, moving from camp to camp and living on the honey, roots, fruits, and leaves they gather as well as the

Operator: Turtle Tours, Box 1147, Carefree, Ariz. 85377; (888) 299-1439 or (480) 488-3688; www.turtletours.com.
Price: Expensive.
Season: September, November, and January.
Length: 16 days.

Accommodations: Tent camps. Five percent discount with BBAT coupon.

game they hunt with their bows and arrows. Their cultural life is rich with dances and songs that recount the ancient legends of the forest. This is still pristine Africa, where tourism has yet to arrive. Participants journey to the Pygmies by boat down the Ugangi and Lobaye Rivers, visiting villages of other ethnic groups along the way. Porters carry all baggage during the treks.

ETHIOPIA

The People and Monuments of Ethiopia

Operator: Geographic Expeditions, 2627 Lombard St., San Francisco, Calif. 94123; (800) 777-8183 or (415) 922-0448; www.geoex.com. *Price:* Expensive. *Season:* January, March, and November. *Length:* 15 days. *Accommodations:* Hotels, lodges, and tent camps. Five percent discount with BBAT coupon.

A particularly beautiful and uplifting country, Ethiopia "often gives one an illusion of living through different centuries," Dervla Murphy once observed. Its history is richer and more extensive than any other African country south of Egypt and spans religions as diverse as Islam, Christianity, Judaism, and, more recently, Marxism, a secular faith Ethiopia wrestled with for years and finally discarded. This comprehensive tour takes in some of the country's most important archaeological sites and scenic wonders, including the Church of St. Mary of Zion, legendary repository of the Ark of the Covenant, and the Simien Mountains— "Switzerland in miniature," Walter Plowden called these impressive crags. The southern portion of the country along the Omo River valley supports one of the richest collections of wildlife in Africa; participants spend several days here observing the wildlife and visiting remote villages where the tribespeople continue to dress in their traditional clothing. A cultural highlight is the visit to Lalibela in the northern part where in the 12th and 13th centuries craftsmen carved 11 monolithic, freestanding churches out of solid rock. (The churches are protected as a World Heritage Site by the United Nations.)

The people of the Karo Mea tribe along the Omo River Valley in southern Ethiopia have had little contact with Westerners

Irma Turtle/Turtle Tours

Overland Expedition to the Omo Valley Tribes

Spilling out of a mountainous plateau southwest of Addis Ababa, the mighty Omo is so isolated that it was not first explored until 1973, a century after Stanley found Livingstone. To venture into the Omo Valley today is to be transported instantly out of a human history measured in years, decades, and centuries and back into the timeless world of ancient Africa. Participants on these rigorous expeditions travel 1,200 miles by four-wheel-drive vehicles into a virgin environment where tourism is nonexistent and tribal traditions remain unchanged. The women dress in skins and pelts decorated with beads, cowries, and pieces of metal. The men still proudly wear the hair bun and scarification that denotes they have killed an enemy. Particularly fascinating are the Mursi tribespeople,

Operator: Turtle Tours, Box 1147, Carefree, Ariz. 85377; (888) 299-1439 or (480) 488-3688; www.turtletours.com.
Price: Expensive.
Season: February, August, and November.
Length: 16 days.
Accommodations: Tent camps and hotels. Five percent discount with BBAT coupon.

whose women wear huge lip plates and whose men participate in ritualistic stick-dueling. The region is also home to a rich variety of wildlife.

GHANA

Culture and Crafts of Western Africa

Operator:
ABA Tours, 45 Auburn St.,
Brookline, Mass. 02146;
(617) 277-0482;
www.abatours@ultranet.com
Price: Moderate.
Season: August and
September.
Length: 14 days.
Accommodations: Hotels and
village guest houses. Five
percent discount with BBAT
coupon.

Ghana is a small country, about the size of Oregon, with a rich culture. The craftspeople here produce indigenous arts that are collected worldwide. The operator, a potter with close ties to many local artisans, puts small groups of travelers in remote villages where they interact with master Kente and Ashanti weavers, potters, basket makers, stool-carvers, and bead makers. Visitors share the locals' daily lives and rituals and observe displays of traditional drumming and dancing. Travelers also visit several famous outdoor markets, such as the Krobo bead market and the Ewe cloth market in the Volta region. Visits are also made to two historically significant slave castles and a game preserve that features a canopy walk 100 feet above the ground. English is the official language of Ghana, a democratic country far more stable than its neighbors, whose people enjoy a reputation for hospitality. The country is a favorite with the American singer Stevie Wonder, who insists he feels more creative here.

MALI

Overland Expedition to Timbuktu

Operator:
Turtle Tours, Box 1147,
Carefree, Ariz. 85377;
(888) 299-1439 or
(480) 488-3688;
www.turtletours.com.

For centuries the name Timbuktu has symbolized ultimate remoteness. In the 16th century it was a major commercial, religious, and intellectual center of the Muslim world and home to 100,000 people. But today Timbuktu is a mere shadow of its former glory. This rigorous expedition travels by four-wheel-drive vehicles through the land of the

A Tuareg woman dressed for a festival near the legendary city of Timbuktu
Irma Turtle/Turtle Tours

Bambara, Dogon, Tuareg, and Peul tribes. The Dogons are best known for their dances on stilts and villages of mud-walled huts built at the foot of sheer cliffs. Participants also visit Djenne, a former religious center with a mosque that is the largest clay building in the world; and Mopti, an important river port with colorful markets. At Kona, on the Niger River, they board a private pirogue for a three-day river journey to Timbuktu.

Price: Expensive.
Season: November–February.
Length: 16 days.
Accommodations: Tent camps and hotels. Five percent discount with BBAT coupon.

NIGER

Festivals of the Wodaabe and Tuareg Nomads

At the end of each summer the Wodaabe and Tuareg people stage spectacular festivals to celebrate the arrival of a plentiful rainy season after a long sea-

Operator:
Turtle Tours, Box 1147,
Carefree, Ariz. 85377;
(888) 299-1439 or
(480) 488-3688;
www.turtletours.com.
Price: Expensive.
Season: September.
Length: 16 days.
Accommodations: Tent
camps. Five percent dis-
count with BBAT coupon.

son of drought. For the handsome Wodaabe, nomadic herders of ancient origin, this is the moment of "Gerewol," a beauty contest in which the men compete with colorful makeup, flashing smiles, and elaborate costumes. For the Tuareg, this is the time for "Tindes," a festival involving dances, camel races, and marriages. Participants on these expeditions spend five days camping with the two groups and sharing their celebrations. For the next five days participants board four-wheel-drive vehicles for an adventure in the legendary Sahara, a region of volcanic mountains fringed by some of the most sublime desert landscapes in Africa. A highlight is a visit to the Tuareg oasis of Iferouane, home to many jewelers still practicing their centuries-old art.

ASIA

Operator:
Adventure
Center/Dragoman,
1311 63rd St., Suite 200,
Emeryville, Calif. 94608;
(800) 227-8747 or
(510) 654-1879;
www.adventure-center.com.
Price: Inexpensive.
Season: August departure.
Length: 9, 13, and 15 weeks.
Accommodations: Tent
camps. Five percent dis-
count with BBAT coupon.

Classic Overland Expedition from London to Kathmandu

Perhaps no other trip gives its participants such insights into history as these lengthy overland expeditions. They pass through the lands of the world's greatest empires, including those of the Greeks, Romans, Byzantines, ancient Persians, Egyptians, Arabs, Ottoman, Sikh, and Hindu Rajputs. Stops at major cities are sandwiched between visits to historic sites, both ancient and modern. Travel is by specially designed 16-ton Mercedes overland vehicles able to traverse all types of terrain quickly and efficiently, no matter how rugged.

"The inscrutability of the East is, I believe, a myth. . . . The ordinary inhabitant is incomprehensible merely to people who never trouble to have anything much to do with him."

FREYA STARK
THE JOURNEY'S ECHO

Across Asia by Train, the Ultimate Rail Adventure

For railway buffs seeking their own "Great Railway Bazaar," this expedition combines the world's two greatest rail journeys: the Trans-Mongolian Express across China and the Trans-Siberian Express across Russia. The trip begins in Beijing and ends in Moscow. Participants have opportunities to leave the train for cultural excursions into such remote regions as Karakorum, Ulan Ude, Lake Baikal, and Irkutsk, visiting native villages along the way. Travel is in comfortable four-berth, air-conditioned compartments.

Operator: Mir Corp., 85 S. Washington St., #210, Seattle, Wash. 98104; (800) 424-7289 or (206) 624-7289; www.mircorp.com.
Price: Expensive.
Season: May–September.
Length: 19 days.
Accommodations: Railroad compartments. Five percent discount with BBAT coupon.

BURMA

Cultural Exploration of Burmese Life

Burma is far less visited than any other Indochinese country. From the ancient ruins of Pagan to the extraordinary markets of Mandalay, to the floating farms of Inle Lake, the country provides fascinating wonders at every turn. Travelers on these trips use trains and air-conditioned minivans to explore one of the most exotic cultures in Asia. The itinerary includes as many local festivals and holiday celebrations as possible. Highlights include a boat ride up the Irrawaddy River, the country's chief highway between Mandalay and Rangoon, and a ride on Inle Lake in a picturesque long lake-boat past villages and farms perched over the water on stilts.

Operator: Journeys International, 107 Aprill Dr., #3., Ann Arbor, Mich. 48103; (800) 255-8735 or (734) 665-4407; www.journeys-intl.com.
Price: Moderate.
Season: Year-round.
Length: 8 and 15 days.
Accommodations: Hotels. Five percent discount with BBAT coupon.

CAMBODIA

A Cultural Tour of Angkor Wat, Asia's "Lost City"

For centuries swallowed up by the dense jungle and lost to outsiders, the vast temple complex of Angkor Wat is today one of the world's great destinations for

Operator:
Geographic Expeditions,
2627 Lombard St.,
San Francisco, Calif. 94123;
(800) 777-8183 or
(415) 922-0448;
www.geoex.com.
Price: Expensive.
Season: Throughout the
year.
Length: 7 days.
Accommodations: Hotels.
Five percent discount with
BBAT coupon.

lovers of archaeology, architecture, and art. The complex was constructed between the ninth and 13th centuries, when the Khmer Empire was at its height. Participants on this cultural tour spend their days in this fascinating complex of temples, gates, and stone carvings with its Elephant Terrace, Terrace of the Leper King, and the stunning Bayon Temple. When they depart, visitors will almost certainly agree with historian Arnold Toynbee, who called the complex "an epic poem." The trip ends with a peaceful day of rafting on the Tonle Sap River.

CHINA

Tibet Overland Odyssey

Tibet, the highest kingdom in the world, has been an ultimate destination for much of this century. Since the time of Marco Polo, the country has traditionally been forbidden to outsiders. Chinese authorities did not open its borders to modern travelers until 1985. These highly affordable trips begin and end in Kathmandu. Travelers spend two nights in ancient Lhasa, visiting the incomparable Potala Palace, a palace of 1,000 rooms and home to the Dalai Lamas, and join Tibetans on the ancient

A highlight of any journey to Tibet is a visit to the famous Potala Palace in Lhasa
Journeys International

pilgrimage trail around the seventh-century Jokhang temple. Then they venture out into the country to see such sights as the Kumbum stupa (Buddhist shrine), Palkhor Monastery, and hilltop fort at the ancient village of Gyantse; and the gold-roofed Tashilhunpo Monastery, founded in 1447 and home to 600 monks. Participants return to Kathmandu by road, driving over the Lalung Leh Pass at 17,102 feet where they enjoy outstanding views of the Himalayas, including Mt. Everest.

INDIA

Festivals of Rajasthan

The operator offers trips to take advantage of five of Rajasthan's finest fairs and festivals. These include the fabulous Pushkar camel fair, an annual event for the Rajasthan desert tribes, who come from great distances to buy and sell livestock and compete in camel races; the three-day Nagaur animal fair, another cauldron of camel-oxen-bullock-horse–trading; the desert festival of Jaisalmer, famous for its Gair dancers, fire dancers, and gypsy dancers; the Holi festival at Jodhpur, the most joyous and exuberant of Hindu festivals celebrating the end of winter and the arrival of spring; and the Dussehra festival of Jaisalmer, an important Hindu festival celebrating the defeat of the demon King Ravana by the forces of Lord Rama. All departures also include visits to Delhi, Udaipur, Jodhpur, Jaisalmer, and the Taj.

The Tribes and Jungles of the North-East Frontier Agency

"The furthest planet in India's teeming solar system," Theo Cruz called the North-East Frontier Area (NEFA), the least-known and least-visited part of the subcontinent. The government opened the area to foreigners only in 1995. This trip focuses on Arunachal Pradesh, the largest of the NEFA states,

Operator:
Journeys International,
107 Aprill Dr., #3.,
Ann Arbor, Mich. 48103;
(800) 255-8735 or
(734) 665-4407;
www.journeys-intl.com.
Price: Moderate.
Season: May–October.
Length: 12 days.
Accommodations: Small hotels. Five percent discount with BBAT coupon.

Operator:
Geographic Expeditions,
2627 Lombard St.,
San Francisco, Calif. 94123;
(800) 777-8183 or
(415) 922-0448;
www.geoex.com.
Price: Expensive.
Season: January, February, March, September, October, and November.
Length: 18 days.
Accommodations: Hotels and deluxe desert camps. Five percent discount with BBAT coupon.

Operator: Geographic Expeditions, 2627 Lombard St., San Francisco, Calif. 94123; (800) 777-8183 or (415) 922-0448; www.geoex.com. *Price:* Expensive. *Season:* January and November. *Length:* 18 days. *Accommodations:* Hotels. Five percent discount with BBAT coupon.

which sits nestled below the snowy peaks of the Himalayan Mountains. Some 21 major tribes live here, most of Mongol and Mon-Khmer descent, far removed from the Aryan-Dravidian peoples of the rest of India. Living in small villages, isolated from each other by the mountainous countryside, each tribe is proudly distinct. In the highlands the Burmese tribes enthusiastically practiced head-hunting until the 1950s.

Indonesians once believed that orangutans could speak but had decided not to do so for fear that humans would put them to work

Earthwatch

INDONESIA

Indonesian Cultural Odyssey

Few regions in Asia are as rich in cultural treasures as the islands of Indonesia. This lengthy expedition focuses on the islands of Sulawesi, Flores, and

Sumba. Four days are spent in Torajaland in Sulawesi, famous for both its great natural beauty and its funerals. After the initial funeral, the bones of the deceased are dug up for a special ceremony. Buffaloes and pigs are slaughtered and then the human remains are placed in wooden coffins, which are deposited in sunken holes carved high up on cliffs with an effigy of the deceased placed nearby. Flores boasts a rugged ridge of mountains with several smoking volcanoes. Its people are famous for their fine music, using instruments such as bamboo slit drums, small gongs, pan pipes, and drums made from parchment stretched over the end of a hollow coconut trunk. The people on the flat, barren island of Sumba produce some of the finest fabrics in Indonesia. Both islands also offer fine dances.

Operator: Asian Pacific Adventures, 9010 Reseda Blvd., #227, Northridge, Calif. 91324; (800) 825-1680 or (818) 886-5190; www.asianpacificadventures.com.
Price: Moderate.
Season: Throughout the year.
Length: 22 days.
Accommodations: Hotels and village homes. Five percent discount with BBAT coupon.

Bali Through an Artist's Eye

Perhaps on no other Asian island have the people developed such a broad selection of sophisticated arts over the past 500 years. For instance, a typical Balinese woman knows the designs of 100 or more different offerings required in the rich ceremonial life of her society. Groups on this trip are limited to six people, a number small enough to visit the studios of artists, woodcarvers, weavers, and basket-makers and learn something of their private and religious ceremonies. Participants also visit numerous museums and temples and spend a day at Tenganan, the ancient walled village where many musical instrument–makers reside and the unique double-ikat gerinsings are woven.

Operator: Asian Pacific Adventures, 9010 Reseda Blvd., #227, Northridge, Calif. 91324; (800) 825-1680 or (818) 886-5190; www.asianpacificadventures.com.
Price: Moderate.
Season: February, April, July, and October.
Length: 15 days.
Accommodations: A private home in Ubud, a mountain village famous for its artists. Five percent discount with BBAT coupon.

"Looking out a train window in Asia is like watching an unedited travelogue without the obnoxious soundtrack."

PAUL THEROUX
THE GREAT RAILWAY BAZAAR: BY TRAIN THROUGH ASIA

Cultural Exploration Among the Tana Toraj People on Sulawesi

Operator:
Outer Edge Expeditions,
4830 Mason Rd.,
Howell, Mich. 48843;
(800) 322-5235 or
(517) 552-5300;
www.outer-edge.com.
Price: Moderate.
Season: May, June, and
August.
Length: 13 days.
Accommodations: Village
guesthouses and hotels.
Five percent discount with
BBAT coupon.

Living in an isolated area and preserving their traditional customs, the Torajan people are noted among anthropologists for their unique starship-shaped houses, hanging graves, effigies to the dead, and massive megaliths. The departures are timed to coincide with the ceremonies called marante sadan, funeral festivals to honor the dead men. After a lengthy celebration, the dead man is launched into the afterlife, his body placed in a cliff grave, and an effigy erected nearby on a stone balcony. The itinerary also includes trekking to outlying Torajan villages, white-water rafting down the Sa'dan River at the base of 3,000-foot-high mountains, and a final two days in Bali.

Expedition to the Heart of Irian Jaya

Largely unexplored until 1975, the isolated frontier of the western half of New Guinea is home to an extraordinary diversity of wildlife and primitive

The Adventure Travel Hall of Fame: MARY KINGSLEY

For most people great travel books lead merely to realms of the imagination, but for an intrepid few they pose an actual invitation. In the 1890s Englishwoman Mary Kingsley sailed off to explore the West African country of Gabon, directly on the equator and once part of the French Congo. It was a risky adventure for the 33-year-old Kingsley, who described the region as "notorious for its deadly climate and diseases, its alarming wildlife and its cannibals." When she returned to England, she set down her obser-

vations and adventures in a best-selling book, Travels in West Africa.

Almost a century later 33-year-old Caroline Alexander spent an evening at her local library in Tallahassee, Florida, where she discovered Kingsley's book and found a kindred spirit. She quickly decided to go to Gabon and follow in the Englishwoman's footsteps. In May 1987 Alexander was on her way, eager to learn how Gabon had changed in the century since Kingsley's visit. Once there she found a country that was still 80 percent jungle, its interior drained by the

tribes, some of whom practiced cannibalism until recent years. Members of this expedition fly to the secluded Baliem Valley of central Irian Jaya, where some 200,000 Dani tribesmen live. The Dani have been slash-and-burn agriculturists for centuries. Expedition members spend several days living in Dani villages with their characteristic dome-roofed huts to observe the customs of these remarkable people. The men wear only long tubular penis sheaths made from dried yellow gourds and armbands fashioned from pigs' scrotums to ward off evil spirits. This is New Guinea as it was 50 years ago.

LAOS

Kingdom of a Million Elephants

Serene and timeless, Laos has escaped the wave of tourism that has engulfed much of Southeastern Asia, a pocket of the Old Asia preserved into modern times. This once-powerful kingdom known as Lang Xang (meaning Million Elephants) dates

Operator:
Outer Edge Expeditions,
4830 Mason Rd.,
Howell, Mich. 48843;
(800) 322-5235 or
(517) 552-5300;
www.outer-edge.com.
Price: Moderate.
Season: January, June, and September.
Length: 15 days.
Accommodations: Hotels and village lodges. Five percent discount with BBAT coupon.

great Ogooué River, and populated with 1 million people divided into 40 tribes, each with its own culture and language.

Determined to parallel Kingsley's journey as closely as possible, Alexander stayed in missions and villages during the course of her travels. In Lambaréné she encountered the ghost of the great Albert Schweitzer, who had set up his hospital there in 1925 and died on the grounds in 1965 after receiving the Nobel Peace Prize in 1952. From there she made her way deep into the interior, following Kingsley's trail through the same mud villages, the same stretches of waterway, rain forest, and empty savanna, before setting out on her own through countryside

that was virtually unreachable a century before. Throughout it all she savored her opportunity for a unique adventure in a faraway part of the world and went at it with scholarly vigor and the awareness and adaptability of a seasoned traveler.

Like Kingsley before her, Alexander returned home and wrote a full account of her travels, One Dry Season: In the Footsteps of Mary Kingsley. Making the trip changed her, she insisted: "It made me feel I could do anything; I could go the distance. Now I can sit in my living room on a rainy afternoon, look at an atlas and make a dream come true. I truly believe that if you get an idea, you can find a way to do it."

Operator:
Geographic Expeditions,
2627 Lombard St.,
San Francisco, Calif. 94123;
(800) 777-8183 or
(415) 922-0448;
www.geoex.com.
Price: Expensive.
Season: November–
February.
Length: 7 days.
Accommodations: Hotels.
Five percent discount with
BBAT coupon.

back to the 14th century. Many aspects of this gilded age have survived the politics and wars of the past century. Highlights include Luang Prabang, the capital of Lang Xang from 1353 to 1545 and today celebrated for its traditional crafts and collection of 30 temples, some dating back 600 years; the limestone caves of Pak-Ou, containing gilded Buddhas of all shapes and sizes; and Pakse, capital of Southern Laos during the height of the Khmer Empire. One day is spent on a private boat traveling down the famed Mekong River to Wat Phu, an early Angkor-period Khmer temple.

LAOS AND VIETNAM

River Odyssey on the Mekong River

Operator:
Asia Transpacific Journeys,
2995 Center Green Ct.,
Boulder, Colo. 80301;
(800) 642-2742 or
(303) 443-6789;
www.southeastasia.com.
Price: Moderate.
Season: January and
November.
Length: 17 days.
Accommodations: Hotels and
guest houses. Five percent
discount with BBAT
coupon.

Participants will find themselves traveling through a land populated by a gracious people who have long since consigned the most recent war to a long history of wars stretching back over 1,000 years. Paradoxically, Americans—more than any nationality—are now welcome in these countries. Participants on this river cruise explore the cultural and scenic wonders of this part of Southeastern Asia from the deck of a handsome teak barge as they travel down the Mekong River through Laos and Vietnam, with frequent stops for villages, nature walks, and temples. A highlight is Luang Prabang, a city of 8,000 famous for its collection of 30 temples, some dating back 600 years.

MALAYSIA

Headhunters, Hornbills, and Orangutans in Sabah, Sarawak, and Borneo

The third-largest island in the world, Borneo represents one of the last frontiers for adventure travel. This expedition focuses on both the anthropological and natural attractions of the island. A full day is spent at the Sepilok Orangutan Reserve, where orphaned primates are conditioned to be returned to the wild. One day is spent on beautiful Turtle Island, where green turtles lay their eggs, for fine snorkeling or scuba diving. And finally, participants board motorized longboats for a journey up the Engari River to an Iban village deep within the jungle. The villagers are former headhunters who are now friendly toward outsiders. Participants will join the Iban in daily activities and be allowed to observe their dancing, traditional games, and animist rituals. (The May group witnesses the Gawai Dayak festival, which celebrates the harvest with dances and banquets.)

Operator: Asian Pacific Adventures, 9010 Reseda Blvd., #227, Northridge, Calif. 91324; (800) 825-1680 or (818) 886-5190; www.asianpacificadventures.com.
Price: Moderate.
Season: May, June, and September.
Length: 14 days.
Accommodations: A traditional Stamang longhouse and hotels. Five percent discount with BBAT coupon.

MONGOLIA

Expedition by Horseback Through Mongolia

The steppes of Mongolia are Asia's Wild West and consist of rolling grasslands stretching to the horizon, unfenced and unpopulated except for small ranching communities. For thousands of years the horse has been an integral part of the nomadic culture in Central Asia. This expedition offers a unique opportunity to take part in the daily life of the Mongolian people. Expedition members spend seven days riding small Mongolian ponies with traditional tack through the historic homeland of Genghis Khan. Local herdsmen act as guides. Two highlights are a visit to a summer camp of the reindeer people near the Siberian border and the annual Naadam Festival, where the warriors proudly display their skills of war in contests of horsemanship, archery, and shooting. The Mongolians are also famous for their warm hospitality toward visitors.

Operator: Boojum Expeditions, 14543 Kelly Canyon Rd., Bozeman, Mont. 59715; (800) 287-0125 or (406) 587-0125; www.boojum.com.
Price: Expensive.
Season: July.
Length: 15 days.
Accommodations: Lodge and tent camps. Five percent discount with BBAT coupon.

"As long as we're traveling toward the unknown, we're on the right track."

RORY NUGENT
THE SEARCH FOR THE PINK-HEADED DUCK

PAKISTAN

Karakoram Highway to Kashgar

Operator: Worldwide Adventures, 1170 Sheppard Ave. West, #45, Toronto, Ont., Canada M3K 2A3; (800) 387-1483 or (416) 633-5666; www.worldwidequest.com. *Price:* Moderate. *Season:* April and September. *Length:* 18 days. *Accommodations:* Hotels. Five percent discount with BBAT coupon.

The Karakoram Highway is one of the highest and most spectacular roads in Asia. It stretches 1,284 kilometers, cuts through the Karakoram Range, and affords unrivaled views of snowcapped peaks, while linking the historic cultures of Swat and the Hunza Valley with Kashgar and Central Asia. Stops are made in the villages of Swat Valley, Gilgit, Hunza Valley, and Kashgar, and at the many colorful bazaars along the way where Pathan tribesmen, Afghan traders, and veiled women trade their wares. This is essentially a vehicle-based trip with a selection of day hikes included.

THAILAND

Elephant Safari Through the Golden Triangle

Operator: Mountain Travel-Sobek, 6420 Fairmount Ave., El Cerrito, Calif. 94530; (888) 687-6235 or (415) 527-8100; www.mtsobek.com. *Price:* Moderate. *Season:* January and November. *Length:* 16 days. *Accommodations:* Houses of village chiefs. Five percent discount with BBAT coupon.

For centuries, the remote mountains of northern Thailand have provided a sanctuary for nomadic tribes. Here some 375,000 non–Thai-speaking minorities live in small scattered villages. To travel among the various hill tribes with their fantastic traditionally embroidered costumes and massive silver jewelry is to be immersed in a cultural and racial potpourri of wondrous diversity. Members of this cultural expedition spend two days riding elephants through dense jungle alive with the sounds of birds and monkeys to visit the villages of these friendly hill tribes. Other activities include two days in a remote Hmong hill-tribe village in the frontier region near the Laos border, and a longtail boat ride on the Mekong River.

VIETNAM

Hill Tribes of Northern Vietnam

The ethnic peoples of northern Vietnam are among the most colorful in Southeast Asia, with cultures that are largely uncontaminated by outside influences. Participants on these cultural expeditions journey out of Hanoi to Hoa Binh to meet the Thai, Muong, and Dao people. Dao women, for example, traditionally wear short skirts of batik material, hand-dyed indigo jackets, and head scarves. Other stops include Hmong villages near Moc Chau and Son La, where the Hmong and Thai ethnic groups live in the hills. In Sa Pa visitors observe an evening festival put on by the Dao, who still follow a nomadic way of life.

Operator: Asian Pacific Adventures, 9010 Reseda Blvd., #227, Northridge, Calif. 91324; (800) 825-1680 or (818) 886-5190; www.asian-pacificadventures.com.
Price: Moderate.
Season: Throughout the year.
Length: 13 days.
Accommodations: Hotels and guest houses. Five percent discount with BBAT coupon.

The Hmong Montagnard, hill-tribe people of northern Vietnam have had little contact with travelers from the outside

Tovya Wager/Asian Pacific Adventures

AUSTRALASIA

AUSTRALIA

Kakadu National Park Cultural Tour

Operator: Adventure Center, 1311 63rd St., Suite 200, Emeryville, Calif. 94608; (800) 227-8747 or (510) 654-1879; www.adventure-center.com. *Price:* Moderate. *Season:* Throughout the year. *Length:* 5 days. *Accommodations:* Tent camps. Five percent discount with BBAT coupon.

Located 150 miles east of Darwin, Kakadu National Park offers overseas visitors a great opportunity to observe aborigines from both a modern and historical perspective. Several hundred aborigines live inside the park boundary, following the traditional ways of their culture. Preserved in the park are an extraordinary collection of aboriginal rock and cave paintings, some dating back 20,000 years. No other Australian national park matches the enormous wealth of wildlife of Kakadu. This is safari country, rich in Australia's nearest approach to big game: wild Asian buffalo, crocodiles, feral pigs, and kangaroos. One-third of the country's 720 bird species have been spotted here.

The Adventure Travel Hall of Fame: TOBIAS SCHNEEBAUM

In 1955 Tobias Schneebaum, a New York City artist, traveled to Peru on a Fulbright fellowship for two years. After a year, seeking relief from the congestion of the big cities, he decided to go into the Amazonian jungle on a search for new opportunities and experiences. Armed with a penknife and the instructions "Keep the river on your right," he set out on an eight-day hike through the jungle to the last outpost of civilization, a small Catholic mission. From there he walked into uncharted jungle on a search for a tribe of cannibals reputed to live there. After a four-day walk he reached a village of Akarama Indians. The warriors, in particular, impressed him. "Some had match-like sticks through their lower lips, others had bones through their noses," he wrote later in his account of his adventure,

PAPUA NEW GUINEA

Cultural Expedition to the Highlands

Until recently some 700 Highland cultures existed in almost total isolation, tribes so colorful and exotic that Papua New Guinea has been called the Human Aviary. On this comprehensive 16-day expedition, members in the company of an anthropologist explore the people, cultures, and tribal art of this remarkable island. Three days are spent visiting villages along the Sepik River, one of the world's centers for tribal art. From Mt. Hagen participants learn about the diversity of the cultures of the Eastern and Western Highlands with visits to Asaro, Chimbu, and Megabo villages to witness sing-sings and tribal celebrations. They then travel to the rarely visited Southern Highlands, home to the Huli clans, to observe the famous wigmen, known for their lavishly decorated wigs of human hair.

Operator: Asia Transpacific Journeys, 2995 Center Green Ct., Boulder, Colo. 80301; (800) 642-2742; (303) 443-6789; www.southeastasia.com.
Price: Expensive.
Season: August.
Length: 13 days.
Accommodations: Hotels and guest houses. Five percent discount with BBAT coupon.

Keep the River on Your Right. "Long, well-combed bangs ran over their foreheads into the scarlet paint of their faces and hair covered the length of their backs and shoulders. Masses of necklaces of seeds and huge animal teeth and small yellow and black birds hung down from their thick necks." For his first meal they fed him roast monkey meat and yucca.

After a few weeks the Akaramas adopted Schneebaum into their tribe. They scraped the hair off his body with a nutria's tooth, painted his body with brilliant colors, and taught him how to use the bow and arrow to hunt small game. He immersed himself in the small rituals of the daily life of his adoptive tribe. Much later he accompanied the Indians on a raid against a neighboring village in which enemy warriors were slaughtered and parts of their bodies eaten in a ceremony of ritualistic cannibalism. After seven months he returned to the civilized world and discovered that the American embassy and Peruvian officials had declared him dead.

CANADA

NUNAVUT

Arctic Dogsled Adventure

Operator: Arctic Odysseys, 2000 McGilvra Blvd. East, Seattle, Wash. 98112; (800) 574-3021 or (206) 325-1977; www.arcti-codysseys.com. *Price:* Expensive. *Season:* March–June. *Length:* 9 days. *Accommodations:* Hotels and igloos. Five percent discount with BBAT coupon.

This expedition provides a superlative cultural experience and the opportunity to learn firsthand about the Inuit lifestyle. Participants travel in the traditional style of the Arctic peoples and go in search of such wildlife as polar bears, walrus, and seals at the edge of the ice floe. They can also fish through the ice for cod and Arctic char. Additionally, from mid-May through June, many of the indigenous and migrating birds can be viewed in their breeding plumage. This is a rigorous but rewarding expedition.

EUROPE

CZECH REPUBLIC

Ballooning over Prague

Operator: The Bombard Society, 333 Pershing Way, West Palm Beach, Fla. 33401; (800) 862-8537 or (561) 837-6610. *Price:* Expensive. *Season:* September. *Length:* 6 days. *Accommodations:* Hotel.

This adventure's participants enjoy an intense cultural immersion in one of Europe's most beautiful and interesting cities. Prague was spared the bombing of World War II and almost half the 3,507 buildings now standing on the city's original medieval ground plan are under landmark protection. Each morning begins with a hot-air balloon flight across a different part of the city, letting participants enjoy 1,000 years of architectural wealth from a bird's-eye perspective. The rest of each day is devoted to exhaustive exploration of the city's cultural and historical attractions.

GEORGIA AND ARMENIA

Transcaucasian Cultural Experience

Beyond the Black Sea's Euro beach resorts and the grand bazaars of Istanbul lies a rugged region that over the centuries has changed hands more often than the keys to a '65 Volkswagen Bug. The operator has designed this adventure as an in-depth exposure to the cultural, spiritual, and culinary traditions of the people in this little-visited region. Participants begin their tour in Tbilisi, the charming capital of Georgia, for visits to the forts, mosques, museums, and basilicas, and then head to higher ground in the Tushetian region. There they visit mountain monasteries, meet villagers, and feast on Caucasus dishes such as shashlik (lamb shish kebab). Crossing into Armenia, travelers end up in Yerevan, a capital city set among orchards and vineyards not far from Mt. Ararat, the biblical resting place of Noah's ark.

Operator: Mir Corp., 85 S. Washington St., #210, Seattle, Wash. 98104; (800) 424-7289 or (206) 624-7289; www.mircorp.com. *Price:* Moderate. *Season:* July–September. *Length:* 15 days. *Accommodations:* Hotels and lodges. Five percent discount with BBAT coupon.

RUSSIA

Evenkian Reindeer Sledding Odyssey

The Evenks are among the few Arctic peoples who have preserved their traditional culture and philosophy while maintaining their nomadic lifestyle of hunting and reindeer-herding in the heart of Siberia in the massive wilderness of the Lena River. The heart of this adventure is an eight-day traditional reindeer sledding trip, allowing the participants a full immersion in the strenuous Evenkian culture as they travel through a landscape of forested tiaiga and mountainous terrain. Wolves, bears, fox, sable, ermine, elk, and deer are prevalent in the region. Travelers can expect wholesome and hearty Evenkian meals, cooked in the traditional forestry manner. This is an adventure that carries a higher risk of inherent dangers, such as extreme cold and attacks from bears and wolves.

Operator: Arctic Odysseys, 2000 McGilvra Blvd. East, Seattle, Wash. 98112; (800) 574-3021 or (206) 325-1977; www.arcticodysseys.com. *Price:* Expensive. *Season:* February and March. *Length:* 14 days. *Accommodations:* Hotels and Evenkian nomadic winter shelters. Five percent discount with BBAT coupon.

LATIN AMERICA

BELIZE

Sacred Caves of the Maya

Operator:
Slickrock Adventures,
P.O. Box 1400,
Moab, Utah 84532;
(800) 390-5715 or
(801) 259-6996;
www.slickrock.com.
Price: Moderate.
Season: January–April.
Length: 5 days.
Accommodations: Jungle
lodge. Five percent dis-
count with BBAT coupon.

Participants on this adventure make a subter-
ranean journey into the sacred underworld of the
Maya. The Maya believed that caves were portals to
the underworld, where their most important gods
dwelled, and therefore were holy places where a
variety of religious rituals were held. Today Mayan
relics can be found in almost every cave in Belize.
Participants on this strenuous caving expedition
visit Mayan ceremonial altars, with their accompanying collections of petroglyphs and artifacts, deep
in the underground world beneath the jungle.
Other attractions include crystal dripstone formations and underground waterfalls.

CHILE

Journey to Easter Island

Easter Island enjoys the distinction of being the
world's most secluded piece of inhabited land. No
other people in history have endured such
extreme cultural isolation, and yet Easter became
home to the most sophisticated Polynesian culture
in the Pacific basin. Among their many achieve-

*"In Easter Island the past is the present, the inhabitants of today less real
than the men who have gone; the shadows of the departed builders still possess the land. Voluntarily or involuntarily, the sojourner must hold com-
mune with those old workers; for the whole air vibrates with a vast purpose
and energy which has been and is no more."*

KATHERINE SCORESBY ROUTLEDGE
THE MYSTERY OF EASTER ISLAND

The enormous statues of Easter Island, 2,500 miles off the coast of Chile, are impressive reminders of the most advanced Polynesian civilization in all the Pacific

James C. Simmons

ments, the ancient Easter Islanders carved 1,000 highly stylized stone statues, some 60 feet high and weighing more than 300 tons. Members of this expedition visit the island's major archaeological sites in the company of local anthropologists. Sites include the quarry at Rano Raraku, where work on 200 statues was abruptly halted; the ceremonial village at Orongo on the rim of Rano Kau volcano; and the restored statues at Ahu Akivi. Participants stay in the village of Hangaroa, where they experience a modern Polynesian culture.

Operator: Nature Expeditions International, 7860 Peters Rd., #F-103, Plantation, Fla. 33324; (800) 869-0639 or (954) 693-8852; www.naturexp.com.
Price: Expensive.
Season: Throughout the year.
Length: 9 days.
Accommodations: Hotels. Five percent discount with BBAT coupon.

MEXICO

By Classic American Train to Copper Canyon

Operator:
Sierra Madre Express,
P.O. Box 26381,
Tucson, Ariz. 85726;
(800) 666-0346 or
(520) 747-0346;
www.sierramadreexpress.com
Price: Expensive.
Season: Throughout the
year.
Length: 7 days.
Accommodations: Train
sleeping compartments
and lodges. Five percent
discount with BBAT
coupon.

The Sierra Madre Express is reminiscent of an era filled with travel lore and impeccable service. Dating from the 1940s, these restored railway cars carry up to 50 passengers in relative comfort through some of the most spectacular countryside in Mexico. All food and drinking water are brought from the United States. Starting and ending their trip in Tucson, participants spend three days in the remarkable Copper Canyon region, where individual canyons are both deeper and wider than our own Grand Canyon. A major attraction of the trip is the time spent among the Tarahumara Indians who live throughout the canyon complex. Known for their long-distance running, the Tarahumara survive in their harsh environment on planted corn and beans and wild fruit. They hunt by running small game to exhaustion. Most Tarahumara make their homes in naturally formed caves hidden in large rock outcroppings. They are the largest—50,000 strong—tribe left in northern Mexico.

Expedition to the Painted Caves of Baja

Operator:
Baja Discovery, P.O. Box
152527, San Diego, Calif.
92195; (800) 829-2252 or
(619) 262-0700;
www.bajadiscovery.com.
Price: Expensive.
Season: April and October.
Length: 7 days.
Accommodations: Tent
camps in palm-studded
canyons and rooms at local
ranches. Five percent discount with BBAT coupon.

Hidden away in the remote mountains of central Baja California are galleries of remarkable rock art hundreds or thousands of years old, which celebrate the world of unknown Indians on a scale unsurpassed in North America. One dynamic mural stretches almost 500 feet, a dense grouping of humans, deer, rabbits, antelope, turtles, and serpents all painted in ochre and black. Elsewhere a 12-foot gray whale breaches on an overhang. Participants on this rigorous seven-day expedition ride mules and walk through remote mountain and canyon country to reach the art sites.

Missions of Baja California

This trip combines Baja's mission history with some of the peninsula's most spectacular wilderness scenery. The 18th-century Spanish padres constructed a chain of over 20 missions, which ran the entire length of California from the southern tip of Baja to present-day San Francisco in the north. Traveling in comfort in an air-conditioned van, participants visit 10 of the historic Spanish missions that dot the length of Baja. These range from the beautifully preserved Jesuit mission church in the oasis village of San Ignacio, dating back to 1786, to the Franciscan Mission San Fernando, whose picturesque adobe ruins lie a short walk away from a rock gallery ablaze with ancient Indian rock paintings. The operator also visits some of the most scenic parts of the Central Desert, which boasts the richest collection of cacti in North America, at least 110 species, of which 60 are endemic.

Operator:
Baja Discovery, P.O. Box 152527, San Diego, Calif. 92195; (800) 829-2252 or (619) 262-0700; www.bajadiscovery.com.
Price: Expensive.
Season: May and October.
Length: 8 days.
Accommodations: Hotels. Five percent discount with BBAT coupon.

PERU

Great Peruvian Rail Adventure

Iron-horse adventurers want more than just another chance to hear that lonesome whistle blow. They want shattering scenery, antique coaches and sleepers, and soul-stirring locomotives making joyful noises in faraway places. Rail buffs will find all this and more on this popular rail expedition,

"When an Australian aborigine suddenly throws up his job and takes to the bush for a few weeks to several years, people say he has gone 'walkabout.' He may have no particular destination, but that does not necessarily mean that he has no purpose. He goes walkabout to get away from it all, to cleanse the soul or possibly just to satisfy a yearning for adventure."

MIKE SAUNDERS
THE WALKABOUTS: A FAMILY AT SEA

Operator:
Trains Unlimited Tours,
P.O. Box 1997,
Portola, Calif. 96122;
(800) 359-4870 or
(530) 836-1745;
www.trainsunltdtours.com.
Price: Expensive.
Season: August.
Length: 16 days.
Accommodations: Hotels.
Five percent discount with
BBAT coupon.

which can be truthfully called "By Railroad Across the Top of the World." The trip begins with a spectacular train ride over what has been called the railway engineering marvel of the world—a 280-mile journey that goes from sea level to 15,693 feet in the first 106 miles. Enjoying breathtaking views, passengers travel over 21 switchbacks, across 61 bridges, and through 66 tunnels. Another exciting rail trip is the 240-mile run from Cusco to Puno on Lake Titicaca, crossing the spine of the Andes at La Raya Pass.

Exploration of the Incan Ruins of the Urubamba Valley

Operator:
Journeys International,
107 Aprill Dr., #3,
Ann Arbor, Mich. 48103;
(800) 255-8735 or
(734) 665-4407;
www.journeys-intl.com.
Price: Moderate.
Season: April, June, July,
and September.
Length: 8 days.
Accommodations: Hotels.
Five percent discount with
BBAT coupon.

Known to the ancient Incas as the "Sacred Valley," the Urubamba Valley offers the visitor the greatest collection of Incan ruins in Peru as well as several well-preserved colonial villages with outstanding Indian markets. Nights are spent in Cusco, the head of the Incan empire. Day trips are made to a variety of ruins, including Quenko, which has a large limestone rock covered with carvings and a cave with altars; Tambo Machy, an Incan bath; and, of course, Machu Picchu, the "lost citadel" of the Incas, where elegant ornamental stonework hints at the site's importance as a ceremonial center. One day is spent hiking the Urubama Valley from the colonial village of Maras to a working model of an Incan farm at Moray and Salinas, a pre-Colombian salt pan still in use today.

MIDDLE EAST

IRAN

Iran Unveiled

After two decades as a closed society hostile to everything and everyone Western, Iran has finally opened its borders to travelers from the outside world. This trip focuses on Iran's wealth of cultural treasures and relics from the many grand Persian empires that rose and fell over the past 4,000 years, best represented by the magnificent ruins of the legendary Persepolis, where Persian kings Darius and Xerxes lived in royal splendor. Other highlights include a visit to the Zagros Mountain villages where Qashgai nomads drive their flocks of sheep and goats from one seasonal pasture to another; a special viewing of traditional wrestling exercises at the "Palace of Strength," complete with drums and singing; and the city of Esfahan, featuring a spectacular collection of beautiful architecture, mosques, ancient bridges, and the most colorful bazaar in Iran.

Operator:
Wilderness Travel,
1102 Ninth St.,
Berkeley, Calif. 94710;
(800) 368-2794 or
(510) 558-2488;
www.wildernesstravel.com.
Price: Moderate.
Season: April, September, and October.
Length: 18 days.
Accommodations: Hotels, with three days of tent camping. Five percent discount with BBAT coupon.

JORDAN

An Expedition to Jordan's Ancient Historical Monuments

The kingdom of Jordan has excited the imagination of Westerners ever since T. E. Lawrence ambushed Turkish troop trains in the desert west of Amman during the First World War. Here the traveler finds some of the most dramatic scenery in the Middle East, plus a rich selection of ruins from the Nabatean, Roman, Byzantine, and Arab civilizations. This trip visits the well-preserved Roman city of Jerash and nearby Qulat al-Rabad Castle, which dates back to the Crusades; the breathtaking desert landscapes of Wadi Rum; the beaches, with their superb coral reefs of the Red Sea off Aqaba; and finally Petra, the celebrated ancient city of the Nabateans, famous for its profusion of temples, tombs, and dwellings, all carved from rose, crimson, and purple limestone.

Operator:
Himalayan Travel,
112 Prospect St.,
Stamford, Conn. 06901;
(800) 225-2380 or
(203) 359-3711;
www.gorp.com/himtravel.htm.
Price: Moderate.
Season: Throughout the year.
Length: 8 days.
Accommodations: Hotels. Five percent discount with BBAT coupon.

SYRIA

Splendors of Syria

Operator:
Journeys International,
107 Aprill Dr., #3,
Ann Arbor, Mich. 48103;
(800) 255-8735 or
(734) 665-4407;
www.journeys-intl.com.
Price: Expensive.
Season: November–April.
Length: 8 days.
Accommodations: Hotels.
Five percent discount with
BBAT coupon.

Rarely visited by American tourists, Syria boasts the finest and most diverse collection of ruins in the Middle East. Damascus lays claim to being the oldest inhabited city in the world. Much of the city has hardly changed since biblical times, and this trip visits a variety of historical sites of world-class importance. Remote in its desert fastness, the Roman complex of Palmyra is a ghost city of colonnaded streets, lavishly decorated tombs, and imposing temples and theaters. The Krak des Chevaliers Castle in the northwestern corner of the country is the best-preserved Crusader castle in the Middle East, so complete that visitors will think they have wandered onto a Hollywood set for a Robin Hood movie. Aleppo offers a Grand Mosque, an Old Bazaar, an ancient caravansary where 1,000 years ago camel caravans spent the nights, and the fifth-century St. Simeon Cathedral, the grandest in the Roman Empire when it was built.

TURKEY

Hot-Air Ballooning over Cappadocia

Operator:
The Bombard Society, 333
Pershing Way,
West Palm Beach, Fla.
33401; (800) 862-8537 or
(561) 837-6610.
Price: Expensive.
Season: September.
Length: 10 days.
Accommodations: Hotels.

Cappadocia, in central Turkey, is an astonishing landscape of dramatic natural beauty. Water and wind erosion have produced a haunting, surrealist region of cones, columns, and canyons. Each morning begins with a low-level hot-air balloon flight over the spectacular landscape. The rest of the days are spent in cultural explorations of the many unique attractions. For 1,000 years, local Christians cut monasteries and churches into the Cappadocian rock. Some 150 of these churches boast some of the most beautiful and famous frescoes in the history of art. The same people also carved entire communities out of the rock, including entire towns set underground. Several days are also spent visiting the sights of Istanbul.

The islanders of Western Samoa are among the friendliest and least spoiled, culturally, in the Pacific

Journeys International

PACIFIC OCEAN

WESTERN SAMOA

Cross-Cultural Opportunities in Margaret Mead Country

Rarely visited by American travelers, the lush green islands of Western Samoa are an unspoiled Pacific paradise. British writer Robert Louis Stevenson contentedly spent the final years of his life here. The people in the countryside outside of Apia, the administrative center, still lead a traditional lifestyle in open-sided, thatch-roofed houses, or fales, in seaside villages ruled over by chiefs. Samoans are among the most generous and hospitable people in the entire Pacific region, often inviting travelers into their homes to share a meal or spend a night.

Operator:
Journeys International,
107 Aprill Dr., #3,
Ann Arbor, Mich. 48103;
(800) 255-8735 or
(734) 665-4407;
www.journeys-intl.com.
Price: Moderate.
Season: Year round.
Length: 8 days.

Accommodations: Hotel and traditional Samoan fales (houses). Five percent discount with BBAT coupon.

Members of this cultural expedition explore all three major inhabited Samoan islands. A highlight is the three days spent on Savai'i Island, the largest and wildest of the islands, where the purest Samoan culture can be found along with over 200 volcanic craters located amidst extensive lava flows.

UNITED STATES

MONTANA, SOUTH DAKOTA, AND WYOMING

Immersion in the Culture of the Northern Plains Indians

Operator: Journeys into American Indian Territory, P.O. Box 929, Westhampton Beach, N.Y. 11978; (800) 458-2632 or (516) 878-8655; www.indianjourneys.com. *Price:* Moderate. *Season:* August. *Length:* 12 days. *Accommodations:* Hotels and motels. Five percent discount with BBAT coupon.

The enormous popularity of the movie *Dances with Wolves* generated considerable sympathy and appreciation for the Plains Indians and their way of life. Participants on this unique trip accompany an anthropologist and his Indian staff on an expedition of cultural discovery. Participants visit several reservations and spend time with individual Indian families, attend private performances of Indian songs and dances, and journey to the Devil's Tower, a Lakota sacred site in the Black Hills of Wyoming. A highlight is the Crow Fair, the "tipi capital of the world," for the powwow dances, hand games, and exhibit of arts and crafts.

Crazy Horse and Custer: The Sioux Wars and the Battle of the Little Bighorn

The operator has built a successful business taking small groups of enthusiasts in the company of notable historians to major sites of American history. This journey through the blood-drenched landscapes of the northern plains where the Sioux Wars unfolded has been a favorite, filling up early. The group visits such rarely seen sites as the spot where Captain William Fetterman and 80 men were annihilated after being decoyed into a trap by the young Crazy Horse; and the Rosebud Battlefield site, where 30 soldiers and civilians held off 800 Sioux warriors. The climax is an extensive study of the Battle of the Little Bighorn on the actual ground where the action unfolded that fateful day.

Operator:
HistoryAmerica Tours,
P.O. Box 797687,
Dallas, Tex. 75379;
(800) 628-8542 or
(972) 713-7171;
www.historyamerica.com.
Price: Moderate.
Season: June.
Accommodations: Motels.
Length: 7 days.

PROFILE

TOVYA WAGER
ASIAN PACIFIC ADVENTURES

"**M**y daughter was born on January 6, 1998, and I firmly believe that her conception happened because of a Bhutanese fertility blessing I had received five months earlier," insists Tovya (pronounced Toe-vee-yuh) Wager, the founder and director of Asian Pacific Adventures. "I was 46 years old at the time. My husband and I had been trying for six years to have a child. We had tried everything. Acupuncture. Herbal treatments. In vitro fertilization. Nothing worked. I had two miscarriages. So we decided to adopt a baby girl in China and started on the paperwork. Then in October of 1996 I escorted one of my groups to Bhutan. One day we visited a religious festival which included a fertility rite. I had worn full Bhutanese religious dress for the occasion. A priest offered to bless me. 'Do you want a boy or a girl?' he asked. 'A girl,' I told him. Then he blessed me with a graphically carved, large wooden phallus and gave me a name for my daughter. I was escorted into the temple behind a fellow cracking a whip to drive off evil spirits. I didn't think too much of it but then five months later I was shocked to discover I was pregnant. We are now obligated to take our daughter to Bhutan to receive the priest's blessing there.

Wager has used her background as a photographer, tribal textile collector, and art educator to carve out a successful niche as an operator specializing in tours focused on providing clients with intense Asian cultural experiences among that region's ethnic minorities. She keeps her business small by choice, carrying just over 300 clients a year, while offering a broad range of itineraries in China, Pakistan, India, Nepal, Bhutan, Borneo, Indonesia, Burma, Vietnam, Laos, and Cambodia.

Wager was born and has lived most of her life in Los Angeles. She took a degree in art and a minor in anthropology at the University of Oregon in Eugene and followed that with a masters in psychology from California Lutheran College in Los Angeles. She taught art for 14 years in high schools in the Los Angeles area.

When China opened its borders to tourists in 1978, Wager decided to be among the first Americans to travel in what had been a closed society. "I've been fascinated with China since I was a child," she reflects. "This sounds funny but I know I was Chinese in another life. My Chinese friends have told me that I am a Chinese person in a Caucasian body. They mean that I really understand, almost intuitively, how the Chinese people think. I feel a close connection to Asian cultures. My soul is more Chinese than Western."

To prepare herself, Wager studied Mandarin Chinese in night school. "I now speak the language fairly fluently, so I can get around there without problems," she says.

Wager's first visit to China in 1979 made her aware of the many different ethnic groups in the country. "People don't realize how many Chinas there are!" she exclaims. "About 94 percent of what we call Chinese are Han, but there are 55 ethnic groups recognized by the government, and I'm sure there are more. I've met people whose lifestyles and features are different but are not listed by the Chinese government as ethnically distinct minorities."

In her travels Wager has visited dozens of these ethnic enclaves, ranging from blond-haired, blue-eyed Moslems descended from the Russian Cossacks to Jewish Chinese people. At first she was obsessed with documenting with her Nikon camera the unique lifestyles of these ethnic cultures. Her early pictures are largely portraits, as she sought to capture her subjects going about their daily business, whether it was a Tibetan horseman smoking a cigarette ("my Tibetan Marlboro man," she calls him) or a Dai seamstress, sewing a costume on a treadle sewing machine in her home.

Wager felt a real sense of urgency about her mission due to the rapid rate of change she saw afflicting China. "Much of the change is for the good, but many of the cultures were losing their unique aspects," she bemoans. "That's what I wanted to document because I knew it would never be the same."

Wager soon gained a reputation as a leading ethnic photographer, exhibiting many of her portraits in galleries, including the Nikon Gallery in Tokyo, and publishing them in magazines and books. Today with the growth of Asian Pacific Adventures that earlier passion has waned somewhat, but she continues to shoot all the photographs that appear in her trip brochure.

During those early years Wager also started collecting Asian tribal textiles. Her collection now runs into the many hundreds of items, some of which she has put on exhibit at selected museums in Los Angeles.

Early on, Wager found herself drawn to China's remote southwestern province of Yunnan, a mountainous region bordering on Burma and Laos. Twenty-four of China's ethnic groups reside there and are more readily accessible than others elsewhere. These isolated minority communities constitute a world apart from the ethnically homogeneous Han culture of modern China. The province's capital, Kunming, was once the headquarters of the famed Flying Tigers, the legendary squadron of U.S. fighter pilots from the early days of World War II who flew out of the Kunming base against the Japanese invaders. Dry, cool, temperatures and a luminous atmosphere make this "city of eternal spring" unusual in China.

In 1985, because of her photographic skills and lengthy experiences with Chinese minorities, Wager was invited to join a National Geographic Society–sponsored expedition down the upper reaches of the Yangtze River. The five men on the expedition were all Chinese, two of them American-born. They camped out all but two nights, sometimes sleeping in caves overlooking the river. They visited villages so remote they were not even listed on the governmental maps of the region.

"You have to have a special personality and mind-set to go on an expedition like that," Wager insists. "You have to know you can encounter danger and be calm and flexible enough to go along with whatever happens."

A highlight came when the group left the river to hike through Tiger Leaping Gorge in a remote section of Yunnan Province. They were the first foreigners into the area since National Geographic Society correspondent Joseph Rock visited it over 50 years before. At one point they met a group of Naxi villagers who, terrified, fled into caves and refused to come out, fearful the foreigners would kidnap them and hold them in slavery.

"We soon learned on this expedition that it was better for me to go first into a new village because the people were not as fearful of me," Wager reflects. "I was less threatening to them because I was a woman. During the days the adults are all out in the fields working, leaving their villages to the older people, women, and children and so unprotected from attack."

On another occasion during this time Wager found herself under arrest by Chinese police in a remote section of Yunnan Province. She had journeyed into a forbidden area to photograph the elusive Yao people, who had seen few foreigners. When she hiked out, she was arrested and jailed by the police for three days. "The guards were drinking tea out of porcelain cups, and I was drinking tea out of a dented metal mug," she recalls. "You definitely knew who the prisoner was. The guards confiscated some of my rolls of exposed film and made me write an essay of self-criticism. It's kind of funny when I think about it now, but then it was, well, very interesting."

Wager started Asian Pacific Adventures in 1986 and had 25 clients that first year. She offered two trips, one to Yunnan Province to visit some of the ethnic cultures there and the other a bicycling tour along a portion of the Yangtze River valley.

"When I first went to China, I decided that it would be great to bring in a group of cyclists and pedal through the countryside," Wager says. "I have always been an avid cyclist. I saw that bicycles would allow us to have a closer cultural interaction with the Chinese people. And the bicycle is the preferred mode of transportation for most rural Chinese."

Over the years Wager refined her concept of the kind of travel experience she wanted to offer. "Here at Asian Pacific Adventures we define quality more in terms of the intensity of experience we can give our clients rather than the number of sites they'll cram into a day," she says. "Our escorts know thoroughly the countries they are presenting. They have friends who welcome them into their homes. They're not just business contacts, but people who live in the villages. All of our trips include time visiting people in their homes. How do people live their daily lives? Well, we show our clients that. To achieve this end we organize many of our departures around local festivals. The people at these events are much more open to mingling with foreigners, and they are usually dressed up for the occasions in their traditional costumes."

Though Asian Pacific Adventures offers a wide selection of tours, each one is limited to just a few departures. Wager strongly believes that there are a few perfect times each year to visit an area in order to catch a particular festival. "Our clients are the sort who will schedule themselves around the tour," she observes. "Convenience isn't their guiding priority."

Wager continues to break through barriers by opening up to group tours areas that had long been closed to outsiders. In 1998 she sent one of the first American groups into Iran. Earlier in 1996 she initiated trips to a part of Yunnan Province famous for a horsemanship festival where Tibetan cowboys display their many skills. "I had visited there in 1985 on my National Geographic expedition," she recalls. "In fact, I looked up a young girl I had met back then. She had grown up and married. But she remembered me right away, and we had a pleasant reunion."

(In 1999 Wager sold her company to Hima Singh, her officer manager for many years, in order to spend more time with her family. Singh moved the company into new quarters but otherwise promises few additional changes. "We will continue to offer the same trips that Tovya developed over the years and maintain the same commitment to cultural interaction for which she became famous," she insists.)

5

RESEARCH EXPEDITIONS

Do your heroes include Howard Carter, Margaret Mead, and Louis Leakey? Do you dream about making a major scientific discovery—perhaps a new species of dinosaur in Utah or an Indian relic from the ruins of a pueblo— that will change what we know about early life in North America?

Historically, many areas of scientific research depended on the help of dedicated amateurs, who have made many of the most important scientific discoveries of modern times. In 1873 Heinrich Schliemann, a retailer who possessed no formal training in archaeology, discovered and excavated the fabled treasures of Troy. And Clyde Tombaugh, a 24-year-old former wheat-farmer with only a high-school education, located the planet Pluto in 1930— after professional astronomers had sought it in vain for decades.

For all those people addicted to National Geographic television specials, there is a way they can live out their fantasies and become a part of a scientific team. Organized research expeditions have grown in popularity over the past decade. Projects as diverse as the excavation of a Pharaoh's temple on the banks of the Nile and the study of moose/wolf dynamics on Isle Royale National Park, Michigan, are now open to untrained, enthusiastic volunteers willing to pay their own way. These are all definitely "working vacations," and living conditions in the field are often spartan. The adventure they offer is of a more cerebral variety than that experienced when climbing a mountain or running a river. The thrill lies in participating in important scientific research and discovery.

Most of the projects team a scientist with a small group of volunteers. The work can sometimes be tedious—digging, sifting, measuring, and cataloging—and it is often physically demanding. The money each volunteer pays underwrites the cost of the project as well as the team's food, lodging, and supplies. An important side benefit is that all expenses, including travel to and from the site, may be tax-deductible.

But the rewards of scientific discovery often bring the volunteers back time after time. Gary Goshgarian, a professor of English at Northeastern University in Boston and veteran of numerous such expeditions, participated in an Earthwatch project searching for shipwrecks off the coast of Spain. One day, off the coast of Mallorca and 135 feet down, he suddenly came upon a pair of perfectly preserved Roman amphoras sitting on the sea bottom. "Imagine the privilege of finding those ancient vases," he recalled later. "Me, a plain old English teacher. I was almost afraid to touch them. It was an incredible moment of infinite discovery. It hit me that when that clay was soft, Bethlehem was just another dusty town and Hannibal was a current event."

AFRICA

KENYA

Medicinal Plants of Kenya

Volunteers on these expeditions work among the Luo tribespeople on the shores of Lake Victoria. In this region Western doctors are a rarity, so most local health needs are treated with traditional herbal remedies that have been handed down through many generations. Volunteers work with a team of ethnobotanical researchers to document the Luo people's vast knowledge of the medicinal properties of numerous local plants to assess the use of botanical medicines for specific diseases. The goal is to develop a database of the herbal medicines, focusing on the rarest species and gathering pertinent information for their conservation.

Operator: Earthwatch, 3 Clock Tower Pl., Suite 100, Box 75, Maynard, Mass. 01754; (800) 776-0188 or (978) 461-0081; www.earthwatch.org.
Price: Moderate.
Season: July and August.
Length: 14 days.
Accommodations: A modern hotel. Ten percent discount with BBAT coupon.

ASIA

INDONESIA

Orangutan Health

Volunteers on this popular expedition to Gungung Leuser National Park in western Sumatra will study and document the feeding behavior of a small group of orangutans in the rain forest. The goal is to learn if they, like their

Operator:
Earthwatch, 3 Clock Tower
Pl., Suite 100, Box 75,
Maynard, Mass. 01754;
(800) 776-0188 or
(978) 461-0081;
www.earthwatch.org.
Price: Moderate.
Season: August–April.
Length: 14 days.
Accommodations: A bunga-
low five minutes' walk from
the park. Ten percent dis-
count with BBAT coupon.

Operator:
University Research
Expeditions Program,
University of California,
One Shields Ave.,
Davis, Calif. 95616;
(530) 752-0692;
www.urep.ucdavis.edu.
Price: Moderate.
Season: July and August.
Length: 14 days.
Accommodations: Guest
house on Bali and private
homes on Flores Island.
homes on Flores Island.

Operator:
Dinosaur Discovery
Expeditions, 550 Jurassic
Ct., Fruita, Colo. 81521;
(800) DIG-DINO or
(970) 858-7282;
www.dinamation.org.

African cousins the gorillas and chimpanzees, eat certain medicinal plants to cure themselves of illnesses and parasites. Volunteers will collect herbs, fruits, soil, and fecal samples for analysis later in a laboratory. Primates studied will include both wild animals and others raised in captivity and reintroduced into the rain forest. Gungung Leuser National Park is also home to 130 mammal species (including gibbons, clouded leopards, Sumatran tigers, elephants, and Sumatran rhinos) and 325 species of birds.

Plants and People: Traditional Knowledge in Eastern Indonesia

Culturally and geographically remote, the eastern islands of the Indonesian archipelago are blessed with a rich selection of native plants. These include hundreds of tree species bearing edible, fleshy fruits. Researchers are curious about where these plants occur naturally, how they are cultivated, whether any are ecologically threatened, and the role they play in the daily lives, ceremonies, and medicine of the local inhabitants. Volunteers will visit the islands of Bali and Flores where they will collect samples, map plant distributions, and photograph plants growing and in use.

MONGOLIA

In the Footsteps of Roy Chapman Andrews

The president of the New York American Museum of Natural History, Roy Chapman Andrews, made history in the 1920s when he led a series of paleontological expeditions into the Gobi Desert, until then largely unexplored by Western observers. On his Third Asiatic Expedition he created a sensation and got his picture on the front page of newspapers around the world when he discovered the world's first dinosaur eggs. This region contains some of the richest deposits of fossilized dinosaur remains in the world. Volunteers on this expedition work with some of the biggest names in American paleontology excavating a wide variety of dinosaur remains. Previous expeditions have made major discoveries. Volunteers also have ample opportunities to become acquainted with the culture of the ancient Mongol people who are their hosts at the research site. A highlight is a 30-kilometer camel trek through the vast Gobi landscape.

Price: Expensive.
Season: August.
Length: 15 days.
Accommodations: Hotels and *gers,* Mongol desert houses. Five percent discount with BBAT coupon.

CANADA

ALBERTA

Excavating the Remains of a Tyrannosaurus Rex Family Group

In 1910, in a remote corner of Alberta, Barnum Brown of the American Museum of Natural History in New York discovered a collection of fossilized remains of nine Albertosaurs, fierce predators in their day. Brown speculated that the animals had died together, indicating they lived together as a family group. Now a washed-out saddle untouched for 90 years, the quarry has recently been reopened. The site lies on the banks of the Red Deer River. Volunteers on this expedition will return to this important site to excavate further the remains still here.

Operator: Dinosaur Discovery Expeditions, 550 Jurassic Ct., Fruita, Colo. 81521; (800) DIG-DINO or (970) 858-7282; www.dinamation.org.
Price: Moderate.
Season: July.
Length: 10 days.
Accommodations: Tent camp. Five percent discount with BBAT coupon.

"Thousands of tired, nerve-shaken, over-civilized people are beginning to find out that going to the mountains is going home; that wilderness is a necessity; and that mountain parks and reservations are useful not only as fountains of lumber and irrigating rivers, but as fountains of life."

JOHN MUIR
OUR NATIONAL PARKS

CARIBBEAN

BAHAMAS

Swimming with Dolphins

Operator:
Oceanic Society Expeditions,
Fort Mason Center, Bldg. E,
San Francisco, Calif. 94123;
(800) 326-7491 or
(415) 441-1106;
www.oceanic-society.org.
Price: Expensive.
Season: May–August.
Length: 7 days.
Accommodations: Shipboard
cabins. Five percent
discount with BBAT
coupon.

Donning snorkeling equipment, participants on this popular project spend several hours each day swimming with pods of Atlantic spotted dolphins who have come to enjoy human companionship. Because these cetaceans are quite friendly and curious about their human observers, volunteers can expect close personal interaction to occur. (Bring an old scarf to attract the dolphins for play.) Researchers use video and acoustic recording equipment to capture continuous sequences of human/dolphin interaction and communication patterns. The project's long-term goal is a better understanding of the system of communication employed by free-ranging dolphins in order to conserve their environment and better respect their needs.

The Adventure Travel Hall of Fame:
DR. ROBERT GRIGGS

In June 1912 the greatest North American volcanic eruption in modern times occurred when Mount Katmai on the Alaskan Peninsula exploded, sending 33 million tons of material into the sky. Because of the remoteness of the area and the fact that not a single life was lost, the eruption, five times larger than that of Mount St. Helens, is remembered today chiefly by a handful of volcanists. By the time it was over, an area the size of the state of Connecticut was covered with a layer of ash up to 10 feet deep. Acid rain disintegrated laundry on clotheslines as far south as Vancouver. The massive amount of debris in the stratosphere eliminated summer temperatures for that year throughout the northern hemisphere.

In 1915 the National Geographic Society sent in a team of three geologists under the leadership of Dr. Robert Griggs, who became the first humans to visit the site after the eruption. All food and water had to be packed in. They passed through country that was completely devastated. "The whole scene looked like the entrance to another world, so foreign was it to anything within our experience," Griggs wrote later. "The

BERMUDA

Underseas Archaeological Investigation of a Shipwreck

The *North Carolina* was a 570-gross-ton Scottish sailing ship built in 1876 and wrecked on a reef just four years later. She went to the bottom carrying a cargo of cotton and miscellaneous cargo. Visitors to the site today can easily make out the ship's three wrought-iron masts, compete with their cable and rigging, lying in ghostly disarray over the rather complete remains of the ship. The researchers are studying not the ship itself but what the North Carolina can tell us about Victorian social history. Certified scuba divers will map and photograph the site, while nondivers help with such tasks as drafting, boat handling, organizing field notes, and working in the laboratory.

Operator: Earthwatch, 3 Clock Tower Pl., Suite 100, Box 75, Maynard, Mass., 01754; (800) 776-0188 or (978) 461-0081; www.earthwatch.org.
Price: Moderate.
Season: August–April.
Length: 21 days.
Accommodations: Men's and women's dormitories. Ten percent discount with BBAT coupon.

---

desolation of the country beggared description." Winds kicked up terrific dust storms and dropped visibility to a few feet. The team found no signs of animal life, except for one moth and several mosquitoes.

Griggs returned in 1916 and climbed a stump, all that remained of the towering, three-peaked, 7,500-foot-high Mount Katmai. From the top he and his team looked down upon a wondrous lake of weird, vitriolic, robin's-egg blue. Around the margins, columns of steam hissed from every crevice. Soon afterward they explored Katmai Pass and found one of the great natural wonders of North America. Over 1,000 fumeroles spewed forth steam, some columns rising over 500 feet into the thin air.

"It was as though all the steam engines in the world, assembled together, had popped their safety valves at once and were letting off surplus steam in concert," Griggs wrote, after naming his discovery the Valley of Ten Thousand Smokes.

Griggs returned to the States to plead for the creation of a national park to protect the Katmai area. Katmai, he argued, was an incomparable laboratory in which the effects of volcanism might be studied. On September 24, 1918, President Woodrow Wilson issued a presidential proclamation establishing the Katmai National Monument, in order to preserve "this wonderland . . . of popular scenic, as well as scientific, interest for generations to come."

TRINIDAD

Snake-Eating Crabs of Tobago

Operator:
Earthwatch, 3 Clock Tower
Pl., Suite 100, Box 75,
Maynard, Mass. 01754;
(800) 776-0188 or
(978) 461-0081;
www.earthwatch.org.
Price: Moderate.
Season: January, February,
August, and September.
Length: 14 days.
Accommodations: Cottages
near the sea. Ten percent
discount with BBAT
coupon.

The Main Ridge Forest Reserve on the small Caribbean island of Tobago is home to one of the Western Hemisphere's most fascinating species of crab. The manicou crab lives in burrows along the stream banks and sports a keen appetite for small snakes, which it hunts during the early nighttime hours. The crabs are in turn eaten by their local human neighbors, who harvest them for popular dishes such as a spicy stew. Volunteers on this expedition will help researchers in their study of the manicou crabs to determine population size, distribution, breeding, and diet. They will monitor the behavior of certain crabs that have been fitted with radio collars. Investigators will have some afternoons free to explore the lush beauty of Tobago's seaside villages, coral reefs, and dense rain forests.

U.S. VIRGIN ISLANDS

Saving the Leatherback Turtle

Operator:
Earthwatch, 3 Clock Tower
Pl., Suite 100, Box 75,
Maynard, Mass. 01754;
(800) 776-0188 or
(978) 461-0081;
www.earthwatch.org.
Price: Moderate.
Season: April–June.
Length: 10 days.
Accommodations: Teams live
in beach cottages with
kitchens and bathrooms.
Ten percent discount with
BBAT coupon.

The deepest-diving breath-holding animal (to depths of 4,000 feet) and the largest of the turtles (weighing up to 1,500 pounds), the leatherback is the most threatened of the marine turtle species of the southeastern United States. It is most vulnerable during the months when the females come ashore at night to lay up to 100 leathery eggs in large pits on sandy beaches. Sixty days later the young turtles all hatch together and scurry toward the ocean. Volunteers on these expeditions make their base on idyllic St. Croix, where their activities include measuring, tagging, and examining female turtles as they lay their eggs; moving unsafe nests to more secure areas; patrolling the beaches to guard against egg poachers; and protecting the hatchlings from predators and obstacles as they race toward the sea.

Over the last decade, Earthwatch volunteers have saved tens of thousands of leatherback turtle hatchlings and released them later into the ocean

Earthwatch

EUROPE

ITALY

Unearthing Horace's Villa

One of ancient Rome's leading satiric and lyric poets, Horace composed over 20 poems about his lavish villa in the lovely Licenza River Valley 35 miles northeast of Rome. Since the Renaissance, archaeologists have studied the area. However, previous excavations were not well documented and did not include the extensive gardens. This project should yield new information as well as consolidate past work. Members of the team will excavate different areas at the site and also record data through notes, drawings, and photographs.

Operator: University Research Expeditions Program, University of California, One Shields Ave., Davis, Calif. 95616; (530) 752-0692; www.urep.ucdavis.edu.
Price: Moderate.
Season: July–September.
Length: 14 days.
Accommodations: Rooms in a recently restored medieval monastery.

"The dreamers of the day are dangerous men, for they may act their dreams with open eyes to make them possible."

T.E. LAWRENCE
SEVEN PILLARS OF WISDOM

ROMANIA

Excavating a Roman Fort on the Danube

Operator:
Earthwatch, 3 Clock Tower Pl., Suite 100, Box 75, Maynard, Mass. 01754; (800) 776-0188 or (978) 461-0081; www.earthwatch.org.
Price: Moderate.
Season: July and August.
Length: 14 days.
Accommodations: Modern bungalow near the site. Ten percent discount with BBAT coupon.

The emperor Trajan waged two campaigns against the Dacians in what is now Romania before finally vanquishing them. His victory gave the Romans undisputed control over both the Danube delta with its rich farmlands and nearby gold and silver mines, and an important gateway to Asia. The Roman army occupied the area for 500 years. Volunteers will help excavate a fort with nearby harbor installations and a settlement at a late Roman site called Halmyris. The most prominent ruins consist of a thick stone wall and two imposing main gates from the fort. The warm, dry summers have helped preserve such fragile artifacts as cereal grains and wooden objects. Romania's foremost classical archaeologist supervises the project.

SPAIN

From Hunter to Farmer: Prehistoric Man in Spain

Operator:
University Research Expeditions Program, University of California, One Shields Ave., Davis, Calif. 95616; (530) 752-0692; www.urep.ucdavis.edu.
Price: Inexpensive.
Season: July and August.
Length: 14 days.
Accommodations: Small hotels or private homes in a nearby village.

Famous for the prehistoric paintings of Alta Mira, the caves and spectacular valleys of northern Spain still have more answers to yield about the evolution of man. Since 1989 archaeologists have uncovered a wealth of artifacts at Peña Oviedo, an isolated 10-mile-long valley that rises dramatically from sea level to 5,000 feet. They theorize that this area contains evidence of the important transition that occurred as prehistoric man began to cultivate rather than hunt and gather food. The important research here will help us understand the cultural interaction between the last hunter-gatherers and the first farmers.

LATIN AMERICA

BELIZE

Seed-Dispersing Behavior of Howler Monkeys

Volunteers on this rain-forest restoration project will have a variety of mixed duties, including collecting data on the behavioral ecology of endangered howler monkeys, banding tropical birds, and conducting experiments on forest restoration methods. Howler monkeys live in groups of four to eight individuals, each troop being comprised of an adult male and females with their young. The male has a distinctive roar that can be heard up to a mile away. Like other primates, howler monkeys display distinctive grooming and play behavior and lavish devoted care on their young. A stable family unit, the troop eats, sleeps, and travels together along aerial pathways. Of particular interest to researchers will be a study of the seed-dispersing activities of howler monkeys and birds. Bird-watching in the area is particularly excellent.

Operator: Oceanic Society Expeditions, Fort Mason Center, Bldg. E, San Francisco, Calif. 94123; (800) 326-7491 or (415) 441-1106; www.oceanic-society.org.
Price: Moderate.
Length: 8 days.
Season: March and April.
Accommodations: Comfortable lodge on the banks of the Belize River. Five percent discount with BBAT coupon.

COSTA RICA

Costa Rica Humpback Whales

Scientists have long known that humpback whales breed in three regions of the North Pacific: the waters off Mexico, Hawaii, and Japan. Recently, researchers have confirmed a fourth breeding area in the waters off Costa Rica's remote Osa Peninsula. Through photographs of marks on the underside of their tail flukes, biologists have matched Costa Rica humpback whales with those that feed off California, suggesting a close association between whales from these two regions. The object of this project is to evaluate the role of Costa Rican waters

Operator: Oceanic Society Expeditions, Fort Mason Center, Bldg. E, San Francisco, Calif. 94123; (800) 326-7491 or (415) 441-1106; www.oceanic-society.org.
Price: Expensive.
Length: 8 days.
Season: February.

Accommodations: Tent camp. Five percent discount with BBAT coupon.

as a breeding ground for the endangered North Pacific humpback whale. Volunteers help to identify preferred locations and habitats of humpback whales, collect environmental data, and assist researchers in observing and recording group size, behaviors, and movement of the whales.

ECUADOR

Ecuador's Rain-Forest Birds

Operator: Earthwatch, 3 Clock Tower Pl., Suite 100, Box 75, Maynard, Mass. 01754; (800) 776-0188 or (978) 461-0081; www.earthwatch.org.
Price: Moderate.
Season: March, May, and December.
Length: 14 days.
Accommodations: Bunks at a research station. Ten percent discount with BBAT coupon.

While Ecuador covers only 1.6 percent of the South American land mass, its rain forests shelter more than 50 percent of the bird species found on the entire continent. The forests of western Ecuador are among the most threatened in the world. Development and excessive logging have reduced them to fragmented patches over the past three decades. Volunteers on this project investigate the ecology of the birds in these rain-forest patches to save them and their dwindling habitat. A major goal is the education of the local people to make them aware of the their forests and to encourage them to participate in conservation efforts to preserve avian biodiversity.

The Adventure Travel Hall of Fame: RORY NUGENT

American traveler Rory Nugent specializes in adventures that are quirky, improbable, and dangerous. In 1986 he traveled to Brazzaville, the capital of the Republic of the Congo, to lay the bureaucratic groundwork for a solo expedition into Lake Télé and the enormous unexplored swamp surrounding it. Only four expeditions had penetrated the region before his arrival. For more than a century rumors had existed of a dinosaur-like creature living there, one the local natives called Mokele-Mbembe, or the god-beast. Some Western scientists have speculated that such creatures might be sauropods, perhaps brontosauruses, hidden away in the Congolese rain forest, the second-largest in the world. For a month

MEXICO

Digging Dinosaurs in the Chihuahuan Desert

Paleontology in Mexico is still in its infancy. These seven-day expeditions allow volunteers to explore some of the richest unexcavated fossil sites in North America. Cretaceous fossils, such as hadrosaurs (duck-billed dinosaurs) and ceratopsians (horned dinosaurs), are common and often in such an excellent state of preservation that skin impressions can be found. They represent the most equatorial dinosaur fauna known in North America. Volunteers will work at two quarries where dinosaur bones are abundant and scattered over the surface, and will also learn how to prepare the plaster jackets that protect the fossil material. Nights are spent in the colonial city of Saltillo, famous for its many preserved historical buildings and monuments.

Operator:
Dinosaur Discovery
Expeditions, 550 Jurassic
Ct., Fruita, Colo. 81521;
(800) DIG-DINO or
(970) 858-7282;
www.digdino.org.
Price: Expensive.
Season: November.
Length: 6 days.
Accommodations: A small, three-star hotel. Five percent discount with BBAT coupon.

Wildlife Study in Dry Tropical Forests

Tropical dry forests are among the most endangered habitats in the world. They once stretched

---

Nugent trekked and paddled with five Africans through a world in which philodendrons towered 70 feet overhead and primitive cycad plants reached heights of 40 feet, hunting and foraging for food and drinking water where they could find it. "I entered Mokele-Mbembe's domain: a pristine world where plants are kings and dinosaurs gods," he noted later in his book Drums Along the Congo. "While the rest of the earth has undergone dramatic geological changes, this steamy chunk of Africa has remained in the Cretaceous period, the sunset years of the dinosaur hegemony." Then, after four weeks, he finally spotted and photographed in the distance a brontosaurus-like creature traveling across the lake. But when he tried to paddle his canoe closer, his guides ordered him back at gunpoint, explaining that "the god can approach man, but man never approaches the god."

Operator:
Earthwatch, 3 Clock Tower
Pl., Suite 100, Box 75,
Maynard, Mass. 01754;
(800) 776-0188 or
(978) 461-0081;
www.earthwatch.org.
Price: Expensive.
Season: January and May.
Length: 11 days.
Accommodations: Rooms at a
field station with bathrooms
and hot showers. Ten per-
cent discount with BBAT
coupon.

for several thousand kilometers across western Mexico and Central America. Today, because of ranching and development, only two percent of these forests remain. Although the areas receive only a fraction of the rainfall of the rain forests, they are home to a wide variety of animal species. Volunteers on this expedition will gather research on the small carnivores (ocelots, jaguarundis, coat- imundis, foxes, coyotes, and pygmy spotted skunks) found in the Chamela forest in the state of Jalisco. The data gathered will help biologists obtain estimates of the diversity, abundance, and habitat preferences for these small animals with an end toward understanding and preserving this reserve.

Operator:
University Research
Expeditions Program,
University of California,
One Shields Ave.,
Davis, Calif. 95616;
(530) 752-0692;
urep.ucdavis.edu.
Price: Inexpensive.
Season: May–July.
Length: 14 days.
Accommodations: Small
palm-covered shelters and
tents with cots.

Brown Pelicans of Baja

Scattered across the Sea of Cortez are dozens of small desert islands that provide sanctuary for mil- lions of marine birds. The island of Isla Piojo sup- ports a colony of breeding brown pelicans, a species just beginning to recover from endangered status due to pollution, fishing, and tourism. El Niño imposed additional stress by reducing the birds' food supply. Volunteers will work with researchers to monitor pelican behavior in the colony, rear captive chicks, and seek an under- standing of the response of these seabirds to cli- mate changes brought on by El Niño.

*"We shall not cease from exploration.
And the end of all our exploring
Will be to arrive back where we started
And know the place for the first time."*

T. S. ELIOT
"LITTLE GIDDING"

PERU

Research on River Dolphins in the Amazonian Rain Forest

Volunteers on these popular expeditions assist in a study of the Amazon's lively pink freshwater dolphins. These are the largest of the river dolphins and endemic to the Amazon River basin. There is a concern that they, like their cousins elsewhere, are at serious risk from human encroachment. Volunteers collect data on the dolphins' movements, social organization, and species communication, gathering the information necessary for the mammals' protection and conservation. Workers also have time to swim with the dolphins, explore the rain forest, and visit Indian settlements along the river.

Operator:
Oceanic Society
Expeditions,
Fort Mason Center, Bldg. E,
San Francisco, Calif. 94123;
(800) 326-7491 or
(415) 441-1106;
www.oceanic-society.org.
Price: Expensive.
Season: July.
Length: 8 days.
Accommodations: Cabins on a traditional wooden riverboat. Five percent discount with BBAT coupon.

Moche Ceremonial Center of Ancient Peru

The Chicama Valley, a coastal desert region just off the Pacific Ocean, harbors the prehistoric remnants of the renowned Moche civilization, known for its representational ceramic vessels and ceremonial centers. The ceremonial site at Mocollope, built around a pyramid, contains valuable clues to understanding the development of Moche society,

Operator:
University Research
Expeditions Program,
University of California,
One Shields Ave.,
Davis, Calif. 95616;
(530) 752-0692;
www.urep.ucdavis.edu.

Volunteers observe the behavior of a group of spinner dolphins in the Midway Islands
R. Shallenberger/Oceanic Society Expeditions

Price: Inexpensive.
Season: July.
Length: 14 days.
Accommodations:
Comfortable hotel in the beach resort town of Huanchaco.

which dates back to A.D. 200–800. The project seeks to answer questions regarding economic and political sources of power and to unravel Moche ideology as expressed in the ornate decorative ceramics for which this culture is known. Volunteers do trowel and brush work, photograph the site, catalog artifacts, and analyze botanical and faunal remains.

THE PACIFIC

MIDWAY ISLAND

Spinner Dolphins Research

Operator:
Oceanic Society Expeditions, Fort Mason Center, Bldg. E, San Francisco, Calif. 94123; (800) 326-7491 or (415) 441-1106; www.oceanic-society.org.
Price: Expensive.
Length: 8 days.
Season: March–August.
Accommodations: Restored military barracks. Five percent discount with BBAT coupon.

Researchers have long known about the existence off Midway Island of a school of about 200 spinner dolphins, famous for their unusual aerial acrobatics—bursting out of the water and rotating rapidly for as many as four revolutions before falling back. The Midway school has never before been studied. Volunteers on this project will assist an investigation into the ecology, behavior, and social organization of the spinner dolphins in an atoll habitat, a subject which has not yet been studied. They will travel daily out into the lagoon in a 22-foot vessel to collect their data, take still photographs of individual dolphins to aid in identification, and shoot video of surface behaviors.

Seabird Monitoring Project

Operator:
Oceanic Society Expeditions, Fort Mason Center, Bldg. E, San Francisco, Calif. 94123; (800) 326-7491 or (415) 441-1106; www.oceanic-society.org.
Price: Expensive.

Midway Atoll supports the largest collection of seabirds in the Central Pacific, with more than 2 million birds visiting here every year. The largest Laysan albatross (gooney-bird) colony in the world is found here, as well as the world's second-largest black-footed albatross colony. At least 13 other species of migratory seabirds also visit here, including shearwaters, petrels, and tropic birds. Volunteers will assist researchers with such tasks as

Volunteers with Oceanic Society Expeditions monitor the 350,000 pairs of Laysan albatrosses nesting on Midway Atoll

Nanette Seto/Oceanic Society Expeditions

population counts, nest monitoring, mapping of nesting areas, monitoring chick hatchings, and chick banding.

Length: 7 days.
Season: March and April.
Accommodations: Restored military barracks. Five percent discount with BBAT coupon.

UNITED STATES

CALIFORNIA

Dolphins and Whales in Monterey Bay

Volunteers on these popular projects work aboard a 55-foot motor vessel. Their primary task is to gather data on the behavior, ecology, communication, and distribution of the Pacific white-sided dolphins resident in the region. A secondary objective is to record all humpback and blue whales that enter the bay and to document their behavior. Both dolphins and whales will be photographed and the pictures compared with those already in an identification file. The Pacific Ocean off Monterey harbors one of the richest and most diverse populations of marine mammals in the world. Pacific

Operator: Oceanic Society Expeditions, Fort Mason Center, Bldg. E, San Francisco, Calif. 94123; (800) 326-7491 or (415) 441-1106; www.oceanic-society.org.
Price: Moderate.
Season: July, August, and September.
Length: 7 days.

Accommodations: A Monterey motel. Five percent discount with BBAT coupon.

white-sided dolphins often swim in schools of more than 1,000 individuals.

COLORADO

Digging the Dinosaurs

Operator: Dinosaur Discovery Expeditions, 550 Jurassic Ct., Fruita, Colo. 81521; (800) DIG-DINO or (970) 858-7282; www.digdino.org. *Price:* Expensive. *Season:* June and July. *Length:* 5 days. *Accommodations:* Hotel. Five percent discount with BBAT coupon.

Dinosaur-lovers seeking hands-on involvement in their favorite subject can join an actual dig under the supervision of paleontologists. The most popular of these are the five-day digging trips sponsored by Dinamation International Society. Unlike other digs located in remote desert areas of the West far from any amenities, these field projects lie within an easy drive of Grand Junction, Colorado, where participants are housed in a hotel instead of tents. These expeditions are particularly popular with youngsters. Volunteers work on a site that was once a water hole, excavating a jumble of skeletons that includes an apatosaurus, an allosaurus, and a nodosaur. Several years ago participants unearthed a new species of apatosaurus, the largest such animal ever found. One enormous vertebra of the animal measured six feet by five feet and weighed at least a ton.

Volunteers on Dinosaurs Discovery Expeditions have made numerous major Discoveries

James C. Simmons

Excavating an Anasazi Pueblo

The Anasazi domain once spread over an area larger than the state of California. They were compulsive builders who, without benefit of the wheel or beasts of burden, raised great apartment structures unequalled until the manufacture of structural steel centuries later. Some 700 years ago the Anasazi people abandoned their cities and tilled fields and moved into other regions of the Southwest to found the great Pueblo cultures in which many of their traditions and customs still survive. Working with trowels and whisk brooms, volunteers on this popular project excavate a sprawling Anasazi ruin forgotten and buried for at least seven centuries. They also dig, wash, sort, and catalog artifacts in the laboratory. The site is located 10 miles from Mesa Verde National Park, in the heart of one of the most archaeologically significant regions in the United States.

Operator: Crow Canyon Archaeological Center, 23390 County Rd. K, Cortez, Colo. 81321; (800) 422-8975 or (970) 565-8975; www.crowcanyon.org. *Price:* Moderate. *Season:* June–September. *Length:* 7 days. *Accommodations:* Comfortable dormitories.

FLORIDA

Monitoring Endangered Manatees

Benign and vulnerable, manatees are slow-moving coastal animals (related to elephants) that feed on sea plants in quiet coastal inlets and rivers. The manatees' greatest threat comes from humans and their speedboats, which have proliferated over the past decade. Last year boats struck and killed 54 of these magnificent animals out of a population of 2,600. Volunteers on this project survey the manatees around Sarasota Bay to learn if certain animals return to favorite secluded spots, how they use different habitats, and their reaction to boats. Participants will also snorkel near the animals to observe their behavior and study and mark on diagrams the scars from motorboat encounters, to be used later in the identification of individual animals.

Operator: Earthwatch, 3 Clock Tower Pl., Suite 100, Box 75, Maynard, Mass. 01754; (800) 776-0188 or (978) 461-0081; www.earthwatch.org. *Price:* Moderate. *Season:* May–October. *Length:* 14 days. *Accommodations:* A furnished shore-side house. Ten percent discount with BBAT coupon.

HAWAII

Studying Humpback Whales

Operator:
Earthwatch, 3 Clock Tower
Pl., Suite 100, Box 75,
Maynard, Mass. 01754;
(800) 776-0188 or
(978) 461-0081;
www.earthwatch.org.
Price: Moderate.
Season: September–May.
Length: 14 and 28 days.
Accommodations: A house
on Maui and a tent camp
on the Lanai beach. Ten
percent discount with
BBAT coupon.

Of all the cetacean species, the gregarious humpbacks are particularly charismatic and delightful. This project focuses on the hauntingly beautiful songs (the most complex of any animal) the whales sing during their winter residence off the islands of Hawaii and Maui. The songs may go on for hours and are specific to groups and areas. Volunteers record the whales' songs and then play them back from underwater microphones to study the behavior they generate. Time is divided between a 17-foot Boston whaler (the playback boat) and an elevated shore station for observation and photography.

Teaching Language to Dolphins

Operator:
Earthwatch, 3 Clock Tower
Pl., Suite 100, Box 75,
Maynard, Mass. 01754;
(800) 776-0188 or
(978) 461-0081;
www.earthwatch.org.
Price: Moderate.
Season: January–April.
Length: 13 days.
Accommodations: Ocean-
facing condominium. Ten
percent discount with
BBAT coupon.

Researchers at the Kewalo Basin Marine Mammal Laboratory in Honolulu have been teaching human language to four bottlenose dolphins. Thus far, the dolphins have learned more than 600 sentences and can understand such grammatical distinctions as direct versus indirect objects. However, they cannot use their skills to communicate with one another because the emphasis in their training has been on language comprehension rather than language production. Volunteers on this popular project assist in the instruction of two young dolphins in an artificial language to see if they can learn to "speak" it. The long-term goal is to determine "the ability of dolphins to exchange information with trainers and amongst themselves." Volunteers serve as trainers, in addition to helping with both the feeding of the dolphins and the weekly tank cleanings.

"Be careful going in search of adventure—it's ridiculously easy to find."

WILLIAM LEAST HEAT MOON
BLUE HIGHWAYS: A JOURNEY INTO AMERICA

An Earthwatch research project in Hawaii seeks to discover if dolphins can learn an artificial language

Earthwatch

NEW MEXICO

Excavating Dinosaurs in the Badlands of Western New Mexico

This expedition is at the cutting edge of dinosaur research. Volunteers will be exploring dinosaur-bearing strata from the middle Cretaceous period and excavating the first significant dinosaur material from the time interval represented by the rock. It is predicted that all the dinosaurs excavated will be new to science. Previously discovered dinosaurs excavated here included several partial hadrosaur skeletons and a fairly complete dromaeosaur (raptor) skeleton with a skull. The site is within walking distance of Anasazi ruins.

Operator: Dinosaur Discovery Expeditions, 550 Jurassic Ct., Fruita, Colo. 81521; (800) DIG-DINO or (970) 858-7282; www.dinamation.org.
Price: Moderate.
Season: May and September.
Length: 5 days.
Accommodations: Motel. Five percent discount with BBAT coupon.

SOUTH DAKOTA

Excavating a Graveyard of Mammoths

Approximately 26,000 years ago, a steep-sided pool lured over 100 Ice Age mammoths to their deaths. Unable to escape, the huge animals drowned or starved to death, gradually filling the pool with

Operator: Earthwatch, 3 Clock Tower Pl., Suite 100, Box 75, Maynard, Mass. 01754;

(800) 776-0188 or (978) 461-0081; www.earthwatch.org. *Price:* Moderate. *Season:* June and July. *Length:* 14 days. *Accommodations:* Dormitory rooms. Ten percent discount with BBAT coupon.

their skeletal remains and creating the largest graveyard of mammoths in North America. Thus far, paleontologists have unearthed the bones of over 45 mammoths, as well as those of a great short-faced bear which stood 11 feet high. Volunteers wield trowels and dental picks to dig, map, record, and preserve the bones. The site lies within the city limits of Hot Springs, a retirement community.

VIRGINIA

Shenandoah Wildlife

Operator: Earthwatch, 3 Clock Tower Pl., Suite 100, Box 75, Maynard, Mass. 01754; (800) 776-0188 or (978) 461-0081; www.earthwatch.org. *Price:* Moderate. *Season:* July and August. *Length:* 7 and 14 days. *Accommodations:* Furnished house. Ten percent discount with BBAT coupon.

This project examines the dynamics within a section of eastern deciduous forest when National Park Service regulations favor one species over another species. The population of white-tail deer is now at an all-time high in the eastern United States, causing a significant alteration in their habitat and thus having an impact on other species. A favorite food of white-tail deer is the acorn, which is also an important foodstuff for many forest mammals, including squirrels and chipmunks. And the overpopulation of deer affects an ecosystem's bird population because deer browse the shrubs that birds depend on for nesting sites, shelter, and berries. Volunteers in this project will examine a broad range of forest phenomena to determine how the density of the white-tailed deer population in the forest affects the entire wildlife community.

"All I wanted to do now was to get back to Africa. We had not left it, yet, but when I would wake in the night I would lie, listening, homesick for it already."

ERNEST HEMINGWAY
THE GREEN HILLS OF AFRICA

WASHINGTON

Orca Survey in Puget Sound

When this long-running project began, marine scientists did not know that orcas could reach 80 years of age or that they lived in matriarchal social groups. Since then researchers on this project have learned an enormous amount about the characteristics of orca society. A major responsibility of volunteers is shooting pictures of individual whales for photo-identification for the purpose of determining individual life histories and the calculation of vital statistics (e.g., birth and death rates) for the area's population. A new focus is determining how the resident population has been affected by the area's mushrooming tourist industry, the growth in numbers of pleasure boats on Puget Sound, and the pollution from nearby communities and industries.

Operator: Earthwatch, 3 Clock Tower Pl., Suite 100, Box 75, Maynard, Mass. 01754; (800) 776-0188 or (978) 461-0081; www.earthwatch.org.
Price: Moderate.
Season: June–September.
Length: 11 days.
Accommodations: A three-bedroom waterfront home, a trailer, and a camper. Ten percent discount with BBAT coupon.

The Northern Cascades Wilderness Ecosystem Project

Grizzly bears, gray wolves, wolverines, and spotted owls once were abundant in the West. But hunting and population pressures have brought all these species to the edge of extinction. However, in the northern Cascades important numbers of these species continue to exist. Volunteers will help wildlife biologists protect the few remaining animals by conducting field research on their behavior and numbers. The team will work in a remote section of the wilderness to determine the location, range, and habitat use of the bears, wolves, wolverines, and spotted owls. The project carries three units of college credit.

Operator: Wildlands Studies, 3 Mosswood Circle, Cazadero, Calif. 95421; (707) 632-5665; www.wildlandsstudies.com/ws.
Price: Inexpensive.
Season: August.
Length: 14 days.
Accommodations: Tent camp.

"Peculiar travel suggestions are dancing lessons from God."

KURT VONNEGUT, JR.
CAT'S CRADLE

PROFILE

MICHAEL PERRY & JAMES KIRKLAND

DINOSAUR DISCOVERY EXPEDITIONS

"A dinosaur dig is like an enormous, three-dimensional jigsaw puzzle," insisted one amateur paleontologist in our group who was, by her own admission, a dinosaur addict. "There are all these pieces scattered around and you have to find them, identify them, and then fit them together."

We were a group of 14 amateur paleontologists at the Mygatt-Moore Quarry to the west of Grand Junction, Colorado, in Rabbit Valley, a forbidding stretch of high desert near the Utah border. We would be working here for the next three days under the supervision of Dr. James Kirkland of Dinosaur Discovery Expeditions (DDE). The site had first been discovered in 1981 but serious digging did not begin until 1985. Tarps were stretched over two working areas to provide some shade for the volunteers.

"This site was once a pond or water hole," Kirkland told us. "We know this because we are finding fossilized roots of horsetails and fish skeletons mixed in with the dinosaur bones. We have a hodgepodge of dinosaur skeletons here. We have already identified eight species, including apatosauruses (which many of you know as a brontosaurus); allosauruses, a large predator similar to a T. rex; and a new species of a nodosaur or Mymoorapelta that looked like a small, armored tank with lots of spines and plates on its back."

Kirkland handed out our excavation kits. Each consisted of a paintbrush, whisk broom, dental pick, small screwdriver, plastic straw, and trowel. Like a drill sergeant, he quickly rattled off the important points we needed to keep in mind:

"Remember, fossilized bones are fragile. Do not dig the ground out from under the bones. Otherwise, they will collapse. Keep the site clear at all times with your whisk brooms and soft brushes. The straws are for blowing dirt away from the most delicate bones. Use your small screwdriver and dental picks to remove the dirt surrounding each bone. If a bone begins to crumble, then get some glue and spray that over the bone to harden it and keep it from fragmenting further. Okay, now let's hit the dirt. In this line of work we spend lots of time on our knees with our noses to the ground looking for small fragments of bones."

Within an hour one of our expedition members made the first discovery—a black apatosaurus tooth, highly worn. Kirkland examined the stubby fossil in his hand. "I never cease to be amazed that a 75-foot long apatosaurus could have a mouth full of these teeth which are not much thicker than a pencil," he told us, as he dropped the tooth into a plastic sandwich bag along with a slip of paper on which he had recorded the pertinent information for later identification.

The fieldwork went slowly. We soon learned that there is little glamour in the life of a paleontologist. Much of the work is tedious—digging, sifting, measuring, and cataloging. The adventure is of a more cerebral variety than that experienced when one climbs a mountain or runs a river. The excitement comes from participating in important scientific research and discovery.

Dinosaur Discovery Expeditions is the largest organization in the world offering a broad range of research expeditions, all of which allow the general public to become directly involved with dinosaur research. The organization's support staff includes some of the biggest names in paleontology today, who teach their volunteers the skills they need to excavate the fossilized bones. The money the volunteers pay funds the costs of these expeditions, some of which go to the remote corners of the world. DDE is a program of the Dinamation International Society (DIS), a nonprofit organization promoting education, research, and preservation in the earth, biological, and physical sciences, with an emphasis on dinosaur paleontology.

"Digging up dinosaurs is a lot like treasure-hunting; you never know what you're going to find," insists volunteer Karen Pankowski. "And whatever you do uncover, you're the first person who's ever seen it. It's incredibly addicting."

A cardinal thrill of paleontology is that of discovery, being the first to uncover a new species. This is the dream motivating each amateur scientist who signs on to one of DDE's projects.

Volunteers with DDE regularly uncover major finds. The staff paleontologists have written over 25 scientific papers about discoveries made by their dedicated volunteers. In early June of 1993 Stephanie Willen, a 14-year-old resident of Boulder, Colorado, working at the Mygatt-Moore Quarry, uncovered an egg from an armored dinosaur (Mymoorapelta maysi), only the third egg ever found in the Jurassic Morrison Formation. In 1997 a 13-year-old boy discovered a mid-Cretaceous Tyrannosaur in New Mexico, near the Arizona border, at a site being worked by DDE crews. Another volunteer uncovered the first late-Jurassic fossilized fish found in North America.

"Ed Fox, one of our volunteers, made an extraordinary discovery during our second expedition into the Gobi Desert in Mongolia in 1997," insists

Kirkland, one of the leaders for that expedition. "He discovered the perfectly preserved and complete skeleton of a Protoceratops, a horned dinosaur. It had apparently been caught in a sandstorm and buried while standing erect. But what was really amazing was that the skull showed borings made by carrion bugs and also had their pupae attached. This was the first record of fossil pupae being found with a skeleton."

Michael Perry, the founder of DDE and DIS, was born in Idaho in 1946 and did his undergraduate and graduate work in biology and ornithology at the University of Utah. "It really proved a natural bridge for me, since dinosaurs are now accepted as the ancestors of birds," he says. His early career was in museum administration. For 18 years he was a director at three different museums in Idaho, Utah, and Colorado. He developed a major interest in dinosaurs while at the Utah Field House of Natural History in Vernal, Utah, from 1973 to 1981. Nearby was Dinosaur National Monument, one of the world's premier paleontological sites.

In 1984 Perry moved to Grand Junction to become the director of the Museum of Western Colorado. A few months later he examined a collection of scrapbooks in the museum's archives. "I was stunned at what I found in those scrapbooks," he recalls today. "There had been important dinosaur finds in the vicinity by local amateurs, as well as turn-of-the-century work by Elmer Riggs for the Field Museum in Chicago. But very little of this had ever been publicized. My immediate reaction was, 'Why aren't we doing something to promote what we have right here?' We in the museum industry know that dinosaurs really attract kids!"

Nearby quarries had yielded the remains of the world's largest and smallest dinosaurs. The largest is the Supersaurus, which stood 40 feet tall and over 100 feet long; its shoulder blade measured eight feet, 10 inches, while its vertebrae were 4.5 feet across. In 1976 the smallest known adult dinosaur, about the size of a modern chicken, was discovered. Perry set about establishing the popular Dinosaur Valley Museum in downtown Grand Junction. But a chance observation by a friend Chris Mays, who had recently founded Dinamation International Corporation, a company devoted to the development of robotic, full-scale dinosaurs, changed the direction of Perry's life.

"Chris had always been impressed with the geology of this area, its beauty, and the amazing abundance of fossils," he remembers. "I think this incredible resource inspired him to suggest the idea of creating a setting for members of the public to participate in the operation of a dinosaur quarry. His initial idea was to create a foundation to help support the science of dinosaur paleontology."

In 1987 Dinamation entered into an agreement with the Museum of Western Colorado to set up the first hands-on dinosaur research project available to the general public. The program began with a series of week-long digs at the Mygatt-Moore Quarry. Dinamation International Corporation handled all the marketing and bookings. The program was inspired, in part, by the success of Earthwatch and the Crow Canyon archaeological dig in southwestern Colorado.

In 1989 Mays created the nonprofit DIS organization to handle the expeditions. In 1990 Perry became the executive director for DIS and incorporated DDE's program into the new organization. (Today DIS is completely separate, legally and financially, from Dinamation International Corporation.) For the first six months he ran the company out of his home before finally renting an office in Fruita. Soon Perry hired James Kirkland, a young paleontologist who had just completed his doctorate at the University of Colorado in Boulder, to run the expeditions at the Mygatt-Moore Quarry. "I took a lot of flak from members of my own profession for not taking a 'real job' like teaching," Kirkland says.

"At the start we encountered a lot of skepticism from the scientific paleontological community," Perry admits. "They thought—wrongly—that we were a commercial enterprise set up to excavate fossil remains to sell to private collectors. Other professionals told me that the public has no business getting involved in the excavation of these precious bones."

DDE forged ahead regardless of the obstacles. "In those early days we survived literally day to day," Kirkland remembers. "Despite how unsure things really were, I knew we were on the ground floor of something monumental."

During the 1991 season a volunteer made the first major discovery at the Mygatt-Moore Quarry. Janet Riehicke unearthed a strangely shaped piece of fossilized bone and approached Kirkland with her find. He immediately recognized it as a plate from an armored dinosaur. Later that season, after his volunteers had excavated additional bones from the creature, he learned they had discovered a new species of ankylosaur.

DIS next decided to explore the option of mounting international expeditions. The first-choice destination was Saltillo, Mexico, in the rich quarries located 186 miles southwest of Laredo, Texas, in rugged but beautiful desert country. The site is important as the southernmost Cretaceous site in North America, contrasting sharply with those in the United States and Canada which had different climates. The Saltillo area has an abundance of bones liberally strewn about the surface of the landscape. Preservation is so good that in some instances volunteers have found the imprint of dinosaur skin on the fossilized bones.

In 1996, which proved to be a banner year, DDE sent the first expedition to the Flaming Cliffs area of the Gobi to work the rich deposits of dinosaur skeletons there. Roy Chapman Andrews made the area famous 75 years before when his third American Museum of Natural History expedition to the Gobi discovered and brought out the first nest of dinosaur eggs known to science. Famed paleontologist Robert Bakker led the 1996 DDE expedition, following in the footsteps of Andrews.

"Our base camp of 13 tents was situated on a small rise where Andrews made most of his discoveries," Perry recalls. "Next to us lived a family of nomad herders. From them we learned much about the lifestyle of Mongols and sampled fermented mare's milk, boiled mutton, warm milk tea, camel yogurt, and dried goat cheese. We rode their camels, enjoyed their company in their felt tents (gers), and laughed with them as we each sang in our native tongues."

A 1996 exploratory expedition to Alaska's North Slope inside the Arctic Circle proved equally productive and thrilling. The paleontologists and their volunteers had to raft down the Colville River to reach the remote site where a rich bone quarry had been found. The excavation presented considerable challenges far beyond the area's severe isolation, poor weather, and short summer season. The fossilized bones were jumbled together in the permafrost, and the ground had to be melted with fires before they could be extracted. The mosquitoes were horrendous. "But the fossil find was fantastic," Perry enthuses. "Our volunteers found themselves excavating a jumble of hadrosaur (or duck-billed dinosaur) skeletons." Over the course of the next two weeks nearly 300 fossils were recovered.

At the start of the 1996 season DDE also sent an expedition to southwestern South Dakota to excavate a partial skeleton of a Tyrannosaurus rex which had been discovered on a cattle ranch. The group recovered the specimen's pelvic girdle and half the skull.

In 1997 DDE mounted an exploratory expedition in search of a lost dinosaur quarry located along the Red Deer River in a remote stretch of Alberta. Using four white-water rafts, the group took 10 days to float 150 miles down the river to reach the site. The site had first been worked by Barnum Brown of the American Museum of Natural History in New York back in 1910 and had not been visited since then. DDE's paleontologists used Brown's original black-and-white photographs and field notes to locate the quarry.

"The expedition made a major discovery of a group of eight skeletons of Albertasaurus, a species of tyrannosaur, that had died together," Kirkland says.

"When DDE returns to this site, our people will investigate such questions as: How did they all end up crowded together in death? Was this a family group killed while crossing the river? Or was the site a predator death trap like the La Brea tar pits in Southern California, where the animals fell in and got stuck?"

Kirkland regrets that his activities with DDE have limited his digging activities in Utah, his major area of interest. In 1992 he participated in the discovery of the Utahraptor, a monstrous predator that stood seven feet tall on its two back legs and reached a length of 20 feet from its head to the tip of its tail. It came equipped with huge, curving claws on its front and hind feet. Steven Spielberg put a similar raptor at the center of his film, *Jurassic Park*. "In its day the Utahraptor was probably the nastiest animal around," Kirkland observes. "He wasn't Einstein, but he was probably the smartest thing on earth at the time."

In 1994 DIS opened the Devil's Canyon Science & Learning Center in Fruita, Colorado, a 22,000-square-foot facility that houses a variety of exhibits, including 13 robotic dinosaurs, and draws over 75,000 visitors a year. DIS is currently planning similar centers in Texas and New Mexico near important dinosaur quarries in those two states.

Perry is proud of the achievements of DIS and DDE in a few short years. "I think it just proves that if you gather the right kind of people together, those who believe that anything is possible, then the sky is really the limit," he says.

WATER ADVENTURES

"An island pleases my imagination,
even the smallest, as a small continent
and integral part of the globe."

Henry David Thoreau,
Walden

6

RIVER RAFTING EXPEDITIONS

O.A.R.S. is one of the country's oldest operators of rafting trips down western American rivers

Rapid Shooters/O.A.R.S.

"Rivers are a constant lure to the adventurous instinct of mankind," Thoreau once observed. Some 3 million Americans agree. Each year that many climb into pontoon boats, paddleboats, dories, sportyaks, and motorized rafts to experience white-water adventure on the rivers of the world. They scream, shout, and hang on tight as their boats plunge over cataracts, fall into holes, and slam through giant waves on rapids boasting names like Hell's Kitchen, Nemesis, Satan's Gut, and Pure Screaming Hell.

Few of these trips require previous rafting experience. Most operators use inflatable oar-powered boats "driven" by expert boatmen who steer the craft using two long oars. The passengers simply hang on and enjoy the ride. Operators also supply all camping equipment and watertight metal boxes in which passengers stash their personal items during the day.

Rivers are the arteries of the world's wilderness areas and provide access to regions too remote and rugged to be explored by other means. River trips are the ideal way to experience great canyon systems. Many of these river trips offer rich experiences viewing wildlife and traditional cultures, and they teach new skills and build self-confidence at the same time they offer excellent opportunities for swimming, fishing, and hiking.

River-running can quickly become addicting. Most river buffs would agree with River Rat in Kenneth Grahame's classic story *The Wind in the Willows:* "Believe me, my young friend, there is nothing—absolutely nothing—half so much worth doing as simply messing about in boats."

AFRICA

ETHIOPIA

Rafting the Omo River

This was the last pocket of unexplored territory in Africa when the outfitter Sobek sent the first expedition down the Omo in 1973. Flowing out of the mountains of southwestern Ethiopia, the river offers an enormous variety of experiences: exciting white water; a 4,000-foot-deep canyon; an abundance of wildlife, including large populations of crocodiles and hippos; and primitive native cultures. This is Old Africa, as it was 150 years ago, before those hardy British explorers opened up the continent to the inquisitive eyes of the Victorian public. This lengthy expedition covers 250 miles in oar-powered inflatable rafts. Considerable time is allowed for hikes up tributary canyons to waterfalls, swims in quiet pools, and visits to native villages.

Operator:
Mountain Travel-Sobek, 6420 Fairmount Ave., El Cerrito, Calif. 94530; (888) 687-6235 or (510) 527-8100; www.mtsobek.com.
Price: Expensive.
Season: October.
Length: 30 days.
Accommodations: Tent camps. Five percent discount with BBAT coupon.

Mursi tribesmen greet members of a Mountain Travel-Sobek expedition on the Omo River in Ethiopia

James C. Simmons

MADAGASCAR

Rafting Four Wild Rivers

Operator:
Remote River Expeditions,
821 Nowita Place,
Venice, Calif. 90291;
(800) 558-1083 or
(310) 823-1083;
www.remoterivers.com.
Price: Expensive.
Season: April–July.
Length: Varies, depending
upon the river.
Accommodations: Tent
camps. Five percent dis-
count coupon.

A naturalist's paradise, Madagascar lies only 250 miles off the coast of Africa in the Indian Ocean, yet it is a world apart. The island is home to many species of flora and fauna found nowhere else. It also represents one of the last frontiers in river raft-ing left for adventurous paddlers to explore. The operator offers rafting expeditions down four sepa-rate rivers. Two of the most exciting are the Mahavavy River, which flows through lightly settled areas, including the Kasijy Forest, home to a dense population of lemurs; and the Mangoky River, which winds through a dry deciduous forest sprin-kled with huge baobab trees and is home to several species of lemurs along with numerous bird species. All four rivers offer excellent wildlife viewing.

ZAMBIA

Rafting the Zambezi

Operator:
Mountain Travel-Sobek,
6420 Fairmount Ave., El
Cerrito, Calif. 94530;
(888) 687-6235 or
(510) 527-8100;
www.mtsobek.com.
Price: Expensive.
Season: August–November.
Length: 15 days.
Accommodations: Tent
camps. Five percent dis-
count with BBAT coupon.

This expedition begins and ends at the foot of spec-tacular Victoria Falls, twice as high as Niagara and a mile wide. One of the most violent rivers in the world, with six big drops larger than the famed Lava Falls on the Colorado, the Zambezi was first run by Sobek in 1981. Expedition members use inflatable oar-powered rafts to navigate the treach-erous white water at the bottom of a deep gorge. Along the way there are two river drops of 20 feet, which must be portaged. The area teems with wildlife, including crocodiles, hippos, baboons, and antelopes. Stops are also made at small fishing villages along the banks. This is a tough, dangerous trip for experienced river-runners only.

"The way I see it, if you want the rainbow you gotta put up with the rain."

DOLLY PARTON

ASIA

CHINA

Rafting the Great Bend of the Yangtze River

The Yangtze received intense media coverage during the mid-1980s when groups of rafters vied to become the first to descend China's most famous river. A decade later this operator, which mounted the third expedition down the river, now runs the 200-mile stretch known as the Great Bend where the Yangtze spills out of the Tibetan plateau. Rafters on these trips enjoy a kaleidoscope of experiences, including Class IV white water, towering mountain peaks, beautiful sand beaches and dunes, and ancient stone towns and monasteries. A Chinese cook prepares all the meals from food native to the region. This is one of the finest adventures in all China.

Operator: Earth River Expeditions, 180 Tow Path Rd., Accord, N.Y. 12404; (800) 643-2784 or (914) 626-2665; www.earthriver.com.
Price: Expensive.
Season: October and November.
Length: 15 days.
Accommodations: Tent camps. Five percent discount with BBAT coupon.

MONGOLIA

Rafting the Chuluut River

Mongolia only recently opened up to international travelers, so few of the people here have had much contact with outsiders. The operator has mounted the country's first rafting expedition in a remote corner of the country. The Chuluut River flows through a shallow canyon in the middle of a landscape of rolling grasslands, largely uninhabited except for small ranching communities. Rafters will find stretches of Class III whitewater. Before the river trip they visit Kharhorin, the ancient capital of Genghis Khan, and make a four-day trip on horseback (with vehicle support) to the put-in spot on the Chuluut. They have plenty of opportunity to mingle with the local "cowboys," a hospitable people who live in yurts.

Operator: Boojum Expeditions, 14543 Kelly Canyon Rd., Bozeman, Mont. 59715; (800) 287-0125 or (406) 587-0125; www.boojum.com.
Price: Expensive.
Season: July and August.
Length: 13 days.
Accommodations: Tent camps. Five percent discount with BBAT coupon.

NEPAL

Rafting the Karnali River

Operator: Dvorak's Kayak and Rafting Expeditions, 17921 U.S. Hwy. 285, Nathrop, Colo. 81236; (800) 824-3795 or (719) 539-3378; www.dvorakexpeditions.com
Price: Expensive.
Season: December–January.
Length: 17 days.
Accommodations: Tent camps and park lodge. Five percent discount with BBAT coupon.

Flowing through the far western corner of Nepal, the Karnali River only recently opened to outsiders. Because Nepal is a small country with elevations ranging from 29,000 feet atop Mt. Everest to sea level on the Gangiatic Plain, its rivers quickly develop intense white-water conditions. The rapids on the Karnali are huge, but fairly straightforward. The expedition finishes with a stay at the famous Tiger Tops Karnali Lodge in the Royal Bhardia National Park, which boasts the highest ratio of tiger sightings in Nepal. Other common species here include one-horned rhinos, Asian elephants, leopards, sloth bears, and barking deer.

CANADA

BRITISH COLUMBIA

Rafting the Chilco, Chilcotin, and Fraser Rivers

Operator: Hyak Wilderness Adventures, 3823 Henning Dr., #203, Burnaby, B.C., Canada V5C 6N5; (800) 663-7238 or (604) 734-8622; www.hyak.com.
Price: Expensive.
Season: July and August.
Length: 6 days.
Accommodations: Tent camps. Ten percent discount with BBAT coupon.

Members of this expedition ride on oar-powered rafts down three swift rivers, each one feeding into the next, through a wilderness largely devoid of signs of human occupation. The Chilco runs through a landscape of forested ridgetops and valleys grassy with small cacti, which support large herds of bighorn sheep and mule deer. The Chilcotin drops into deep canyons and tumbles over impressive rapids. The Fraser drains 92,000 square miles with 10 times the flow of the Colorado, hurling itself past relics of the 1858 gold rush and through Moran Canyon, whose sheer walls rise 2,000 feet high. The summer climate is ideal—hot, dry, and free of bugs.

One-Day Adventure on the Thompson River

The Thompson is British Columbia's most popular river trip. A chief reason is that it flows through the desert region of the province's interior, where rafters can almost always count on warm, sunny weather. The river spills out of the western edge of Jasper National Park and rushes down the flank of the Rockies through the driest country in Canada, where the sun bakes the naked hillsides and little grows but cactus and sagebrush. The operator's one-day trip travels the 25-mile stretch through the lower Thompson Valley and White Canyon, a section which offers the best white water and most spectacular scenery. The Thompson becomes more challenging lower down, with rafters experiencing 19 major rapids in the last two hours of their ride. The operator also offers a two-day trip and return transportation from Vancouver for all trips.

Operator: Hyak Wilderness Adventures, 3823 Henning Dr., #203, Burnaby, B.C., Canada V5C 6N5; (800) 663-7238 or (604) 734-8622; www.hyak.com.
Price: Inexpensive.
Season: July–September.
Length: 1 day. Ten percent discount with BBAT coupon.

QUEBEC

Rafting the Great Whale River

Participants on these trips will find a rafting experience that is rich in both white-water adventure and cultural interaction with the Cree Indians. These people have lived for the past 5,000 years in this remote stretch of northern Quebec and are now fighting an extended war with the provincial government, which wants to build a series of dams and flood vast parts of their ancestral lands. As guests of the Whapmagoostui band of the Cree nation, rafters run one of their beautiful threatened rivers (which boasts numerous Class IV rapids), sleep in teepees under the magical pulsing light of the aurora borealis, share Indian customs, and learn firsthand of their struggle for survival. They will also see beluga whales, caribou, wolves, and rare freshwater seals.

Operator: Earth River Expeditions, 180 Tow Path Rd., Accord, N.Y. 12404; (800) 643-2784 or (914) 626-2665; www.earthriver.com.
Price: Expensive.
Season: August.
Length: 5 days.
Accommodations: Tepees. Five percent discount with BBAT coupon.

Rafting the Magpie River

Operator:
Earth River Expeditions,
180 Tow Path Rd.,
Accord, N.Y. 12404;
(800) 643-2784 or
(914) 626-2665;
www.earthriver.com.
Price: Expensive.
Season: August.
Length: 8 days.
Accommodations: Tent
camps. Five percent discount with BBAT coupon.

Beginning on Newfoundland's Labrador Plateau in eastern Quebec, the Magpie River flows untouched through hundreds of miles of lake-dotted virgin forests of pine and multicolored moss, hurtling down steep granite gorges and off spectacular falls before emptying into the St. Lawrence River. Floatplanes provide access to this remote wilderness. Rafters on this trip explore a region which, aside from the occasional explorer, few people have ever seen. A highlight of the trip is Magpie Falls, where the river hurtles 80 feet off the Laurentian Plateau in a thunderous crescendo of spray and sound.

EUROPE

ICELAND

Iceland Adventures

Iceland lies just south of the Arctic Circle, astride the great crack in the earth's surface known as the Mid-Atlantic Rift, and is famous for its active volca-

---

The Adventure Travel Hall of Fame:
ROBERT FULTON, JR.

In 1931 the American Robert Fulton, Jr., purchased a heavy-duty, 750-pound Douglas 600-cc motorcycle in London and set out on an epic, 40,000-mile, two-year journey around the world. Most of the storage space on his cramped bike was taken up by film gear. A camera buff, he brought along an old Bell & Howell 35-mm movie camera, 4,000 feet of film, and a Leica still camera. He stashed a revolver under his skid plate. Whenever possible, he traveled off the main roads into areas that had experienced little contact with the West. It was the end of what he later called the "global middle ages," where isolation from all but the communal family kept one village and region cut off from the next. Turkey and

noes, geysers, and glaciers. The country's grasslands, bogs, moorlands, and marshes are home to 241 species of birds. About the size of Ohio but with only two percent of that state's population, Iceland is relatively undiscovered as an adventure destination. The operator combines rafting, hiking, boating, and wildlife tours into one package to explore the many natural wonders of Iceland. Two days are spent rafting the Austari Jokulsa River, which offers challenging Class IV and V rapids on a run through an isolated landscape that displays the unique beauty and raw nature for which Iceland is famous.

Operator: Destination Wilderness, P.O. Box 1965, Sisters, Ore. 97759; (888) 423-8868 or (541) 549-1336; www.wildernesstrips.com.
Price: Expensive.
Season: Late June–mid-September.
Length: 7 and 8 days.
Accommodations: Hotels and trekker's huts. Ten percent discount with BBAT coupon.

LATIN AMERICA

CHILE

Rafting the Futaleufu River

"The Rio Futaleufu is the gem of Chile," Lars Holbeck insists in his *Whitewater Guide to Chile*. The operator pioneered this river, which has in the past few years become a favorite with many interna-

---

Syria presented him with the worst road conditions of his trip. In Turkey, while driving through the desert at night, he roared onto a concrete bridge across a 200-foot-wide dry riverbed. He was three-quarters of the way across before he realized that the bridge was missing a span, and he crashed into the river bottom. When he came to he was in the hut of a local villager who had carried him a half-mile to his house.

Lodging was scarce in many parts of the world then. In the Middle East, India, and Pakistan, Fulton often wound up staying in British and French forts. In Haiphong, Vietnam, he boarded a freighter for Hong Kong and soon realized that the captain was smuggling opium. He continued his trip through a China barely removed from the feudal era. His expedition came to an end in Japan. In 1937 he published his book, One Man Caravan, which chronicled his motorcycle trip. Fulton later became a photographer for Life magazine.

Chile's Futaleufu River serves up some of the most challenging white water in South America

James Beal/Earth River Expeditions

Operator:
Earth River Expeditions, 180 Tow Path Rd., Accord, N.Y. 12404; (800) 643-2784 or (914) 626-2665; www.earthriver.com. **Price:** Expensive. **Season:** January–March. **Length:** 10 days. **Accommodations:** Tent camps. Five percent discount with BBAT coupon.

tional river-runners. The 100-mile-long "Fu" begins in the high Andes and then rushes toward the Pacific, slicing through deep canyons and past snowcapped peaks and towering spires. Tributaries tint the river a deep azure color. Long stretches of Class IV and V rapids abound, offering some of the best white-water adventure in the Western Hemisphere. These trips begin in the town of Puerto Varas in the heart of the lovely Chilean Lake District. Forty-five minutes after putting in the boats, rafters run Inferno Gorge with a series of back-to-back Class V rapids bearing names like Wall Shot, Orgasm, and Exit. A layover day is scheduled at the scenic Zeta Rapids where rafters can hike, ride horses, kayak, or fish for trout. A classy touch is provided by the presence of a professional Chilean masseuse, who accompanies the group for the entire trip.

ECUADOR

Rafting the Headwaters of the Amazon on the Rio Upano

One of the newest playgrounds for river-runners, Ecuador offers scores of rivers that rush down the eastern side of the Andes into the Amazon basin.

The operator pioneered a rafting program in the country and made the first descent of the Rio Upano, a world-class white-water trip with its Class III and IV rapids. For the first part the river alternates between wide valleys and narrow, intimate canyons. Then the river enters a towering canyon where spectacular waterfalls cascade hundreds of feet down and the constricted river produces a series of challenging rapids. Visits are made with small groups of Shuar Indian families who live in traditional palm-thatched houses along the riverbank. The nearby jungle abounds with a wide variety of bird species, including parrots.

Operator:
River Odysseys West,
P.O. Box 579,
Coeur d'Alene, Idaho
83816; (800) 451-6034 or
(208) 765-0841;
www.rowinc.com.
Price: Expensive.
Season: November–mid-
February.
Length: 11 days.
Accommodations: Hotels and
tent camps. Ten percent
discount with BBAT
coupon.

PERU

Rafting the World's Deepest Canyon

Colca Canyon in southern Peru is twice as deep as the Grand Canyon of the Colorado and just as impressive. From its crystalline waters, towering walls open to vistas of soaring snow-covered Andean peaks. The river offers numerous stretches of Class V rapids caused by truck-size boulders that have fallen from the ramparts, littering the canyon floor. Rafters can expect to see wild alpacas, llamas, condors, and otters. A special highlight is the run through Chocolate Canyon, where the walls are an incredible Hershey's brown. This is a tough, dangerous expedition for experienced river-rafters only.

Operator:
Earth River Expeditions,
180 Tow Path Rd.,
Accord, N.Y. 12404;
(800) 643-2784 or
(914) 626-2665;
www.earthriver.com.
Price: Expensive.
Season: July.
Length: 12 days.
Accommodations: Shore
camps. Five percent dis-
count with BBAT coupon.

MIDDLE EAST

TURKEY

White-Water Excitement on the Coruh River

Spilling out of the sparsely settled northeastern corner of Turkey, the Coruh flows through the Black Mountains before finally reaching the Black

Operator:
Mountain Travel-Sobek,
6420 Fairmount Ave.,
El Cerrito, Calif. 94530;
(888) 687-6235 or
(510) 527-8100;
www.mtsobek.com.
Price: Expensive.
Season: June.
Length: 16 days.
Accommodations: Tent
camps. Five percent discount with BBAT coupon.

Sea. Members of this expedition ride oar-powered rafts through a densely forested canyon almost as deep as the Grand Canyon, past snowcapped peaks, Seljuk castles, ruins of ancient monasteries, and villages so remote they don't even appear on a map. The rapids are world-class. Participants also experience numerous cultural encounters along the way with the friendly shore people in their traditional costumes, few of whom had ever met an American before Sobek mounted the first expedition into the area. One highlight is a visit to the village of Isper, a center for traditional rug-weaving.

PACIFIC OCEAN

FIJI

Pacific Islands Paddling Adventure

Operator:
Destination Wilderness,
P.O. Box 1965,
Sisters, Ore. 97759;
(888) 423-8868 or
(541) 549-1336;
www.wildernesstrips.com.
Price: Expensive.
Season: October–March.
Length: 7 and 14 days.
Accommodations: Tent
camps, grass beach cottages, and hotels. Ten percent discount with BBAT coupon.

Few travelers realize that Viti Levu, Fiji's largest island, boasts some of the finest wilderness in the South Pacific. Here mountains rise over 4,000 feet above the sea and serve as the watershed for the isolated rivers cascading down toward their rendezvous with the sea. The rushing water has carved verdant canyons, filled with hanging gardens of exotic plants, which support a rich profusion of wildlife, including some 70 bird species, including parrots, mynahs, cuckoos, kingfishers, and hawks. The only way to explore this dense tropical paradise is by raft. One day is spent rafting the Luva River, a warm-up run for a four-day rafting expedition down the Navua River. Paddlers then fly to the atoll island of Kandavu and board a motor launch for the smaller island of Ono where several days are spent sea-kayaking along the coast and snorkeling in the crystal-clear waters offshore. Participants have ample opportunity during both legs of the trip to experience the traditional Fijian culture found in the smaller, more isolated villages. Paddlers can book either segment of the trip separately or both together.

UNITED STATES
ALASKA

Down the Tatshenshini

To raft the Tatshenshini through British Columbia to the Pacific is to experience nature on a grand scale. The river slices through mountains over 14,000 feet high and passes more than 20 glaciers. Splendid scenery, not white water, makes this one of the world's premier wilderness river trips. Participants on this expedition experience one of the richest concentrations of wildlife in Alaska, including grizzly bears, Dall sheep, moose, and bald eagles. A highlight is the layover day at iceberg-studded Alsek Bay, so remote that no cruise ship or tour bus has ever reached there. Rafters watch bergs the size of tall buildings calve off the seven-mile-wide Alsek Glacier; paddle among the scores of floes, fantasy creations in blue ice; and hike up the tongue of ice.

Operator: Alaska Discovery, 5310 Glacier Hwy., Juneau, Alaska 99801; (800) 586-1911 or (907) 780-6226; www.akdiscovery.com. *Price:* Expensive. *Season:* June–September. *Length:* 10 days. *Accommodations:* Tent camps. Five percent discount with BBAT coupon.

Rafting the Alsek River

Rafting enthusiasts seeking a more challenging river experience than the Tatshenshini offers will

Rafters on Alaska Discovery's trip down the Tatshenshini River travel past ice-covered mountains and glaciers, dodging icebergs along the way

Alaska Discovery

Operator:
Alaska Discovery, 5310
Glacier Hwy.,
Juneau, Alaska 99801;
(800) 586-1911 or
(907) 780-6226;
www.akdiscovery.com.
Price: Expensive.
Season: July and September.
Length: 12 days.
Accommodations: Tent
camps. Five percent discount with BBAT coupon.

find the Alsek River more to their satisfaction. From headwaters high up in the Yukon Territory, the Alsek River flows fast and deep through unspoiled wilderness before finally merging with the Tatshenshini in one of the most spectacular confluences in North America. This is a truly wild river, with Class III and IV rapids rushing through the bottom of deep canyons. The nearest road and human settlement lie dozens of miles away. This is a rafting expedition for experienced river-runners only.

Rafting the Kongatut River

Operator:
Alaska Discovery,
5310 Glacier Hwy.,
Juneau, Alaska 99801;
(800) 586-1911 or
(907) 780-6226;
www.akdiscovery.com.
Price: Expensive.

This expedition begins and ends in the Land of the Midnight Sun as participants paddle through the imposing and remote wilderness of the Arctic National Wildlife Refuge. The Kongatut flows quickly, with few rapids, through the Brooks Range foothills and tundra country ablaze with wildflowers. The major attraction is the profusion of wildlife, including the annual migration of the

The Adventure Travel Hall of Fame: BILL BEER AND JOHN DAGGETT

In 1955 Bill Beer and John Daggett, two young insurance salesmen from California, were looking for a fun, cheap vacation. The pair were skilled surfers and swimmers but had no river experience when they struck on the idea of running the Colorado River from Lee's Ferry to Pierce Ferry, through the entire length of the Grand Canyon. They were undeterred by the fact that only about 200 people had made the trip to date. Because they could not afford a boat and all the necessary equipment, they decided to swim the 280 miles! Their equipment matched

the "Budget Cheap" dictum—war-surplus rubber boxes designed to protect radio gear, made from corded neoprene and sealable (a bargain at 89 cents each!), thin rubber shirts found at a sale in a dive shop for $15 each, swim fins, inflatable Mae West lifejackets, and wool long johns—scant protection against the 51-degree water.

In April the pair arrived at Pierce Ferry on Lake Meade to scout their take-out point and leave one car. Just before dawn they were awakened by the explosion of an atomic bomb at the Nevada test site just 30 miles away. Then on Easter morning they

180,000-strong Porcupine caribou herd. Rafters also can expect to see wolves, bear, Dall sheep, and thousands of nesting birds. The fishing is excellent, and the dinner menu often includes fresh char and grayling. The final night is at the traditional Eskimo settlement of Kaktovik.

Season: June.
Length: 11 and 12 days.
Accommodations: Tent camps. Five percent discount with BBAT coupon.

ARIZONA

The Colorado River Through the Grand Canyon

Ever since Teddy Roosevelt declared in 1903 that the Grand Canyon is "the one great sight every American must see," it has been the premier American natural attraction. "The canyon is at least two things besides spectacle," naturalist Joseph Wood Krutch wrote. "It is a biological unit and the most revealing single page of earth's history anywhere open on the face of the globe." Each year millions of tourists arrive at the small village of

arrived at their Lee's Ferry departure site. They put on their funny-looking swimming gear and carried their heavy boxes to the water's edge. A nearby sign warned, "No Swimming." They waded into deep water and swam out to the main current, which quickly caught them up and swept them on their way.

The pair swam through all the river's rapids, including the legendary Lava Falls. However, they soon learned that their greatest danger came not from the thunderous rapids but the numbing cold they had to endure each day. "On first getting into the water we felt pain everywhere on the surface of our bodies from the shock of the cold water," Beer recollected in his memoir of the experience, We Swam the Grand Canyon.

Beer and Daggett had given several interviews with journalists before their departure from Los Angeles with the stipulation that none of the stories run until after they had entered the river. During the escapade the Park Service conducted a futile airplane search and the media believed them dead. But 26 days later the pair emerged at Pierce Ferry, having successfully completed their remarkable journey. They were only the 219th and 220th people in history to make the trip through the entire Grand Canyon.

Grand Canyon to stare off into the awesome gorge below, at its monumental buttes and erosion-scarred slopes. But only a handful experience its full impact, riding the muddy chaos of the Colorado for 300 miles through some 200 rapids. This is the world's supreme river trip, the standard against which all others are measured. The U.S. Park Service allows some 17,000 people a year to know the special enchantment of the canyon by seeing it from the bottom up, one mile below the distant rims. These visitors have a variety of options available.

Motorized Inflatable Boats

Operator:
Canyoneers, P.O. Box 2997, Flagstaff, Ariz. 86003; (800) 525-0924 or (520) 526-0924; www.canyoneers.com.
Price: Expensive.
Season: April–mid-September.
Length: 7 days.
Accommodations: Shore camps.

Most people ride the motor-driven pontoon boats that slam with a shock through the toughest white water. These big boats are virtually unflippable and provide the most stable ride through the major rapids. The trips travel the length of the Grand Canyon.

"Running the big rapids is like sex. Half the fun lies in the anticipation. Two-thirds of the thrill comes with the approach. The remainder is only ecstasy—or darkness."

EDWARD ABBEY

Operator:
Dvorak's Kayak and Rafting Expeditions, 17921 U.S. Hwy. 285, Nathrop, Colo. 81236; (800) 824-3795 or (719) 539-6851; www.dvorakexpeditions.com
Price: Expensive.
Season: May–September.
Length: The trip through the entire canyon takes 12 days, although the operator allows rafters to book shorter segments.
Accommodations: Shore camps. Five percent discount with BBAT coupon.

Oar-Powered Inflatable Boats

These trips all use smaller, oar-powered inflatable rafts that are free of the noise and smoke associated with outboard motors. Typically, five or six rafts launch together and travel as a group. Most operators limit group size to 25 persons.

"Climbing K-2 or floating down the Grand Canyon in an inner tube: There are some things one would rather have done than do."

EDWARD ABBEY
A VOICE CRYING IN THE WILDERNESS

Wooden Dories

For pure adventure and a nonstop rush of adrenaline, go with the 17-foot-long-by-seven-foot wide wooden boats. These are small dories that ride low in the water and can easily capsize or break up against the rocks. This is the ultimate way to challenge Lava Falls and Crystal Rapid, two of North America's biggest drops.

Operator: Grand Canyon Dories, P.O. Box 216, Altaville, Calif. 95221; (800) 877-3679 or (209) 736-0805; www.oars.com.
Price: Moderate.
Season: April–September.
Length: The trip through the entire canyon from Lee's Ferry to the Grand Wash Cliffs takes 19 days, but clients can book a variety of shorter segments.
Accommodations: Shore camps. Five percent discount with BBAT coupon.

Small wooden dories offer the most exciting ride through the big rapids along the Colorado River at the foot of the Grand Canyon

Bert Sagara/O.A.R.S.

"Travel allows you to experiment with a thousand different ways of life. Most of us go through life being the way we are not because we want to, but because that's the pigeonhole we're stuck in. But travel shows us we can be what we want. You're as free as a bird."

ROBERT FULTON, JR.
ESCAPE MAGAZINE, JANUARY 1997

The Tuolumne River boasts some of the wildest white water conditions in the United States

Sierra Mac River Trips

CALIFORNIA

Lower Klamath

Operator: O.A.R.S., P.O. Box 67, Angels Camp, Calif. 95222; (800) 346-6277 or (209) 736-4677; www.oars.com. *Price:* Moderate. *Season:* June–October. *Length:* 3 days. *Accommodations:* Shore camps. Five percent discount with BBAT coupon.

These popular trips are ideal for families with young children seeking a scenic float on a warm, gentle section of the Klamath River that flows through northern California's mountains and valleys. This is California's second-largest river and one of the first rivers in the state to be granted National Wild and Scenic status. The Klamath runs free for 180 miles to the ocean. These easy trips offer an abundance of scenic beauty, diverse wildlife, and recreational opportunities. The rapids are exciting but not intimidating, perfect for young children.

Gastronomic Adventure on the Tuolumne

Plunging down a gradient of 60 feet per mile, through the grandeur of an unspoiled Sierra mountain canyon, the Tuolumne has some of the finest white water in the West, secluded tributary streams, and relics from an earlier generation of gold-seekers. Eagles, river otters, and ring-tailed cats all call the nearby forests home. Dubbed the

"California Roll," this expedition on oar-powered rafts blends high river adventure and haute cuisine. A top San Francisco chef prepares gourmet dinners, served with vintage wines, crystal, and white linens in a wilderness setting. "We invite you to discover how a 20-year-old bottle of California Cabernet safely descends the Class IV rapids of this wild river," teases owner/host Marty McDonnell. A typical five-course dinner includes artichoke hearts with roast leg of lamb, baby-chicken tamales with South Texas salsa, mesquite-grilled albacore tuna, and chocolate truffle cake. No less an authority than Craig Claiborne, the late food guru of the *New York Times,* has pronounced the California Roll "magnifique."

Operator: Sierra Mac River Trips, P.O. Box 366, Sonora, Calif. 95370; (800) 457-2580 or (209) 532-1327; www.sierramac.com. *Price:* Expensive. *Season:* June–October. *Length:* 3 days. *Accommodations:* Shore camps. Five percent discount with BBAT coupon.

White-Water Rafting School

This intensive white-water week is designed for beginners to advanced rafters. The course covers the fundamental skills of reading white water and maneuvering boats. The instruction follows a written manual and is tailored to meet students' individual needs. Lectures cover safety procedures and equipment. Students also learn raft-rigging, equipment maintenance and repair, and camp cooking. Field instruction takes place on a variety of California wild rivers, including the Main and Upper Tuolumne, Giant Gap, and North Fork of the American. At the end of the course each student receives a personal written evaluation.

Operator: Sierra Mac River Trips, P.O. Box 366, Sonora, Calif. 95370; (800) 457-2580 or (209) 532-1327; www.sierramac.com. *Price:* Moderate. *Season:* April and May. *Length:* 7 days. *Accommodations:* Motel. Five percent discount with BBAT coupon.

COLORADO

A Classical-Music Journey down the Dolores River

Since 1985 the operator has brought professional musicians and their instruments from major orchestras into some of the wildest canyons of the West. They provide four scheduled performances on the trips, but rafters soon get used to hearing a

Operator:
Dvorak's Kayak and Rafting
Expeditions,
17921 U.S. Hwy. 285,
Nathrop, Colo. 81236;
(800) 824-3795 or
(719) 539-6851;
www.dvorakexpeditions.com
Price: Moderate.
Season: June.
Length: 4 and 7 days.
Accommodations: Shore
camps. Five percent dis-
count with BBAT coupon.

Mozart quartet or a Vivaldi flute concerto while traveling down the river at the bottom of a deep canyon. The highlight is a formal recital in an immense amphitheater near the campsite. All this takes place on the Dolores River, a joy to run. This lovely alpine stream spills out of the southern San Juan range and rushes through the foothills and tablelands, cutting a canyon some 2,500 deep. With an average gradient of 20 feet per mile and one sec-tion approaching a 60-foot drop per mile, the Dolores offers an abundance of Class II and III rapids. Stops are made on these trips for hikes into tributary canyons, visits to Anasazi ruins, and fish-ing breaks. (The operator also offers a classical music journey down the Green River.)

IDAHO

Snake River Through Hell's Canyon

Operator:
Hughes River Expeditions,
P.O. Box 217,
Cambridge, Idaho 83610;
(800) 262-1882 or
(208) 257-3477;
www.hughesriver.com.
Price: Expensive.
Season: Late
May–September.
Length: 3, 4, 5, and 6 days.
Accommodations: Shore
camps. Five percent dis-
count with BBAT coupon.

As the Snake River flows along the border between Idaho and Oregon, it carves Hell's Canyon, the deepest in North America. At one point the canyon drops 7,900 feet from the craggy heights of the Seven Devils Mountains to the churning rapids and eddies of the river below, eclipsing the Grand Canyon by 2,000 feet. Rafters on these expeditions ride through some of the wildest white water in the West—full-bodied, roller coaster–style rapids. This is an area steeped in frontier history, from 8,000-year-old Indian sites and abandoned pioneer cab-ins to the gory Deep Creek, where in 1887 a group of cowboys brutally murdered 31 Chinese placer miners. The Snake also offers excellent fishing for rainbow trout, smallmouth bass, and steelhead.

Down the "River of No Return"

Idaho's celebrated Main Salmon River flows fast, cold, and rough through the second-deepest canyon in North America (the Grand Canyon is the third!). When the Lewis and Clark expedition saw the mile-deep canyon and raging rapids, they understood why the Indians called it the "River of No Return." Participants on these trips ride oar-powered inflatable rafts through some of the most legendary rapids in North America. Along the way they visit abandoned cabins, hidden waterfalls, hot springs, and Indian pictographs. Camps are set up on white-sand beaches. The surrounding forests abound in a wide variety of wildlife, including bighorn sheep, bear, cougars, and eagles.

Operator:
Silver Cloud Expeditions,
P.O. Box 1006,
Salmon, Idaho 83467;
(208) 756-6215;
www.silvercloudexp.com.
Price: Expensive.
Season: June–September.
Length: 5 and 6 days.
Accommodations: Shore camps. Five percent discount with BBAT coupon.

Lodge-to-Lodge Rafting Trip on the Main Salmon River

For those river-runners who prefer the amenities of a soft bed and hot shower at night, the operator offers a lodge-based rafting adventure for the 80-mile run down the Main Salmon River.

Operator:
Echo: The Wilderness Company, 6529 Telegraph Ave., Oakland, Calif. 94609; (800) 652-3246 or (510) 652-1600; www.echotrips.com.
Price: Expensive.
Season: June and July.
Length: 4 days.
Accommodations: Wilderness lodges. Five percent discount with BBAT coupon.

Echo: The Wilderness Company offers a popular lodge-to-lodge rafting trip down the Main Salmon River
George Wuerthner/Echo: The Wilderness Company

"The first condition of right thought is right sensation—the first condition of understanding a foreign country is to smell it."
T. S. ELIOT
"RUDYARD KIPLING"

The Middle Fork of the Salmon

Operator: Rocky Mountain River Tours, P.O. Box 2552, Boise, Idaho 83701; (208) 345-2400; in summer P.O. Box 207, Salmon, Idaho 83467; (208) 756-4808. *Price:* Expensive. *Season:* Late May–September. *Length:* 6 days, with 4-day trips in the early season. *Accommodations:* Shore camps. Five percent discount with BBAT coupon.

The Middle Fork snakes its way through the heart of the 2.2-million-acre Salmon Wilderness Area in central Idaho, amid a spectacular blend of mountains, forests, and deep canyons. With an average drop of 27 feet per mile and more than 100 rapids, it offers a superb combination of thrilling white water, extraordinary scenery, and abundant wildlife. Rafters descend from an elevation of 5,700 feet to 3,000 feet, riding through dense forests to end in the rugged granite gorge of Impassable Canyon. Stops are also made at several abandoned homesteads, masterpieces of frontier handiwork with handmade furniture inside finely cut and fitted log cabins.

Through Bruneau Canyon

Operator: Hughes River Expeditions, P.O. Box 217, Cambridge, Idaho 83610; (800) 262-1882 or (208) 257-3477; www.hughesriver.com. *Price:* Expensive. *Season:* May and early June. *Length:* 4 days. *Accommodations:* Shore camps. Five percent discount with BBAT coupon.

The Bruneau River twists through the Pacific Northwest's most dramatic desert canyon. Sheer basalt cliffs tower more than a thousand feet above the boats. The white water is excellent, the most celebrated stretch being "Five Mile Rapids" where the rapids hit with machine-gun frequency. Because of the river's difficulty the operator uses special small oar-powered boats, each one carrying only two passengers and a boatman. Bruneau Canyon is rich in mule deer, otters, birds of prey, and other types of wildlife. Short hikes are also made up tributary canyons to visit the remains of an old whiskey still, two hot springs, and several large caves. Although only a handful of people have experienced the Bruneau, it has become a favorite with river guides and boaters.

Rafting the Lochsa River

Of all the rivers in Idaho, none offers more continuous, explosive white water than the Lochsa ("LOCK-saw"), which well lives up to its name, an Indian word meaning "rough water." From its headwaters in the Bitterroot Mountains to its confluence with the Selway and Clearwater Rivers, the Lochsa pounds and churns through more than 40 major rapids rated Class III to V. The river is not dammed; therefore, the water flow depends strictly on the snowpack. The water level is highest and the rapids are most demanding in late May and early June. The river run is through a deep, thickly forested canyon. The operator uses 16-foot paddle-assisted oar-rafts. This is a river for experienced rafters who are also strong swimmers.

Operator:
River Odysseys West, P.O. Box 579, Coeur d'Alene, Idaho 83816; (800) 451-6034 or (208) 765-0841; www.rowinc.com.
Price: Moderate.
Season: May and June.
Length: 1, 2, and 3 days.
Accommodations: Tent camps. Ten percent discount with BBAT coupon.

MAINE

One-Day Adventure on the Kennebec River

Huge waves crashing through a deep forested gorge, combined with the Class IV white-water excitement of Magic Falls, create a natural roller-coaster ride that makes the Kennebec an ideal rafting adventure. When the first rafter ran the river in 1976, he was told that he would never survive. He not only survived, he also spawned a multimillion-dollar industry. More than 55,000 people now run the Kennebec each year on those days when the Yankee Nuclear Power Plant releases excess water from its dam. The flow of 6,000 cubic feet per second insures plenty of thrills for the 13-mile adventure, with the first five miles being one continuous white-water run. The rapids grow in a crescendo, each one bigger than the one before.

Operator:
New England Outdoor Center, P.O. Box 669, Millinocket, Maine 04462; (800) 766-7238 or (207) 723-5438; www.raftingmaine.com.
Price: Moderate.
Season: May–September.
Length: 1 day. Five percent discount with BBAT coupon.

"I do not know why it is, but the instant I am on an elephant I do not feel afraid for myself or anybody else. When the tall grass shakes and the elephants begin to scream, I ask whether it is a tiger or a rhinoceros in exactly the same tone I should ask the servants whether it is a partridge or a pheasant."

FANNY EDEN
INDIAN JOURNALS, 1837–1838

One-Day Adventure on the Penobscot River

Operator:
New England Outdoor
Center, P.O. Box 669,
Millinocket, Maine 04462;
(800) 766-7238 or
(207) 723-5438;
www.raftingmaine.com.
Price: Moderate.
Season: May–September.
Length: 1 day. Five percent
discount with BBAT
coupon.

The west branch of the Penobscot challenges even the most experienced rafter. To make the river accessible to all rafters and to eliminate 1.5 miles of flat water, the operator begins the adventure on the lower, calmer stretch of the river. After a lunch break with a riverside cookout, paddlers are then bused upstream to the headwaters for the formidable run through the white water of Ripogenus Gorge. The big drops there sport such intimidating names as Exterminator (a Class V rapid), Staircase, and Cribworks, with the latter considered the most challenging white water in the East.

MARYLAND

The Upper Yough

Operator:
Appalachian Wildwaters,
P.O. Box 100,
Rowlesburg, W.Va. 26425;
(800) 624-8060 or (304)
454-2475; www.awrafts.com.
Price: Moderate.
Season: April–November.
Length: 1 day. Five percent
discount with BBAT
coupon.

The Indians called it Youghiogheny, meaning "river which flows in all directions." With the steepest riverbed east of the Rockies, it starts in West Virginia, rushes through Maryland, and finishes in Pennsylvania. Appalachian Wildwaters runs an 11-mile section in western Maryland popularly known as the Upper Yough (pronounced "yok" to rhyme with "rock"). The 115-foot-per-mile gradient in the main section of the run and the nonstop nature of the rapids make the Upper Yough one of the most challenging stretches of white water anywhere. The names of the rapids—Triple Drop, Snaggle Tooth, and Meat Cleaver—hint at the violence of this stretch of the river. Trips in four-person paddle rafts are scheduled for Monday through Friday when a power company opens the floodgates of a dam and releases a rush of water. The Upper Yough is for experienced rafters only.

"One day's exposure to mountains is better than cartloads of books."

JOHN MUIR

MASSACHUSETTS

Rafting the Upper Deerfield River

The Deerfield River originates in southern Vermont, drains a total area of some 665 square miles, and journeys 70 miles, dropping over 2,000 feet, before it joins the Connecticut River in Massachusetts. Ten hydroelectric dams block the river but release water on a regular basis. The Deerfield provides the finest white-water conditions within easy access to Boston and Providence, and Class II and III rapids boasting names such as Microwave, Freight Train, and Pinball. These 10-mile trips are guaranteed to get the adrenaline rushing!

Operator: Zoar Outdoor, P.O. Box 245, Charlemont, Mass. 01339; (800) 532-7483 or (413) 339-4010; www.zaroutdoor.com.
Price: Inexpensive.
Season: April–mid-October.
Length: 4 to 6 hours. Ten percent discount with BBAT coupon.

NORTH CAROLINA

The Nantahala River

Nestled in a deep gorge along the southern edge of the Great Smoky Mountains National Park, the Nantahala is the most popular river in the Southeast. More than 150,000 people each year succumb to its beauty and playfulness to run the river in paddleboats, canoes, and kayaks. The Nantahala is dam-fed, so its flow is consistent and dependable throughout the year. A float along this lovely river is quiet serenity, laced with some exciting Class II and III rapids so the ride is never dull. This is the perfect river adventure for families and novices. The trip covers eight miles.

Operator: USA Raft, P.O. Box 277, Rowlesburg, W.Va. 26425; (800) USA-RAFT or (828) 488-2175; www.usaraft.com.
Price: Inexpensive.
Season: Late March–October.
Length: 4 hours. Five percent discount coupon with BBAT coupon.

OREGON

The Rogue River

One of the original rivers protected under the National Wild and Scenic Rivers Act, the Rogue boasts a 40-mile section that flows through the

Operator:
Sundance River Center,
14894 Galice Rd., Merlin,
Ore. 97532; (888) 777-7557
or (541) 479-8508;
www.sundanceriver.com.
Price: Moderate.
Season: April–mid-
September.
Length: 4 days.
Accommodations: Operator
offers a choice of tent-camp
and lodge-based trips. Five
percent discount with
BBAT coupon.

rugged coastal Mountain Range in Oregon's southeastern corner. The white water on this stretch contains numerous Class II and III rapids. Warm water, beautiful sandy beaches perfect for campsites, and a wild, nearly pristine landscape make the Rogue one of the Pacific Northwest's most popular rivers. The most fearsome cataracts are Rainie Falls, which drops a full 10 feet, and Blossom Bar, a gigantic rock-garden below the boiling waters of Mule Creek Canyon. Be sure to visit the cabin where Zane Grey wrote many of his novels and fished for Chinook salmon and steelhead trout. Participants have a choice of oar boats, paddle rafts, or inflatables.

Wine and Whitewater on the Rogue

Operator:
Echo: The Wilderness
Company, 6529 Telegraph
Ave., Oakland, Calif. 94609;
(800) 652-3246 or
(510) 652-1600;
www.echotrips.com.
Price: Moderate.
Season: June.
Length: 4 days.
Accommodations: Tent
camps. Five percent dis-
count with BBAT coupon.

This operator has a long and popular history of offering wine-tasting trips down the Rogue River. A Napa Valley wine expert accompanies each departure and gives informal talks on all aspects of wine making. Evenings are spent tasting a variety of sparkling wines, including the pinots and chardonnays that are blended to make them.

"Travel is a vanishing act, a solitary trip down a pinched line of geography to oblivion."

PAUL THEROUX
THE OLD PATAGONIAN EXPRESS

Half-Day Trip on the McKenzie River

Operator:
Destination Wilderness,
P.O. Box 1965, Sisters, Ore.
97759; (888) 423-8868 or
(541) 549-1336;
www.wildernesstrips.com.
Price: Inexpensive.
Season: October–March.
Length: Half-day. Ten percent discount with BBAT
coupon.

For rafters who want a half-day adventure, the McKenzie River in central Oregon offers crystal-clear waters and fine Class II and III white-water stretches. The operator runs trips on both the upper and middle portions of the McKenzie, where the rapids come in quick succession, and the river winds its way through a verdant forest. These trips are great for those looking for fun but not overwhelming rapids and great mountain scenery—in short, a great escape for those people with busy schedules.

TENNESSEE

The Nolichucky River

Rafters have only recently discovered the action on the Nolichucky, which flows out of the Blue Ridge Mountains in North Carolina and rushes 150 miles through Tennessee. Thus it lacks the crowds often found on more-accessible and better-known rivers. Paddlers put in across from Polly's General Store in the tiny town of Poplar, North Carolina, and run the Nolichucky for nine miles through the Pisgah and Cherokee National Forests, at the bottom of one of the most scenic gorges in the Southeast. Towering cliffs loom above the rapids. The banks are lined with wild flowering laurel and rhododendron. Boaters can look forward to as many as 25 Class II to IV rapids. No previous rafting experience is necessary.

Operator: USA Raft, P.O. Box 277, Rowlesburg, W.Va. 26425; (800) USA-RAFT or (828) 488-2175; www.usaraft.com. *Price:* Inexpensive. *Season:* Late March–October. *Length:* 4 hours. Five percent discount coupon with BBAT coupon.

UTAH

The Colorado River Through Cataract Canyon

This trip enjoys legendary status among professional river-runners but is relatively unknown to the neophyte. Cut by the Colorado River through Canyonlands National Park in southern Utah, Cataract Canyon is an eerie labyrinth of sandstone crevices, a wilderness accessible only by raft. For the first two days participants on these expeditions ride lazily down a peaceful river, enjoying days filled with visits to ancient Anasazi Indian ruins and pictographs, swims in tributary streams, and explorations of side canyons. Three miles below its confluence with the Green River, the Colorado becomes a churning sluice as it squeezes through Cataract Canyon, generating one of the country's most treacherous white-water stretches. The famed cataract The Big Drop falls 80 feet in less than a mile. The operator offers trips aboard oarboats and larger J-rig rafts.

Operator: Sheri Griffith Expeditions, P.O. Box 1324, Moab, Utah 84532; (800) 332-2439 or (435) 259-8229; www.GriffithExp.com. *Price:* Moderate. *Season:* May–September. *Length:* 3, 4, and 5 days. *Accommodations:* Shore camps. Five percent discount with BBAT coupon.

Water fights are a popular distraction on the river during the heat of the day

Sheri Griffith Expeditions

Champagne and Caviar on the Colorado River

Operator: Sheri Griffith Expeditions, P.O. Box 1324, Moab, Utah 84532; (800) 332-2439 or (435) 259-8229; www.GriffithExp.com. *Price:* Expensive. *Season:* June and August. *Length:* 4 days. *Accommodations:* Shore camps. Five percent discount with BBAT coupon.

Through Cataract Canyon. For those river-runners who seek to add some evening luxury to their daytime white-water adventures, the operator adds haute cuisine and high culture to her usual river experience—chamber music, gourmet meals, linens, and crystal. These rafting expeditions are designed to pamper. Camp attendants, for example, set up and take down the tents. Tuxedoes and evening gowns are strictly optional!

The Green River

Operator: Sheri Griffith Expeditions, P.O. Box 1324, Moab, Utah 84532; (800) 332-2439 or (435) 259-8229; www.GriffithExp.com. *Price:* Moderate. *Season:* June and July. *Length:* 4 and 5 days. *Accommodations:* Shore camps. Five percent discount with BBAT coupon.

This formidable wilderness was a favorite hiding place a century ago for the outlaws Butch Cassidy and the Sundance Kid. Today the combination of spectacular scenery and drops of 30 feet in less than a mile make this trip a river-runner's white-water favorite. Between mad, churning white-knuckle passages, there is plenty of time for drifting past 2,000 foot-high cliffs and hiking up tributary canyons to Indian ruins and fern grottoes with waterfalls. Wildlife is common, and rafters can see herds of deer and bighorn sheep from the river. Clients have a choice of oar boats or paddleboats.

The Yampa River Through Dinosaur National Monument

The last undammed major tributary of the Colorado, the Yampa cuts a 200-mile course through the 2,000-foot-deep canyons of northeast Utah's Dinosaur National Monument. The U.S. Park Service severely limits the number of rafters permitted on the river each summer. The white water is excellent; Warm Springs Rapid is one of the longest and technically most difficult in the Southwest. Although a few hardy hermits settled in the canyon in the 19th century, much of this wilderness is virtually unexplored. Rafters on these four- and five-day expeditions may find the isolation overwhelming. Don't miss the impressive gallery of Indian petroglyphs—bighorn sheep and hunters with bows and arrows—at Jones Hole. Because it flows freely, the Yampa can be rafted only during the late spring runoff in May and June.

Operator: Sheri Griffith Expeditions, P.O. Box 1324, Moab, Utah 84532; (800) 332-2439 or (435) 259-8229; www.GriffithExp.com. *Price:* Moderate. *Season:* June and July. *Length:* 4 and 5 days. *Accommodations:* Shore camps. Five percent discount with BBAT coupon.

Women-Only Rafting Trips

This operator pioneered women-only wilderness experiences on Western rivers. She created trips that provide a supportive, non-competitive setting in which women can learn outdoor skills taught by

Operator: Sheri Griffith Expeditions, P.O. Box 1324, Moab, Utah 84532;

Sheri Griffith Expeditions pioneered the concept of women-only rafting expeditions on the Colorado River

Sheri Griffith Expeditions

(800) 332-2439 or (435) 259-8229; www.GriffithExp.com. **Price:** Moderate. **Season:** June, July, and August. **Length:** 3 and 4 days. **Accommodations:** Shore camps. Five percent discount with BBAT coupon.

well-trained river boatwomen. These trips underscore the fact that women relate to one another differently in "survival" situations when men are not around. As the operator states in her catalog: "Women-only trips offer the opportunity to discover our selves, each other, and the world around us without the self-imposed restrictions that are present in everyday life." She offers women-only trips down the Colorado River through Cataract Canyon and Westwater Canyon.

Rafting Expeditions for the Disabled

Operator: Dvorak's Kayak and Rafting Expeditions, 17921 U.S. Hwy. 285, Nathrop, Colo. 81236; (800) 824-3795 or (719) 539-6851; www.dvorakexpeditions.com **Price:** Moderate. **Season:** Check with operator for dates. **Length:** Check with operator. Five percent discount with BBAT coupon.

Only recently, because of advances in equipment and the development of access points, has river rafting become available to physically disabled people. Experts now recognize that certain adventure-travel experiences can provide important steps toward rehabilitation after a disabling injury. On the river, disabled participants find themselves free to explore their limits—and many discover that their sense of accomplishment can be more powerful than their sense of being "handicapped." This outfitter has been a leader in providing rafting trips for a wide variety of disabled adventurers, offering trips down several rivers, including a six-day Green River expedition. Boats are specially rigged for safety, and camping sites are chosen for their accessibility. A trained nurse accompanies each group. Participants in these trips include people confined to wheelchairs as well as those suffering from deafness, blindness, muscular dystrophy, cerebral palsy, and multiple sclerosis.

WEST VIRGINIA

White-Knuckled Excitement on the Gauley

Operator: Appalachian Wildwaters, P.O. Box 100, Rowlesburg, W.Va. 26425; (800) 624-8060 or (304) 454-2475; www.awrafts.com.

Located 30 miles southeast of Charleston, the Gauley drops almost 100 feet a mile through spectacular scenery in one of the East's finest whitewater runs. In the autumn it guarantees 50 or more Class III to VI rapids with hair-raising names such as Pure Screaming Hell. The Upper Gauley requires previous experience. This river is runnable for only 21 days each autumn, when Summersville Lake is lowered to prepare for winter snows and spring thaws.

Challenging the Cheat

The 150-mile long Cheat River is one of the largest uncontrolled watersheds in the eastern United States. A major flood in 1985 rearranged some of the rapids, exposed some ledges, and made some drops even steeper. New drops have been christened with names such as Terminator and Cyclotron, while at the same time, old menaces like Devil's Trap remain. During the spring runoff, rafters encounter Class III to V rapids. Few rivers offer such a challenging run for experienced paddlers. Autumn on the Cheat brings spectacular foliage. This 12-mile-long trip is for experienced white-water paddlers or those "willing to assume risks somewhat in excess of those inherent in any raft trip."

Paddling the Tygart

Commercial river-running came late to the Tygart, but it has quickly established its popularity with experienced river buffs. The Arden section opens with stretches of gentle white water that build in size until paddlers hit such formidable rapids as Deception, Undercut, and Premonition. The grand finale is Seven Wells Falls, which the operator insists is "the most powerful runnable rapid in the Monongahela River Basin." The short but intense Valley Falls features a 25-foot water slide and a 14-foot vertical waterfall. Constant releases from the Tygart Lake Dam guarantee rafters a plentiful supply of water. Passengers ride in four- and 10-person rafts. No previous rafting experience is necessary.

Price: Moderate.
Season: March–November.
Length: The Upper Gauley run covers 15 miles and takes 6 hours; the Lower Gauley, 11 miles and 4 hours. Five percent discount with BBAT coupon.

Operator:
Appalachian Wildwaters, P.O. Box 100, Rowlesburg, W.Va. 26425;
(800) 624-8060 or
(304) 454-2475;
www.awrafts.com.
Price: Inexpensive.
Season: March–August.
Length: 7 hours. Five percent discount with BBAT coupon.

Operator:
Appalachian Wildwaters, P.O. Box 100, Rowlesburg, W.Va. 26425;
(800) 624-8060 or
(304) 454-2475;
www.awrafts.com.
Price: Moderate.
Season: March–August.
Length: The trip covers seven miles and takes 6 hours. Five percent discount with BBAT coupon.

The New: The Grand Canyon of the East

Operator:
Appalachian Wildwaters,
P.O. Box 100, Rowlesburg,
W.Va. 26425; (800) 624-
8060 or (304) 454-2475;
www.awrafts.com.
Price: Moderate.
Season: March–November.
Length: Half-day and 2-day
trips.
Accommodations: Shore
camp. Five percent dis-
count with BBAT coupon.

One of the most popular rivers in America with river-runners, the New is the white-water equivalent of a roller-coaster ride. The lower New features spectacular white-water runs at the foot of a deep gorge known as the "Grand Canyon of the East," which is run in 10-person paddle rafts. No previous experience is necessary. The upper New provides the perfect trip for beginners and families, being a gentle run through some of the state's most beautiful mountain scenery.

WYOMING

The North Platte River Through Northgate Canyon

Operator:
Dvorak's Kayak and
Rafting Expeditions,
17921 U.S. Hwy. 285,
Nathrop, Colo. 81236;
(800) 824-3795 or
(719) 539-6851;
dvorakexpeditions.com
Price: Moderate.
Season: May–July.
Length: 2 and 3 days.
Accommodations: Tent
camps. Five percent dis-
count with BBAT coupon.

Mark Twain once joked that if the North Platte were turned on edge, it just might make a respectable river. But he was talking about the lower sections. The upper North Platte is as beautiful a mountain river as can be run in the Rockies. The hundreds of boaters who paddle the rapids of Northgate Canyon, where the river drops 470 feet in 18 miles, know the river is not all sandbars and flat water. Fine scenery, excellent white water, and great trout-fishing make the upper North Platte a first-rate experience. Rafters on these trips cover 35 miles.

PROFILE

MARTY MCDONNELL
SIERRA MAC RIVER TRIPS

"We invite our clients to discover how a 20-year-old bottle of California cabernet safely descends the Class IV rapids of this wild river," teases Marty McDonnell, the owner of Sierra Mac River Trips. His three-day California Roll rafting trip down the wild Tuolumne River blends high river adventure and haute cuisine. A top chef from a leading Texas culinary school prepares gourmet dinners, served with vintage wines, crystal, and white linens in a wilderness setting.

Back in 1985 McDonnell's passenger list for this popular trip included the late Craig Claiborne, then food editor for the *New York Times*, who was on his first white-water rafting trip. His review focused as much on the thrills as the food: "Within seconds of our departure, I felt myself surrounded by the perils in question: wild currents, boulders large and small that would loom suddenly ahead of our craft, deep chutes, straight-down tumbles of eight feet and more. . . . The trip had all the qualities (mainly speed and terror) of an out-of-control roller coaster ride."

But that evening Claiborne traded the thrills of the river for the culinary creations of chef Armando G. Dominguez. "The food for our first evening began with a 'mandala' of seasonal vegetables with a tarragon dipping sauce and assorted imported cheeses, followed by sausages flavored with aged tequila and a variety of mustards, deep-fried quail eggs with chili croutons, a filet mignon grilled over mesquite and served with roast garlic butter, wild rice blended with chanterelle mushrooms and sun-dried tomatoes, buttered spinach, a string bean salad with hazelnuts and cream, and, for dessert, fresh figs with raspberries," an enthusiastic Claiborne wrote later in his *Times* review.

Sierra Mac River Trips is a boutique among the department stores of operators who offer a broad spectrum of trips on both international and domestic rivers. McDonnell's specialty is the celebrated Tuolumne River with its long stretches of Class IV and V white-water runs. The Tuolumne drains the northern reaches of Yosemite and thunders through nine miles of rapids on the upper portion and 18 on the lower. In 1999 Sierra Mac River Trips took some 1,000 clients (40 percent repeaters) down California's wildest river, long considered the mecca for technical rafting

in the western United States.

"River-running has become a religion for me," McDonnell admits. "I live for the high-water trips. Then it's like the difference between riding a pony and an elephant. It's much more powerful. When you are connected to the river during the high water, there's much greater energy, which I find more thrilling."

McDonnell was born in 1950 in Mill Valley, across the bay from San Francisco. He readily admits that his older sister Candy was the single biggest influence in his young life. She was one of California's first kayakers, skilled enough to compete in a national slalom on the Feather River. She let her younger brother tag along and encouraged him to build his own kayaks and take them out to the ocean, where he rode them through the surf. He opened a little shop selling and renting kayaks and kayaking equipment.

In 1962, at his sister's urging, young McDonnell and his parents signed on for a rafting trip down the Sacramento River run by Bryce Whitmore's Wilderness Waterways, the first outfitter on the Stanislaus and the main Tuolumne Rivers. He was only 12 at the time but big and tall for his age, and that summer he discovered he had an intuitive grasp of white-water rafting. Whitmore promised to train and then hire him as a river guide after his 15th birthday.

In the meantime, in 1963 McDonnell and his family took a two-week camping trip to British Columbia where they ran the Canoe River, a major tributary of the Columbia. The two children were in kayaks, the parents in a yellow raft. "This trip introduced me to the magic of the wilderness," McDonnell recalls. "We were alone on the river. For the first time I found myself immersed in the rhythms of nature away from the distractions of modern civilization."

The summer after he turned 15 McDonnell went to work for Whitmore's Wilderness Waterways. At 18 he entered Sonoma State College and majored in philosophy while leading river trips during his summers. Then during Marty's junior year Whitmore decided to move to Oregon and focus on the Rogue River. He sold his young guide his Tuolumne and Stanislaus operations. For his first two years McDonnell ran Wilderness Waterways strictly as a summer business while he competed his degree.

"Even at that young age I knew I wanted to go into business for myself," McDonnell says. "Upon graduation I went full-time into rafting as my career of choice and have never regretted that decision."

In 1972, the first year officially for Sierra Mac River Trips, McDonnell carried 1,200 clients, mostly on the Stanislaus River. Soon afterwards he started running trips down the Klamath, Merced, and south fork of the American. He decided from the first to concentrate his efforts on California rivers.

"What was important for me was to be able to go on my own trips on a regular basis," McDonnell reflects. "I got into this business to be on the river. I decided to focus on one watershed, get to know it real well, and do an excellent job of providing rafting trips. And I also wanted to concentrate on those rivers offering Class IV and V white-water experiences, a niche no one else had taken. We encourage our clients to have had previous white-water experience but it is not mandatory. We start our more demanding trips with a two-hour training seminar. Afterwards, if we feel someone does not possess those skills necessary to manage the river, then we send them back in the van."

The young McDonnell soon began to fantasize about rafting the upper Tuolumne, which the current Sierra Mac River Trips catalog calls "the most challenging run in the U.S. and the standard by which Class V runs are measured." Back then it was considered unrunnable, with a gradient twice as steep as any other American river. In one mile-long section the river plummets 200 feet.

To prepare for this first descent McDonnell quickly demonstrated himself to be an innovator and a Benjamin Franklin of the river. He modified his Huck Finn rafts, which had four tubes side-by-side. He eliminated the two center tubes, which made the resulting craft much more agile, maneuverable, and faster. He called his creations "spider boats" or "catarafts."

In 1972 McDonnell and his friend Walt Harvest, a strong rafter, launched the first run of the Cherry Creek stretch of the upper Tuolumne River. They wore helmets, unusual for rafters in those early days, and took climbing gear along in case they had to line their rafts through rapids or belay them down the sheer walls of the canyon if they portaged. They launched just before dawn. They were two miles downstream, scouting a rapid they named Corkscrew, when the sun finally climbed above the canyon wall. McDonnell later wrote up the experience for a guidebook on California rivers:

"It was like a dream come true. To our amazement, we found that we were able to run one after another of these fearsome chutes and drops. The rapids that later became Mushroom, Lewis's Leap, and Flat Rock Falls caused us the most hesitation. We could hardly believe we were really doing it. Our euphoria almost ran away with us. . . . We ran the upper Tuolumne twice more that spring, and by the time the summer came around our concept of rafting had been transformed. After that, though we continued to respect it, the main Tuolumne looked almost flat."

Today McDonnell offers regularly scheduled one-day trips down a nine-mile stretch of the upper Tuolumne. Because of the powerful Class V white water the company requires all rafters take a training seminar and pass a Class V paddler's test before allowing them on the river.

Sierra Mac River Trips also offers one-, two-, and three-day trips down an 18-mile stretch of the main Tuolumne from Meral's Pool to Ward's Ferry. Other favorites on the same watershed are one-day trips down the Giant Gap section of the north fork of the American, another river with Class V white water lying at the bottom of a 2,000-foot-deep canyon; and the Chamberlain Falls section of the same river, which offers Class IV white water.

McDonnell reflects today on what makes his company distinctive from the other operators in the area: "One area in which we differ from our competitors lies in the age and maturity of our guides. Most have had 10 or 12 years experience on these rivers. We also put six guides with every group of 20 clients, which is rare in this industry. And our trips offer true wilderness experiences. Over 100,000 people run the American River each year, compared to the 7,500 on the lower Tuolumne and 250 or so on the upper Tuolumne. On our trips our clients will go the entire time without seeing another group of rafters."

McDonnell has also been a major force in the conservation movement for California river preservation. He was heavily involved in the losing struggle to save the Stanislaus River from drowning after the U.S. Army Corps of Engineers built a controversial dam. Then he switched his attention to the Tuolumne when three dams there were proposed. The lessons he and other conservationists had learned from the first battle for the Stanislaus were instrumental in their success at saving the Tuolumne. In 1984 McDonnell flew to Washington, where he testified before a Congressional committee. Soon afterwards the Tuolumne received federal certification as a wild and scenic river, thus saving it from destruction. Then a few years later another fight loomed over the Clavey River, the Tuolumne's major tributary, which two major irrigation districts wanted to dam. Because of the efforts of McDonnell and others the permits to construct the dam were denied.

"Our focus now is to educate the public on how important it is to manage a river as a watershed resource, to look at the broader picture," McDonnell says. "We set up a visitors' center to do just this sort of education."

Through Sierra Mac River Trips McDonnell also operates one of the most highly acclaimed white-water rafting schools in the western United States. The week-long course is designed primarily for sports enthusiasts rather than people who want to become professional river guides.

A recent innovation at Sierra Mac River Trips has been custom trips for couples seeking a wilderness experience in which to get married or renew their wedding vows. McDonnell has his minister's license and performs the ceremonies. Recently, a wedding party chartered one of his California Roll trips. He performed the wedding service that first evening in camp as the sun set. "It was a fairy-tale experience," he says.

"Rafting takes me away from all the hassles of the complex society in which we live," observes McDonnell. "For me the river means freedom. I guess it's the Huck Finn in me!"

7

CANOE EXPEDITIONS

"The movement of a canoe is like a reed in the wind," Sigurd F. Olson observed years ago in *The Lonely Land.* "Silence is a part of it, and the sounds of lapping water, bird songs, and the wind in the trees. . . . A man is part of his canoe and therefore part of all it knows. The instant he dips his paddle, he flows as it flows, the canoe yielding to his slightest touch and responsive to his slightest whim and thought."

The romance of the canoe tugs at our imagination in ways a raft or kayak can never do. The canoe has figured in history and adventure on the North American continent from the earliest days. Its design remains virtually unchanged since the 17th century when the legendary French voyageurs heaped steel knives, red wool blankets, tomahawks, mirrors, and other trade items into 35-foot-long birch-bark canoes and set out for the unexplored interior of North America.

Modern canoes are made of aluminum, magnesium, plastic and glass fibers, molded plywood, or canvas over wood frames. But they still allow the adventurous traveler to paddle into the American past on routes once taken by the voyageurs. In 1979 a newlywed couple from Bend, Oregon, made the first transcontinental canoe journey. Paddling an estimated one million strokes each, Cathy and Greg Jensen completed their canoe and portage journey from Astoria, Oregon, to Savannah, Georgia, in eight months.

Canoes are fast, light, and highly maneuverable. With each stroke you come to know your boat better until, after a time, it becomes an extension of your own body, as Olson noted. Once you have mastered some of the basic skills and strokes, you can join any number of organized canoeing trips into wilderness areas inaccessible by other means. A guided canoe trip down a wild river differs in fundamental ways from a rafting experience. You, not the guide, are in charge. Your strokes, not those of the guide, count. Your skill with a paddle determines how you fare in white water and whether or not you collide with rocks or roll over in a hole. And a good guide provides solid instruction, allowing his or her people to raise their levels of paddling experience while building their self-confidence.

A swiftly moving river has long been a source of fascination, and the canoe a perfect way to indulge that fascination. "A canoe trip has become simply a rite of oneness with a certain terrain," John McPhee wrote in *The Survival of the Bark Canoe,* "a diversion of the field, an act performed not because it is necessary but because there is value in the act itself."

AFRICA

ZAMBIA

Canoe Safari

The quiet of canoe travel means paddlers enjoy some of the finest African wildlife viewing possible. On this trip they travel down the Lower Zambezi River, an excellent way to approach the wildlife that live in the river or come to its banks to drink. Participants can expect to see, as they paddle by, hundreds of hippos and numerous other animals, including elephants and lions, at the water's edge. The area is also rich in exotic birds. At the end of the river portion, participants travel by vehicle through Lower Zambezi National Park for wildlife viewing that includes large populations of buffaloes, waterbucks, zebras, elephants, lions, leopards, and many species of birds.

Operator: Himalayan Travel/The Imaginative Traveler, 110 Prospect St., Stamford, Conn. 06901; (800) 225-2380 or (203) 359-3711; www.gorp.com/himtravel.htm
Price: Moderate.
Season: Throughout the year.
Length: 6 days.
Accommodations: Riverside camps. Five percent discount with BBAT coupon.

CANADA

NEWFOUNDLAND

Newfoundland Sampler

Newfoundland is a land of magnificent contrasts, with its rugged coasts, majestic fjords, fast-running rivers, and open valleys. Paddlers on this trip explore from the picturesque fishing village of Burgeo to the dramatic landscape of Gros Morne National Park, spending three days of leisurely paddling on the coastline near Burgeo, a seascape of rocky islands, sandy beaches, and sheer cliffs where an abundance of marine life can be observed in the crystal-clear waters. They then canoe the Lloyds River, for hundreds of years used by the local Indians for their seasonal migrations; the Humber

Operator: Battenkill Canoe, 6328 Historic Route 7A, Arlington, Vt. 05250; (800) 421-5268 or (802) 362-2800; www.battenkill.com.
Price: Moderate.
Season: July–September.
Length: 7 days.
Accommodations: Inns and guest houses. Five percent discount with BBAT coupon.

The Soper River on Baffin Island offers hardy paddlers the challenge of canoeing Canada's northernmost river

Martin Brown/Sunrise County Canoe

River, a remote waterway rarely visited by outsiders; and the Grandy's River which ends in a breathtaking waterfall. A stay is also made in Gros Morne National Park, which was proclaimed a UNESCO World Heritage site in 1987.

NORTHWEST TERRITORIES

The Ultimate Northern Canoe Trip

Operator:
Sunrise Expeditions, Cathance Lake, Grove Post Office, Maine 04638; (800) RIVER-30 or (207) 454-7708; www.expeditionlogistics.com
Price: Expensive.
Season: July and August.
Length: 9 days.
Accommodations: Tent camps. Five percent discount with BBAT coupon.

The Soper River on Baffin Island is the northernmost navigable river in the eastern Arctic, and it is navigable for only a short time each year. Flowing only during July to mid-August, the river is frozen the rest of the year. The first descent by canoe was not made until July 1990. Members of these expeditions paddle through spectacular and dramatic northern landscape—flowering tundra and narrow gorges, with thin wisps of waterfalls drifting off steeply terraced escarpments. The river also offers a fair amount of Class II and III white water. At the end of the trip, paddlers spend two days at Lake Harbour, an Inuit village renowned for the excellence of its soapstone carvings.

QUEBEC

The Ashuapmushuan River

Sometimes called the Chamouchouane, the Ashuapmushuan River flows out of the Ashuapmushuan Reserve and picks up the flow of the Riviere du Chef to become a river of major proportions. This was the major means of access to the northern interior for 18th-century French explorers. Canoeists on this trip paddle just under 100 miles through a wilderness devoid of human signs. The white-water stretches are long and runnable, with the exception of a few Class IV and V drops that require portaging. A special treat is the Chauirere Falls which has several drops, the biggest 60 feet. (This is portaged.) The pike fishing is excellent. The operator runs this trip at the height of the summer blueberry season.

Operator:
Allagash Canoe Trips,
P.O. Box 713,
Greenville, Maine 04441;
(207) 695-3668.
Price: Moderate.
Season: August.
Length: 7 days.
Accommodations: Tent camps. Five percent discount with BBAT coupon.

YUKON TERRITORY

In the Footsteps of the Klondikers

The fifth-longest river system in North America, the Yukon flows almost 2,000 miles to empty into the Bering Sea. In 1898 over 30,000 gold-seekers made their way down the river to the gold fields near Dawson City. The Yukon's banks are still littered with abandoned relics from that exciting period—Indian camps, trappers' cabins, old Northwest Mounted Police posts, and steamboat wrecks. Members on these paddling expeditions launch their canoes on the Big Salmon River, a tributary of the Yukon River. The mighty Yukon flows wide, deep, and fast through a landscape of rolling hills and steep bluffs heavily timbered with forests of pine, fir, and poplar.

Operator:
Wilderness Inquiry, 1313
Fifth St., SE, Box 84,
Minneapolis, Minn. 55414;
(800) 728-0719 or
(612) 379-3858;
www.wildernessinquiry.org.
Price: Moderate.
Season: July.
Length: 16 days.
Accommodations: Tent camps. Five percent discount with BBAT coupon.

"Travelling is more fun—hell, life is more fun—if you treat it as a series of impulses."

BILL BRYSON
NEITHER HERE NOR THERE: TRAVELS IN EUROPE

EUROPE

ICELAND

Canoeing the Land of Fire and Ice

Operator:
Sunrise Expeditions,
Cathance Lake,
Grove Post Office, Maine
04657; (800) RIVER-30 or
(207) 454-7708;
www.expeditionlogistics.com
Price: Expensive.
Season: July.
Length: 10 days.
Accommodations: Tent
camps. Five percent dis-
count with BBAT coupon.

Iceland lies just south of the Arctic Circle, astride the great crack in the earth's surface known as the Mid-Atlantic Rift, and is famous for its active volcanoes, geysers, and glaciers. The vast, uninhabited, and intensely surreal interior is technically Europe's greatest wilderness and its only desert. This is a stark and imposing tundra, characterized by immense black lava fields, volcanic craters, snow-capped peaks, ice caves, and bizarrely shaped headlands. In Icelandic folklore this region was the home of legendary outlaws and an assortment of mythical creatures. Paddlers on these rigorous expeditions run two rivers, neither of which had been run before 1994—the lunar-like Tungnaa, which flows from Europe's largest glacier; and the Pjorsa, which features spectacular gorges and miles of moderate Class II white water.

LATIN AMERICA

COSTA RICA

Canoeing the Rain Forests

Operator:
Battenkill Canoe, P.O. Box
65, Historic Route 7A,
Arlington, Vt. 05250;
(800) 421-5268 or
(802) 362-2800;
www.battenkill.com.
Price: Moderate.
Season: December–March.
Length: 11 days.

A beautiful, peaceful Central American country, Costa Rica is a gem of wonderful natural diversity. The country's rivers are the finest for canoeing in all the region. Participants on these trips experience a variety of rivers, beginning with a paddle down the Rio Peñas Blancas through a river corridor carved out of dense rain forest. Next, they travel along the Rio Arenal, a quiet, isolated river dominated by a volcano. Other highlights include the Rio Frio through the Caño Negro Wildlife Refuge,

Canoes offer visitors to Costa Rica an unparalleled way to explore the wonders of a tropical rain forest

Battenkill Canoe

a remote haven for birds, caymans, sloths, howler monkeys, and numerous other animals; the Rio San Juan, along the border with Nicaragua; and the Sarapiqui River, which flows through rain forest and farmland and offers a variety of small rapids. This is one of the best adventures going in Costa Rica.

Accommodations: Lodges. Five percent discount with BBAT coupon.

UNITED STATES

ALASKA

Noatak River Canoeing

The Noatak spills out of the Brooks Range and flows 400 miles west to Kotzebue Sound, running its entire length north of the Arctic Circle. These expeditions begin with a bush-plane flight from Bettles. Canoeists paddle the upper reaches of the Noatak, which offers the most spectacular scenery. Wildlife observation and fishing are excellent. The late-August trip includes a chance to see Arctic caribou migrating to the south slope of the Brooks Range. The sight of these animals thundering across the tundra and swimming the river is one of North America's great wildlife spectacles.

Operator:
Alaska Discovery,
5310 Glacier Hwy.,
Juneau, Alaska 99801;
(800) 586-1911 or
(907) 780-6226;
www.akdiscovery.com.
Price: Expensive.
Season: August.
Length: 10 days.
Accommodations: Tent camps. Five percent discount with BBAT coupon.

FLORIDA

Northern Florida Rivers

Operator:
St. Regis Canoe Outfitters,
P.O. Box 318,
Lake Clear, N.Y. 12945;
(888) 775-2925 or
(518) 891-1838;
www.canoeoutfitters.com.
Price: Moderate.
Season: March.
Length: 8 days.
Accommodations: Bed-and-breakfasts. Five percent discount with BBAT coupon.

Far from the crowded tourist meccas of Orlando and Miami, northern Florida offers a canoeist's paradise with some 500 miles of free-flowing rivers. Canoeists on these trips paddle a different river each day and return to the comfort of a B&B each evening. Often they find themselves traversing a wilderness area of ancient pine and cypress trees where signs of people are rare. Along the way they explore isolated sandy beaches, silent swamps, and refreshing springs while paddling the Santa Fe, Itchetucknee, Suwanee, Oclockonee, Aucilla, and Wacissa Rivers.

By Canoe Through Everglades National Park

Another of the country's unique ecosystems, the

The Adventure Travel Hall of Fame: VERLEN KRUGER

The world champion for long-distance canoeing is undoubtedly Verlen Kruger, a man obsessed with exploring the North American continent by canoe. In 1971 he traversed 7,000 miles of Canadian and Alaskan waters, following a historic fur-trade route from Montreal to the Bering Sea. Then in late April of 1980 he and his son-in-law started out on a 3.5-year, 28,000-mile canoe odyssey around the North American continent. "The canoe is my home," he would insist to curious well-wishers along the way. "It isn't just a canoe trip anymore, this is my life." After 20,000 miles,

when they were in Santa Barbara, California, his son-in-law suddenly had to return home for a family emergency. Kruger, a man in his early sixties, then invited Valerie Fons, a 31-year-old woman whose only previous canoe experience was on placid lakes and bays, to join him for the most dangerous portion of his Ultimate Canoe Challenge—becoming the first people to circumnavigate Baja California's 2,411 miles of desert coasts in canoes. Fons quickly agreed and then quit her job, sold her car, rented her house, put her furniture in storage, assembled her gear, settled her affairs, and had her long hair cut short.

Everglades are characterized by hundreds of square miles of water slowly migrating through sawgrass prairies toward the sea. The largest subtropical wilderness in North America, it teems with wildlife, including over 300 species of birds. Paddlers on this expedition travel through the maze of mangrove islands, bays, and channels of the Ten Thousand Islands area of the park. Alligators and manatees are common in this area. This trip offers a perfect opportunity to people seeking a greater understanding of the trials, tribulations, and fragile beauty of one of our finest national parks.

Operator: Wilderness Inquiry, 1313 Fifth St. SE, Box 84, Minneapolis, Minn. 55414; (800) 728-0719 or (612) 379-3858; www.wildernessinquiry.org. *Price:* Moderate. *Season:* January–March. *Length:* 6 days. *Accommodations:* Tent camps set up on the sandy beaches of subtropical keys. Five percent discount with BBAT coupon.

"Tourists don't know where they've been. Travelers don't know where they're going."

PAUL THEROUX
THE HAPPY ISLES OF OCEANIA

The pair departed Santa Barbara on October 25, 1982. At first seasickness nearly caused Fons to give up, but Kruger linked their canoes together, paddled for both of them, and encouraged her to keep going. As her strength returned, she adjusted to life in a 17-foot, one-person canoe. "I couldn't help but think of the various conditions of the sea as its different moods," she wrote later in her book, Keep It Moving: Baja by Canoe. "I knew when the sea was angry and I knew when it was being coy. The sea played by its own rules, and to succeed Verlen and I had to accept them. I had not been able to change the sea one bit, but it was changing me." On February 2 the pair reached San Felipe, the final stop for Fons's portion of Kruger's Ultimate Canoe Challenge. His son-in-law rejoined the expedition, and the two men continued paddling another 4,800 miles before arriving home in Lansing, Michigan.

In April of 1984 Fons rejoined Kruger and the two raced the entire 2,348-mile length of the Mississippi in 23 days, 10 hours, and 20 minutes, setting a new world record for the fastest time canoeing downstream on the Mississippi and earning a place in the Guinness Book of World Records. On April 3, 1986, they were married. Two months later they departed from Inuvik, Northwest Territories, on a 21,000-mile canoe voyage down the Pacific coasts of North, Central, and South America to Cape Horn, Chile.

IDAHO

In the Footsteps of Lewis and Clark on the Missouri River

Operator:
River Odysseys West,
P.O. Box 579, Coeur
d'Alene, Idaho 83816;
(800) 451-6034 or
(208) 765-0841;
www.rowinc.com.
Price: Expensive.
Season: June–mid-
September.
Length: 3 and 5 days.
Accommodations: Tent
camps. Ten percent dis-
count with BBAT coupon.

This is a river trip for history buffs, especially fans of Stephen Ambrose's best-selling history, *Undaunted Courage,* about the Lewis and Clark expedition. Today's travelers journey down the river on modern replicas of the 34-foot canoes used by the early voyageurs, or fur traders, who first explored the area. (They are also similar in size to the dugouts used by the Lewis and Clark expedition when they passed through here.) Each canoe carries up to 14 paddlers. The four-day trips focus on the White Cliffs area, while the six-day trips continue on for another 60 miles through the badlands of the Missouri River breaks. Side trips allow visits to long-abandoned homesteads; collections of tipi rings, century-old relics of Blackfeet Indian encampments; and a hideout used by Butch Cassidy, the Sundance Kid, and their Hole-in-the-Wall gang. The lack of white water makes this an especially good trip for families.

MAINE

St. John River

Operator:
Allagash Canoe Trips,
P.O. Box 713,
Greenville, Maine 04441;
(207) 695-3668.
Price: Moderate.
Season: May.
Length: 7 days.
Accommodations: Tent
camps. Five percent dis-
count with BBAT coupon.

Many consider this the most magnificent paddle in the eastern United States. Almost every site along the 140-mile river is a place of historical interest, strewn with turn-of-the-century artifacts left by lumberjacks who lived, worked, and died in the wild Maine woods. Paddlers on this trip fly to the headwaters by floatplane from Moosehead Lake. With only a few miles of lake paddling at the start, the rest is all river travel, often interspersed with Class I and II rapids. The longest and wildest free-flowing river left in the eastern United States, the St. John is flanked by beautiful woodland abundant in wildlife.

A party of paddlers explores the Maine wilderness along St. John River

Allagash Canoe Trips

Saint Croix River

Flowing out of a chain of wilderness lakes, the Saint Croix runs through the beautiful woodlands of eastern Maine along the border with Canada. Its long stretches of easy white water with only a few precipitous drops make this an ideal river for novices. In the 19th century the Saint Croix was popular with the timber industry for floating logs to the mills, but now nature has reclaimed the area. Bald eagles are common once again, and paddlers can expect to see moose, black bear, deer, and loons. The small-

Operator: Sunrise Expeditions, Cathance Lake, Grove Post Office, Maine 04638; (800) RIVER-30 or (207) 454-7708; www.expeditionlogistics.com
Price: Moderate.
Season: June–early October.
Length: 4 or 6 days.
Accommodations: Tent camps. Five percent discount with BBAT coupon.

"And suddenly a puff of wind, a puff faint and tepid and laden with strange odors of blossoms and aromatic wood, comes out of the still night— the first sigh of the East on my face."

JOSEPH CONRAD
"YOUTH"

A couple relaxes in camp in the Boundary Waters Canoe Area, America's only wilderness set aside for canoeists

Gunflint Northwoods Outfitters

mouth bass fishing is excellent. The operator specializes in instruction, including lessons in the long-forgotten art of poling. The most popular month to paddle the Saint Croix is September, when the trees are ablaze with color and thousands of migrating birds fill the skies overhead.

MINNESOTA

The Boundary Waters Wilderness

Operator:
Gunflint Northwoods
Outfitters, 143 S.
Gunflint Lake, Grand
Marais, Minn. 55604;
(800) 328-3325 or
(218) 388-2296;
www.gunflintoutfitters.com.
Price: Moderate.
Season: July and September.
Length: 7 days.
Accommodations: Tent
camps. Five percent discount with BBAT coupon.

Dividing the United States and Canada along 200 miles of border, the Boundary Waters Canoe Area (BWCA) encompasses a million acres and a thousand lakes. It is America's only wilderness canoeing country. On the Canadian side of the border, Ontario's Quetico Provincial Park adds another million acres of water wilderness to the area. In BWCA, 300-year-old pines shelter a host of wildlife, ranging from moose and Canadian lynxes to black bear, otters, bald eagles, and wolves. This magnificent country is one of the last intact wilderness areas left in the "Lower 48." Canoeists on these expeditions journey deep into the heart of the wilderness, following in the footsteps of 17th-century voyageurs who traveled these waters in massive, 35-foot birch-bark canoes.

Lodge-to-Lodge Canoeing in the Boundary Waters

Canoeists on these expeditions spend four nights in lodges and two nights camping. The trip begins at Gunflint Lodge on historic Gunflint Lake, the place where early explorers launched their journeys deep into the interior of North America. Guests stay in cabins, most with fireplaces. The serene BWCA waterways offer quiet paddling, plentiful wildlife, and excellent fishing. The second night is at Nor'Wester Lodge, a family resort dating back to the 1930s and furnished with family heirlooms and antiques. Canoeists then circle back to Gunflint before running the famous Granite River, actually a series of small interconnected lakes with numerous waterfalls and rapids. The operator provides all equipment, a guide, and camp cook.

Operator:
Gunflint Northwoods Outfitters, 143 S. Gunflint Lake, Grand Marais, Minn. 55604; (800) 328-3325 or (218) 388-2296; www.gunflintoutfitters.com.
Price: Moderate.
Season: July–September.
Length: 7 days.
Accommodations: Lodges and tent camps. Five percent discount with BBAT coupon.

"One of the best places you can go in a canoe is the wilderness. And what, you may ask, is so great about that? The silence, for one thing. In real wilderness, silence is not just quiet, which is the absence of noise. It is the voice of the living earth, unmuddied by aural clutter."

ROBERT KIMBER
A CANOEIST'S SKETCHBOOK

NEW YORK

Canoeing Adirondack Park

Long a mecca for canoeists, New York's glorious Adirondack Park covers more than 6 million acres and boasts almost 3,000 lakes and ponds and 1,500 miles of rivers. Particularly popular are the Saranac Lakes and the St. Regis Canoe Wilderness area. This operator offers a dozen varieties of canoe expeditions through various regions of Adirondack Park, ranging in time from one to nine days, including both camping and lodge-to-lodge trips. Guides maintain a relaxed pace with stops for wildlife observation, short hikes into the forest, swimming, and fishing.

Operator:
St. Regis Canoe Outfitters, P.O. Box 318, Lake Clear, N.Y. 12945; (888) 775-2925 or (518) 891-1838; www.canoeoutfitters.com.
Price: Inexpensive to moderate.
Season: April–mid-October.
Length: Check with operator.
Accommodations: Tent camps. Five percent discount with BBAT coupon.

NORTH CAROLINA

Canoe School

Operator: Nantahala Outdoor Center, 13077 Hwy. 19 West, Bryson City, N.C. 28713; (888) 662-1662 or (828) 488-2175; www.noc.com. *Price:* Moderate. *Season:* March–October. *Length:* 2 and 4 days. *Accommodations:* A rustic motel near the Nantahala Center or camping along a river.

The Nantahala Outdoor Center sponsors the country's finest and most comprehensive canoe school. White-water courses ranging from three days to a week are offered in five skill levels, from novice to expert. Special courses for women, people over 40, handicapped persons, and children are also scheduled. The beginners' five-day course includes three days practicing techniques in the slower waters of the Nantahala River, then two days of instruction in white-water canoeing. On the final day they make a run through a major rapid under instructors' watchful eyes. Other classes for intermediate and advanced canoeists are offered on the Chattooga and Ococee rivers.

"When Dr. David Livingstone was working in Africa, a group of friends wrote him: 'We would like to send other men to you. Have you found a good road into your area yet?' According to a member of his family, Dr. Livingstone sent this message in reply: 'If you have men who will come only if they know there is a good road, I don't want them. I want men who will come if there is no road at all."

LEWIS TIMBERLAKE
TIMBERLAKE MONTHLY

The Adventure Travel Hall of Fame: DON STARKELL

On June 1, 1980, divorced father Don Starkell and his two teenage sons departed from Winnipeg in a 21-foot canoe and started paddling south. Twenty-three months later, two of them swept down the Amazon River to Belem, Brazil, on the Atlantic. Their route had taken them down the entire length of the Mississippi River, along the Gulf coasts of Texas and Mexico, down the Caribbean coast of Central America, along the coasts of Columbia and

Battenkill Canoe offers popular inn-to-inn canoeing trips which allow paddlers the opportunity to explore a variety of the state's wild rivers

Battenkill Canoe

TEXAS

Rio Grande Canoeing

The Rio Grande marks the boundary between the United States and Mexico. Much of the time it flows through a haunted desert landscape of volcanic hills and mountains and deep gorges, an area now protected as Big Bend National Park. Canoeists on these expeditions paddle the lower canyons, the most isolated and spectacular section of all. The river flows between sky-scraping cliffs and past banks overgrown with tamarisk and bam-

Operator:
Sunrise Expeditions,
Cathance Lake, Grove Post
Office, Maine 04638;
(800) RIVER-30 or
(207) 454-7708;
www.expeditionlogistics.com
Price: Moderate.
Season: March and April.

Venezuela, then 500 miles up the Orinoco River to the Rio Negro, and into the Amazon at Manaus. By trip's end father and son (the second son had dropped out at Veracruz, Mexico) had paddled more than 20 million strokes and covered 12,192 miles. Along the way they encountered piranhas, wild pigs, and hungry crocodiles. They had been arrested, mistaken for spies, and attacked by coastal pirates and drug smugglers. They had survived terrifying hurricanes, food poisoning, and near-starvation. After their return to Canada, Starkell reflected in his book, Paddle the Amazon, "Our trip taught us an awful lot about how small we are in the broad scope of things—and about the importance of faith and determination in overcoming that smallness."

Length: 7 days.
Accommodations: Tent camps. Five percent discount with BBAT coupon.

boo. Stops are made for hikes up tributary canyons and soaks in hot springs. This trip appeals to both beginning and intermediate canoeists.

VERMONT

Vermont River Sampler

Operator: Battenkill Canoe, 6328 Historic Route 7A, Arlington, Vt. 05250; (800) 421-5268 or (802) 362-2800; www.battenkill.com.
Price: Expensive.
Season: May–October.
Length: 5 days.
Accommodations: Country inns. Five percent discount with BBAT coupon.

After bicyclists, hikers, and cross-country skiers discovered the delights of traveling inn-to-inn through Vermont, it was only a matter of time before the canoeists fell into step. What all seek is a spirited adventure vacation but not at the expense of luxury. Inns offer the twofold advantages of comfort and excellent food. Canoeists on these trips paddle down the Batten Kill River, a swift tributary of the Hudson River and an excellent river for beginners; the upper Connecticut, which runs through unspoiled rural New England scenery at its finest; the Lamoille River, with wide-open views of valleys and interesting geological rock formations; and the White River, an excellent mixture of flat-water and quick water, with Class I and II rapids to spice up the paddling.

PROFILE

BRUCE KERFOOT
GUNFLINT NORTHWOODS OUTFITTERS

"I was raised in the wilderness of northern Minnesota and learned my woods skills from the Chippewa Indians who lived in the area and worked for my parents' small outfitting company," Bruce Kerfoot recalls today. "After my 14th birthday, the Indians began teaching me what I needed to know to survive. When they went on a moose hunt, spent a few days on a remote lake harvesting whitefish, or checked their traplines, they invited me along. As I got older and began to assume greater responsibilities guiding fishermen on canoe trips in the Boundary Waters Canoe Area Wilderness, my Indian friends always kept an eye on me from a distance to make certain I never got into a situation I couldn't handle."

Today Kerfoot's Gunflint Northwoods Outfitters is the largest company in the big Boundary Waters Canoe Area Wilderness. The third generation of Kerfoots to run the business, he has seen the simple fishing camp run by his grandparents in the late 1920s grow over the years to encompass a year-round lodge with a dining room noted for its chef and fine wine cellar, 25 modern log cabins, a store, and an outfitting business that runs a variety of guided canoe trips throughout the surrounding region. Altogether the company handles over 8,000 clients a year, about a third of the total number visiting the area, 20 percent of whom sign on one of the guided canoe trip departures for which the Kerfoots are famous. (Another 1,500 or so take advantage of the outfitting services and go into the wilderness on their own.) During winter months Kerfoot also offers guests a variety of other adventures, including cross-country skiing, lodge-to-lodge dogsledding, and snowshoeing.

The Boundary Waters Canoe Area Wilderness encompasses 1,100,000 acres of largely pristine wilderness, including over 1,000 lakes. The U.S. Forest Service has managed to preserve its primitive character to a great degree through careful management of the numbers of visitors allowed, of the timing and duration of each visit, and of the actual put-in points where canoeists are allowed to enter the wilderness.

Canoes have always been the primary means of transportation about the area. "Our waterways have always been our highways," Kerfoot notes. "Even today we have few roads into the wilderness. The culture of the

Chippewa Indians was based entirely on canoes. And when the French-Canadian traders first came into the area in the 18th century, they paddled birch-bark canoes for fur-trading companies. And canoes were the principal way we got around when I was a boy growing up."

Gunflint Lodge was a small fishing camp when Kerfoot's grandparents took it over in 1927. His mother, Justine, had graduated from Northwestern University with a degree in zoology and finished one year of graduate studies when the Great Depression settled in and she decided to join her parents at their fishing camp. Little did she know at the time that she would serve as the owner and operator for 51 years, until her retirement in 1979.

Bruce was born in 1938 during the Winter of the Great Snows. When Justine went out snowshoeing, she carried her infant son on her back in a papoose-carrier a local Chippewa woman had given her. Bruce and his two sisters grew up leading a frontier existence in extreme isolation. As he recalls today:

"We never gave our isolation a second thought. Our home was a three-room log cabin my mother had built. Every Saturday night my sisters and I took a bath in our kitchen in a galvanized metal tub Mom also used for the laundry. We each had only two sets of clothes. We got around back then by canoes in summer and dogsleds in winter. Our only neighbors were a small group of Chippewa Indians, and one a week would come by our small fishing camp for a visit. We were too remote to pick up any transmissions from radio stations. During each fall we stockpiled enough supplies to see us through the long winter. We bought sacks of wild rice from the Indians at 25 cents a pound and cartons of canned goods from a small store in the little community of Grand Marais 45 miles away. Mom shot us deer. Venison and fresh fish were all the meat we ate. The only vegetables I ate as a boy were from a can. Mom handled all our schooling at home, which was true of most of the kids I knew whose families lived out in the woods. We had no electricity, of course, so we had to do our studying in the evening with the help of a kerosene lantern. I took my last two years of high school at the public school in Grand Marais where I boarded with a family. Before my high-school graduation ceremony I had never worn a coat and tie."

Kerfoot graduated in 1960 from Cornell University, with a major in hotel administration. He then spent two years in the Army and then returned to his parents' lodge. "I was never tempted to resettle in a large city," he says. "I worked one summer with a travel agency in the Twin Cities. But my wilderness upbringing made me too independent to work for someone else or live in a large city. So I returned to the lodge and have been there ever since."

When Kerfoot began working at Gunflint Outfitters, the operation catered strictly to a clientele of serious fishermen and offered them rather primitive

accommodations. "Small, uncomfortable cabins with no inside plumbing and a cook whose previous experience was cooking for lumberjacks in a timber camp was what our business was back then," he says. Under his supervision over the years Gunflint Trail Outfitters was transformed from a small fishing camp to a complex of handcrafted log cabins surrounding one of the finest lodges in northern Minnesota. There have been other changes as well. Kerfoot adds:

"We now have a modern paved road into the area and electricity to the lodge and cabins. This means more people. Our summer population has more than doubled. In our county we now have 4,000 residents. It's getting crowded. I've a neighbor living within a mile now! I may have to put curtains on our cabin windows!"

Over 25,000 people each summer visit the area to canoe and stay in the lodges and cabins scattered along the Gunflint Trail. A large portion book their wilderness experiences through Gunflint Northwoods Outfitters. Kerfoot's small store has 125 canoes for rent and sells a selection of wilderness foods, fishing tackle, outdoor clothing, and other items.

Kerfoot has been active in local environmental politics. "I've tried to maintain a balance between preservation and reasonable recreational use of our wilderness," he says. "Before, we had a problem developing with canoeists leaving behind too much plastic and glass. So I persuaded the other outfitters not to provide anything in cans or bottles. Now most of us don't even use twist-ties. That helps keep our wilderness free from non-biodegradable garbage. Most of us also agreed not to allow snowmobiling during the winter months. We emphasize the silent sports that are compatible with our wilderness values."

Kerfoot and his neighbors are seeing a different mix of people visiting them now, more honeymooners and families. Recently he has expanded his business to target families interested in adventure-travel experiences that are both fun and educational. "We have interpretative naturalists on hand who lead nature walks. One of our most popular programs allows children and their parents to go out by canoes in the company of a naturalist to a remote piece of shoreline and then explore a dense forest environment to learn exactly what the complexities are. Another popular program is an early morning paddle in canoes for a breakfast cookout. We get the children involved with helping us fix breakfast and thus teach them some wilderness skills in the process. On another program we take kids into the forest and teach them how to read animal tracks, recognize the different forest edibles, and identify the different trees and birds they see. And, of course, on our overnight guided canoe trips we have special departures for families with younger children. We are making a big push in the area of family adventure travel."

8

KAYAK EXPEDITIONS

In the world of water sports, few adventures can match the thrill and immediacy of paddling one's kayak through a stretch of boiling white water at the bottom of a deep canyon. "Kayaking is to rafting as skiing is to tobogganing," insists Dana Olson, head of the Snake River Kayak and Canoe School. "There's something about being under your own power, in control of your kayak or skis, that's a real rush."

Elegantly simple in design, these sleek boats were original created over 5,000 years ago by Eskimo hunters, who shrank seal or other animal skins over a wooden frame. The kayak transformed Eskimo culture, giving its hunters mobility in the ice-filled seas and increasing their range enormously.

In the 1860s people began using kayaks recreationally to run European rivers. In the 1920s, enthusiasts first ventured into coastal waters. Today, expeditions by sea kayak have become increasingly popular with adventurous paddlers. One expedition paddled the 3,852 miles from Lisbon, Portugal, to the Virgin Island of St. Thomas, and another voyaged 9,400 miles around the entire coast of Australia.

Learning to kayak is easier and less dangerous than most people realize. Numerous kayak schools exist throughout the country, where novices can master the basic skills in small groups and a safe environment.

Students in the Sundance Kayak School tackle Upper Black Bar Falls

Sundance Expeditions

When Mark Billington and three friends paddled sea kayaks from Seattle to Ketchikan in southeastern Alaska and back, they encountered high winds, heavy rain, and large waves. But afterwards he recalled, "Those days gave my life a little more meaning, brought my values into focus, back to the basics of man's existence, back to the values of our ancestors, of quest and survival."

AUSTRALASIA

AUSTRALIA

Daintree Coastal Sea Kayak

The northern islands of the Great Barrier reef are among the loveliest and most isolated in Australia. Kayakers paddle among a variety of these tropical islands where two World Heritage areas meet—the Wet Tropics National Park and the Great Barrier Reef Marine Park. They travel through an area rich in marine life, including giant sea turtles, rare dugongs, manta rays, and dolphins. The opportunities for snorkeling and fishing over fringing coral reefs are excellent.

Operator: Adventure Center, 1311 63rd St., Suite 200, Emeryville, Calif. 94608; (800) 227-8747 or (510) 654-1879; www.adventure-center.com.
Price: Moderate.
Season: May–September.
Length: 7 days.
Accommodations: Beach camps. Five percent discount with BBAT coupon.

NEW ZEALAND

Exploring the Bay of Islands by Sea Kayak

Outside magazine calls New Zealand "an international hot spot for sea kayaking." These trips focus on the Bay of Islands, a 100-square-mile maritime park on the top of North Island, the homeland of the Maori civilization. Paddlers explore a vast sheltered bay blessed with a balmy subtropical climate, white-sand beaches, warm water, abundant fish and birdlife, and a treasure trove of green islands sporting wild basalt formations, sea caves, and Maori ruins. An additional attraction is kayak surfing at

Operator: New Zealand Adventures, HCR 56, Box 575, John Day, Ore. 97845; (541) 932-4925.
Price: Moderate.
Season: December–April.
Length: 5 and 10 days.
Accommodations: Shore camps. Five percent discount with BBAT coupon.

several beaches. Paddlers also have plenty of opportunity to enjoy the area's excellent fishing.

Running Seven Wild Rivers

Operator:
Dvorak's Kayak and Rafting Expeditions, 17921 U.S. Hwy. 285, Nathrop, Colo. 81236; (800) 824-3795 or (719) 539-6851; www.dvorakexpeditions.com
Price: Moderate.
Season: November–February.
Length: 10 and 17 days.
Accommodations: Tent camps and hotels. Five percent discount with BBAT coupon.

The rugged Kiwi backcountry has long been the domain of trekkers and campers. Kayakers have only recently begun to enjoy the opportunities offered by the variety of white-water rivers that spill out of the New Zealand mountain ranges. Unlike the United States, in New Zealand dams are fairly rare. And the water in nearly all of the country's wild rivers and lakes is still pure enough to drink, one more indication of their undeveloped state. Members of this expedition paddle seven rivers on both North and South Islands. These include the Motu, which starts flowing slowly through narrow rock canyons; the Rangitaiki, Rangitata, and Mohaka, all short but challenging paddles; the Kawarau, which boasts the Chinese Dogleg, the country's wildest rapid; the Shotover, which flows through historic gold camps before running into a mining tunnel, capped with a Class IV rapid; and finally the Landsborough, which requires a helicopter ride to reach its headwaters and the start of the paddle.

"I went to Asia, then, not only to see Asia, but also to see America, from a different vantage point and with new eyes. I left one kind of home to find another: to discover what resided in me and where I resided most fully, and so to better appreciate—in both senses of the word—the home I had left. The point was made best by one great traveler who saw the world without ever leaving home, and, indeed, created a home that was a world within— Thoreau: 'Our journeying is a great-circle sailing.'"

PICO IYER
VIDEO NIGHT IN KATHMANDU

CANADA

BRITISH COLUMBIA

A Lodge-Based Kayak Exploration of the Inside Passage

Located off the Canadian coast, Vancouver Island encompasses 10,000 square miles, most of it heavily wooded wilderness with 6,000-foot mountains. To the east, on the mainland of British Columbia, is the rugged Coast Range—its highest peak reaching nearly 14,000 feet. In between lies a beautiful glacier-carved channel called the Inside Passage. With a maze of beautiful islands, placid waterways, and excellent weather, this is one of North America's finest areas for kayaking. Participants on these trips spend their daylight hours leisurely exploring the splendid scenery of the Inside Passage in their kayaks. Wildlife is abundant, with pods of orca whales a common sight for paddlers. Trip members are flown in by chartered seaplane.

Operator: Northern Lights Expeditions, P.O. Box 4289, Bellingham, Wash. 98227; (800) 754-7402 or (360) 734-6334; www.seakayaking.com.
Price: Expensive.
Season: September.
Length: 6 days.
Accommodations: A four-star fishing lodge, the only structure on a remote island. Five percent discount with BBAT coupon.

Paddling Through Canada's Galapagos

Set 500 miles north of Vancouver, the Queen Charlotte Islands are often called the "Galapagos of the North." One-fourth of all the nesting seabirds on the Canadian Pacific Coast are found here, as well as the second-greatest concentration of nesting eagles in the world. The Haida Indians settled the area centuries ago, built great longhouses, and carved giant totem poles out of cedar trunks. From misty alpine heaths through lush primeval forests, past rich intertidal areas to the open sea, the Queen Charlotte Islands are a virtual layer-cake of life zones, each distinct from the rest and each one a great treasurehouse of biological marvels. The operator offers a variety of trips by sea kayak that allow paddlers to explore myriad bays, islets, channels, and the open coast with its wealth of natural and cultural history. Paddling distances

Operator: Ecosummer Expeditions, 936 Peace Portal Dr., P.O. Box 8014-240, Blaine, Wash. 98231; (800) 465-8884 or (604) 214-7484; www.ecosummer.com.
Price: Moderate.
Season: May–early September.
Length: 14 days.
Accommodations: Tent camps. Five percent discount with BBAT coupon.

are short, and paddlers have ample opportunity to visit important Indian sites, soak in hot springs, hike on picturesque alpine slopes, snorkel in clear waters filled with marine life, and fish for salmon. No previous experience with sea kayaks is required.

NORTHWEST TERRITORIES

Kayaking the Thomsen River, Banks Island

Operator:
Whitney & Smith
Legendary Expeditions,
P.O. Box 2097,
Banff, Alb., Canada
T0L 0C0; (403) 678-3052;
www.legendaryex.com.
Price: Expensive.
Season: June and July.
Length: 15 days.
Accommodations: Tent
camps. Five percent discount with BBAT coupon.

Banks Island—the westernmost island in the Canadian Arctic Archipelago—is the setting for this kayak expedition through one of Canada's newest national parks. Called Aulavik, meaning "a place where people travel," the park encompasses over 10,000 square miles of windswept tundra. Running through the heart of the park is the Banks River, a serene and slowly meandering waterway located some 600 miles north of the Arctic Circle. Kayakers will find themselves in an excellent position to observe the island's rich selection of wildlife, including the world's largest herd of musk oxen, some 70,000 animals, many of which graze along the banks of the river. They may also see groups of the endangered Peary caribou, the smallest of the caribou species, which migrate through the park each summer.

Kayaking the Fjords of Ellesmere Island

Operator:
Whitney & Smith
Legendary Expeditions,
P.O. Box 2097, Banff, Alb.,
Canada T0L 0C0;
(403) 678-3052;
www.legendaryex.com.
Price: Expensive.
Season: August.
Length: 15 days.
Accommodations: Tent
camps. Five percent discount with BBAT coupon.

A land of rugged mountains and immense glaciers, Ellesmere Island is a true Arctic desert, receiving only two more inches of precipitation annually than the Sahara. The area abounds in wildlife—mammoth musk oxen, Arctic hares by the hundreds, the rare Peary caribou, polar bears, wolves, and numerous species of birds. Because of the region's extreme isolation, many of these animals lack an instinctive fear of humans and often approach closely to satisfy their curiosity. Clients on this rigorous expedition kayak the great fjords much as the Inuit hunters did just a few decades

The fjords of Ellesmere Island with their many glaciers spilling into the sea offer sea kayakers one of the top Arctic adventures

Steve Smith/Whitney & Smith

ago, past spectacular scenery that includes hanging glaciers, glaciers flowing into the sea, and icebergs of all shapes and sizes. The operator has sent over 30 kayaking trips into the region over the past 15 years and knows the area intimately.

QUEBEC

Kayaking with Beluga Whales

This popular sea-kayaking adventure takes place off the mouth of the wild, unspoiled wilderness of the Saguenay River, which has carved one of North America's most imposing fjords. At this spot in the cold waters of the St. Lawrence River dozens of beluga whales congregate, along with a selection of fin, minke, and blue whales. This important feeding area offers some of the finest whale-watching in the northeast.

Operator:
Worldwide Adventures, 1170 Sheppard Ave. West, #45, Toronto, Ont., Canada M3K 2A3; (800) 387-1483 or (416) 633-5666; www.worldwidequest.com.
Price: Moderate.
Season: July and August.
Length: 8 days.
Accommodations: Tent camp. Five percent discount with BBAT coupon.

"When you have caught the rhythm of Africa, you find that it is the same in all her music."

ISAK DINESEN
OUT OF AFRICA

CARIBBEAN

BAHAMAS

By Sea Kayak Through the Exuma Islands

Operator: Ecosummer Expeditions, 936 Peace Portal Dr., P.O. Box 8014-240, Blaine, Wash. 98231; (800) 465-8884 or (604) 214-7484; www.ecosummer.com.
Price: Moderate.
Season: February–April.
Length: 7 and 14 days.
Accommodations: Shore camps on secluded beaches. Five percent discount with BBAT coupon.

Close to the southern coast of Florida, the Bahamas have long been a popular tourist destination. Many adventure travelers have stayed away, thinking that all the islands must be despoiled by high-rise hotels and crowds of Americans. However, scattered over 100 miles of ocean southeast of Nassau are the Exuma Islands, an archipelago of 365 islands devoid of tourist facilities. Recently the government created a national park to protect the area. The uninhabited islands offer idyllic paddling conditions—perfect weather, crystal-clear waters, and spectacular marine life for snorkelers to watch. Participants have a choice of expeditions through the islands, using two-person folding sea kayaks and paddling an average of 10 miles a day. No previous sea-kayaking experience is required.

The Adventure Travel Hall of Fame: THE 1981 POLISH COLCA EXPEDITION

In southern Peru, far from the usual tourist haunts, lies the world's deepest canyon, Colca Canyon. At 10,607 feet it is twice as deep as the Grand Canyon. Condors nest in the steep canyon walls, soaring in twos and threes and swooping down to the river. The canyon is virtually devoid of vegetation and people. The only green oasis along its entire length is Hacienda Canco, where several Indian families live in complete isolation from civilization. At the bottom of the gorge the Colca River, brutal and intimidating, rushes on its way.

Until 1981 Colca Canyon was unexplored, its existence largely unknown even to well-traveled and educated Peruvians living less than a 100 miles away. On May 12 of that year five Polish kayakers launched an expedition down the Colca. For two years the group had been away from their native Poland, wandering through Central and South America on a search for virgin rivers to run. They planned to run the entire

EUROPE

GREECE

Inn-to-Inn Sea Kayaking in Crete

The sea kayak is a perfect way to escape the crowds of tourists that collect each summer on Greece's most popular island. It allows adventuresome visitors an opportunity to enjoy deserted beaches and rarely visited fishing villages. Kayakers on this popular trip paddle along a southern coast marked by crystal-clear waters, magnificent mountains rearing up from the water's edge, and deep, forested gorges plunging down from the highlands. Each day of paddling brings numerous opportunities for cappuccino stops at seaside tavernas, cliff-jumping and exploration, snorkeling dips, and visits to ancient chapels and dark sea caves. A van transports all personal gear.

Operator: The Northwest Passage, 1130 Greenleaf Ave., Wilmette, Ill. 60091; (800) RECREATE or (847) 256-4409; www.nwpassage.com.
Price: Expensive.
Season: May, September, and October.
Length: 7 days.
Accommodations: Seaside inns and hotels. Five percent discount with BBAT coupon.

─────────────────────────

canyon in five days and had brought food for seven. Instead they found themselves caught up in the worst ordeal of their lives, the Colca battering them with a ferocity they did not believe possible.

Later, expedition leader Jerzy Majcherczyk wrote about their nightmare: "Each day we made about four kilometers, using all our wits to fight incredible difficulties we had never encountered before—boulders completely blocking the river; almost continual cascades in some sectors; vertical walls that closed in over this place that would have been hell for anyone, but even more for us as its first explorers and

navigators. . . . The river defended its virginity with a fury and we had to fight for every meter. On the eighth day we had to start rationing food. By the 10th day, still inside the canyon, we ate our last rations. Difficult before, navigation now became insanity."

Finally, emaciated and exhausted the group reached the stony beaches of Hacienda Canco and departed the river. Afterwards, Majcherczyk summed up the philosophy that had brought him through his ordeal: "Every time things go black, there is a gift from God. We are crazy Poles, but we are also very lucky."

GREENLAND

Kayaking with the Inuit Hunters

Operator: Whitney & Smith Legendary Expeditions, P.O. Box 2097, Banff, Alb., Canada T0L 0C0; (403) 678-3052; www.legendaryex.com. **Price:** Expensive. **Season:** August. **Length:** 15 days. **Accommodations:** Tent camps. Five percent discount with BBAT coupon.

Participants on these kayaking expeditions paddle along the coast of Greenland's northwestern corner, an area lying just 800 miles from the North Pole. One of the world's last communities of Inuit people leading traditional lives can be found here at Qaanaaq, the world's most northern settlement. Kayakers will have ample opportunity to learn about this remarkable polar culture as they explore the waters around Inglefield Fjord with its tidewater glaciers, towering granite mountains, and profusion of wildlife. Groups of migrating narwhals are also common in the waters here. Visits will also be made to Inuit hunting camps along the shore.

IRELAND

Kayaking the Dingle Coast

Operator: Trek & Trail, P.O. Box 906, Bayfield, Wis. 54814; (800) 354-8735 or (715) 779-3595; www.trek-trail.com. **Price:** Expensive. **Season:** September. **Length:** 9 days. **Accommodations:** Tent camps on uninhabited islands and local B&Bs at the beginning and end. Five percent discount with BBAT coupon.

National Geographic Traveler has called the Dingle Peninsula one of the most beautiful places on earth. This is a land of sheer cliffs, rounded hills, and lush lowland bogs, studded with medieval castles and abbeys. Ireland is virgin ground for sea kayaks. This small band of paddlers will explore uninhabited islands offshore, including a nine-mile open-sea crossing to Skellig Michael Island to visit the well-preserved beehive stone cells of a sixth-century outpost of Christianity and observe thousands of nesting puffins. This adventure is for advanced kayakers only.

"The Zambesie, Congo, Shanghai, Zomba, Samba Falls—I number these among the places I would seek merely for their names."

CAROLINE ALEXANDER
ONE DRY SEASON IN THE FOOTSTEPS OF MARY KINGSLEY

Sea kayaks are a perfect way to explore the isolated beauty of the barrier reef off Belize's coast

Lucy Wallingford/Slickrock Adventures

LATIN AMERICA

BELIZE

Belize Adventure Week

These trips are composed of a series of adventurous sporting events leading paddlers through many of the natural wonders that have made Belize famous. Participants begin with several days of sea kayaking from Glovers Atoll, the country's newest National Marine Reserve. They then take a charter boat to the mainland for a series of adventures, including a mountain-bike trip through the jungle on trails linking remote Mayan villages; visiting a newly discovered Mayan ceremonial cave; exploring the Mayan ruins at Xunantunich; running a Class IV section of the Macal River by kayak or raft; and ending up with a kayak exploration of the Caves Branch River through five miles of underground caverns.

Operator: Slickrock Adventures, P.O. Box 1400, Moab, Utah 84532; (800) 390-5715 or (801) 259-6996; www.slickrock.com.
Price: Expensive.
Season: January–April.
Length: 9 days.
Accommodations: Thatch-roof cabanas on the beach and screened cabins in the jungle. Five percent discount with BBAT coupon.

MEXICO

Sea Kayaking in the Sea of Cortez

Operator:
Baja Expeditions, 2625
Garnet Ave., San Diego,
Calif. 92109;
(800) 843-6967 or
(858) 581-3311;
www.bajaex.com.
Price: Moderate.
Season: March, April, May,
October, November, and
December.
Length: 7 days.
Accommodations: Shore
camps. Five percent discount with BBAT coupon.

Few areas offer novices a better opportunity to learn sea kayaking than the coasts of Baja. Calm waters, lovely sand beaches, and numerous bays make this a paradise for paddlers. This trip focuses on the remarkable desert island of Espiritu Santo located near La Paz. The island is twice the size of Manhattan and inhabited only by itinerant fishermen. The rugged volcanic landscape is studded with spectacular desert vegetation, including elephant trees, giant cardon cactus, and wild fig trees. Participants on these expeditions explore the 25 miles of shoreline with its numerous sandy coves and inlets, visit a large rookery of sea lions, snorkel with schools of brilliantly colored tropical fish, and hike into remote desert canyons. Paddling time is about four hours a day. A motor-driven support boat accompanies the group.

Sea Kayaking Among Gray Whales

Operator:
Baja Expeditions, 2625
Garnet Ave., San Diego,
Calif. 92109;
(800) 843-6967 or
(619) 581-3311;
www.bajaex.com.
Price: Moderate.
Season: January–March.
Length: 7 days.
Accommodations: Shore
camps. Five percent discount with BBAT coupon.

Paddlers on this expedition explore the unusual environment of Magdalena Bay on Baja's Pacific side, winter home to hundreds of migrating gray whales. They travel over 5,000 miles to the warm waters of Baja where they mate and bear their young. Kayakers observe a wide range of whale behavior at close quarters, paddle through the channels of a mangrove swamp for excellent bird-watching, explore the dunes of the barrier island, and beachcomb along 50 miles of uninhabited shoreline.

Kayaking the Yucatan Coast

The Mayan civilization reached its height in the Yucatan Peninsula. The carefully restored Mayan complexes here are among the most impressive in all the Americas. Kayakers on these popular winter trips explore a different aspect of this popular part of Mexico, one few tourists ever see: they have a unique opportunity to paddle through the ancient waterways of the Mayans. The mangrove channels were once used by early traders from Belize and Guatemala. Among the sites the paddlers visit are a remote guardhouse ruin built of massive carved stones and a complex of ruins at Chunyaxche, an inland seaport archaeologists believe dates back to the first century. Boaters also have ample opportunity for visits to local markets, sightseeing the famous ruins, long beach walks, swimming, and sunning on deserted beaches.

Operator:
Trek & Trail, P.O. Box 906, Bayfield, Wis. 54814; (800) 354-8735 or (715) 779-3320; www.trek-trail.com.
Price: Expensive.
Season: January–April.
Length: 8 days.
Accommodations: Villas overlooking the sea. Five percent discount with BBAT coupon.

PANAMA

Kayaking Among the Kuna Indians of the San Blas Islands

Famous for their colorful, embroidered molas (textile artworks), Panama's Kuna Indians strive to preserve their traditional lifestyle in the face of tremendous cultural, economic, and environmental pressures. For centuries they have lived on the archipelago of tropical islands known as the San Blas, an area essentially unspoiled by modern development. Participants on these paddling expe-

Operator:
Mountain Travel-Sobek, 6420 Fairmount Ave., El Cerrito, Calif. 94530; (888) 687-6235 or (510) 527-8105; www.mtsobek.com.
Price: Moderate.

The Cuna Indians of the San Blas Islands of Panama hold to their traditional ways against all encroachments of modern life

James C. Simmons

Season: Late December–mid-March.
Length: 15 days.
Accommodations: Hotel and beach camping. Five percent discount with BBAT coupon.

ditions can expect some unique cultural interaction as they visit colorful Indian villages, meet the village leaders, and sample the local cuisine. The nearby jungle-covered coast is famous for its nearly 1,200 species of birds, while the warm waters abound in rays, moray eels, and a variety of richly hued tropical fish. (The San Blas Islands are a snorkeler's paradise.)

THE PACIFIC

MICRONESIA

Sea Kayaking Through the Palau Archipelago

Operator: Wilderness Travel, 1102 Ninth St., Berkeley, Calif. 94710; (800) 368-2794 or (510) 558-2488; www.wildernesstravel.com.
Price: Expensive.

Paddlers on this adventure use their kayaks to explore at leisure one of the of most legendary atolls in the Pacific. Palau is a giant coral lagoon filled with islands sheltering more species of marine life than any similar-sized area in the world. It's a snorkeler's paradise, with a dazzling abundance and array of rainbow-colored fish, sponges,

The Adventure Travel Hall of Fame: RUNNING THE AMAZON, 1985

Until the summer of 1985 no one had ever traveled the full length of the 4,200-mile Amazon River, whose source is a snowfield more than 18,000 feet high in Peru's Andes Mountains. In late August of that year nine men and a woman embarked on that incredible journey—on foot, by raft, and by kayak—through some of the planet's last truly unexplored areas. American journalist Joe Kane joined the small, underfunded, inter-

national, and motley group of adventurers. Six months later only two finished and a six-man support team had dwindled to two.

The expedition encountered its greatest dangers in the remote canyon of the violent, wild Apurimac River. In just 300 miles the river at the bottom of a gorge 10,000 feet deep plunges 13,000 vertical feet, a gradient five times that of the Colorado River through the Grand Canyon. "The gorge walls were nearly vertical," Kane wrote in his book,

and corals. The famous rock islands are a maze of unsurpassed beauty, tropical gardens atop limestone ridges set in glass-clear waters. Palau rates among the top three snorkeling destinations in the world. Paddlers have plenty of time for swimming, snorkeling, beachcombing, and local exploration.

Season: Throughout the year. *Length:* 13 days. *Accommodations:* Hotels and tent camps. Five percent discount with BBAT coupon.

TONGA ISLANDS

By Sea Kayak Through the Kingdom of Tonga

Scattered to the south of Samoa, the Tongan islands are a Polynesian kingdom largely forgotten by the 20th century. King Taufa'ahau Tupou IV has ruled benignly since his coronation in 1967. Tonga consists of three major island groups, totaling 270 square miles. Members of this expedition head for the beautiful Vava'u group of 34 high and thickly forested islands, most of which are uninhabited. Few tourists penetrate this area, where a traditional Polynesian culture still prevails. Paddling distances are short, and members enjoy considerable leisure time to snorkel over coral reefs, visit native villages,

Operator: Ecosummer Expeditions, 936 Peace Portal Dr., P.O. Box 8014-240, Blaine, Wash. 98231; (800) 465-8884 or (604) 214-7484; www.ecosummer.com. *Price:* Moderate. *Season:* July–November. *Length:* 14 days. *Accommodations:* Shore camps on deserted beaches. Five percent discount with BBAT coupon.

Running the Amazon. *"We could not portage, we could not climb out, we could not pitch camp. As the gorge cooled through the night, boulders popped out of the ramparts."* The challenge, according to Kane, was for the expedition members in their kayaks and rafts to determine *"how to pick a safe line through the Apurimac pinball machine."*

The Apurimac canyon also gave birth to the ruthless Shining Path movement, a clandestine guerrilla army that terrorized Peru for years. At one point the expedition was ambushed by guerrillas who, a few hours later, captured the entire group. The river-

runners experienced several hours of tense negotiations before the guerrillas finally allowed them to continue.

At the beginning Kane was drafted as a kind of kayak Boswell to record the paddlers' accomplishment. He walked and rafted the first leg of the trip, then found himself one of the kayakers at the River Ene, about 3,500 miles from the Amazon's mouth. Finally, as his teammates dropped out one by one, he ended up paddling into the placid waters of the Atlantic with Polish kayaker Piotr Chmielinski. Before the trip, Kane had never sat in a kayak.

Length: 7 days. *Accommodations:* Tent camps. Five percent discount with BBAT coupon.

and explore the idyllic islands. The operator supplies two-person sea kayaks. No previous sea-kayaking experience is necessary.

UNITED STATES

ALASKA

Granite Fjord's Sea Kayaking

Operator: Alaska Discovery, 5310 Glacier Hwy., Juneau, Alaska 99801; (800) 586-1911 or (907) 780-6226; www.akdiscovery.com. *Price:* Expensive. *Season:* June–August. *Length:* 7 days. *Accommodations:* Tent camps. Five percent discount with BBAT coupon.

In 1879 John Muir enthused of the Tracy Arm–Fords Terror Wilderness that "the fjord is shut in by sublime Yosemite cliffs, nobly sculptured, and adorned with waterfalls, fringes of trees, and patches of flowers." Today's visitors will find the area's pristine wilderness unchanged. Sea kayakers paddle along the base of 3,000-foot-high granite cliffs at the bottom of narrow fjords and past icebergs broken off from the spectacular Dawes Glacier. Opportunities for day hikes to explore the surrounding shore abound. Floatplanes take clients in and out of this wilderness.

Exploring Glacier Bay by Sea Kayak

Operator: Alaska Discovery, 5310 Glacier Hwy., Juneau, Alaska 99801; (800) 586-1911 or (907) 780-6226; www.akdiscovery.com. *Price:* Moderate. *Season:* July–August. *Length:* 8 days. *Accommodations:* Tent camps. Five percent discount with BBAT coupon.

Since naturalist John Muir explored Glacier Bay in 1879, this scenic wilderness in southeastern Alaska has taught the world much of what it knows about the behavior of great glaciers. There are 16 active glaciers within the park's boundaries; everywhere visitors look are long ribbons of ice flowing to the sea, resculpting the land in the process. Most people view them from the deck of a luxury cruise ship, but the glaciers are much more impressive when approached in a two-person sea kayak. The ice sheets loom high above paddlers gliding among icebergs. Seals slither off the ice floes and splash into the sea. A floatplane flies participants into a remote section of the park. Kayakers can expect to travel 10 to 20 miles a day, leaving plenty of time for day hikes, wildlife

With 16 active glaciers and a profusion of wildlife, Glacier Bay offers kayakers a wealth of experiences

Alaska Discovery

photography, and glacier climbs on these trips. No previous kayaking experience is required.

One-Day Sea-Kayaking Adventure on Glacier Bay

In addition to their eight-day trip on Glacier Bay, Alaska Discovery offers a popular one-day adventure kayaking Bartlett Cove and the Beardslee Islands. Each group, accompanied by a professional guide, ranges in size from two to 12 guests. The day begins with instruction in the necessary kayaking skills. The pace is leisurely, with a focus on natural history, wildlife observation, and the park's scenic beauty. The operator also offers a popular three-day kayaking adventure that centers on the Hubbard Glacier, Alaska's largest.

Operator: Alaska Discovery, 5310 Glacier Hwy., Juneau, Alaska 99801; (800) 586-1911 or (907) 780-6226; www.akdiscovery.com. *Price:* Moderate. *Season:* July–August. *Length:* 1-day trips depart daily mid-May–mid-September; 3-day trips depart weekly throughout the same period. Five percent discount with BBAT coupon.

ARIZONA

Kayaking the Grand Canyon

The 226 miles of the Colorado River through the Grand Canyon stand as the Mount Everest of whitewater kayaking. The canyon's combination of spec-

Operator: Orange Torpedo Trips, P.O. Box 1111, Grants Pass, Ore. 97526; (541) 479-5061;

www.orangetorpedo.com.
Price: Moderate.
Season: April and September.
Length: 12 days.
Accommodations: Tent camps. Five percent discount with BBAT coupon.

Operator: Wilderness Inquiry, 1313 Fifth St., S.E., Box 84, Minneapolis, Minn. 55414; (800) 728-0719 or (612) 379-3858; www.wildernessinquiry.org
Price: Moderate.
Season: March–May & October. *Length:* 6 days.
Accommodations: Shoreline camps. Five percent discount with BBAT coupon.

Operator: Orange Torpedo Trips, P.O. Box 1111, Grants Pass, Ore. 97526; (541) 479-5061; www.orangetorpedo.com.
Price: Moderate.
Season: May–September.
Length: 2 and 3 days.
Accommodations: Choice of camping or spending nights at riverside lodges. Five percent discount with BBAT coupon.

tacular scenery and exciting rapids make this the supreme challenge for all serious paddlers. Instructors accompany each group to provide assistance and advice on the best routes through such legendary rapids as Lava Falls. Oar-powered rafts carry all camping equipment and supplies. This expedition is for advanced kayakers only.

Lake Powell Kayak Adventure

The world's second-largest man-made lake, 186-mile-long Lake Powell straddles the Arizona–Utah border and draws some 3.6 million visitors each year to its red sandstone–walled canyons. It is an inland desert sea with 1,900 miles of shoreline and 96 major side canyons, many of which contain abandoned cliff-dwelling Anasazi villages dating back more than 500 years. Kayaks provide a perfect way to explore the less-visited portions of this magnificent shoreline.

CALIFORNIA

The Klamath River

Running along the border between Oregon and California, the Klamath offers excellent white water, impressive canyons, moderate water temperatures, and abundant wildlife. The operator provides 10-foot inflatable plastic kayaks which have proven their effectiveness with thousands of first-time paddlers since 1969. (Hard-shell kayaks, by contrast, can be tippy and require a longer training period.) After just a few hours, even beginners will find themselves eagerly anticipating rapids boasting such names as Hell's Corner, Satan's Gate, and the Cauldron.

COLORADO

The Dolores River

Running north for 120 miles through near-wilderness country in southwestern Colorado, the Dolores is one of the major tributaries of the mighty Colorado River. The upper reaches flow through ponderosa pine and Douglas fir forests. Downstream the river enters the desert-like world of Slickrock Canyon, where walls of slick sandstone streaked with desert varnish rise straight out of the water. Here, paddlers have plenty of opportunity to explore Indian ruins and pictographs. Hanging Flume Canyon holds visible relics from an 1891 mining operation. Support rafts carry all camping equipment.

Operator: Dvorak's Kayak and Rafting Expeditions, 17921 U.S. Hwy. 285, Nathrop, Colo. 81236; (800) 824-3795 or (719) 539-6851; www.dvorakexpeditions.com
Price: Moderate.
Season: April–June.
Length: 12 days, with the option of shorter trips of 3 to 10 days.
Accommodations: Shore camps. Five percent discount with BBAT coupon.

The Gunnison River

Better known as the "Baby Grand," the Black Canyon of the Gunnison plunges 2,400 feet. Other canyons may be longer or deeper, but no other offers such an atmosphere of profound gloom. Boaters ride beneath looming cliffs of ebony-like schist, and must hike a mile down a steep trail to reach the river's edge. (Packhorses carry all camping equipment and boats.) This lack of easy access makes the Gunnison a very private wilderness for those willing to make the extra effort. The river offers fine white water and excellent game-viewing. These expeditions are raft-supported.

Operator: Dvorak's Kayak and Rafting Expeditions, 17921 U.S. Hwy. 285, Nathrop, Colo. 81236; (800) 824-3795 or (719) 539-6851; www.dvorakexpeditions.com
Price: Expensive.
Season: May–September.
Length: 1 and 2 days.
Accommodations: Shore camps. Five percent discount with BBAT coupon.

"Men go out into the void spaces of the world for various reasons. Some are actuated simply by a love of adventure, some have the keen thirst for scientific knowledge, and others again are drawn away from the trodden path by the 'lure of little voices,' the mysterious fascination of the unknown."

BRITISH ANTARCTIC EXPLORER SIR ERNEST SHACKLETON

IDAHO

The Lower Salmon

Operator:
Orange Torpedo Trips, P.O.
Box 1111, Grants Pass, Ore.
97526; (541) 479-5061;
www.orangetorpedo.com.
Price: Moderate.
Season: July and August.
Length: 3, 4, and 5 days.
Accommodations: Tent
camps. Five percent dis-
count with BBAT coupon.

When Lewis and Clark were thinking about float-ing down the Salmon River their Indian guides advised against it, saying they would never return. However, as thousands of modern river-runners can testify, you can come back from the River of No Return. Many return again and again to experi-ence the thrills and spills the great river offers at every turn. Boaters on this trip cover 50 miles of river on the Lower Salmon, paddling 10-foot inflat-able plastic kayaks that allow even novice kayakers to enjoy themselves when taking a roller-coaster ride through the Class III rapids. Boaters travel through a series of magnificent canyons—the Green, Cougar, Snow Hole, and Blue Canyons—before coming out into the Snake River. The trip concludes with a thrilling 52-mile jet-boat ride down the scenic Hell's Canyon of the Snake River to Lewiston. (Hell's Canyon is the deepest canyon in North America.)

Operator:
Mountain Travel-Sobek,
6420 Fairmount Ave.,
El Cerrito, Calif. 94530;
(888) 687-6235 or
(510) 527-8105;
www.mtsobek.com.
Price: Expensive.
Season: Mid-May–mid-
September.
Length: 7 days.
Accommodations: Waterfront
inns. Five percent discount
with BBAT coupon.

MAINE

Sea Kayaking Among the Maine Islands

The southern coast of Maine is a kayaker's dream—a series of lovely bays dotted with chains of small islands supporting a profusion of wildlife. Ospreys ride the wind currents overhead, while curious seals poke their heads out of the water to watch the occasional visitor pass by. Paddlers can also look forward to lobster feeds and clambakes with all the trimmings.

MICHIGAN

Isle Royale Kayaking Adventure

This isolated wilderness park, the least-visited National Park in the country, lies in the western reaches of Lake Superior and is famous as a habitat for wolf and moose. American Indians mined copper here long before the first European trappers entered the area. Paddlers travel by sea kayaks along the sheltered coastline from Rock Harbor on the island's northeastern shore to Chippewa Harbor on its southern coast. They have plenty of opportunities for hikes back into the interior, along trails springy with moss that wind past beaver ponds and glades ablaze with wild iris. A visit is made to the Rock Harbor Lighthouse.

Operator: Wilderness Inquiry, 1313 Fifth St., SE, Box 84, Minneapolis, Minn. 55414; (800) 728-0719 or (612) 379-3858; www.wildernessinquiry.org. *Price:* Moderate. *Season:* July and August. *Length:* 6 days. *Accommodations:* Tent camps. Five percent discount with BBAT coupon.

OREGON

Kayak School on the Rogue River

The oldest kayak school in the western United States, Sundance Expeditions's popular program for beginners opens with a deliberately unchallenging first day and concludes with a descent of the Rogue. Students spend their first five days working a 12-mile stretch of the river to learn the basics—paddling strokes, eddy turns, ferrying current, and how to roll. Accommodations are in the comfortable Sundance River House located on the banks of the river. Boaters then test their new skills on a four-day, 40-mile wilderness kayak trip through the spectacular Rogue River Gorge. The off-water agenda includes swimming, hiking, and catching a tan while contemplating the river and rapids ahead. Rafts carry all camping equipment and personal baggage. (Sundance also offers special classes in intermediate and advanced kayaking techniques.)

Operator: Sundance River Center, 14894 Galice Rd., Merlin, Ore. 97532; (888) 777-7557 or (541) 479-8508; www.sundanceriver.com. *Price:* Moderate. *Season:* May–mid-September. *Length:* 9 days. *Accommodations:* Dormitory rooms and tent camps. Five percent discount with BBAT coupon.

VERMONT

Inn-to-Inn Kayaking on Lake Champlain

Operator:
Paddleways,
P.O. Box 65125,
Burlington, Vt. 05406;
(802) 660-8606; www.pad-
dleways.com.
Price: Moderate.
Season: July–mid-September.
Length: 3 and 4 days.
Accommodations: Country
inns.

The locals jokingly refer to Lake Champlain Valley as "New England's West Coast." And in a sense it is—a west coast composed of the sixth-largest freshwater body in the United States. Long and slender, it stretches 110 miles along two-thirds of the Vermont–New York border. Paddlers on these popular adventures explore by water the shorelines of Vermont and New York with ample opportunities for swimming, sunbathing, and strolls along deserted beaches or through pretty lakeside villages.

WISCONSIN

Paddle Through Time

The operator uses this popular paddle as an opportunity to teach the techniques of sea kayaking while giving boaters the chance to explore the wonders of Lake Superior. They visit two historic lighthouses, hike along wilderness trails, and explore

"Being in a sea kayak is only a half-step away from swimming. A kayak is to boating what a 10-speed bicycle is to highway travel. On the open sea, I have to suppress the natural inclination to panic because I'm beyond the distance a man could possibly swim to the safety of land. When waves rush over the kayak, I have the sensation of being waist-deep in a vast expanse of rough water, a human cork of sorts. But it is this nakedness, this exposure to the elements, that gives kayaking its thrill. The boat becomes an extension of my body. My legs are a single Fiberglas appendage; my arms form a double-ended paddle. It is an atavistic manifestation of man as amphibious animal."

DANIEL MORRISON
"THICKER THAN WATER,"
IN AMERICAN WAY, SEPTEMBER 1, 1989

rugged sea caves and cliffs at Sand Island and Squaw Bay. The final day is spent visiting five spots in the Apostle Islands National Lakeshore, an archipelago of 22 islands known for its sea caves, sandy beaches, lighthouses, and sunken shipwrecks. These islands are close to the mainland and are protected from Lake Superior's swells.

Operator: Trek & Trail, P.O. Box 906, Bayfield, Wis. 54814; (800) 354-8735 or (715) 779-3595; www.trek-trail.com.
Price: Moderate.
Season: June–August.
Length: 3 days.
Accommodations: Tent camps on uninhabited islands. Five percent discount with BBAT coupon.

WYOMING

Kayaking Yellowstone National Park

Sea kayaks are a fresh way to view the natural wonders of Yellowstone National Park. The Park Service has long declared Yellowstone Lake to be a motor-free zone, so the operator uses kayaks as a way of getting people onto the South and Southeast Arms of this fabulous body of water. September is the most popular time for this program, after most of the tourists have departed for home. Sea kayaks provide an excellent way to get close to some of the park's wildlife as they come down to the lakeshore to drink.

Operator: O.A.R.S., Box 67, Angels Camp, Calif. 95222; (800) 346-6277 or (209) 736-4677; www.oars.com.
Price: Expensive.
Season: July and September.
Length: 3 and 5 days.
Accommodations: Tent camps. Five percent discount with BBAT coupon.

PROFILE

KEN LEGHORN

ALASKA DISCOVERY

"The sun disappeared behind a mass of clouds as we turned into the inlet, struggling against a current thick with glacial silt," Elizabeth Royte, a writer for Condé Nast Traveler, wrote later in her article about an Alaska Discovery sea-kayak trip through Glacier Bay. "A cold wind swept off the frigid surface of McBride Glacier, a half mile ahead. All around our tiny kayaks the water swirled, bearing large chunks of ice. So many of nature's forces seemed to be warning us away. Even the icebergs' shapes—ethereal and ghostly as they silently drifted by— spoke of desolation. Then a great booming filled the air as a slab of blue ice fell in slow motion from the glacier's front into the churning water. 'Stay back,' our guide called, halting the group a quarter mile from McBride. Stationed in front of the great gray glacier, we paddled just enough to keep our kayaks in place, shivering in the wind, mesmerized by this fantastical sight. Our whole world was ice and water. Everything around us was huge, ancient, and uncontrollable. Glaciers like this carve bedrock and scour out valleys. They move mountains. Looming 150 feet over our heads and almost two miles wide, McBride filled us with a tremendous sense of insignificance. We were out of our element, to be sure, but this was in part why we had come."

Alaska Discovery is the oldest sea-kayaking company in Alaska and the only operator permitted by the park service to take clients into the dramatic wilderness of Glacier Bay National Park, which scientists call "an open book on the last Ice Age." The company offers a variety of expeditions by sea kayaks along the coast of southeastern Alaska, along with rafting and canoeing expeditions on both the Kongakut and Noatak Rivers in the extreme northern part of the state and the Tatshenshini and Alsek Rivers in the southeast. Annually, the company carries more than 650 clients on their multiday trips and another 4,000 on their one- and half-day trips.

"All of our trips are quite popular in that almost all our departures go out fully booked," says Ken Leghorn, the company's president. "Our trips that focus on wildlife observation are especially popular. Sea kayaks are one of the best ways for people to see Alaska's profusion of wildlife, both the big and small species."

Leghorn was born in New York but raised in Massachusetts, near Boston. In the seventh grade he attended a summer camp sponsored by the Massachusetts Audubon Society, and this gave him an early orientation toward conservation. "Recently, I read through a diary I had kept in seventh grade in which I had written, 'When I grow up, I want to protect the wilderness and wildlife,'" he recalls. "Most of my reports in high school were on this subject. We lived in a rural area where not many kids were around, so I spent much of my free time bird-watching. And when I was 14, my parents sent me to a summer camp in eastern Canada where I was introduced to camping."

At Williams College in Massachusetts, Leghorn developed strong interests in winter camping, skiing, and Alaska; the latter he picked up from a close friend from Juneau. In 1976 he traveled to Alaska to attend the National Outdoors Leadership School for a summer course.

"That started my love affair with Alaska," Leghorn admits. "I returned to college for one more year. Then after graduation in 1978 I packed my car and headed off toward Fairbanks. I had a serious interest then in the classical violin and had set up an audition with the Arctic Chamber Orchestra. But I never got beyond Juneau. I fell in love with that city and never left. Within two days I landed a job with the Department of Fish and Game for the state of Alaska. The appeal of Alaska for me lay in the vastness of its wilderness and the degree to which it was unspoiled. And having a strong interest in conservation and resource management, Alaska appealed to me because it was our last chance to do it right."

Leghorn also joined the Juneau Symphony Orchestra, where he has played violin for over 20 years while also serving as the concertmaster. He quit his job with the state after two years and started guiding for Alaska Discovery, a company founded in 1972 by Chuck Horner primarily to help protect Admiralty Island from development and logging by running groups of tourists on canoe trips through its interior in an attempt to publicize its natural wonders.

"When Leghorn took over Alaska Discovery, sea kayaking was still in its infancy. The company then ran only a handful of trips, most to Admiralty Island and Glacier Bay. Later he made a decision to focus his company's attention chiefly on trips in southeastern Alaska, a 600-mile-long panhandle with over 10,000 miles of shoreline and more than 1,000 islands. Fewer than 70,000 people live here, most in the capital city of Juneau. "Tidewater glaciers are just one of the phenomena that make southeastern Alaska so special," he insists. "I love glaciated areas for their stark beauty, explicit geology, profound silence, and for their excellent camping, hiking, and placid paddling."

Glacier Bay National Park today is the chief jewel in Alaska Discovery's crown. The company offers eight- and five-day trips in Glacier Bay, along with a popular one-day version. There are 16 active glaciers within the park's boundaries, and everywhere are long ribbons of ice flowing to the sea, resculpting the land in the process. The area is also home to a rich selection of wildlife. Seals, bears, otters, porpoises, humpback whales, moose, lynxes, beavers, and deer abound, along with more than 200 species of birds and fish. But few of these are seen by the 200,000 visitors each year who arrive aboard the giant cruise ships and never step ashore.

Kayaks also make wonderful viewing platforms for the observation of humpback whale behavior. These magnificent creatures exist in abundance, with a large number always concentrated just off Point Aldophus where the feeding seems to go on nonstop. Writer Rob Seideman was on one of Alaska Discovery's trips to the area and wrote later:

"The whale surfaced to breathe with a loud whoooosh! It moved slowly through the water, then dove down, leaving behind a spellbinding impression of its enormous tail. We all stopped paddling. Our eyes scanned the surface of the water for 5, 10, 15 minutes. Then all of a sudden, right in front of us, the whale burst from the surface and into the air. The whale breached a half-dozen more times, rolled about like a dog scratching its back, and with its head and body submerged, slapped the water repeatedly with its tail. The sound was like a succession of sonic booms, and the show left us stunned."

Another major draw has been the giant Alaskan brown bears which abound along the coast. These are the largest, most dangerous carnivores in North America, reaching up to nine feet when standing on their hind legs and weighing more than 1,200 pounds in old age.

"We see bears on every trip," insists Leghorn. "However, we rarely have problems with bears in our camps because our guides follow strict rules about the storage, preparation, and disposal of food. However, on one of our trips to Icy Bay a client was in his tent reading Alaska Bear Tales, a book of horror stories about bear attacks. Suddenly a large brown bear wandered into camp and stuck his head through the front entrance of his tent. The guy looked up from his book, saw the bear, and screamed. The bear took off. This was one of the few times we ever had a bear in camp. So we figured that this bear knew our client was reading about him!"

In fact, Alaska Discovery's trips to Admiralty Island remain a perennial favorite with clients in part because of the large population of brown bears that call the rain forest here home. The company offers both a 2.5-day sea-kayaking and camping adventure and a one-day trip in which clients fly down on a floatplane from Juneau, board sea kayaks, and spend much of the day at the Stan Price Pack Creek Brown Bear Sanctuary, one of Alaska's top viewing areas for the coastal grizzlies. During July and August Pack Creek is alive with thousands of salmon making their way against all odds to the shallow headwaters where they spawn and then, exhausted, die. The stream becomes a fast-moving food chain for hundreds of eagles, herons, gulls, and, of course, bears.

The bears at Pack Creek were also responsible for introducing Leghorn to Susan Warner, his future wife and a wildlife biologist who spent three summers there studying the impact of humans on bear behavior. She gave a slide-show presentation in Juneau in 1991 and afterwards met Leghorn when he came up to introduce himself as "the guy who runs those groups of tourists into Pack Creek." They married the next year. Like her husband, Warner has played an active role in Alaskan conservation and spent two years in Washington lobbying on behalf of the nonprofit Southeast Alaska Conservation Council.

Leghorn has also been active and successful in organized efforts to promote state conservation. He served for 11 years on the board of the Alaska Conservation Foundation (ACF) and was chairman for three years. ACF is the chief fund-raiser for all the environmental groups in Alaska, raising over $2 million annually. In 1996 he started a "Dollar-a-Day for Conservation" program whereby Alaska Discovery asks each client to contribute one dollar for each day they are in the wilderness. Each season the company raises over $3,500 from the clients and then matches that amount from corporate profits, with all the money being donated to the Southeast Alaska Conservation Council to support a wide variety of projects.

How much previous experience at sea kayaking do people need for Alaska Discovery's trips? "We assume that all our clients are novices," Leghorn says. "Our itineraries are geared toward novices. That first day we instruct our clients in basic kayaking skills. The waters where we paddle are normally quite placid. And we spend lots of time ashore for wildlife-viewing. We also keep our group size small, with most of our trips running to 10 guests and two guides."

In 1995 First Daughter Chelsea Clinton and friends signed on to Alaska Discovery's Ultra Expedition, a combination trip featuring the bears of Admiralty Island, whale-watching off Point Adolphus, and paddling in Glacier Bay National Park. Leghorn and his wife were the guides for that trip. As he recalls:

"Chelsea accompanied a 15-year-old friend and her family. Two Secret

Service agents also went along, as well as a father-daughter combination from Kentucky. Chelsea really enjoyed the experience. She was a strong paddler and a tremendous help with the camp chores."

9

SAILING ADVENTURES

"I must down to the seas again, to the lonely sea and the sky; And all I ask is a tall ship and a star to steer her by," British poet John Masefield wrote in 1902.

A century ago they filled the sea lanes. Their graceful forms, square-rigged and fast, inspired countless poets, novelists, and painters. They were the tall ships, bound for Singapore with cargoes of silk and spice, or fighting their way through the fierce seas around Cape Horn, carrying grain and coal between England and Australia. But where cargo delivery is involved, schedules are important; and the newly developed steamships made their own power—no need for the right winds, no worry about becalming. So the majority of tall ships, no longer essential, were "retired." The very few that remained intact became permanently docked maritime museums or, in some cases, naval training ships for a few nations of the world.

Today, however, the tall ships have returned—once again to inspire poets, novelists, painters, and dreamers. Modern travelers can choose from numerous sailing expeditions open to public participation, and can realize two of the most enduring fantasies of our time: the thrill of the ship's surge as a freshening wind fills her sails and she answers the call of her elements; and the exquisite joy of finding that certain atoll, that white-sand island with palm trees, coral reefs, and clear blue water, that existed (one thought) only in dreams.

The choice of ships for today's traveler spans the spectrum, ranging from square-rigged tall ships built as the 19th century became the 20th, to fast racing sloops incorporating the most recent advances in design and technology. Some cruise the fjords of Norway while others hug the wild coasts of Chile or island-hop across Micronesia. Both the novice and the experienced sailor are welcomed on board. Life aboard is rarely passive, as most participants quickly join in the work of sailing the ship. Smaller vessels offer excellent opportunities for one-on-one instruction in sailing and navigation. And sailing on old schooners combines maritime traditions with an active adventure cruise.

"Glorious it is when wandering time is come."

OLD ESKIMO SONG

Many of the exotic islands lying east of Bali have no regularly scheduled transportation to them and so can only be visited by private sailing ship

Andy Freeberg/Wilderness Travel

ASIA

INDONESIA

Sailing the Savu Sea

Operator:
Wilderness Travel,
1102 Ninth St.,
Berkeley, Calif. 94710;
(800) 368-2794 or (510)
558-2488;
www.wildernesstravel.com.
Price: Expensive.
Season: July–September.
Length: 12 days.
Accommodations: Shipboard
cabins. Five percent discount with BBAT coupon.

The Savu Sea lies east of Bali and west of Timor, a region of Indonesia that few travelers ever penetrate. Participants on this adventure explore this exotic region with its hundreds of untouristed islands aboard the two-masted tall ship Adelaar, which has eight air-conditioned cabins. A full day is spent on Komodo Island, home to the legendary Komodo dragons, the world's largest and most fearsome lizards. These carnivorous monitor lizards measure up to 10 feet in length and can weigh 350 pounds. Other ports of call include Flores, a long, narrow, rugged island dotted with active volcanoes, where three days are spent exploring the rich sights; Lomblen Island, where the villagers still hunt sperm whales from small sailboats for their sole source of protein; and Savu Island, which offers visitors walled, unspoiled villages, lively rituals, traditional dances, and splendid handwoven textiles.

REPUBLIC OF THE MALDIVES

Sail Expedition Through the Maldive Islands

A chain of some 1,300 coral atolls located in the Indian Ocean 400 miles southwest of Sri Lanka, the Maldive Islands support a population of about 200,000 people. Only 200 of the islands are inhabited. Participants on these expeditions travel from atoll to atoll on a dhow, the traditional Arab sailing vessel. Days are spent visiting native villages, enjoying some of the best snorkeling in Asia, and beachcombing on palm-fringed islands. A Maldivian proverb says it all: "Here the world ends and paradise begins."

Operator: Worldwide Adventures, 1170 Sheppard Ave. West, #45, Toronto, Ont., Canada M3K 2A3; (800) 387-1483 or (416) 633-5666; www.worldwidequest.com.
Price: Moderate.
Season: November–March.
Length: 6 days.
Accommodations: Nights are spent on the dhow or camped on shore. Five percent discount with BBAT coupon.

THAILAND

Clipper Ship Adventure in the Andaman Sea

The *Star Flyer,* a modern clipper ship, began service in 1991. Her four masts tower 220 feet over the deck and fly 36,000 square feet of sail. She is the perfect way to explore one of the Far East's loveliest and least-explored regions, the little ports and scores of islands dotting the Andaman Sea along the west coasts of Thailand and Malaysia. The warm waters support a fishing culture that still uses the old ways to harvest the bounty of the sea. An abundance of coral reefs, most in pristine condition, makes this a paradise for snorkelers. The ports of call include the Batong Group of islands, characterized by towering rock formations and beautiful beaches; Ko Rok Nok, one of the Lanta group of islands, in the heart of a national maritime park; and Khai Nok, an idyllic paradise with spectacular views of Phuket's coastline.

Operator: Star Clippers, 4101 Salzedo Ave., Coral Gables, Fla. 33146; (800) 442-0551 or (305) 442-0550; www.starclippers.com.
Price: Moderate to expensive, depending upon the cabin.
Season: November–March.
Length: 7 days.
Accommodations: Shipboard cabins. Five percent discount with BBAT coupon.

ATLANTIC OCEAN

Transatlantic Crossing

Operator:
Star Clippers,
4101 Salzedo Ave.,
Coral Gables, Fla. 33146;
(800) 442-0551 or
(305) 442-0550;
www.starclippers.com.
Price: Moderate to expensive, depending upon the cabin.
Season: April–May and September–October.
Length: 31 days, although passengers can book shorter segments.
Accommodations: Shipboard cabins. Five percent discount with BBAT coupon

For serious sailors, the transatlantic crossing is the epitome of sailing experiences. Following the trade winds in a 2,300-mile northeastern arc across the Atlantic, the *Star Flyer,* a modern clipper ship, is the first commercial sailing vessel in more than 120 years to carry passengers on regularly scheduled trips across the Atlantic. She makes two annual ocean crossings from Barbados to Cannes, France. She boasts a length of 360 feet, surpassing by 25 feet the Great Republic, the largest clipper ship of the 19th century. *Star Flyer* is also the world's tallest sailing ship, with four masts that soar 220 feet above the deck and fly 36,000 square feet of sail. On one 1991 trip she recorded 14.8 knots westbound off the Azores. For much of the voyage passengers never see land or another ship, only empty horizon in every direction. The staff offers daily classes in navigation and knot-tying.

AUSTRALASIA

AUSTRALIA

Operator:
Adventure Center,
1311 63rd St., Suite 200,
Emeryville, Calif. 94608;
(800) 227-8747 or
(510) 654-1879;
www.adventurecenter.com.
Price: Moderate.
Season: Year-round.
Length: 4 and 7 days.
Accommodations: Shipboard cabins. Five percent discount with BBAT coupon

Sail Cruise Along the Barrier Reef

Off the east coast of Australia lie islands of astonishing beauty, all the more remarkable for their accessibility. The larger ones have succumbed to development as resorts. But hundreds of the smaller islands are uninhabited and unspoiled. Members of this seven-day expedition board the *Coral Trekker,* a square-rigged Norwegian-built wooden ship, for a cruise among the deserted islands and coral reefs of the Whitsunday Passage off North Queensland. The days are filled with snorkeling, swimming, sailing, windsurfing, and

The *Star Flyer* is a modern clipper ship capable of traveling at speeds of 15 knots in the open ocean

Star Clippers

island visits. A fully qualified dive master accompanies each group. Sail instruction is also available for those who wish it.

NEW ZEALAND

North Island Sailing Expedition

North of Auckland lie some of the Pacific's finest sailing locations, blessed with strong winds, spectacular natural settings, and fast yachts. A major attraction is the Bay of Islands Maritime and Historic Park, 86 islands and 500 miles of coastline, a sailor's paradise because of its sheer variety. The sun-washed cliffs around the islands are deeply cut by caves and arches and further highlighted with dramatic rock formations. The area also has excellent fishing and snorkeling. Participants on these trips have a choice of several vessels.

Operator: Ocean Voyages, 1709 Bridgeway, Sausalito, Calif. 94965; (800) 299-4444 or (415) 332-4681; www.oceanvoyages.com.
Price: Moderate.
Season: October–February.
Length: 10 to 21 days.
Accommodations: Shipboard cabins. Five percent discount with BBAT coupon.

"Civilization is falling from me little by little. All the joys of a free life are mine. I have escaped everything."
PAUL GAUGUIN
1890, IN A LETTER HOME AFTER HE HAD ARRIVED IN TAHITI

CARIBBEAN

Instructional Sail Cruise Through the American and British Virgin Islands

Operator: Annapolis Sailing School, P.O. Box 3334, Annapolis, Md. 21403; (800) 638-9192 or (410) 267-7205; www.usboat.com/annapway. *Price:* Moderate. *Season:* Throughout the year. *Length:* 5 and 7 days. *Accommodations:* Shipboard cabins. Five percent discount with BBAT.

The Annapolis Sailing School, the country's oldest and largest, offers sail cruises of the Virgin Islands out of its Christiansted office on St. Croix. These are not only tropical vacations with numerous opportunities for swimming, snorkeling, and beachcombing, but also instructional courses in which students learn the art of sail cruising by living aboard a yacht and sailing under the watchful eye of an expert instructor. The boats include a Gulfstar 50-foot ketch-rigged luxury yacht and a 24-foot Rainbow sloop.

WEST INDIES

By Tall Ship Through the Leeward Islands

Operator: Windjammer Barefoot Cruises, P.O. Box 120, Miami Beach, Fla. 33119; (800) 327-2601 or (800) 432-3364 in Florida; www.windjammer.com. *Price:* Moderate. *Season:* Throughout the year. *Length:* 6 days. *Accommodations:* Shipboard cabins.

The last of the great Portuguese Grand Banks schooners, the 248-foot *Polynesia* was featured in National Geographic articles and a book by famous sea captain Alan Villiers. Now completely refurbished, she unfurls her 11 sails from 192-foot masts and departs from St. Maarten on cruises, carrying 126 passengers to some of the loveliest islands in the Caribbean. Sailing distances are short, and passengers spend most of their days ashore, exploring the sights. On the first and third Mondays of each month the *Polynesia* sails for Saba, St. Barts, St. Kitts, and Statia; on the second and fourth Mondays she heads for Antigua, St. Barts, Montserrat, and Nevis.

By Tall Ship Through the Grenadines

Perhaps the least known but among the loveliest of the Windward Islands, the Grenadines consist of

Passengers on the 248-foot Mandalay experience sea travel from another era

Windjammer Barefoot Cruises

100 islands and rocks scattered along a submerged ridge between Grenada and St. Vincent. Many are uninhabited, most have no airstrips, and all are ignored by the big cruise ships. The islands boast exotic names like Bequia, Mustique, Petit St. Vincent, and Isles des Saintes. The Grenadines are the playground for the 72 passengers on the tall ship *Mandalay*, which sails among them. Originally built in 1923 for financier E.F. Hutton, in her day the Mandalay was one of the most luxurious personal yachts in the world, flying more than 22,000 square feet of sail. She arrives at each port early in the day, allowing passengers ample time for whatever activities beckon ashore.

Sail Cruising in the Grenadines

In addition to great scenic beauty, lovely beaches, and friendly people, the Grenadines also offer

Operator: Windjammer Barefoot Cruises, P.O. Box 120, Miami Beach, Fla. 33119; (800) 327-2601 or (800) 432-3364 in Florida; www.windjammer.com. **Price:** Moderate. **Season:** Throughout the year. **Length:** 14 days. **Accommodations:** Shipboard cabins.

Operator:
Ocean Voyages, 1709
Bridgeway, Sausalito, Calif.
94965; (800) 299-4444 or
(415) 332-4681;
www.oceanvoyages.com.
Price: Expensive.
Season: Throughout the
year. *Length:* 10, 14, and 21
days.
Accommodations: Shipboard
cabins. Five percent discount with BBAT coupon.

excellent sailing conditions with consistent, moderate winds. These sail cruises are for people who want a more intimate experience with the boat, sea, and islands than is possible on a larger ship. Group size is kept small (between two and six). The yachts include the *Infinity,* a Danish-built 46-foot sloop designed for offshore cruising and racing. Their captains know the islands extremely well, and all are ready to give hands-on sailing instruction to participants who show an interest. A highlight of the cruises is always the Tobago Cays, a group of uninhabited coral atolls that offer some of the finest snorkeling in the Caribbean.

EUROPE

FRANCE

Sailing on a Clipper Ship to Sardinia and Corsica

The magnificent clipper ships were the most celebrated of the tall ships of the last century, setting speed records that still stand. The *Star Flyer,* a modern clipper that started service in 1991, is 360 feet

The passengers on the Star Clippers ships join the crew to raise the sails
Alan Littell/Star Clippers

long, more than 25 feet longer than the *Great Republic,* the 19th century's largest clipper ship. She is also the world's tallest sailing ship: her four masts stretch 220 feet above the deck and fly 36,000 square feet of sail. Each summer she is positioned on the Mediterranean coast of France for sailing trips to the exotic islands just to the south—Corsica, Sardinia, and Elba. Considerable time is allowed for shore visits at such places as Costa Smeralda, a Sardinian enclave of private seaside resorts developed by the Aga Khan; Bonifacio, Corsica's almost-landlocked harbor and ancient citadel town perched high atop a granite cliff; and Portoferrai, Elba, where Napoleon waited out his first exile.

Operator:
Star Clippers, 4101 Salzedo Ave., Coral Gables, Fla. 33146; (800) 442-0551 or (305) 442-0550; www.starclippers.com.
Price: Moderate to expensive, depending upon the cabin.
Season: June–September.
Length: 7 days.
Accommodations: Shipboard cabins. Five percent discount with BBAT coupon.

GREECE

Sailing on a Clipper Ship to the Greek Isles and Turkey

The magnificent clipper ships of the last century were the largest and tallest sailing ships ever constructed and set scores of speed records, many of which still hold today. The *Star Flyer,* a modern clipper ship, began service in 1991. With her four 220-foot masts that fly 36,000 square feet of sail, she is the perfect way to visit the legendary Greek islands and Turkish coast. Its 2,000 islands and a coastline of tiny fishing villages, major historical sites, peaceful bays, and whitewashed towns make Greece a sailing paradise. Ports of call include Rhodes, whose capital is a bustling mecca for both sightseers and shoppers alike; Santorini, thought to be the source of the myth of Atlantis after a volcanic eruption 2,000 years ago devastated the island's Minoan civilization; and Mykonos, a favorite resort long popular with artists and writers. Turkish stops include Bodrum, which boasts splendid classical ruins and a fine medieval castle; and Cesme, a charming seaside town with a rich maritime history. Participants have ample time for secluded beaches, shore excursions, and the lively taverna.

Operator:
Star Clippers, 4101 Salzedo Ave., Coral Gables, Fla. 33146; (800) 442-0551 or (305) 442-0550; www.starclippers.com.
Price: Moderate to expensive, depending upon the cabin.
Season: May–October.
Length: 8 days.
Accommodations: Shipboard cabins. Five percent discount with BBAT coupon.

SWEDEN

Sailing Through the Stockholm Archipelago

Operator:
Ocean Voyages, 1709
Bridgeway, Sausalito, Calif.
94965; (800) 299-4444 or
(415) 332-4681;
www.oceanvoyages.com.
Price: Moderate.
Length: 7 days.
Accommodations: Shipboard
cabins. *Season:* July and
August. Five percent discount with BBAT coupon.

The collection of islands known as the Stockholm Archipelago is unique in Europe. Consisting of more than 24,000 islands in every conceivable shape and size, this island world actually starts in Stockholm. The islands near the city are virtually suburbs of the Swedish capital. Other parts are uninhabited and still among the wildest areas in Europe. Some of the islands are forest-clad and rise sharply from the sea; others are low, naked slabs of rocks called "skerries." Because so few tourists visit the Stockholm Archipelago, there are no bars, souvenir stands, or facilities for mass tourism. These sail expeditions offer the ideal way to explore these fascinating islands. Participants travel in groups of six or fewer on 40-foot sailing yachts.

The Adventure Travel Hall of Fame: GRAHAM MACKINTOSH

In 1982 Graham Mackintosh, a 30-year-old British schoolteacher, read a book about an English couple who rowed across the Pacific Ocean and had been forced into Ensenada, Mexico, for repairs. Their description of that seaport had gripped his imagination. While visiting friends in Los Angeles, he took a bus to Ensenada where he "paced that town as moved as a Moslem in Mecca." Soon afterwards he conceived the idea of hiking the entire coastline of Baja California. He was quick to admit that he was an unlikely candidate for such a stunt. "I had never been good at anything except catering to my own comfort and safety," he admitted afterwards in his memoir, Into a Desert Place: A 3,000 Mile Walk Around the Coast of Baja California. "I was the kind of guy who was happiest feet up front of the television or drinking beer in an English pub."

Mackintosh refused to let himself be daunted by the diabolical coastal geography of the Baja peninsula. One grizzled Baja veteran who had been up and down the Gulf side by boat, plane, and burro pointed out to him

LATIN AMERICA

BELIZE

Exploring the Barrier Reef

Just off Belize lies the largest barrier reef in the Western Hemisphere, second in size worldwide only to Australia's. Scattered along the 100-mile length are scores of small islands, most with beautiful sandy beaches and swaying palm trees. Many support large rookeries of reddish egrets, frigate birds, herons, and red-footed boobies. Known throughout the world for its pristine beauty and diversity of marine life, the reef is shallow enough to allow even the least-experienced snorkeler the opportunity to enjoy the myriad life forms. Participants on these cruises travel on a 48-foot sailboat built by one of the last of Belize's traditional shipwrights. After leaving the historic harbor of

Operator: Ecosummer Expeditions, 936 Peace Portal Dr., P.O. Box 8014-240, Blaine, Wash. 98231; (800) 465-8884 or (604) 214-7484; www.ecosummer.com. *Price:* Moderate. *Season:* January–mid-April. *Length:* 7 days. *Accommodations:* Shipboard cabins. Five percent discount with BBAT coupon.

---

at least three long stretches that were physically impassable. "There's nothing but sheer cliff and rugged, treacherous mountains," the man declared authoritatively. As for the Pacific coast, he asked, "Why do you think there's no road? Because there's no way through. If anyone could get by, there'd be a road or trail. There isn't because it's so damned rugged."

Yet on April 25, 1983, Mackintosh strapped on his 60-pound backpack, picked up a gallon bottle of water in each hand, and began trudging southward along the beach in San Felipe. "Looking and feeling like something from another planet, I walked past a group of bemused tourists," he later wrote. "I walked on head high, even though

the pack and the burden of my anxieties were doing their best to crush me."

Two years and some 3,000 miles later, Mackintosh nonetheless had accomplished the impossible. Before completing his adventure, he went through seven pairs of hiking boots. He also plunged into quicksand, endured two scorpion bites, suffered innumerable falls, and survived a charge by a rabid wild burro. Yet his worst moments were those occasions when his water supplies ran low and he faced the agony of a slow death from thirst. "You can see it coming," he says. "You've got time to worry about it." In 1986 he won the British Adventurous Traveler of the Year award for his feat

Season: Late December–mid-March.
Length: 15 days.
Accommodations: Hotel and beach camping. Five percent discount with BBAT coupon.

Belize City, the group sails to the remote parts of the reef, visiting several of the most famous atolls, including Lighthouse with its spectacular Blue Hole. Pastimes include snorkeling, sea kayaking, and beachcombing.

MIDDLE EAST

TURKEY

Sailing Turkey's Turquoise Coast

Operator: Geographic Expeditions, 2627 Lombard St., San Francisco, Calif. 94123; (800) 777-8183 or (415) 922-0448; www.geoex.com.
Price: Moderate.
Season: May, June, September, and October.
Length: 17 days.
Accommodations: Shipboard cabins. Five percent discount with BBAT coupon.

When Antony wanted to impress Cleopatra, he took her to the spectacular southern coast of Turkey lying between modern Bodrum and Antalya. Participants on this expedition follow in the wake of the Roman general and his Egyptian queen past isolated coves, spectral ruins, and small fishing villages. Their ship is the traditional Turkish gulet, air-conditioned for the comfort of modern travelers. Twelve days are spent on board, providing a leisurely exploration of this fabled coast with considerable time allowed for day trips to archaeological sites. The stops include Termessos with its extraordinary 2,000-year-old rock-hewn tombs; the Greek ghost town of Kayakoy, abandoned in 1923; Ephesus, one of the richest Greco-Roman sites in the world; Myra, with its spectacular Lycian rock tombs hewn into a cliff above a fine late Roman amphitheater; and the sunken ruins of an ancient city off Kalekoy, which provide some of the most exciting snorkeling in the Mediterranean.

"I must down to the seas again,
to the lonely sea and the sky.
And all I ask is a tall ship and
a star to steer her by."

JOHN MASEFIELD
"SEA FEVER"

A sail yacht in French Polynesia provides a perfect escape to the idyllic tropical island of our dreams where we can dwell, if only for a day, in tranquility, happiness, and security amidst natural beauty

Ocean Voyages

THE PACIFIC

FRENCH POLYNESIA

Sailing in the Wake of Captain Cook

Few places excite the traveler's imagination more than the fabled islands of French Polynesia, where the sweet scent of tiare blossoms promises Edens still uncorrupted. Novelist James Michener called Bora Bora "the most beautiful island in the world." The operator has several yachts for sails between Huahine and Bora Bora with stops at Raiatea and Tahaa. Sailing distances are short, allowing passengers ample time to snorkel over coral reefs, play Robinson Crusoe on deserted motus (small

Operator:
Ocean Voyages, 1709 Bridgeway, Sausalito, Calif. 94965; (800) 299-4444 or (415) 332-4681; www.oceanvoyages.com.
Price: Moderate.
Season: April–December.
Length: 7 days.
Accommodations: Shipboard cabins. Five percent discount with BBAT coupon.

islands), and experience a traditional lifestyle in villages where few foreigners ever go. The French skipper is ready to teach passengers the skills of reef sailing. Sail on the Archipels and discover the beauty of the South Seas. Others have had to mutiny for it.

MICRONESIA

Palau

Operator:
Ocean Voyages, 1709 Bridgeway, Sausalito, Calif. 94965; (800) 299-4444 or (415) 332-4681; www.oceanvoyages.com.
Price: Expensive.
Season: Throughout the year.
Length: 7 and 14 days.
Accommodations: Shipboard cabins. Five percent discount with BBAT coupon.

This portion of Micronesia consists of hundreds of islands with secluded beaches and greenhouse vegetation, connected by channels of clear water. Palau is best known for its underwater life. The huge diversity of corals is perhaps unequaled by any other place in the world. More than 1,500 species of tropical fish have been documented in Palau. Many of these can easily be seen by snorkeling in three to 20 feet of water. The operator has the *Eclipse*, an attractive 48-foot sloop, positioned in these waters. The ship offers accommodations for up to six passengers and is equipped for scuba diving, and passengers' interests determine the itiner-

---

The Adventure Travel Hall of Fame: EDMUND JAMES BANFIELD

As a figure of the popular imagination, the beachcomber has loomed large in the myth and fantasy of the 20th century, inspiring countless thousands of travelers to go to the Pacific in search of their own Isle of Dreams, that unprofaned sanctuary, an island removed from the haunts of man where one may dwell in tranquillity, happiness, and security amid a closeness to nature.

Few realized more fully this ideal than the legendary Edmund James Banfield, a British-born journalist who in 1896 settled on idyllic Dunk Island within Australia's Great Barrier Reef. His mature age and chronic poor health made him vulnerable in his isolation. But the tonic of sun and sea, fresh air and freedom worked a miracle. On Dunk he enjoyed another 25 years of life, surprising the doctors who had given him

ary. Options include snorkeling over reefs, climbing to marine lakes (including the acclaimed Jellyfish Lake), bird-watching, swimming, and beachcombing.

PITCAIRN ISLAND

Sailing in the Wake of the Bounty Mutineers

Two centuries after young Fletcher Christian seized H.M.S. *Bounty* from its hard-driving captain, Lt. William Bligh, the colony founded by nine mutineers and 19 Polynesians still survives on this remote Pacific island, located 1,200 miles southeast of Tahiti. Increasingly cut off from the outside world with each passing year, the islanders depend upon these sail expeditions to bring them much-needed supplies. Rising sheer from the depths of the sea, Pitcairn has no fringing reef, harbor, sheltered bay, or even a beach. Participants on these expeditions spend two weeks in the homes of the islanders, exploring this legendary Pacific island and getting to know her people. These trips begin

Operator: Ocean Voyages, 1709 Bridgeway, Sausalito, Calif. 94965; (800) 299-4444 or (415) 332-4681; www.oceanvoyages.com. *Price:* Expensive. *Season:* Check with operator. *Length:* 21 days. *Accommodations:* Shipboard cabins and family homes on Pitcairn Island. Five percent discount with BBAT coupon.

just six months to live. Banfield's wife, Bertha, a charming and forbearing woman, supported her husband through the harsh realities of life in a tropical paradise.

Banfield's years on Dunk Island were times of enormous professional productivity. Completely revitalized, he wrote three books and several hundred articles. No other beachcomber has reflected so profoundly upon his experiences. "Small must be the Isle of Dreams, so small that possession is possible," he insisted in his best-selling book, Further Confessions of the Beachcomber.

"A choice passion is not to be squandered on that which, owing to exasperating bigness, can never be fully possessed."

Early in life, Banfield had discovered Thoreau's Walden. The American writer reshaped the Englishman's values and cast a long shadow over his stay on Dunk. Banfield died in 1923. His tombstone bears Thoreau's celebrated injunction: "If a man does not keep pace with his companions, perhaps it is because he hears a different drummer. Let him step to the music which he hears."

and end on the island of Mangareva (one of the Gambier Islands, in the Tuamotu Archipelago), just two days' sail from Pitcairn and boasting its own exotic history.

Your own idyllic Pacific island is there, waiting to be discovered

James C. Simmons

UNITED STATES

ALASKA

Exploring the Inside Passage

Operator: Ocean Voyages, 1709 Bridgeway, Sausalito, Calif. 94965; (800) 299-4444 or (415) 332-4681; www.oceanvoyages.com.
Price: Moderate.
Season: June–August.
Length: 7 and 14 days.
Accommodations: Shipboard cabins. Five percent discount with BBAT coupon.

Southeast Alaska has long been popular with thousands of travelers for its spectacular scenery, fantastic profusion of wildlife, splendid isolation, and numerous colorful towns, some of great historic interest. Avoiding most of the usual ports of call, participants on these cruises explore parts of the Alaskan coast that are still untouched frontier. Wildlife-viewing is superb. Grizzlies feeding on salmon, bald eagles riding the wind currents, and orcas splashing about are just some of the common sights. Fishing is excellent, with salmon, red snapper, cod, and halibut the catches of the day. Travel is on the elegant 70-foot motor yacht *Midnight Sun.*

CALIFORNIA

California Dreaming on the Deck of a Tall Ship

The *Californian*, a 145-foot recreation of an 1840s revenue cutter, was built by the Nautical Heritage Society of California. The state's official tall ship, she is a gaff-rigged topsail schooner with two masts rising more than 100 feet above the deck and nine sails sporting 7,000 square feet of canvas. Today her chief purpose is to serve as a unique sail-training vessel for students aged 15 to 19. Each participant receives a manual, stands a watch, and works closely with the professional crew in learning to sail and navigate the ship. Lectures on history, seamanship, and earth sciences are included.

Operator: Nautical Heritage Society, 1064 B Calle Negocio, San Clemente, Calif. 92673; (800) 432-2201 or (949) 369-6773; www.californian.org. *Price:* Moderate. *Season:* Throughout the year. *Length:* 5 days. *Accommodations:* Shipboard cabins. Five percent discount with BBAT coupon.

Sailing Amid the Channel Islands National Park

These islands beckon, not with the sensuality of the South Seas but with dramatic mountaintops and jagged shorelines of awesome cliffs and deep caves. Teeming with wildlife, they have been called an "American Galapagos." Nearly half the world's 100,000-plus population of California sea lions visits its San Miguel. Santa Barbara Island is a major seabird rookery and has perhaps the world's largest breeding colony of Xantus' murrelet and the only nesting place in America of the black storm petrel. Anacapa is the only breeding place in the country for the California brown pelican. In winter months it is possible to follow and photograph California

Operator: Ocean Voyages, 1709 Bridgeway, Sausalito, Calif. 94965; (800) 299-4444 or (415) 332-4681; www.oceanvoyages.com. *Price:* Moderate. *Season:* Throughout the year. *Length:* 7 days. *Accommodations:* Shipboard cabins. Five percent discount with BBAT coupon.

"There is something about long journeys. You're lucky if you manage one in a lifetime, and by the time you're done you're swearing, 'By God, I'll never do it again.' But then some evening, months or years later, while you're browsing through the atlas, whistling or humming or eating, wop! A few weeks later you're gone."

MARK JENKINS
OFF THE MAP: BICYCLING ACROSS SIBERIA

grey whales during their migration between the Bering Sea and Baja California lagoons. Participants on these expeditions discover the wonders of the Channel Islands from the deck of the classic sailing yacht Sea Maiden.

FLORIDA

Instructional Cruise to the Dry Tortugas

Operator: Annapolis Sailing School, P.O. Box 3334, Annapolis, Md. 21403; (800) 638-9192 or (410) 267-7205; www.usboat.com/annapway. *Price:* Expensive. *Season:* November–April. *Length:* 8 days. *Accommodations:* Shipboard cabins. Five percent discount with BBAT.

Located 68 miles south of Key West, the Dry Tortugas have a gaudy history of pirates and boat-wreckers. Today they are bird sanctuaries to thousands of sooty and noddy terns, cormorants, and frigate birds. They also offer excellent snorkeling over coral reefs in crystal-clear water. It was here that treasure hunter Mel Fisher discovered *Nuestra Senora de Atocha,* perhaps the richest Spanish wreck in history. A major attraction is Fort Jefferson, a perfectly preserved hexagonal fort, built in 1860 and notorious after the Civil War as an American "Devil's Island" for its use as a federal prison. The Annapolis Sailing School offers instructional sail cruises for advanced students to the Dry Tortugas out of St. Petersburg. This is both a true open-water cruising course, providing instruction in

A highlight of the Annapolis Sail School's instructional cruise to the Dry is a visit to Fort Jefferson, which dates back to the time of the Civil War

James C. Simmons

nighttime sailing and watch-keeping, and a vacation with plenty of opportunity to enjoy these historic islands.

HAWAII

Sailing the Other Hawaii

"The loveliest fleet of islands that lie anchored in any ocean," Mark Twain wrote, after his residency here in 1866. There is another Hawaii, of coral reefs, quiet anchorages, jagged pinnacles of black lava rock, and deserted beaches, that lies far beyond the tourist haunts. With groups of eight or fewer, these expeditions cruise among the wild places of Lanai, Maui, Molokai, and Oahu. Strong winds on the channel crossings often mean exciting, fast sails. Days are filled with wilderness hikes, swims in quiet pools at the bases of waterfalls, snorkeling over coral reefs, and coastal sailing excursions. The winter months also offer excellent opportunities to observe humpback whales. Participants have a choice of several yachts.

Operator:
Ocean Voyages, 1709 Bridgeway, Sausalito, Calif. 94965; (800) 299-4444 or (415) 332-4681; www.oceanvoyages.com.
Price: Moderate.
Season: Year-round.
Length: 7 days.
Accommodations: Shipboard cabins. Five percent discount with BBAT coupon.

MAINE

Windjamming on the Grace Bailey

Built in 1882 and designed to carry hard pine from South Carolina and Georgia to lumber mills in

"While on my sailboat I rejoice in the thought of . . . nature outside the boat, society within, and just an inch of planking between the world of the one and the world of the other. The essence of being afloat is feeling the eggshell containment of an orderly domestic life suspended over the deep. The continuous slight motion of the boat, swinging on its anchor on the changing tide, is a reminder of how fragile our tenure is here."

JONATHAN RABIN
"AT SEA," OUTSIDE, SEPTEMBER 1996

The passengers on the historic windjammer *Grace Bailey* join the crew to furl the sails

Maine Windjammer Cruises

Operator: Maine Windjammer Cruises, P.O. Box 617, Camden, Maine 04843; (800) 736-7981 or (207) 236-2939; www.mainewindjammer-cruises.com.
Price: Moderate.
Season: June–early September.
Length: 2 and 5 days.
Accommodations: Shipboard cabins. Ten percent discount with BBAT coupon.

New York, the *Grace Bailey* has been fully restored with careful attention to the preservation of historical accuracy. She and two other schooners take passengers on unstructured cruises, their direction and pace dictated by the winds and currents. They sail through Penobscot Bay, a 30-mile-wide waterway dotted with hundreds of islands, many etched in pink granite and covered with teal-colored forests, and stop at several whitewashed fishing villages. A highlight is an old-fashioned New England lobster bake, cooked over a driftwood fire on an uninhabited island—steamed lobsters, clams, corn, cheeses, salads, and vegetable buffet. The fall foliage cruises are particularly popular.

MARYLAND

Instructional Sail Cruises on Historic Chesapeake Bay

Operator: Annapolis Sailing School, P.O. Box 3334, Annapolis, Md. 21403; (800) 638-9192 or (410) 267-7205; www.usboat.com/annapway.
Price: Moderate.

Perhaps no American body of water offers finer sailing opportunities than Chesapeake Bay, over 195 miles long and up to 30 miles wide. This was, of course, a major reason why the federal government located its naval academy here. The oldest sailing school in the country, with 120 boats and over 100,000 students graduated to date, the

Annapolis Sailing School offers instructional cruises. Students learn sail cruising not from classroom instruction but by living aboard a yacht and actually sailing, under the careful supervision of an expert instructor. These are vacations as well as courses, so students have time to explore the scenic harbor towns.

Season: April–October.
Length: 5 days.
Accommodations: Shipboard cabins. Five percent discount with BBAT.

WASHINGTON

Sailing Among the San Juan Islands in Puget Sound

Numbering over 200 jade-green islands, the San Juans lie in the shadow of the magnificent Olympic Mountains. They offer idyllic sailing conditions with scores of peaceful harbors, excellent beaches, and picturesque villages. Passengers stop at a different island each day and have ample opportunity to explore ashore. Excellent opportunities exist to observe pods of killer whales. Passage is on the 50-foot sailing yacht *Northwind,* which has four large private cabins, each with its own bathroom. These are sheltered waters, so no need to bring your seasickness medicines! The captain offers interested participants hands-on instruction in sailing and navigation. The operator also has longer trips up the Inside Passage.

Operator: Sail the San Juans, 2275 Lake Whatcom Blvd., PMB 186, Bellingham, Wash. 98226; (800) 729-3207 or (360) 671-5852; www.stsj.com.
Price: Moderate.
Season: May–October.
Length: 6 and 13 days.
Accommodations: Shipboard cabins. Five percent discount with BBAT coupon.

Aboard the Lady Washington

This is a replica of the tall ship commanded by Capt. Robert Gray, who in 1792 laid the United States's claim to the Pacific Northwest. She is an authentic reproduction, both in materials and in shipbuilding techniques of the tall ships that sailed when the United States comprised 13 colonies. Construction on the 112-foot long, square-rigged ship was completed in 1989. She sails out of Grays Harbor Historical Seaport in Aberdeen for half-day trips along the Washington coast. Particularly popular are her whale-watching cruises.

Operator: Grays Harbor Historical Seaport, P.O. Box 2019, Aberdeen, Wash. 98520; (800) 200-5239 or (360) 532-8611.
Price: Inexpensive.
Season: Throughout the year.
Length: Half-day.

PROFILE

CAPTAIN RAY WILLIAMSON
MAINE WINDJAMMER CRUISES

When the Age of Sail gave way to the Age of Steam, the faster and more efficient steamships replaced the magnificent sailing ships on the trade routes of the world. Only a handful survived, most to serve as training ships for the world's navies or as maritime museums. The others were salvaged for their lumber or left to rot in forgotten corners of the world's ports.

But one fleet of windjammers survives for those travelers who thrill to the pleasure of planting their feet on a sharply angled teak deck while sails billow overhead and the ship runs before the winds. The Maine Windjammer Association includes 10 traditional schooners, most of which have been designated National Historic Landmarks. Privately owned and operated, the ships carry between 20 and 40 passengers each on three-, four-, and six-day cruises along the Maine coast, going where the winds take them and anchoring at nights in small island harbors.

The Gulf of Maine has long enjoyed a reputation as one of the finest sailing grounds in the world. In the 1870s hundreds of ruggedly built coastal schooners sailed from these waters, delivering lumber, granite, ice, and fish all along the Atlantic from Maine to the Caribbean and returning with their holds filled with casks of molasses, rum, and sugar. Today only 14 of the windjammers are left to continue the tradition. And it is doubtful if any of these would have survived had it not been for the vision of one Frank Swift. An artist from rural Maine, he looked about him in the middle of the Depression and decided that vacationers from Boston might well enjoy a sail retreat from the pressures of city life. So he bought one schooner, modified the cargo hold to carry passengers, and offered week-long cruises along the Maine coast at a cost of $25, meals included. "On our first cruise in 1936 we had just three lady passengers from Boston," he recalled in later years. "The next time, I believe, we took off without any passengers." But he persevered. By the early 1940s he had built a flourishing business that ensured a steady growth of his fleet. Swift retired in 1961, 25 years after he had introduced his first windjammer cruise on Penobscot Bay, leaving a rich legacy in his wake.

Following in Swift's footsteps, a number of sea captains began offering windjammer cruises of their own in the 1950s. In 1977 they formed

the Maine Windjammer Association to promote themselves. Today the Association's fleet includes two of Frank Swift's original schooners, the *Grace Bailey* and the *Mercantile*, along with America's two oldest commercial coasting schooners, an oyster-fishing schooner and a three-masted ram schooner, both built in 1871.

The major player in this area is Ray Williamson. His company, Maine Windjammer Cruises, owns three sail ships, including the historic vessels *Grace Bailey* and *Mercantile*. These carry more than 1,400 passengers during the summer season on a variety of five-day, four-day, three-day, and weekend cruises out of the port of Camden. The operation is very much a family affair. Ray runs the entire operation and during the summer season works as the captain on the *Grace Bailey* while his wife Ann cooks in the galley and their two young daughters help out.

Born in Montreal but raised on Long Island, New York, Williamson's love of sailing developed out of a youthful passion for surfing. "I surfed from a young age," he recalls today. "But the waves were only good in the early morning. So I looked around for another activity on the ocean for the rest of the day. That turned out to be sailing. At the age of 18 I bought a Sea Snark, an 11-foot Styrofoam sailboat. I learned how to sail by reading a 12-page instructional booklet that came with the little craft."

Soon Williamson moved up to a 21-foot boat, which he rebuilt and sailed for two years, before turning that in on a 35-foot sailboat. In 1975 he and his wife-to-be moved to St. Croix in the Caribbean when Ann took a job in Christiansted teaching kindergarten. Ray landed a job as a social worker and then found himself increasingly preoccupied with a sail charter operation taking passengers out on day trips to nearby Buck Island, a park situated about six miles from Christiansted, for snorkeling and sunbathing. "In time I found myself getting tired of making the same run each day," Williamson recalls. "Also the boat I was captaining was the biggest in the harbor, so I felt I was confined in my ability to advance in St. Croix."

In 1982 Williamson read an article in *Wooden Ship* magazine about the Maine windjammers. "This is it," he told Ann. "We're moving to Maine." Within a few months he had relocated his family to Camden and signed on with Maine Windjammer Cruises as a deckhand on the *Mattie* (now the *Grace Bailey*) earning $60 a week. The next year he was made captain of the 40-foot *Mistress*; the following year he captained the 80-foot *Mercantile*. In 1986 he bought all three schooners.

His little fleet contains two of the most historic ships on the Maine coast. The *Grace Bailey*, launched in 1882, was originally designed to carry

timber from South Carolina and Georgia to Edwin Bailey's lumber mills on Long Island, New York. She was named after Edwin's daughter who was born that same year. The *Grace Bailey* was also registered for foreign trade and made numerous voyages to and from the West Indies. Captain Frank Swift bought her in 1939 and made her the flagship of his Maine Windjammer Cruises fleet.

"The *Grace Bailey* is the finest example of a coastal schooner still afloat," Williamson insists. "Of all the windjammers operating today off the coast of Maine she is the most authentic. When we restored her, we kept most of her original features intact. The lounge, for example, still has the original hand-carved paneling from the 1880s."

A second ship, the *Mercantile*, was built in 1916 on a beach near the town of Little Deer Isle, Maine. She carried fish, granite, and other general cargo as well as wood from Maine's coastal islands to fuel the lime kilns of Rockport. A shoal-draft vessel, she was designed to take on and discharge cargo in out-of-the-way places inaccessible to vessels drawing a deeper draft. In 1943 Swift added her to his fleet of windjammers carrying commercial passengers.

In 1989 Williamson embarked on a lengthy, detailed restoration of the *Mercantile*. The job proved long and arduous, requiring not only the expert attentions of skilled shipwrights but also the acquisition of materials from all over the country, including white oak from southern New England, yellow pine from the Carolinas, and Douglas fir from Oregon. Equally important and often difficult to locate were the tools, hardware, and fastenings needed to make the restoration as authentic as possible. In the end many of these had to be handmade using 19th-century techniques.

In 1990 both ships were entered on the National Register of Historic Places, an indication that they have been deemed worthy of preservation and protection as part of the nation's historic and architectural heritage.

A third ship, the *Mistress*, a newer vessel built in 1960 on Deer Isle, blends the traditional design of a coastal schooner with the modern accommodations necessary for today's passenger trade. The 60-foot ship carries only six passengers, making it seem more like a private yacht.

When Williamson took over the fleet in 1986, the captains of the Maine windjammers were all offering only six-day cruises. His ships were going out with just a 40 percent occupancy. "To fill the cabins on my three ships I introduced the concept of shorter cruises, lasting four days and weekends, to allow more people to fit them into their busy schedules," he recalls. "Our weekend trips are intended as an introduction to windjamming. But all our trips follow the same basic formula. Our focus is always on sailing. We provide informal instruction on sailing and navigation to those passengers who express an interest. Each evening we anchor near a different port. Our passengers can go ashore then or in the morning before our departure. A highlight of our six- and four-day cruises is always a New England lobster bake, cooked over a driftwood fire on a deserted island."

10

EXPEDITIONARY CRUISING

"Why take a cruise when you can take an expedition?" asks the advertisement for one major operator.

Why, indeed! Expeditionary cruise ships sail to such remote regions as Antarctica, the outlying islands of Polynesia, and the Arctic, areas that are virtually inaccessible by any other means. Their passengers book into these cruises not for the food and entertainment but for the adventure, wildlife, and exotic cultures. The more remote the destination, the stronger the appeal. And these are expeditionary cruises in the true sense of the word, with risks no ordinary cruise ship would experience. In the late summer of 1988, for example, the passengers on the 236-foot *Explorer* found themselves trapped in pack ice 50 miles northeast of Point Barrow, Alaska, as they attempted to navigate the historic and perilous Northwest Passage. A Coast Guard icebreaker finally freed them. (In 1984 the *Explorer* became the first passenger ship in history to make the journey pioneered by Norwegian explorer Roald Amundsen in 1906.)

Unlike conventional cruise ships, expeditionary ships are smaller, with shallow drafts, allowing them easy access to areas closed to the larger vessels. Some have reinforced hulls and bows to allow them to push through polar ice packs. Each carries a fleet of agile, swift Zodiac inflatable boats to facilitate safe landings in remote wilderness areas. And most carry a staff of naturalists, anthropologists, and historians, who lecture on the regions being visited.

The 21st century will see the expansion of expeditionary cruises below the surface of the world's oceans. The first fleet of tourist submarines already carries thousands of awed passengers as deep as 150 feet to view reefs, shipwrecks, and fish life. And now in production is a radically different kind of submarine—a craft with a clear acrylic hull that will make passengers feel as though they have become a part of the undersea environment.

"Planes are like Seven League Boots. I could be in New Zealand or Easter Island tomorrow."

PAUL THEROUX
THE HAPPY ISLES OF OCEANIA

Antarctica offers visitors spectacular mountain and ice scenery, great concentrations of wildlife, and the opportunity to explore our globe's last major frontier

James C. Simmons

ANTARCTICA

Cruising the Antarctic Peninsula

Inhospitable as Antarctica may be to humans, its waters support a fantastic concentration of wildlife. In the south polar regions the number of species is severely limited, but each is represented by such an abundance of individuals that the effect is overwhelming. The Antarctic area is completely free of onshore predators. As a result, birds and mammals have never been conditioned to fear anything on land and human visitors can approach to within a few feet. The accessibility and profusion of wildlife translate into a paradise of opportunity for both the naturalist and photographer. Members of this expedition explore the wonders of the Antarctic Peninsula on the *Marine Discoverer*, a comfortable Russian research vessel. They enjoy frequent shore excursions to explore the sights.

Operator: Marine Expeditions, 30 Hazleton Ave., Toronto, Ont., Canada M5R 2E2; (800) 263-9147 or (416) 964-9069; www.marineex.com.
Price: Expensive.
Season: November–March.
Length: 14 days.
Accommodations: Shipboard cabins.

Wildlife Cruise to South Georgia Island and the Falkland Islands

Located 1,200 miles east of Cape Horn, South Georgia Island is an inhospitable but beautiful

Operator:
Marine Expeditions, 30
Hazleton Ave., Toronto,
Ont., Canada M5R 2E2;
(800) 263-9147 or
(416) 964-9069;
www.marineex.com.
Price: Expensive.
Season: November and
December.
Length: 24 days.
Accommodations: Shipboard
cabins.

world of craggy mountains of alpine proportions. Around its fringes, the pebble beaches and grassy slopes teem with one of the richest concentrations of wildlife in the world. Fur and elephant seals carpet the shores, multitudes of gentoo and king penguins come and go from rookeries, while thousands of seabirds nest among the clumps of hardy tussock grass. For 60 years South Georgia was the center of the Antarctic whaling industry. Visitors to the former administrative center of Grytviken can explore at leisure the elaborate gadgetry of a major whaling station. Everything was left behind when the station was abandoned; nothing was salvaged. Most visitors make their way to the town's small cemetery to pay homage at the grave of the famous Antarctic explorer Sir Ernest Shackleton. During the expedition passengers also visit the Falkland Islands, a paradise for birders, and the Antarctic Peninsula.

ATLANTIC OCEAN

Visiting the Wreck of the Titanic

Operator:
Zegrahm Expeditions,
192 Nickerson St., #200,
Seattle, Wash. 98109;
(800) 628-8747 or
(206) 285-4000;
www.zeco.com.
Price: Expensive.
Season: August and
September.
Length: 9 days.
Accommodations: Shipboard
cabins.

The technology of deep-diving submersibles has finally advanced to the point where just about any part of the ocean floor, no matter how deep, is now reachable. The operator employs the MIR I and II submersibles (Russian deep-diving vessels capable of reaching ocean depths of 20,000 feet, used in the filming of James Cameron's film) to take clients down to the most famous shipwreck in history, that of the H.M.S. *Titanic,* lying almost 15,000 feet down in the cold Atlantic waters off Nova Scotia. Once the wreck is reached, the MIR's large halogen-mercury-iodine lights illuminate the *Titanic's* ruined remains, lying in the midst of an extensive debris field. The ship broke into two large sections, the demolished stern and the bow separated by nearly 2,000 feet. The MIRs spend up to three hours exploring the wreckage and debris field.

By Deep-Diving Submersible to Undersea Hydrothermal Vents

Near the Azores, 7,875 feet below on the ocean's floor, lie the "Rainbow Vents," a field of tall sediment chimneys that exist in a state of constant eruption. Beyond its geological significance, the site is a biological wonderland of alien marine life. Great numbers of white crabs, blind shrimp, mussels, clams, and glowing jellyfish thrive in the waters around the vents. Dives to the site are made aboard the MIR I and II submersibles, vessels capable of diving to ocean depths of 20,000 feet. Once the site is reached, the submersible will turn on its powerful halogen-mercury-iodine lights to illuminate the otherworldly scene.

Operator: Zegrahm Expeditions, 192 Nickerson St., #200, Seattle, Wash. 98109; (800) 628-8747 or (206) 285-4000; www.zeco.com.
Price: Expensive.
Season: September.
Length: 13 days.
Accommodations: Hotel.

AUSTRALASIA

AUSTRALIA

Cruising the Great Barrier Reef

The world's largest living structure, Australia's Great Barrier Reef covers an area the size of England and Scotland combined. Only a tiny portion of the massive reef breaches the ocean's surface in the form of islands and outcroppings. A handful of the hundreds of islands are inhabited or developed for tourists. The others are rarely visited except by occasional fishermen and sailors. *The Coral Princess,* a 115-foot, luxurious, fully air-conditioned catamaran, cruises between Townsville and Cairns each week, exploring the picturesque islands and superb reefs in the heart of the world's largest marine park. Passengers spend no more than half a day at a time actually cruising; the rest of their time is spent ashore exploring the islands or snorkeling over the reefs.

Operator: Adventure Center, 1311 63rd St., Suite 200, Emeryville, Calif. 94608; (800) 227-8747 or (510) 654-1879; www.adventure-center.com.
Price: Expensive.
Season: Throughout the year.
Length: 4 days.
Accommodations: Shipboard cabins. Five percent discount with BBAT coupon.

CANADA

Exploring Canada's Maritime Provinces and Coastal Maine

Operator:
American Canadian
Caribbean Line, P.O. Box
368, Warren, R.I. 02885;
(800) 556-7450 or
(401) 247-0955;
www.accl-smallships.com.
Price: Expensive.
Season: July and August.
Length: 16 days.
Accommodations: Shipboard
cabins. Five percent discount with BBAT coupon.

The coasts of eastern Canada and Maine present an incomparable mix of weathered promontories, sheltered coves, historic islands, picturesque fishing villages, and an abundance of whales, seabirds, and seals. *The Caribbean Prince* carries 80 passengers on a cruise from Quebec to Warren, Rhode Island. Highlights along the way include Cape Breton Island, site of Canada's largest historical park; Bonaventure Island, home to 200,000 birds, including a huge gannet colony; delightful Prince Edward Island, home of Anne of Green Gables; Nova Scotia's bustling port of Halifax; the picturesque seaport of Bar Harbor, Maine; Acadia National Park, made famous by Longfellow's poem

Passengers go to shore to explore the coastal wilderness in a remote area of Canada's maritime coast

James C. Simmons

The 40-foot boat, *Spirit Bear*, allows the kayaking clients of Northern Lights Expeditions to expand greatly their paddling range

Northern Lights Expeditions

"Evangeline"; and Newport, Rhode Island, a popular summer watering hole for the rich and famous.

BRITISH COLUMBIA

Small-Ship and Sea-Kayaking Adventure in the Canadian Inside Passage

In 1997 the operator introduced the concept of the "mother ship" to sea kayaking. Instead of camping or staying at a lodge, clients live aboard the 40-foot classic wooden vessel *Spirit Bear*, thereby greatly increasing their range for day trips and providing the means to visit three or four entirely unique and different habitats, such as fjords, river mouths (where they can watch grizzly bears feeding), and small outer islands. The kayaks ride on the deck until a new launch point is reached. Clients paddle during the day and sometimes meet the boat for lunch and then again in the late afternoon. In just a couple of hours in the evening they can move to a new location 40 miles away. The use of a live-aboard ship greatly increases their freedom of movement. "This concept of the mother ship will revolutionize sea kayaking," insists the operator. Group size is limited to four guests and a guide. No previous sea-kayaking experience is necessary.

Operator: Northern Lights Expeditions, P.O. Box 4289, Bellingham, Wash. 98227; (800) 754-7402 or (360) 734-6334; www.seakayaking.com.
Price: Expensive.
Season: June–September.
Length: 8 days.
Accommodations: Shipboard cabins. Five percent discount with BBAT coupon.

NORTHWEST TERRITORIES

By Deep-Diving Submersible to the H.M.S. Breadalbane Under the Arctic Ice

Operator:
Zegrahm Expeditions, 1414
Dexter Ave. North, #327,
Seattle, Wash. 98109;
(800) 628-8747 or
(206) 285-4000;
www.zeco.com.
Price: Expensive.
Season: March and April.
Length: 8 days.
Accommodations: Specially
designed living quarters on
the ice.

The Breadalbane was a 500-ton, three-masted, wooden sailing ship that sank in 1853 off Beechey Island in the Canadian Arctic. She had sailed into these treacherous waters in a futile search for the famous Arctic explorer Sir John Franklin. The ship now sits upright 350 feet down, fully intact and perfectly preserved in the cold waters. From a base on the ice, adventuresome travelers can visit this northernmost shipwreck by means of two deep-diving submersibles. Once at the shipwreck, the submersibles turn on their powerful flood-lights to illuminate the site. Visibility in the clear waters is 150 feet.

The Adventure Travel Hall of Fame:
H. M. TOMLINSON

On his way to the office one dreary November morning in 1909 H. M. Tomlinson, a journalist in his mid-thirties, comfortably settled, with a family, suddenly caught a glimpse of himself as a squirrel trapped inside a revolving wheel. Moments later he met an old acquaintance, now the skipper of a tramp steamer, Capella, soon to carry 5,200 tons of Welsh coal on an experimental voyage across the Atlantic to Para, Brazil, and then 2,000 miles to the upper reaches of the Amazon.

Tomlinson admitted to feeling restless. "Then why don't you chuck it?" his friend asked mischievously. Tomlinson was stunned.

"How shall we live if not in bonds?" he asked. "Give it up," his friend insisted, "and come with me."

The temptation proved too great. A few days later Tomlinson quit his job with the newspaper, kissed his wife and children good-bye, and signed on to the Capella as her purser. The risks to his life were substantial. The Amazon River was still largely untouched frontier. Yellow fever, malaria, dysentery, and beri-beri were rampant. The small settlements along the river were graveyards for foreigners.

The Capella's voyage up the Amazon assumed the quality of a nightmare that refused to end at daybreak. On January 30,

EUROPE

BRITAIN

Exploring the Wild Coasts of Britain and Ireland

Members of this expedition board the *Caledonia Star* to visit areas where few other cruise ships venture. A fleet of Zodiac inflatable boats allows the freedom to land on isolated beaches and approach closely the otherwise inaccessible cliffside seabird rookeries. Stops are made at the islands of Scilly, where legend tells us King Arthur once ruled over a lovely land before it vanished beneath the ocean; the Skellig Islands, home to tens of thousands of nesting seabirds and site of a perfectly preserved eighth-century monastic settlement; the Aran

Operator: Special Expeditions, 720 Fifth Ave., New York, N.Y. 10019; (800) 762-0003 or (212) 765-7740; www.expeditions.com.
Price: Expensive.
Season: June.
Length: 14 days.
Accommodations: Shipboard cabins.

1910, the ship finally arrived at its destination where a railroad was being constructed. Tomlinson found himself slowly seduced by the jungle beyond. He listened to the laborers' tales of a land where the sun never shone and where headhunting Indians sometimes lurked in the shadows, waiting for an opportunity.

When a line boss offered to take him to the construction site, Tomlinson eagerly accepted. For almost two weeks and 200 miles the pair journeyed by train, canoe, and mule through the dense jungle. They bedded down in the construction camps and shared jokes and meals (of toucan, parrot, and monkey) with the American and English engineers. When they finally arrived back at the railhead, Tomlinson realized to his horror that they were just 60 minutes too late to catch the last train to Puerto Velho for a week. He would miss his ship! His companion commandeered a handcart and a crew to take them the 60 miles back. Tomlinson took his turns, hysterically pumping away at the handle of the hand-cart in order to catch the ship he feared he would miss.

On March 10, 1910, the Capella—with Tomlinson on board—sailed from Puerto Velho. Within a month he was back in England to "the orderly hedges, the clean roads, and the geometrical patterns of the fields that gave assurance once more of order and security." Soon afterwards he published a memoir of his trip, The Sea and the Jungle, a lyrical classic of self-discovery.

Passengers on a Special Expeditions cruise along the wild coasts of Britain and Ireland explore an abandoned village on remote St. Kilda Island

James C. Simmons

Islands, with their imposing prehistoric monuments; Iona Island, where Shakespeare's Macbeth is reputed to have been buried; the Orkney Islands, rich in antiquities; and the Isle of Noss in the Shetland group, the site of one of Europe's largest seabird colonies.

NORWAY

Beyond the North Cape

Operator: Special Expeditions, 720 Fifth Ave., New York, N.Y. 10019; (800) 762-0003 or (212) 765-7740; www.expeditions.com. *Price:* Expensive. *Season:* July and August. *Length:* 19 days. *Accommodations:* Shipboard cabins.

Sculpted by the last Ice Age into an extraordinary landscape of deep fjords, plunging mountains, and craggy islands, the Norwegian coast is the most dramatic in Europe. Passengers on this cruise board the *Caledonia Star* to explore 1,500 miles of diverse coastal scenery, from the tidy medieval quarters of Bergen's waterfront district to the brooding glaciers of Spitzbergen. The cruise itinerary includes Geiranger Fjord, often thought to be the most beautiful in Norway; the remote Lofoten archipelago, where granite mountains dwarf storybook fishing villages; Tromso, the largest town north of the Arctic Circle and a staging point for numerous early Arctic expeditions; and Bear Island, with its abundant populations of fulmars, kittiwakes, guillemots, and gulls. Three days are spent exploring Spitzbergen, visiting old whaling stations, and searching for polar bears and walruses.

SWEDEN

Exploring the Stockholm Archipelago by Small Ship

Scattered along Sweden's eastern coast lie some 24,000 islands, skerries, and islets. The archipelago is really two environments: the wooded, protected inner part and the barren, wild outer islands, home to seabirds, seals, and a handful of hardy fisherfolk. Participants travel through this corner of Scandinavia on their private boat, the 128-foot *Swedish Islander,* which also carries bicycles and fishing equipment. Stops are made at Mariefred, dominated by the imposing Gripsholms Castle, one of the most famous in Sweden; Roslagen, which has inspired many of Sweden's most beloved artists and writers; and Ängso National Park, Sweden's first protected reserve and a haven for wildflowers and abundant birdlife.

Operator: Special Expeditions, 720 Fifth Ave., New York, N.Y. 10019; (800) 762-0003 or (212) 765-7740; www.expeditions.com.
Price: Expensive.
Season: June–August.
Length: 8 days.
Accommodations: Small inns.

LATIN AMERICA

BELIZE

Cruising Belize's Coral Coast

Belize lays claim to the world's second-longest barrier reef, boasting over 200 islands ranging in size from a few hundred square yards to big Ambergris Cay, some 25 miles long. All but one of the Western Hemisphere's large atolls can be found here. The United Nations has recently proposed this splendid natural resource for designation as a World Heritage Site. Without a private yacht, however, the

Operator:
American Canadian
Caribbean Line, P.O. Box
368, Warren, R.I. 02885;
(800) 556-7450 or
(401) 247-0955;
www.accl-smallships.com.
Price: Expensive.
Season: December–March.
Length: 12 days.
Accommodations: Shipboard
cabins. Five percent dis-
count with BBAT coupon.

reef is virtually inaccessible—except by the small cruise vessel *Caribbean Prince*, which carries up to 80 passengers on cruises along the entire length of the reef. Numerous stops are made at deserted islands, with their white, sandy beaches topped by palm trees swaying in the sunshine, for some of the finest snorkeling in the Caribbean. Three days are also spent exploring rarely visited northeastern Guatemala, where the ship cruises up the Rio Dulce at the bottom of a jungle-filled gorge to Lake Izabal, the largest in the country.

BRAZIL

Exploring the Amazon Basin Above Manaus by Houseboat

Operator:
Journeys International, 107
Aprill Dr., #3., Ann Arbor,
Mich. 48103;
(800) 255-8735 or
(734) 665-4407;
www.journeys-intl.com.
Price: Moderate.
Season: Throughout the
year.
Length: 8 days.
Accommodations: Shipboard
cabins. Five percent dis-
count with BBAT coupon.

Like the sinuous veins of an enormous leaf, the tangled tributaries of the Amazon writhe across an area two-thirds the size of the United States. Members of this expedition explore the pristine Amazonian rain forest from their very own motorized houseboat with a local captain, cook, and guide. After a tour of the isolated jungle metropolis of Manaus, participants board the *Amazon Explorer*, specially designed to navigate the shallow waters of the Amazon's tributaries, inland lakes, and island archipelagos beyond the range of the larger ships. They visit Lake Januaca and its tributaries, looking for exotic bird species such as hoatzins and horned screamers. They then cruise up the Rio Cuieiras through a

"It is only when a man goes out into the world with the thought that there are heroisms all round him and with the desire all alive in his heart to follow any which may come within sight of him that he breaks away, as I did, from the life he knows and ventures forth into the wonderful mystic twilight land where lie great adventures and great rewards."

SIR ARTHUR CONAN DOYLE
THE LOST WORLD

region of lakes and virgin rain forest to explore the Anavilhanas Archipelago, a collection of several hundred forest-covered islands; and visit the region drained by the Rio Negro for short hikes into the forest beyond the riverbanks.

MEXICO

Among the Blue Whales

The blue whale is in the record books as the largest animal ever to live: one female was measured at 98 feet; another weighed in at 329,000 pounds. These behemoths live almost exclusively on shrimp-like creatures called krill. Blue whales are found throughout the world's oceans, but the opportunity for extended observation of their behavior is rare. An exception occurs each spring in an area south of Isla Carmen in the Sea of Cortez where numbers of blue whales congregate to feed, mate, and nurse their young. The expeditionary cruise vessel *Don Jose* takes 20 passengers on cruises into this special area to allow them an extended opportunity to observe and photograph the big whales' activities from close range. Travelers can also expect to see other whale species, including humpback, sperm, fin, pilot, minke, gray, and killer. Daily land excursions on desert islands or at fishing villages are also included.

Operator:
Baja Expeditions,
2625 Garnet Ave.,
San Diego, Calif. 92109;
(800) 843-6967 or
(858) 581-3311;
www.bajaex.com.
Price: Expensive.
Season: March and April.
Length: 8 days.
Accommodations: Shipboard cabins. Five percent discount with BBAT coupon.

Circumnavigating the Baja California Peninsula

The Sea of Cortez is the world's largest deepwater gulf, nearly 11,000 feet deep at its mouth. John Steinbeck, Joseph Wood Krutch, and Erle Stanley Gardner are three who spent long periods of time on and around the Sea of Cortez, and found themselves seduced by its breathtaking scenery, remoteness, and wondrous profusion of wildlife. This is a naturalist's paradise. Its many islands, most uninhabited, hold plant and animal species found

Operator:
Special Expeditions,
720 Fifth Ave., New York,
N.Y. 10019; (800) 762-0003
or (212) 765-7740;
www.expeditions.com.
Price: Expensive.
Season: January–March.
Length: 9 days.
Accommodations: Shipboard
cabins.

nowhere else, earning them the reputation as a Mexican Galapagos. Of the region's 110 species of cacti, for example, 60 are endemic to the Sonoran Desert. The isolation of populations has speeded the process of evolutionary change, much as it has in the Galapagos. Passengers on this cruise circumnavigate much of the Baja peninsula, putting ashore on such rarely visited islands as Isla Espiritu Santo, Los Islotes, and Isla Santa Catalina.

PANAMA

Cruise Along the Caribbean and Pacific Coasts

Operator:
American Canadian
Caribbean Line, P.O. Box
368, Warren, R.I. 02885;
(800) 556-7450 or
(401) 247-0955;
www.accl-smallships.com.
Price: Expensive.
Season: January–March.
Length: 12 days.
Accommodations: Shipboard
cabins. Five percent discount with BBAT coupon.

For thousands of years the tiny isthmus of Panama has served as the land bridge between the North and South American continents. The existence of this link has had a profound effect on the distribution of plants, animals, and humans. Barely 50 miles wide at its narrowest point, Panama "funnels" the millions of birds which annually move between the temperate and tropic zones. These popular cruises explore the coastal wilderness areas on both sides of the isthmus. Several days are spent in the San Blas Islands among the Kuna Indians, famous for their colorful textile art form, the mola, which is produced mainly by the women. The ship then

---

The Adventure Travel Hall of Fame: THE FIRST TRAVERSE OF BAFFIN ISLAND

In March 1994 John Dunn and five companions set out to become the first adventurers to travel the 1,880-mile length of Baffin Island, the earth's fifth-largest island, much of it located above Canada's Arctic Circle. Over the next six months they skied the first 1,045 miles, kayaked the next 605 miles, and hiked the final 230 miles. Their route took them through three of Baffin's nine Inuit communities, where they picked up food. Twice they were resupplied by small plane. Except for a few hunters and their families, they

passes through the world-famous Panama Canal to the Pacific Ocean, to visit several of the exotic islands in that area. A visit is also made to Darien to meet the Choco Indians, whose small settlements can be reached only by plane or ship. Plenty of time is allowed for beachcombing, swimming, and snorkeling at deserted beaches.

THE NORTH POLE

Cruise to the North Pole

Passengers board the Russian icebreaker *Yamal* (with a displacement of 23,000 tons, 75,000 total horsepower, a 48-mm-thick hull, and a bright-red paint job) for this adventuresome cruise through the thick pack ice to the North Pole. Once there, they will disembark and explore the surrounding pack ice, finishing the day with a barbecue on the ice. The ship's open-bridge policy allows passengers to watch navigation and icebreaking operations around the clock. On the way back the ship will stop at Franz Josef Land, a remote world of dense pack ice, towering volcanic mountains, icebergs, and glaciers, not discovered until 1873. Throughout the cruise passengers have the opportunity for extended "flightseeing" from the ship's helicopter. Several naturalists accompany the passengers.

Operator:
Quark Expeditions, 980 Post Rd., Darien, Conn. 06820; (800) 356-5699 or (203) 656-0499; www.quark-expeditions.com.
Price: Expensive.
Season: August.
Length: 15 days.
Accommodations: Shipboard cabins.

met no other people along the way. Hauling heavy sleds loaded with 250 pounds of supplies and confronting temperatures that dropped as low as minus 42 degrees, the small group spent most of the first few weeks just trying to keep warm. They had to make hazardous crossings of the frozen pack ice covering the fjords that cut into the island's northeastern coast. In the middle of Baffin Island they traded their sleds for folding kayaks to paddle and portage through a maze of lakes and rivers, often following the traditional route of Inuit caribou hunters. Finally, the group reached the southernmost tip of the island after 192 days of intense but exhilarating physical exertion and cold.

THE PACIFIC

FRENCH POLYNESIA

By Freighter to the Marquesas Islands

Operator:
Compagnie Polynesienne de Transport Maritime, 2028 El Camino Real S., Suite B, San Mateo, Calif. 94403; (415) 574-2575; www.aranui.com.
Price: Moderate to expensive, depending on type of accommodation.
Season: Year-round.
Length: 16 days.
Accommodations: Shipboard cabins. Five percent discount with BBAT coupon.

In 1985 the cargo ship *Aranui* began monthly service from Tahiti to all six inhabited Marquesas Islands, among the most isolated and legendary in the Pacific. Up to 100 passengers ride deck-passage; the others travel in comfort in air-conditioned cabins, eat meals prepared by a French chef, and are cared for by an English-speaking hostess. Ample shore time is allowed. Of particular interest are Atuona on Hiva Oa, where French artist Paul Gauguin lived out his final years and is buried; the enormous stone tikis of Puamau, also on Hiva Oa; and Hanavave, a tiny village of 200 tucked away in the spectacular Bay of Virgins on Fatu Hiva. Full-day stops are also made at Takapoto, Ahe, and Rangiroa atolls in the Tuamotu group. This just may be the best adventure going in the Pacific.

VANUATU

The Islands of the Coral Sea

East of Australia lies a great arc of islands known as Melanesia. Here the visitor finds dense rain forests, grassy volcanic ridges deeply cut by plunging valleys, cascading mountain falls, precipitous cliffs, and idyllic atolls. The islands are home to a rich diversity of primitive cultures, many of which have managed to endure without significant disruption by outside influences. Participants on this seagoing expedition board their ship *Marine Spirit* in Fiji for an anthropological voyage to many of

"To lie about a far country is easy."

AMHARIC PROVERB

The celebrated French painter Paul Gauguin lies buried on Hiva Oa, one of the Marquesas Islands visited by the freighter *Aranui*
James C. Simmons

the most remote and fascinating islands in the Coral Sea, including Vanuatu's Pentecost Island, famous for its spectacular festival in which men dive off 90-foot-high platforms with vines tied to their feet to prevent them from hitting the ground; Solomon Islands' Nendo Island, where the men still use red-feather money to buy brides; Guadalcanal, capital of the Solomon Islands and the site of a long, fierce WWII battle between U.S. Marines and Japanese soldiers; Papua New Guinea's New Britain with its capital of Rabaul set at the foot of three volcanoes, and New Ireland, an island so remote that the people still retain all their traditional customs and culture.

Operator: Marine Expeditions, 30 Hazleton Ave., Toronto, Ont., Canada M5R 2E2; (800) 263-9147 or (416) 964-9069; www.marineex.com.
Price: Expensive.
Season: May.
Length: 19 days.
Accommodations: Shipboard cabins.

UNITED STATES

ALASKA

Prince William Sound Aboard the Discovery

Southeastern Alaska is where you go for a vivid glimpse of what most of the Northern Hemisphere looked like 10,000 years ago when the last ice age

Operator:
Geographic Expeditions,
2627 Lombard St., San
Francisco, Calif. 94123;
(800) 777-8183 or (415)
922-0448; www.geoex.com.
Price: Expensive.
Season: June and August.
Length: 2 and 5 days.
Accommodations: Shipboard
cabins. Five percent dis-
count with BBAT coupon.

was in retreat. Everywhere you look are long ribbons of ice flowing to the sea, resculpting the land
in the process. Prince William Sound is also home
to a rich selection of wildlife. Seals, bears, otters,
beavers, and deer abound, with more than 200
species of birds and fish along the sound's 3,000
shoreline miles of bays, coves, and deep fjords.
Visitors on this cruise explore this wonderland
from the deck of the 65-foot *Discovery*, with its six
snug cabins. Plenty of opportunity is allowed for
shore walks and close-up tours on inflatable rafts.

Seeing the Inside Passage from the Deck of a Minesweeper

Operator:
The Boat Company,
811 First Ave., #454,
Seattle, Wash. 98104;
(206) 624-4242;
www.theboatcompany.com.
Price: Expensive.
Season: Late-May–mid-
September.
Length: 6 to 9 days.
Accommodations: Shipboard
cabins.

Southeastern Alaska, with its 10,000 miles of
rugged coastline, towering glaciers, and abundance of wildlife, ranks today as one of the most
popular cruising destinations in the United States.
The major cruise ships, however, are little more
than floating hotels. For those who prefer a more
intimate experience, there are the *Observer* and the
Liseron, two wooden vessels originally commissioned as World War II minesweepers. Small and
maneuverable, with shallow drafts, they can easily
enter the coves and inlets that the big ships cannot,
where much of the wildlife can be found. Carrying
a maximum of just 24 passengers plus naturalists,
the two ships explore the Tongass National Forest.
Stretching 500 miles from the Canadian border to
north of Skagway, the Tongass is the nation's largest
national forest.

*"Travel is necessary to understanding man. Such delicate goods as justice,
love, honor, and courtesy are valid everywhere, but they are variously
molded, often differently handled, and sometimes nearly unrecognizable if
you meet them in a foreign land. The art of learning fundamental common
values is perhaps the greatest gain of travel to those who wish to live at
ease among their fellows."*

FREYA STARK
PERSEUS IN THE WIND

NEW YORK

Cruising the Erie Canal

This itinerary will delight the sailor, historian, engineer, architect, and lover of flora and fauna. Two ships carry 80 passengers each and have been designed with special shallow drafts and retractable pilot houses to allow them to pass under numerous low bridges. Passengers board in Warren, Rhode Island, then sail along the New England shoreline and up the Hudson River, past the manor homes of Franklin Roosevelt, Martin Van Buren, Washington Irving, and Frederick Vanderbilt. The heart of the cruise is the passage up the historic Erie Canal and through its numerous locks. Next the ships travel along the St. Lawrence Seaway to Montreal and Quebec, then to the scenic Saguenay River, a breeding ground for beluga whales. The cruise ends in Montreal and the passengers return to Providence, Rhode Island, by chartered bus. The last two cruises of each year feature New England fall foliage.

Operator: American Canadian Caribbean Line, P.O. Box 368, Warren, R.I. 02885; (800) 556-7450 or (401) 274-0955; www.accl-smallships.com.
Price: Expensive.
Season: June–mid-October.
Length: 12 days.
Accommodations: Shipboard cabins. Five percent discount with BBAT coupon.

PROFILE

SVEN-OLOF LINDBLAD
SPECIAL EXPEDITIONS

Our expeditionary cruise ship, the *Polaris*, bobbed gently in the swells. Overhead thousands of gannets, puffins, and storm petrels wheeled in the wind currents. Rafts of puffins rode the ocean's surface. Just off our bow the mysterious Skellig Islands, two sea-besieged citadels steeped in Irish history and legend, rose like apparitions out of the sea some eight miles west of County Kerry, Ireland.

I had come to this remote place with Special Expeditions of New York City. Each spring the company sends one of its expeditionary cruise ships along the wildest coasts in all Europe to explore the islands off the coasts of Britain, Ireland, and Scotland, among the most legendary in Europe. Steeped in ancient ruins, rare bird life, and history, they boast remarkable archaeological sites that reveal the many layers of human settlements over the centuries, from Stone and Bronze Age people to Picts, Celts, Romans, and Vikings.

We were a group of 64 passengers plus a teaching staff of four naturalists, an archaeologist, and a historian. They turned our ship into a floating seminar, giving slide-show presentations and lectures before each landing and accompanying the passengers ashore for additional presentations in the field.

Our main destination that day was Skellig Michael, a deeply eroded and weathered rocky thumb some 44 acres big and 715 feet high. We landed and walked along a paved path to a set of 600 perfectly preserved stone steps which led up from the sea through spongy mats of seapink. Like modern pilgrims, we climbed the flagstone steps, passing out of history into another world, one of enchanted myth. At the top, 550 feet above the sea, we came abruptly upon a stone wall (also perfectly preserved), passed through a doorway, and found ourselves in one of the most remarkable and least-visited archaeological sites in Ireland— the nearly intact buildings of a sixth-century monastic community. For many years this little settlement represented the westernmost outpost of Christianity in Europe, at a time when Islam posed a threat from the south and pagan Vikings raided from the north.

Awestruck, we wandered through the complex. The site is quite small, just over 300 feet long and 150 feet wide. Six ancient beehive-

shaped huts, two boat-shaped oratories, a medieval church, and a small graveyard studded with stone crosses fill the compound. The church is in a state of picturesque collapse, but the other buildings are remarkably intact. The cells and oratories are all dry-built of corbel construction.

"What is impressive about Skellig Michael is the completeness of the site," Dr. Richard Hall, our archaeologist from York, England, told us. "Here one can get in touch with the ancient way of life led by those Irish monks and hermits. We are seeing what the monks saw all those centuries ago."

Expeditionary cruises have been growing in popularity with travelers in recent years, carrying thousands of passengers to such remote regions as Antarctica, the Arctic, the outlying islands of Polynesia, the Indonesian archipelago, and up the Amazon River. Passengers on these trips are not looking for the food and entertainment but for the adventure, wildlife, and exotic cultures they know they will experience. The more remote the destination, the stronger the appeal. Travelers have come to recognize that expeditionary cruises, as opposed to the more traditional big-ship cruises, do have strong appeal for adventurous travelers. And they also allow access to many areas not easily reached by land.

Sven-Olof Lindblad's Special Expeditions is a leader in the field of expeditionary cruising. His fleet of highly specialized cruise ships carries more than 11,000 passengers annually to some of the world's most remote wildernesses. The company's sea and land programs are staffed with expedition leaders, naturalists, historians, and cultural authorities who are knowledgeable experts on the flora, fauna, culture, and history of the regions they visit. All of his ships are equipped with the highly agile, motorized, Zodiac inflatable rafts for spontaneous, up-close observation of marine and land animals.

"We believe that travel should stimulate and enrich the mind without sacrificing the elements of physical comfort," Lindblad insists. "We reflect this point of view in our selection of destinations which focus on the natural world and its inhabitants. We give travelers a true sense of adventure and limit the number of participants to allow a spirit of camaraderie to develop. Itineraries are kept flexible so that we can exploit unexpected sightings—a pod of whales off the coast of Baja California, a gathering of polar bears on a remote stretch of Spitzbergen Island north of the Arctic Circle, and the chance to photograph trees along the Sepik River in New Guinea lit by thousands of synchronous fireflies."

Recently, Lindblad commissioned a study of his company's demographics and developed a profile of his clients: "They come from all walks of occupational life. Generally, they are highly educated. They have high income, but they are less into material things, more interested in experiential things. They are concerned about their environment, but not rabid about it."

Born in Zurich, Switzerland, in 1950, Lindblad traveled extensively as a boy with his father, Lars-Eric, the founder of Lindblad Travel and the man who almost single-handedly developed the concept of organized adventure travel tours. Lars-Eric opened up such exotic areas as Antarctica, the Arctic, Tibet, Patagonia, Bhutan, the Falkland Islands, Tierra del Fuego, Easter Island, the Galapagos Islands, and much of China to organized tours. The pioneering expeditionary cruise ship he commissioned, the *Lindblad Explorer*, was the first to carry passengers to the far-flung and rarely visited corners of the world's oceans, pushing the frontiers of cruising far beyond what any thought possible. "Being the son of Lars-Eric Lindblad was a little tough if you wanted to go into the travel business because he didn't leave much to discover," his son admits today.

Curiously, in his youth Sven-Olof showed little interest in his father's business. Instead of heading to college, he spent several years in East Africa, photographing elephants and cheetahs in Tsavo National Park in Kenya. For a time he assisted famed primatologist Dian Fossey in her work among the gorillas of Rwanda. And he even worked on a film crew documenting the destruction of African wildlife and the habitats that support them. During this time he developed a strong commitment to conservation. As he recalls today: "When I was in Tsavo one day, for the fun of it, I decided to go out alone and see how many black rhinos I could count. I counted 59. Today you are lucky to see one in two weeks!"

Eventually, Lindblad went to work for Lindblad Travel and in 1979 started Special Expeditions as a division of his father's company. "I gravitated to small ships because they allow the freedom to move into environments that are otherwise inaccessible, while living decently on board," he recalls today. After two years, he spun Special Expeditions off as a separate company. The two Lindblads, however, remained close, and the son adopted the credo on which his father had based his company: "I believe in freedom, creativity, and conversation. And further, I believe that tourism is the handmaiden of them all. I believe in creating new possibilities for human experience and understanding."

In 1986 Lindblad acquired the *Polaris*, a 238-foot-long cruise ship with cabins for 80 passengers, and used it for a series of cruises along the wilder coasts of Europe, across the North Atlantic, up to the Canadian Arctic, down the coast of South America, and 2,000 miles up the Amazon River. "The ship was small enough so we could manage the logistics of putting people ashore in almost any environment without undue impact, and large enough so there would be no sacrifices to comfort and service," he observes. (Today Lindblad stations the *Polaris* in the Galapagos Islands on a year-round basis while using the *Caledonia Star* for his northern Atlantic cruises.)

Expeditionary cruising at its best gives opportunism a good name. A flexible itinerary is the secret of its success. A sudden change in the weather, for instance, can force itinerary changes. But much more exciting is the possibility of an unexpected landing at a site that has not been visited before. On those occasions, expeditionary cruising becomes exploratory in the true sense of the word.

From the start Lindblad's major goal of Special Expeditions has been to target the growing market for environmentally conscious adventure travelers. He followed after his father in his commitment to ecotourism. "Tourism is clearly a double-edged sword," he admits. "We have a strong commitment to visiting a place, learning about it, and leaving it intact. If we want to conserve a place a legitimate way, tourism can become more meaningful and play a critical role. We're not involved in environmental protection purely because we're altruists. It's because it's good business. The well-being of the environment is critical to our business. I believe that ecotourism is absolutely the wave of the future. People will demand to travel with companies that take these kinds of issues seriously."

11

FAMILY ADVENTURE TRAVEL

Family adventure-travel vacations have taken off in recent years and now represent the fastest growing area within the large organized adventure travel industry. As they depart for summer vacation this year, many families will forego Disney World and opt instead for a white-water rafting trip or a biking expedition. According to one recent survey, adventure trips are ranked by consumers as among the five most popular family vacation choices. After *Outside* magazine published a special guide to family adventure-travel vacations, Nancy Zimmerman, an executive editor, insisted, "The point we're trying to make is if you're an active adult used to adventures, that doesn't have to end just because you have kids."

There are a good many reasons for this growing popularity. Wilderness trips provide a sure way for families to come together, free from the artificial diversions that grab children's attention at home but provide little basis for real education. And adventure travel for children is often educational and fun at the same time, an unbeatable combination for both kids and their parents. These trips can also give children a tremendous sense of accomplishment. A child as young as five can lead a llama along a trail, according to author Candyce Stapen, who described the experience of a Maine llama trek she took with her children as "like wandering through the woods with Big Bird."

Younger children on Journeys International treks in Nepal can always ride in baskets on the backs of porters when they are too tired to walk

Journeys International

Florine Herendeen signed up with her husband, their six-year-old son, Nolan, and three-year-old daughter, Kellyn, for a Journeys International family trip to Costa Rica. There they watched sea turtles nesting on a beach, visited Arenal volcano, went rafting on the gentle Corobici River, and took a horseback ride through Rincon de la Viega National Park. "I see changes in my own six-year-old," Florine observed a few weeks after their return. "He now has a new appreciation for nature and is noticing the wildlife around our own home."

AFRICA

TANZANIA

Wildlife Week for Families

This is a big-game safari especially designed for families with older children. The itinerary includes three of the premier viewing areas for wildlife in East Africa—Lake Manyara National Park, noted for its tree-climbing lions, enormous hippo population, and excellent birding; Ngorongoro Crater, an enormous volcanic crater that's home to lions, elephants, rhinos, zebras, and a host of other animals; and Serengeti National Park, which holds the largest concentration of wildlife in East Africa. Visits are also made to local families in a Masai tribal village.

Operator: Journeys International, 107 Aprill Dr., #3, Ann Arbor, Mich. 48103; (800) 255-8735 or (734) 665-4407; www.journeys-intl.com.
Price: Expensive.
Season: June and July; other departures by special arrangement.
Length: 8 days.
Accommodations: Lodges and semipermanent tent camps. Five percent discount with BBAT coupon.

"All journeys are rhapsodies on the theme of discovery. We travel as seekers after answers we cannot find at home."
PHIL COUSINEAU
THE ART OF PILGRIMAGE

ASIA

NEPAL

Annapurna Family Trek

Operator:
Journeys International,
107 Aprill Dr., #3,
Ann Arbor, Mich. 48103;
(800) 255-8735 or
(734) 665-4407;
www.journeys-intl.com.
Price: Moderate.
Season: December; other
departures by special
arrangement.
Length: 16 days.
Accommodations: Tent
camps. Five percent dis-
count with BBAT coupon.

The 10th-highest mountain in the world, Annapurna lies in the midst of some of the Himalayas' most magnificent scenery. This trek has been toned down to suit the needs of younger explorers. Hiking distances are kept short and are along well-kept trails. Porters or pack animals carry most personal gear, food, and equipment. Young children under 50 pounds have the options of hiking or being carried in specially-designed porter baskets. The itinerary for this trip includes the Gurung village of Landrung and a visit to a local school; the village of Chandrakot, where travelers can observe a constant flow of religious pilgrims and Tibetan pony caravans; and lovely Phewa Lake where the group sets up camp in a grove of giant sacred Bodhi trees.

AUSTRALASIA

AUSTRALIA

Australia Family Odyssey

Operator:
Journeys International,
107 Aprill Dr., #3,
Ann Arbor, Mich. 48103;
(800) 255-8735 or
(734) 665-4407;
www.journeys-intl.com.
Price: Expensive.
Season: July and August;
other departures by special
arrangement.

Few Americans realize that Australia has the world's second-oldest national park system. Families on this expedition visit some of the most celebrated parks. Several days are spent in the heart of the Outback at Ayers Rock and Alice Springs, which can include a climb to the top of Ayers, the world's largest rock, rising almost 1,000 feet above the surrounding desert. Two nights are spent at a working cattle station (ranch) where kangaroos, wallabies, and dingoes abound; children can explore the surrounding area from the back of a camel on an escorted ride. Special arrangements have been made for a visit to the Outback "School of the Air" where teachers conduct classes via radio for children who live hundreds of miles away. Several days are also spent on Australia's famed tropical coast for a visit to the Great Barrier Reef.

Length: 13 days.
Accommodations: Hotels and ranch bunkhouses. Five percent discount with BBAT coupon.

CANADA

BRITISH COLUMBIA

Marine Science Camp

One of North America's leading operators of sea-kayaking trips, Ecosummer Expeditions also runs an experiential learning and skill-building program for students and their families who are interested in taking a closer look than usual at the natural sciences. Staffed with accredited teachers, naturalists, and field biologists and set in some of the most beautiful coastal wilderness in western Canada, the camp allows students to work side-by-side with professionals who have both the firsthand knowledge and the passion to share it. The learning environment is built around one of the richest coastal envi-

Operator:
Ecosummer Expeditions,
936 Peace Portal Dr.,
P.O. Box 8014-240,
Blaine, Wash. 98231;
(800) 465-8884 or
(604) 214-7484;
www.ecosummer.com.
Price: Moderate.
Season: April–June.
Length: 7 days.

A camel ride is just one of the many adventures children can enjoy while on a Journeys International's family trip to Australia
Journeys International

Accommodations: Dormitory-style rooms at research base. Five percent discount with BBAT coupon.

ronments in the natural world and includes a field station equipped with light and stereo microscopes, live tanks, plankton trawling gear, and a host of other learning aids and research materials. A major focus of the program is tidepool ecology.

EUROPE

ITALY

Tuscan Fantasy

Operator:
Ciclismo Classico,
30 Marathon St.,
Arlington, Mass. 02474;
(800) 866-7314 or
(781) 646-3377;
www.ciclismoclassico.com.
Price: Expensive.
Season: June–early
September.
Length: 7 days.
Accommodations: Restored
farmhouse. Five percent discount with BBAT coupon.

The leading player in bike and hiking tours of Italy, this operator also offers an idyllic, villa-based learning experience for families in this popular cultural adventure. Home base is a fully restored, 15th-century farmhouse offering panoramic views, a pool, tennis courts, and horseback riding. Local cycling trips are combined with lectures on Tuscan history and art, cooking lessons from a Tuscan chef, and tours of medieval villages. There are beginning bicycle clinics for the children, along with a variety of games and activities. While the adults are off cycling to Monte Secchieta, the highest point in Tuscany, the children will be enjoying their own

The Adventure Travel Hall of Fame: BIKING THE ALASKA RANGE

In the summer of 1995 a team of three adventurers— Roman Dial, Paul Adkins, and Carl Tobin—set out on one of the most arduous mountain-bike journeys ever undertaken, a seven-week, 775-mile expedition to traverse the rugged Alaska Range from the Yukon border in the east to the base of the Aleutian Range in the west. They passed through a wilderness of boulders, brush, and belly-deep bogs, following game trails and gravel bars. They also rafted rivers, pedaled across glaciers, and climbed icy mountains to complete their ambitious, high-country journey. They traveled light, carrying just 20 pounds each in food, gear,

adventures, perhaps visiting a gelateria to learn how Italian ice cream is made or joining some Italian children in a soccer game.

LATIN AMERICA

BELIZE

Belize Wildlife Adventure

The least-populated country in Central America, with a Caribbean rather than a Latin culture, Belize offers families rain forests, pine-covered mountains, Mayan ruins, caves, and the world's second-longest barrier reef. Canoeing, swimming, birding, and horseback-riding are among the options on this children-friendly wildlife expedition. The highlights include a trip along the Macai River by motorized canoe; a visit to the cave of Che Chem Ha and its cache of 1,500-year-old pots left by the Maya; a visit to the magnificent Mayan ruins of Tikal, just across the border in Guatemala; and snorkeling at Southwater Caye in the heart of the barrier reef.

Operator: Journeys International, 107 Aprill Dr., #3, Ann Arbor, Mich. 48103; (800) 255-8735 or (734) 665-4407; www.journeys-intl.com.
Price: Expensive.
Season: February and June; other departures by special arrangement.
Length: 8 days.
Accommodations: Lodges. Five percent discount with BBAT coupon.

and clothing. They saved weight by sleeping in a floorless tent and using bike tools as silverware. Because the park service prohibits any mechanized travel within the Denali Wilderness, the trio had to hike the 60 miles across the backcountry to be reunited with their bikes at the western border. They completed history's first traverse of the Alaskan Range following caribou and bear trails through Lake Clark National Park. After weeks of survival on freeze-dried meals and high-energy bars, they celebrated with a meal of pasta and garden-fresh peas and tomatoes. "A half-dozen flat tires, just as many hard spills, sore legs, sprained wrists, and aching backs all came with the territory," Roman Dial wrote in an article in the May 1997 issue of National Geographic. "But so did memories of sublime wilderness—of the glacier-hung mountains still free of names, of misty valleys dotted with caribou, and of braided rivers."

COSTA RICA

Family Adventure in the Rain Forest

Operator:
Journeys International, 107
April Dr., #3, Ann Arbor,
Mich. 48103;
(800) 255-8735 or
(734) 665-4407;
www.journeys-intl.com.
Price: Moderate.
Season: February; other
departures by special
arrangement.
Length: 8 days.
Accommodations: Hotels.
Five percent discount with
BBAT coupon.

Costa Rica's commitment to environmental preservation and democratic tradition make it the ideal destination in Latin America for families. This itinerary allows parents and their children an opportunity to explore one of the country's finest rainforest reserves and observe two memorable events—volcanic eruptions and leatherback sea turtles nesting on a Caribbean beach. The child-friendly activities include a visit to Arenal, Costa Rica's most active volcano, and a swim in nearby thermal pools; a two-hour rafting trip down the gentle Corobici River; an exploration of the cloud forest reserve at Monteverde, home to neon-colored poison dart frogs, huge bullet ants, spectacular hummingbirds, and toucans; and the beach at Tamarindo where hundreds of large female leatherback turtles come ashore at night to lay their eggs in the warm sand.

ECUADOR

Galapagos Wildlife Odyssey

Operator:
Journeys International, 107
April Dr., #3,
Ann Arbor, Mich. 48103;
(800) 255-8735 or
(734) 665-4407;
www.journeys-intl.com.
Price: Expensive.
Season: Dates throughout
the year.
Length: 11 days.
Accommodations: Shipboard
cabins. Five percent dis-
count with BBAT coupon.

The Galapagos Islands offer one of the premier wildlife-viewing experiences in the world. Because most of the animals do not have natural enemies on their islands, they are unperturbed when human visitors approach closely. This makes the islands ideally suited for young people. As fascinating as the encounters on land are, those that take place in the warm waters offshore are even more exciting. Parents are urged to bring snorkeling masks so their children can enjoy the schools of brightly colored reef fish and the frisky sea lions, eager to play once you join them in their watery realm. Passage among the islands is aboard a comfortable yacht; for older children, instruction in the fundamentals of sailing is another option.

Older children will find numerous occasions for close encounters with local wildlife on the journeys International trip to the Galapagos Islands
Journeys International

UNITED STATES

CALIFORNIA

Lodge-Based Kayaking Adventure on the Klamath River

The operator insists this is a great trip for families with older children and for first-timers. Located along the border between California and Oregon, the Klamath offers impressive canyons, moderate water temperature, and abundant wildlife. The operator provides 10-foot inflatable plastic kayaks which have proven their effectiveness with thousands of first-time paddlers since 1969. (Hard-shell kayaks, by contrast, can be tippy and require a longer training period.) The operator also offers a camping version of this trip.

Operator:
Orange Torpedo Trips, P.O. Box 1111, Grants Pass, Ore. 97526; (541) 479-5061; www.orangetorpedo.com.
Price: Moderate.
Season: May.
Length: 3 days.
Accommodations: Lodge.
Five percent discount with BBAT coupon.

"Traveler, there is no path. Paths are made by walking."

ANTONIO MACHADO
SPANISH POET

COLORADO

Kids' Dinosaur Camp

Operator:
Dinosaur Discovery
Expeditions, 550 Jurassic
Ct., Fruita, Colo. 81521;
(800) DIG-DINO or
(970) 858-7282;
www.digdino.org.
Price: Moderate.
Season: July and August.
Length: 5 days.
Accommodations: Motel. Five
percent discount with
BBAT coupon.

"After 'Mommy,' 'Daddy,' 'yes,' and 'no,' often a child's fifth word is 'stegosaurus,'" director Steven Spielberg quipped after the release of his film *Jurassic Park.* "Kids are completely dino-savvy at a very young age." Dinosaur Discovery Expeditions offers families the chance to experience the wonders of paleontology. Their Kids' Dinosaur Camp is specially geared for children ages six to 12. Each five-day kids' session runs concurrently with each regular five-day adult expedition. Parents and their children are offered separate instruction and activities. While the children are uncovering "planted" bone replicas in a mock quarry, their parents are

Young children with an interest in dinosaurs can become up close and personal with their favorite creatures at the Kid's Dinosaur Camp where they are taught how to excavate fossilized bones

James C. Simmons

painstakingly excavating fossils in a separate authentic quarry. The camp counselors offer children many activities in which their favorite subjects predominate.

Family Archaeological Excavation Program

Here's a family trip designed for parents whose children love the Discovery Channel, especially the programs on archaeology. Once a year the operator offers a special program of a week of learning about the archaeological process and excavation. The busy schedule includes an introduction to the local ecology, hands-on experiences with ancestral Puebloan lifestyles, archaeological excavation at Shields Pueblo, and a tour of spectacular Mesa Verde National Park. Each family is housed in its own Navajo-style log cabin (hogan). Minimum age for the program is 12.

Operator:
Crow Canyon
Archaeological Center,
23390 County Rd. K,
Cortez, Colo. 81321;
(800) 422-8975 or
(970) 565-8975;
www. crowcanyon.org.
Price: Moderate.
Season: July.
Length: 7 days.
Accommodations: Navajo-style hogans.

Family Llama Trek Along the Continental Divide

Llamas—the animal one devoted fan described as "the front end of a camel and the caboose of an ostrich wedded to the personality of a teddy bear"—are now in use by the hundreds on trails as pack animals in many parts of the Western wilderness. The animals are smaller and more docile than horses and mules and not nearly as intimidating to people with little experience handling large animals. They are particularly great for parents with children who still want to camp out but don't want the hassle of 60-pound backpacks. Children will enjoy leading a llama along the trail and in the process making a new friend. The operator offers a popular llama trek along the Continental Divide on a section of the famous Colorado Trail.

Operator:
Paragon Guides, P.O. Box
130, Vail, Colo. 81658;
(877) 926-5299 or
(970) 926-5299;
www.paragonguides.com.
Price: Expensive.
Season: August and
September.
Length: 4 days.
Accommodations: Tent camp
one night, mountain huts
the other nights. Five percent discount with BBAT
coupon.

"Glorious it is when wandering time is come."

ESKIMO SONG

IDAHO

Family Fun on the Salmon

Operator:
River Odysseys West,
P.O. Box 579,
Coeur d'Alene, Idaho
83816;
(800) 451-6034 or
(208) 765-0841;
www.rowinc.com.
Price: Moderate.
Season: July and August.
Length: 5 days.
Accommodations: Tent
camps. Ten percent dis-
count with BBAT coupon.

The Salmon River provides families with a magical mixture of sun, sand, and warm water perfect for swimming. There's enough white water to get the kids' adrenaline flowing, but not enough to worry their parents. The expansive white-sand beaches are just the thing for nighttime camping—or a game of volleyball. The operator offers several departures designed just for families. An extra guide accompanies the trips to keep an eye on the little ones (ages five to 16). The days are packed with fun-filled, nature-oriented games and activities, ranging from building sand castles to nature hikes. There's even a special kids' menu at all meals. And parents will appreciate the fact that each evening the staff does all the work of setting up camp and preparing the meals.

MAINE

Easy Canoe Adventure on the West Branch of the Penobscot

Operator:
Allagash Canoe Trips,
P.O. Box 713,
Greenville, Maine 04441;
(207) 695-3668;
alcanoe@moosehead.net.
Price: Inexpensive.
Season: July or by special
arrangement.
Length: 5 days.
Accommodations: Tent
camps. Five percent dis-
count with BBAT coupon.

The scenic upper West Branch of the Penobscot River provides an excellent experience for families seeking to introduce their children to the wonders of wilderness canoeing. The distance covered on this trip is short, with no white water to frighten the younger children but plenty of good activities for them to enjoy, such as swimming in the warm water, watching (from a safe distance) the moose feeding along the banks, and the evening campfires. A stop is made at historic Chesuncook Village, a great place to camp, swim, and pick berries.

Family Sailing Adventure Along the Coast

The operator's fleet of fine windjammer ships includes the lovely *Mistress*, a combination traditional schooner and private yacht. With accommodations for just six passengers, she provides an intimate setting for family vacations. Children of all ages will find plenty to do, both on board and ashore exploring deserted islands. The cruises are unstructured and can be customized to suit each family's interests. They sail through Penobscot Bay, a 30-mile-wide waterway dotted with hundreds of islands, many etched in pink granite and covered with teal-colored forests. A highlight is an old-fashioned New England lobster bake, cooked over a driftwood fire on an uninhabited island—steamed lobsters, clams, corn, cheeses, salads, and vegetable buffet.

Operator: Maine Windjammer Cruises, P.O. Box 617, Camden, Maine 04843; (800) 736-7981 or (207) 236-2939; www.mainewindjammer-cruises.com.
Price: Moderate.
Season: June–early September.
Length: 2, 3, 4, and 5 days.
Accommodations: Shipboard cabins. Ten percent discount with BBAT coupon.

MARYLAND

Kid Ship Sailing School

Long recognized as the finest sailing school in the United States, the operator now offers a special sailing school for children ages five through 15. Kid

The Mistress, a small windjammer, serves as an intimate setting for family sail adventures along the Maine coast

Robert Jenks/Maine Windjammer Cruises

Operator:
Annapolis Sailing School,
P.O. Box 3334,
Annapolis, Md.;
(800) 638-9192 or
(410) 267-7205;
www.usboat.com/annapway.
Price: Inexpensive.
Season: June–August.
Length: 2, 3, and 5 days.
Accommodations: Not
included. Five percent discount with BBAT coupon.

Ship's fleet consists of a variety of centerboard sailing dinghies that are safe, responsive, and just the right size for younger sailors. Kids' classes are coordinated with adult classes at the Annapolis Sailing School so the family can learn together. Instruction includes all the nuts and bolts of sailing, including nautical theory and terminology. Parents and children get together at lunch.

MASSACHUSETTS

Windjamming Off Cape Cod

Operator:
Coastwise Packet Company,
P.O. Box 429, Vineyard
Haven, Mass. 02568;
(508) 693-1699;
www.coastwisepacket.com.
Price: Moderate.
Season: Mid-June–mid-September.
Length: 6 days.
Accommodations: Shipboard
cabins.

Launched in 1964, the clipper schooner *Shenandoah* was designed and built expressly for passenger service, incorporating the best of 19th-century maritime tradition. She measures 152 feet overall and flies 7,000 square feet of sail from topmasts that soar 94 feet up. Her cabins are spartan but comfortable. Berthed on the island of Martha's Vineyard, the *Shenandoah* sails on cruises in the wakes of the whalers, clippers, and privateers that once crowded the busy ports in this area. Many of the cruises are focused on children, teaching the youngsters about their maritime heritage and numerous skills of sailing. They become part of the crew and help with the deck-swabbing, galley duty,

The Adventure Travel Hall of Fame: JOSEPH F. ROCK

Explorer, botanist, writer, and photographer, Joseph F. Rock was the National Geographic Society's man in China from 1913 to 1935, mounting one marathon expedition after another through the unmapped mountains and kingdoms of premodern China. Braving bandits and courting kings, his adventures yielded 10 memorable articles in the society's magazine. Setting out for months at a time, he traveled in style. One such expedition in the 1920s included 26 mules and 17 men, who were accompanied by 190 soldiers for protection from bandits. His baggage included tents, a folding bed, chairs, a table, a portable rub-

and sail-hauling. Three chaperones supervise the children. The wind and tide determine each cruise's itinerary, but the ports of call may include Nantucket, Block Island, New Bedford, New London, and Mystic.

Family Rafting on the Lower Deerfield River

For families in the Boston or Providence area who might be looking for a half-day family rafting experience, this is the perfect trip. The entire trip, including dinner and swim stops, takes just four or five hours. Families paddle through farmland and the rolling Berkshire foothills along the historic Mohawk Trail. While the Deerfield's upper stretches sport challenging rapids, the same river on this lower portion is much more subdued. Guides provide insight into the natural and cultural history of the area, thus turning the trip into a learning experience for the youngsters.

Operator:
Zoar Outdoor, P.O. Box 245, Charlemont, Mass. 01339; (800) 532-7483 or (413) 339-4010; www.zaarooutdoor.com.
Price: Inexpensive.
Season: May–early September.
Length: 4 to 5 hours. Ten percent discount with BBAT coupon.

"The world is a traveler's inn."

Afghan folk saying

ber bathtub, and table linen and china. He even brought a battery-powered phonograph, on which he played opera for the astonished nomads and monks he met in his travels. His expense account to the Society included such items as: "Chair coolies, 4 coolies at 80¢ a day." The sedan chair was the limousine that he needed to impress the kings, warlords, and village leaders in the remote wilderness, along with the white shirt, tie, and jacket he always wore at these

meetings. "You've got to make people believe you're someone of importance if you want to live in these wilds," he once remarked to his editors back in Washington, D.C. As an adventurer, he was intrigued by the cultures of China's minority peoples and frequently found himself the first white man they had ever seen. "Unless I can work in the wilderness and the unexplored regions," Rock once wrote, "I would have no incentive to living."

Echo: The Wilderness Company has for years run popular family rafting trips on Oregon's Rogue River that include specialized activities just for the kids

Echo: The Wilderness Company

MICHIGAN

Betsie River Pedal and Paddle

Operator: Michigan Bicycle Touring, 3512 Red School Rd., Kingsley, Mich. 49649; (231) 263-5885; www.bikembt.com. *Price:* Moderate. *Season:* June–August. *Length:* 3 days. *Accommodations:* Deluxe rooms at Crystal Mountain Resort. Five percent discount with BBAT coupon.

This trip provides a fun combination of easy biking and canoeing that is perfect for families with younger children. The cycling each day is through level to gently rolling farmland. On the afternoon of the first day participants gather at the Betsie River for a two-hour canoe trip. A designated wild and scenic river, the Betsie's shallow, warm, clear waters meander peacefully through unspoiled wilderness. A highlight of the second day, and one the kids will love, is a visit to a country candy kitchen, carrying on a tradition of Old World German candy-making; the owners handcraft 50 varieties of maple-syrup candies.

MINNESOTA

Family Canoe Trip Through the Boundary Waters Canoe Area Wildernes

Operator: Gunflint Northwoods Outfitters, 143 S. Gunflint Lake, Grand Marais, Minn.

Straddling the border with Canada, the Boundary Waters Canoe Area spreads over 1 million acres and a thousand lakes. It is America's premier canoeing wilderness. The area is home to numerous species of wildlife, including moose, black bears, and Canadian lynxes. For those parents who want to take their children on a canoe adventure but don't want the hassle of getting the whole crew packed and on the water, the operator has the perfect solution— guided, fully outfitted canoe trips for the entire family, with special attention to making the experience both fun and educational for the youngsters.

NEBRASKA

Wagon Train Along the Oregon Trail

If there is a single thing that sums up the westward expansion of America in the 19th century, it is the familiar covered wagon. The early pioneers braved hardships, but they also knew the community of fellowship, of sharing triumphs and failures, and of working together for survival. Starting at Independence, Missouri, and ending in the Willamette Valley, the Oregon Trail was one of two principal routes by which the West was settled. Modern families can now experience this important part of American history in a living re-creation of the wagon train. The wagons are authentic replicas of the pioneers' covered wagons, modified to include rubber tires and foam-padded seats. The pace is the same as in the 19th century, about three miles an hour. The wagons follow a stretch of the original Oregon Trail through the Nebraska wilderness. Campfire cooking, staff dressed in period costumes, and encounters with "wild" Indians turn this family vacation into an adventure of learning for the young people.

OREGON

Rafting the Rogue River

Warm water, beautiful sandy beaches perfect for campsites, and a wild, nearly pristine landscape

55604;
(800) 328-3325 or
(218) 388-2296;
www.gunflintoutfitters.com.
Price: Moderate.
Season: June and July; other times by special arrangement.
Length: 7 days.
Accommodations: Two nights in a lodge, five nights camping. Five percent discount with BBAT coupon.

Operator:
Oregon Trail Wagon Train, Rt. 2, Box 502, Bayard, Neb. 69334;
(308) 586-1850.
Price: Inexpensive.
Season: June–August.
Length: 1 and 4 days.
Accommodations: Covered wagons. Five percent discount with BBAT coupon.

Operator:
Echo: The Wilderness
Company, 6529 Telegraph
Ave., Oakland, Calif. 94609;
(800) 652-3246 or
(510) 652-1600;
www.echotrips.com.
Price: Moderate.
Season: July.
Length: 4 days.
Accommodations: Tent
camps. Five percent dis-
count with BBAT coupon.

make the Rogue one of the Pacific Northwest's most popular rivers. For years this operator has been running special departures set aside for families with children. Each of these popular Kids' Trips features a "Fun Director," a special staff person who organizes games and educational activities for the children. The operator has found these trips appeal most strongly to children aged seven to 11.

UTAH

River Trip for Families

Operator:
Sheri Griffith Expeditions,
P.O. Box 1324,
Moab, Utah 84532;
(800) 332-2439 or
(435) 259-8229;
www.GriffithExp.com.
Price: Moderate.
Season: June and July.
Length: 4 and 5 days.
Accommodations: Shore
camps. Five percent dis-
count with BBAT coupon.

This operator pioneered family-only vacations, evolving a type of river adventure specially designed for parents with children from three to 16 years of age. The guides are also teachers, enlisting the imaginations of all in setting up a learning environment for kids and adults alike. The base is Coyote Run Camp, a 20-acre camp in which the children sleep in teepees (and their parents in a homestead, if they like). There are short rafting trips on calm portions of the Colorado River through beautiful scenery with no rapids to scare the younger children. The activities include nature walks and evening campfires, complete with ghost stories for the older children. The operator also offers a special family-rafting expedition through the Majestic Canyon of the Colorado River.

WYOMING

One-Day Wildlife Safari in Yellowstone National Park

Few places in the United States offer parents a more exciting opportunity to introduce their children to wildlife than Yellowstone, the richest nature preserve in the "Lower 48." The operator has refined his one-day Discovery Safaris into the park's backcountry to accommodate the needs of families with children. Travel is by customized four-wheel-drive vehicles with sliding roof hatches for comfortable viewing. Snacks and refreshments are provided, along with binoculars and spotting scopes. When a family books, the operator reserves the vehicle for their exclusive use. The daily programs are adjusted to the pace of the children along. There are also interpretive walks and other wildlife activities outside the vehicle. Children and their parents can expect to see a wide variety of species, including moose, bison, bighorn sheep, elk, coyotes, bald eagles, beavers, and mule deer.

Operator:
Great Plains Wildlife Institute, P.O. Box 7580, Jackson Hole, Wyo. 83002; (307) 733-2623; www.wildlifesafari.com.
Price: Moderate.
Length: 1 day.
Season: Year-round. Ten percent discount with BBAT coupon.

Northern Yellowstone Wildlife and Wildflower Extravaganza

This camping trip is a perfect way for families to escape the crowds that overwhelm Yellowstone National Park in the vicinity of the Old Faithful Visitor Center. The northern range is the warmest and driest part of the park and an important breeding ground for many of the park's larger mammals, such as elk, bison, mule deer, black bears, and pronghorn antelopes. The spectacular Black Canyon of the Yellowstone River is here. Campers have plenty of opportunities for easy day hikes

Operator:
Big Wild Adventures, 5663 West Fork Rd., Darby, Mont. 59829; (406) 821-3747.
Price: Moderate to expensive, depending on the number of people.
Season: May–September.
Length: 7 days.
Accommodations: Tents. Five percent discount with BBAT coupon.

Sheri Griffith Expeditions' Coyote Run Camp along the banks of the Colorado River provides younger children with a perfect introduction to rafting

Sheri Griffith Expeditions

along trails through the forests, lush meadows of grass and sagebrush, and splendid blooms of spring wildflowers.

Jackson Lake Kayak Adventure

Operator:
O.A.R.S., Box 67, Angels Camp, Calif. 95222; (800) 346-6277 or (209) 736-4677; www.oars.com.
Price: Expensive.
Season: June–September.
Length: 1, 2, and 5 days.
Accommodations: Tent camps. Five percent discount with BBAT coupon.

The special appeal of the Grand Teton Mountains lies in their precipitous rise from the lake-studded valley of Jackson Hole, the tallest peak stabbing the sky at nearly 14,000 feet. For visitors fed up with the swelling tide of tourists at Jackson Hole, no better escape exists than these leisurely trips on Jackson Lake. The operator is the only concessionaire authorized to take clients on overnight camping trips on this world-renowned alpine lake in the heart of Grand Teton National Park, through a game-rich wilderness teeming with moose, deer, bear, otter, beaver, eagle, osprey, and Canada geese. Participants have ample time to hike through flower-strewn meadows or fish for trout. This is a perfect trip for novice kayakers and families with older children.

Families who book into the one-day wildlife viewing safaris in Yellowstone National Park offered by the Great Plains Wildlife Institute get the exclusive use of the vehicle

Great Plains Wildlife Institute

ART OF TRAVEL

Tips on Successful Adventure Travel from a 19th-Century Expert

The 19th century was the great age of adventure travel. Vast blank spaces in the Middle East, Africa, Australia, North America, and Asia beckoned. From 1850 onward, hundreds of men and a handful of women made journeys into remote and savage regions. Traveling largely alone and for a variety of reasons, they endured enormous hardships, often risked death on an almost-daily basis, and left behind a library of travel books.

For many of these Victorian travelers Francis Galton's *Art of Travel, or Shifts and Contrivances Available in Wild Countries* was an indispensable bible. The idea for a handbook of practical information on mounting adventure-travel expeditions came to the author during a two-year exploration of southwestern Africa. *Art of Travel* first appeared in 1855 and became an immediate success, going through numerous editions and several revisions over the next 20 years. In it Galton touched on a wide variety of subjects, from how to handle the death of an expedition member to which insects were safe to eat. The book provides a fascinating window on Victorian attitudes toward exploring the world beyond Europe.

ON TRAVEL

To Those Who Mediate Travel—If you have health, a great craving for adventure, at least a moderate fortune, and can set your heart on a definite object which old travellers do not think impracticable, then—travel by all means. If, in addition to these qualifications, you have scientific taste and knowledge, I believe there is no career, in time of peace, can offer you more advantages than that of a traveller.

ON SERVANTS

Engaging Natives—On engaging natives, the people with whom they have lived, and to whom they have become attached and learnt to fear, should impress upon them that, unless they bring you back in safety, they must never show their faces again, nor expect the balance of their pay, which will only be delivered to them on your return.

Reluctant Servants—Great allowance should be made for the reluctant cooperation of servants; they have infinitely less interest in the suc-

cess of the expedition than their leaders, for they derive but little credit from it. . . . It will, perhaps, surprise a leader who, having ascertained to what frugal habits a bush servant is inured, learns on trial how desperately he clings to those few luxuries which he has always had. Thus, speaking generally, a Cape servant is happy on meat, coffee, and biscuit; but if the coffee or biscuit has to be stopped for a few days, he is ready for mutiny.

Natives' Wives—If some of the natives take their wives, it gives great life to the party. They are of very great service and cause no delay; for the body of a caravan must always travel at a foot's pace, and a woman will endure a long journey nearly as well as a man, and certainly better than a horse or bullock. They are invaluable in picking up and retaining information and hearsay gossip, which will give clues to much of importance, that, unassisted, you might miss. Mr. [Samuel] Hearne, the American traveller of the last century, in his charming book writes as follows: "Women were made for labour: one of them can carry or haul as much as two men can do. They also pitch our tents, make and mend our clothing, keep us warm at night; and in fact there is no such thing as travelling any considerable distance or for any length of time in this country without their assistance."

"Women," he said again, "though they do everything are maintained at a trifling expense; for as they always stand cook, the very licking of their fingers in scarce times is sufficient for their subsistence."

ON HEALTH

Precautions in Unhealthy Places—There are certain precautions which should be borne in mind in unhealthy places . . . such as never to encamp to the leeward of a marsh; to sleep close in between large fires, with a handkerchief gathered around your face; to avoid starting too early in the morning; and to beware of unnecessary hunger, hardship, and exposure.

Tooth-ache—Tough diet tries teeth so severely that a man about to undergo it should pay a visit to a dentist before he leaves England. An unskilled traveller is very likely to make a bad job of a first attempt at tooth-drawing. By constantly pushing and pulling an aching tooth, it will in time loosen and perhaps, after some weeks, come out.

Blistered Feet—To prevent the feet from blistering, it is a good plan to soap the inside of the stocking before setting out, making a thick lather all over it. A raw egg broken into a boot, before putting it on, greatly softens the leather. Of course, the boots should be well greased when hard walking is anticipated.

Washing Oneself; Warmth of Dirt—There is no denying the fact, though it be not agreeable to confess it, that dirt and grease are great protectors of the skin against inclement weather, and that therefore the leader of the party should not be too exacting about the appearances of his less warmly clad followers. Daily washing, if not followed by oiling, must be compensated by wearing clothes. . . . In Europe we pass our lives in a strangely artificial state; our whole body swathed in many folds of dress, excepting the hands and face—the first of which are frequently gloved. We can afford to wash, but naked men cannot.

Proceedings in Case of Death—If a man of the party dies, write down a detailed account of the matter, and have it attested by the others, especially if accident be the cause of his death. If a man be lost, before you turn away and abandon him to his fate, call the party formally together, and ask them if they are satisfied that you have done all that was possible to save him, and record their answers. After death it is well to follow the custom at sea—i.e. to sell by auction all the dead man's effects among his comrades, deducting the money they fetch from the pay of the buyers, to be handed over to his relatives on the return of the expedition.

ON FOOD

Insects—Most kinds of creeping things are eatable and are used by the Chinese. Locusts and grasshoppers are not at all bad. To prepare them, pull off the legs and wings and roast them with a little grease in an iron dish, like coffee. Even gnats that swarm on the Shire River are collected by the natives and pressed into cakes.

Seizing Food—On arriving at an encampment, the natives commonly run away in fright. If you are hungry or in a serious need of anything that they have, go boldly into their huts, take just what you want, and leave fully adequate payment. It is absurd to be over-scrupulous in these cases.

ON CAMPING

Buried, or in Holes—A European can live through a bitter night on a perfectly dry sandy plain without any clothes besides what he has on, if he buries his body pretty deep in the sand, keeping only his head above ground.

ON SAVAGES

General Remarks—A frank, joking but determined manner, joined with an air of showing more confidence in the good faith of the natives than you really feel, is the best. It is observed that a sea-captain generally succeeds in making an excellent impression on savages; they thoroughly appreciate com-

mon sense, truth, and uprightness; and are not half such fools as strangers usually account them. If a savage does mischief, look on him as you would a kicking mule or a wild animal whose nature is to be unruly and vicious, and keep your temper quite unruffled.

Flogging—Different tribes have very different customs in the matter of corporal punishment; there are some who fancy it a disgrace and a serious insult. A young traveller must therefore be discriminating and cautious in the licence he allows to his stick, or he may fall into sad trouble.

Resisting an Attack—In picking out the chiefs, do not select the men that are the most showily ornamented, for they are not the chiefs; but [rather shoot at] the biggest and the busiest. Of all European inventions, nothing so impresses and terrifies savages as fireworks, especially rockets. . . . A rocket, judiciously sent up, is very likely to frighten off an intended attack and save bloodshed.

ON RETURNING HOME

Complete Your Collections—When your journey draws near its close, resist restless feelings; make every effort before it is too late to supplement deficiencies in your various collections; take stock of what you have gathered together, and think how the things will serve in England to illustrate your journey or your book. Keep whatever is pretty in itself, or is illustrative of your everyday life or that of the savages, in the way of arms, utensils and dresses. Make careful drawings of your encampment, your retinue, and whatever else you may in indolence have omitted to sketch, that will possess an after-interest. Look over your vocabularies for the last time, and complete them as far as possible. Make presents of all your traveling gear and old guns to your native attendants, for they will be mere litter in England, costly to house and attractive to moth and rust; while in the country where you have been traveling, they are of acknowledged value, and would be acceptable as keepsakes.

GEOGRAPHICAL INDEX

OPERATORS INDEX

HOW TO USE THE COUPONS

A few points to bear in mind regarding the coupons:

• Each coupon is good for one trip for one person. Couples must purchase two copies of n order to get two coupons for
a particular trip. Please do not ask operators to apply one coupon toward two or more people booking a particular trip.

• Many operators have extended these discounts to all the trips listed in their catalogs and not solely to those described in Readers should first check with individual operators to see what restrictions,
if any, apply to any particular coupon. The coupons cannot be used in conjunction with other discounts.

• Most of the discounts are for 5 percent; some are for 10 percent. Readers should check the individual trip descriptions to learn the amount of the discount a particular operator offers.

• All coupons expire on June 30, 2003. After that date they are worthless. Some operators may decide to set earlier expiration dates.

• Readers must submit thcoupon when booking a trip. Under
no circumstances will an operator accept a photocopy or other duplicate. The reader will then receive a credit for the amount of the discount against the final payment for the trip.

ABA TOURS

THE BIG BOOK OF ADVENTURE TRAVEL
DISCOUNT COUPON
NAME

Good for One Person on One Trip
Expires June 30, 2003

ABOVE THE CLOUDS TREKKING

THE BIG BOOK OF ADVENTURE TRAVEL
DISCOUNT COUPON
NAME

Good for One Person on One Trip
Expires June 30, 2003

ADVENTURE CENTER

THE BIG BOOK OF ADVENTURE TRAVEL
DISCOUNT COUPON
NAME

Good for One Person on One Trip
Expires June 30, 2003

ALASKA DISCOVERY

THE BIG BOOK OF ADVENTURE TRAVEL
DISCOUNT COUPON
NAME

Good for One Person on One Trip
Expires June 30, 2003

ALASKAN BICYCLE ADVENTURES

THE BIG BOOK OF ADVENTURE TRAVEL
DISCOUNT COUPON
NAME

Good for One Person on One Trip
Expires June 30, 2003

JAMES C. SIMMONS

AVALON TRAVEL PUBLISHING

EMERYVILLE, CALIFORNIA

JAMES C. SIMMONS

AVALON TRAVEL PUBLISHING

EMERYVILLE, CALIFORNIA

ALLAGASH CANOE TRIPS

THE BIG BOOK OF ADVENTURE TRAVEL
DISCOUNT COUPON

NAME

Good for One Person on One Trip
Expires June 30, 2003

AMERICAN CANADIAN CARIBBEAN LINE

THE BIG BOOK OF ADVENTURE TRAVEL
DISCOUNT COUPON

NAME

Good for One Person on One Trip
Expires June 30, 2003

ANNAPOLIS SAILING SCHOOL

THE BIG BOOK OF ADVENTURE TRAVEL
DISCOUNT COUPON

NAME

Good for One Person on One Trip
Expires June 30, 2003

APPALACHIAN WILDWATERS

THE BIG BOOK OF ADVENTURE TRAVEL
DISCOUNT COUPON

NAME

Good for One Person on One Trip
Expires June 30, 2003

ARCTIC ODYSSEYS

THE BIG BOOK OF ADVENTURE TRAVEL
DISCOUNT COUPON

NAME

Good for One Person on One Trip
Expires June 30, 2003

JAMES C. SIMMONS
AVALON TRAVEL PUBLISHING
EMERYVILLE, CALIFORNIA

JAMES C. SIMMONS
AVALON TRAVEL PUBLISHING
EMERYVILLE, CALIFORNIA

ASIAN PACIFIC ADVENTURES

THE BIG BOOK OF ADVENTURE TRAVEL
DISCOUNT COUPON

NAME

Good for One Person on One Trip
Expires June 30, 2003

ASIA TRANSPACIFIC JOURNEYS

THE BIG BOOK OF ADVENTURE TRAVEL
DISCOUNT COUPON

NAME

Good for One Person on One Trip
Expires June 30, 2003

BACK-COUNTRY

THE BIG BOOK OF ADVENTURE TRAVEL
DISCOUNT COUPON

NAME

Good for One Person on One Trip
Expires June 30, 2003

BACKROADS

THE BIG BOOK OF ADVENTURE TRAVEL
DISCOUNT COUPON

NAME

Good for One Person on One Trip
Expires June 30, 2003

BAJA DISCOVERY

THE BIG BOOK OF ADVENTURE TRAVEL
DISCOUNT COUPON

NAME

Good for One Person on One Trip
Expires June 30, 2003

The
BIG
Book
of
ADVENTURE
TRAVEL

JAMES C. SIMMONS
AVALON TRAVEL PUBLISHING
EMERYVILLE, CALIFORNIA

The
BIG
Book
of
ADVENTURE
TRAVEL

JAMES C. SIMMONS
AVALON TRAVEL PUBLISHING
EMERYVILLE, CALIFORNIA

BAJA EXPEDITIONS

THE BIG BOOK OF ADVENTURE TRAVEL
DISCOUNT COUPON

NAME

Good for One Person on One Trip
Expires June 30, 2003

BATTENKILL CANOE

THE BIG BOOK OF ADVENTURE TRAVEL
DISCOUNT COUPON

NAME

Good for One Person on One Trip
Expires June 30, 2003

BICYCLE AFRICA

THE BIG BOOK OF ADVENTURE TRAVEL
DISCOUNT COUPON

NAME

Good for One Person on One Trip
Expires June 30, 2003

BIG WILD ADVENTURES

THE BIG BOOK OF ADVENTURE TRAVEL
DISCOUNT COUPON

NAME

Good for One Person on One Trip
Expires June 30, 2003

BOOJUM EXPEDITIONS

THE BIG BOOK OF ADVENTURE TRAVEL
DISCOUNT COUPON

NAME

Good for One Person on One Trip
Expires June 30, 2003

JAMES C. SIMMONS
AVALON TRAVEL PUBLISHING
EMERYVILLE, CALIFORNIA

JAMES C. SIMMONS
AVALON TRAVEL PUBLISHING
EMERYVILLE, CALIFORNIA

CICLISMO CLASSICO

THE BIG BOOK OF ADVENTURE TRAVEL
DISCOUNT COUPON

NAME

Good for One Person on One Trip
Expires June 30, 2003

CLASSIC ADVENTURES

THE BIG BOOK OF ADVENTURE TRAVEL
DISCOUNT COUPON

NAME

Good for One Person on One Trip
Expires June 30, 2003

COMPAGNIE POLYNESIENNE DE TRANSPORT MARITIME

THE BIG BOOK OF ADVENTURE TRAVEL
DISCOUNT COUPON

NAME

Good for One Person on One Trip
Expires June 30, 2003

DESERT ADVENTURES

THE BIG BOOK OF ADVENTURE TRAVEL
DISCOUNT COUPON

NAME

Good for One Person on One Trip
Expires June 30, 2003

DESTINATION WILDERNESS

THE BIG BOOK OF ADVENTURE TRAVEL
DISCOUNT COUPON

NAME

Good for One Person on One Trip
Expires June 30, 2003

The **BIG** Book of ADVENTURE TRAVEL

JAMES C. SIMMONS
AVALON TRAVEL PUBLISHING
EMERYVILLE, CALIFORNIA

The **BIG** Book of ADVENTURE TRAVEL

JAMES C. SIMMONS
AVALON TRAVEL PUBLISHING
EMERYVILLE, CALIFORNIA

DINOSAUR DISCOVERY EXPEDITIONS

THE BIG BOOK OF ADVENTURE TRAVEL
DISCOUNT COUPON

NAME

Good for One Person on One Trip
Expires June 30, 2003

DVORAK'S KAYAK AND RAFTING EXPEDITIONS

THE BIG BOOK OF ADVENTURE TRAVEL
DISCOUNT COUPON

NAME

Good for One Person on One Trip
Expires June 30, 2003

EARTH RIVER EXPEDITIONS

THE BIG BOOK OF ADVENTURE TRAVEL
DISCOUNT COUPON

NAME

Good for One Person on One Trip
Expires June 30, 2003

EARTHWATCH

THE BIG BOOK OF ADVENTURE TRAVEL
DISCOUNT COUPON

NAME

Good for One Person on One Trip
Expires June 30, 2003

EASY RIDER TOURS

THE BIG BOOK OF ADVENTURE TRAVEL
DISCOUNT COUPON

NAME

Good for One Person on One Trip
Expires June 30, 2003

JAMES C. SIMMONS
AVALON TRAVEL PUBLISHING
EMERYVILLE, CALIFORNIA

JAMES C. SIMMONS
AVALON TRAVEL PUBLISHING
EMERYVILLE, CALIFORNIA

ECHO: THE WILDERNESS COMPANY

THE BIG BOOK OF ADVENTURE TRAVEL
DISCOUNT COUPON

NAME

Good for One Person on One Trip
Expires June 30, 2003

ECOSUMMER EXPEDITIONS

THE BIG BOOK OF ADVENTURE TRAVEL
DISCOUNT COUPON

NAME

Good for One Person on One Trip
Expires June 30, 2003

EURO-BIKE & WALKING TOURS

THE BIG BOOK OF ADVENTURE TRAVEL
DISCOUNT COUPON

NAME

Good for One Person on One Trip
Expires June 30, 2003

EUROPEDS

THE BIG BOOK OF ADVENTURE TRAVEL
DISCOUNT COUPON

NAME

Good for One Person on One Trip
Expires June 30, 2003

GEOGRAPHIC EXPEDITIONS

THE BIG BOOK OF ADVENTURE TRAVEL
DISCOUNT COUPON

NAME

Good for One Person on One Trip
Expires June 30, 2003

JAMES C. SIMMONS
AVALON TRAVEL PUBLISHING
EMERYVILLE, CALIFORNIA

JAMES C. SIMMONS
AVALON TRAVEL PUBLISHING
EMERYVILLE, CALIFORNIA

GRAND CANYON DORIES

THE BIG BOOK OF ADVENTURE TRAVEL
DISCOUNT COUPON

NAME

Good for One Person on One Trip
Expires June 30, 2003

GREAT PLAINS WILDLIFE INSTITUTE

THE BIG BOOK OF ADVENTURE TRAVEL
DISCOUNT COUPON

NAME

Good for One Person on One Trip
Expires June 30, 2003

GUNFLINT NORTHWOODS OUTFITTERS

THE BIG BOOK OF ADVENTURE TRAVEL
DISCOUNT COUPON

NAME

Good for One Person on One Trip
Expires June 30, 2003

HIMALAYAN TRAVEL

THE BIG BOOK OF ADVENTURE TRAVEL
DISCOUNT COUPON

NAME

Good for One Person on One Trip
Expires June 30, 2003

HUGHES RIVER EXPEDITIONS

THE BIG BOOK OF ADVENTURE TRAVEL
DISCOUNT COUPON

NAME

Good for One Person on One Trip
Expires June 30, 2003

The BIG Book of ADVENTURE TRAVEL

JAMES C. SIMMONS
AVALON TRAVEL PUBLISHING
EMERYVILLE, CALIFORNIA

The BIG Book of ADVENTURE TRAVEL

JAMES C. SIMMONS
AVALON TRAVEL PUBLISHING
EMERYVILLE, CALIFORNIA

HURRICANE CREEK LLAMA TREKS

THE BIG BOOK OF ADVENTURE TRAVEL
DISCOUNT COUPON
NAME

Good for One Person on One Trip
Expires June 30, 2003

HYAK WILDERNESS ADVENTURES

THE BIG BOOK OF ADVENTURE TRAVEL
DISCOUNT COUPON
NAME

Good for One Person on One Trip
Expires June 30, 2003

JOURNEYS INTERNATIONAL

THE BIG BOOK OF ADVENTURE TRAVEL
DISCOUNT COUPON
NAME

Good for One Person on One Trip
Expires June 30, 2003

JOURNEYS INTO AMERICAN INDIAN TERRITORY

THE BIG BOOK OF ADVENTURE TRAVEL
DISCOUNT COUPON
NAME

Good for One Person on One Trip
Expires June 30, 2003

KOLOTOUR BICYCLE HOLIDAYS

THE BIG BOOK OF ADVENTURE TRAVEL
DISCOUNT COUPON
NAME

Good for One Person on One Trip
Expires June 30, 2003

JAMES C. SIMMONS
AVALON TRAVEL PUBLISHING
EMERYVILLE, CALIFORNIA

JAMES C. SIMMONS
AVALON TRAVEL PUBLISHING
EMERYVILLE, CALIFORNIA

MAINE WINDJAMMER CRUISES

THE BIG BOOK OF ADVENTURE TRAVEL
DISCOUNT COUPON

NAME

Good for One Person on One Trip
Expires June 30, 2003

MICHIGAN BICYCLE TOURING

THE BIG BOOK OF ADVENTURE TRAVEL
DISCOUNT COUPON

NAME

Good for One Person on One Trip
Expires June 30, 2003

MIR CORP

THE BIG BOOK OF ADVENTURE TRAVEL
DISCOUNT COUPON

NAME

Good for One Person on One Trip
Expires June 30, 2003

MOUNTAIN TRAVEL-SOBEK

ABB00

THE BIG BOOK OF ADVENTURE TRAVEL
DISCOUNT COUPON

NAME

Good for One Person on One Trip
Expires June 30, 2003

NATURAL HABITAT ADVENTURES

THE BIG BOOK OF ADVENTURE TRAVEL
DISCOUNT COUPON

NAME

Good for One Person on One Trip
Expires June 30, 2003

JAMES C. SIMMONS

AVALON TRAVEL PUBLISHING

EMERYVILLE, CALIFORNIA

JAMES C. SIMMONS

AVALON TRAVEL PUBLISHING

EMERYVILLE, CALIFORNIA

NATURE EXPEDITIONS INTERNATIONAL

THE BIG BOOK OF ADVENTURE TRAVEL
DISCOUNT COUPON

NAME

Good for One Person on One Trip
Expires June 30, 2003

NAUTICAL HERITAGE SOCIETY

THE BIG BOOK OF ADVENTURE TRAVEL
DISCOUNT COUPON

NAME

Good for One Person on One Trip
Expires June 30, 2003

NEW ENGLAND HIKING HOLIDAYS

THE BIG BOOK OF ADVENTURE TRAVEL
DISCOUNT COUPON

NAME

Good for One Person on One Trip
Expires June 30, 2003

NEW ENGLAND OUTDOOR CENTER

THE BIG BOOK OF ADVENTURE TRAVEL
DISCOUNT COUPON

NAME

Good for One Person on One Trip
Expires June 30, 2003

NEW ZEALAND ADVENTURES

THE BIG BOOK OF ADVENTURE TRAVEL
DISCOUNT COUPON

NAME

Good for One Person on One Trip
Expires June 30, 2003

JAMES C. SIMMONS
AVALON TRAVEL PUBLISHING
EMERYVILLE, CALIFORNIA

JAMES C. SIMMONS
AVALON TRAVEL PUBLISHING
EMERYVILLE, CALIFORNIA

THE NORTHWEST PASSAGE

THE BIG BOOK OF ADVENTURE TRAVEL

DISCOUNT COUPON

NAME

Good for One Person on One Trip
Expires June 30, 2003

NORTH WIND GUIDED HIKING & WALKING TOURS

THE BIG BOOK OF ADVENTURE TRAVEL

DISCOUNT COUPON

NAME

Good for One Person on One Trip
Expires June 30, 2003

NORTHERN LIGHTS EXPEDITIONS

THE BIG BOOK OF ADVENTURE TRAVEL

DISCOUNT COUPON

NAME

Good for One Person on One Trip
Expires June 30, 2003

O.A.R.S.

THE BIG BOOK OF ADVENTURE TRAVEL

DISCOUNT COUPON

NAME

Good for One Person on One Trip
Expires June 30, 2003

OCEAN VOYAGES

THE BIG BOOK OF ADVENTURE TRAVEL

DISCOUNT COUPON

NAME

Good for One Person on One Trip
Expires June 30, 2003

JAMES C. SIMMONS

AVALON TRAVEL PUBLISHING

EMERYVILLE, CALIFORNIA

JAMES C. SIMMONS

AVALON TRAVEL PUBLISHING

EMERYVILLE, CALIFORNIA

OCEANIC SOCIETY EXPEDITIONS

THE BIG BOOK OF ADVENTURE TRAVEL

DISCOUNT COUPON

NAME

Good for One Person on One Trip
Expires June 30, 2003

ORANGE TORPEDO TRIPS

THE BIG BOOK OF ADVENTURE TRAVEL

DISCOUNT COUPON

NAME

Good for One Person on One Trip
Expires June 30, 2003

OREGON TRAIL WAGON TRAIN

THE BIG BOOK OF ADVENTURE TRAVEL

DISCOUNT COUPON

NAME

Good for One Person on One Trip
Expires June 30, 2003

OUTER EDGE EXPEDITIONS

THE BIG BOOK OF ADVENTURE TRAVEL

DISCOUNT COUPON

NAME

Good for One Person on One Trip
Expires June 30, 2003

PARAGON GUIDES

THE BIG BOOK OF ADVENTURE TRAVEL

DISCOUNT COUPON

NAME

Good for One Person on One Trip
Expires June 30, 2003

JAMES C. SIMMONS
AVALON TRAVEL PUBLISHING
EMERYVILLE, CALIFORNIA

JAMES C. SIMMONS
AVALON TRAVEL PUBLISHING
EMERYVILLE, CALIFORNIA

REI ADVENTURES

THE BIG BOOK OF ADVENTURE TRAVEL
DISCOUNT COUPON

NAME

Good for One Person on One Trip
Expires June 30, 2003

REMARKABLE JOURNEYS

THE BIG BOOK OF ADVENTURE TRAVEL
DISCOUNT COUPON

NAME

Good for One Person on One Trip
Expires June 30, 2003

REMOTE RIVER EXPEDITIONS

THE BIG BOOK OF ADVENTURE TRAVEL
DISCOUNT COUPON

NAME

Good for One Person on One Trip
Expires June 30, 2003

RIM TOURS

THE BIG BOOK OF ADVENTURE TRAVEL
DISCOUNT COUPON

NAME

Good for One Person on One Trip
Expires June 30, 2003

RIVER ODYSSEYS WEST

THE BIG BOOK OF ADVENTURE TRAVEL
DISCOUNT COUPON

NAME

Good for One Person on One Trip
Expires June 30, 2003

JAMES C. SIMMONS
AVALON TRAVEL PUBLISHING
EMERYVILLE, CALIFORNIA

JAMES C. SIMMONS
AVALON TRAVEL PUBLISHING
EMERYVILLE, CALIFORNIA

ROCKY MOUNTAIN RIVER TOURS

THE BIG BOOK OF ADVENTURE TRAVEL
DISCOUNT COUPON

NAME _____

Good for One Person on One Trip
Expires June 30, 2003

RYDER- WALKER ALPINE ADVENTURES

THE BIG BOOK OF ADVENTURE TRAVEL
DISCOUNT COUPON

NAME _____

Good for One Person on One Trip
Expires June 30, 2003

SAIL THE SAN JUANS

THE BIG BOOK OF ADVENTURE TRAVEL
DISCOUNT COUPON

NAME _____

Good for One Person on One Trip
Expires June 30, 2003

SHERI GRIFFITH EXPEDITIONS

THE BIG BOOK OF ADVENTURE TRAVEL
DISCOUNT COUPON

NAME _____

Good for One Person on One Trip
Expires June 30, 2003

SIERRA MAC RIVER TRIPS

THE BIG BOOK OF ADVENTURE TRAVEL
DISCOUNT COUPON

NAME _____

Good for One Person on One Trip
Expires June 30, 2003

JAMES C. SIMMONS
AVALON TRAVEL PUBLISHING
EMERYVILLE, CALIFORNIA

JAMES C. SIMMONS
AVALON TRAVEL PUBLISHING
EMERYVILLE, CALIFORNIA

SIERRA MADRE EXPRESS

THE BIG BOOK OF ADVENTURE TRAVEL
DISCOUNT COUPON

NAME

Good for One Person on One Trip
Expires June 30, 2003

SILVER CLOUD EXPEDITIONS

THE BIG BOOK OF ADVENTURE TRAVEL
DISCOUNT COUPON

NAME

Good for One Person on One Trip
Expires June 30, 2003

SILVER LINING TOURS

THE BIG BOOK OF ADVENTURE TRAVEL
DISCOUNT COUPON

NAME

Good for One Person on One Trip
Expires June 30, 2003

SKY TREKKING ALASKA

THE BIG BOOK OF ADVENTURE TRAVEL
DISCOUNT COUPON

NAME

Good for One Person on One Trip
Expires June 30, 2003

SLICKROCK ADVENTURES

THE BIG BOOK OF ADVENTURE TRAVEL
DISCOUNT COUPON

NAME

Good for One Person on One Trip
Expires June 30, 2003

JAMES C. SIMMONS
AVALON TRAVEL PUBLISHING
EMERYVILLE, CALIFORNIA

JAMES C. SIMMONS
AVALON TRAVEL PUBLISHING
EMERYVILLE, CALIFORNIA

SOUTHERN YOSEMITE MOUNTAIN GUIDES

THE BIG BOOK OF ADVENTURE TRAVEL
DISCOUNT COUPON

NAME

Good for One Person on One Trip
Expires June 30, 2003

ST. REGIS CANOE OUTFITTERS

THE BIG BOOK OF ADVENTURE TRAVEL
DISCOUNT COUPON

NAME

Good for One Person on One Trip
Expires June 30, 2003

STAR CLIPPERS

THE BIG BOOK OF ADVENTURE TRAVEL
DISCOUNT COUPON

NAME

Good for One Person on One Trip
Expires June 30, 2003

SUNDANCE RIVER CENTER

THE BIG BOOK OF ADVENTURE TRAVEL
DISCOUNT COUPON

NAME

Good for One Person on One Trip
Expires June 30, 2003

SUNRISE EXPEDITIONS

THE BIG BOOK OF ADVENTURE TRAVEL
DISCOUNT COUPON

NAME

Good for One Person on One Trip
Expires June 30, 2003

JAMES C. SIMMONS

AVALON TRAVEL PUBLISHING

EMERYVILLE, CALIFORNIA

JAMES C. SIMMONS

AVALON TRAVEL PUBLISHING

EMERYVILLE, CALIFORNIA

TAHOE TRIPS & TRAILS

THE BIG BOOK OF ADVENTURE TRAVEL
DISCOUNT COUPON

NAME

Good for One Person on One Trip
Expires June 30, 2003

TIMBERLINE BICYCLE TOURS

THE BIG BOOK OF ADVENTURE TRAVEL
DISCOUNT COUPON

NAME

Good for One Person on One Trip
Expires June 30, 2003

TRAINS UNLIMITED TOURS

THE BIG BOOK OF ADVENTURE TRAVEL
DISCOUNT COUPON

NAME

Good for One Person on One Trip
Expires June 30, 2003

TREK & TRAIL

THE BIG BOOK OF ADVENTURE TRAVEL
DISCOUNT COUPON

NAME

Good for One Person on One Trip
Expires June 30, 2003

TURTLE TOURS

THE BIG BOOK OF ADVENTURE TRAVEL
DISCOUNT COUPON

NAME

Good for One Person on One Trip
Expires June 30, 2003

JAMES C. SIMMONS
AVALON TRAVEL PUBLISHING
EMERYVILLE, CALIFORNIA

JAMES C. SIMMONS
AVALON TRAVEL PUBLISHING
EMERYVILLE, CALIFORNIA

USA RAFT

THE BIG BOOK OF ADVENTURE TRAVEL
DISCOUNT COUPON

NAME

Good for One Person on One Trip
Expires June 30, 2003

VERMONT BICYCLE TOURING

THE BIG BOOK OF ADVENTURE TRAVEL
DISCOUNT COUPON

NAME

Good for One Person on One Trip
Expires June 30, 2003

WHITNEY & SMITH LEGENDARY EXPEDITIONS

THE BIG BOOK OF ADVENTURE TRAVEL
DISCOUNT COUPON

NAME

Good for One Person on One Trip
Expires June 30, 2003

WILDERNESS INQUIRY

THE BIG BOOK OF ADVENTURE TRAVEL
DISCOUNT COUPON

NAME

Good for One Person on One Trip
Expires June 30, 2003

WILDERNESS TRAVEL

THE BIG BOOK OF ADVENTURE TRAVEL
DISCOUNT COUPON

NAME

Good for One Person on One Trip
Expires June 30, 2003

JAMES C. SIMMONS

AVALON TRAVEL PUBLISHING

EMERYVILLE, CALIFORNIA

JAMES C. SIMMONS

AVALON TRAVEL PUBLISHING

EMERYVILLE, CALIFORNIA

THE WORLD OUTSIDE

THE BIG BOOK OF ADVENTURE TRAVEL
DISCOUNT COUPON

NAME

Good for One Person on One Trip
Expires June 30, 2003

WORLDWIDE ADVENTURES

THE BIG BOOK OF ADVENTURE TRAVEL
DISCOUNT COUPON

NAME

Good for One Person on One Trip
Expires June 30, 2003

YELLOWSTONE LLAMAS

THE BIG BOOK OF ADVENTURE TRAVEL
DISCOUNT COUPON

NAME

Good for One Person on One Trip
Expires June 30, 2003

ZOAR OUTDOOR

THE BIG BOOK OF ADVENTURE TRAVEL
DISCOUNT COUPON

NAME

Good for One Person on One Trip
Expires June 30, 2003

JAMES C. SIMMONS
AVALON TRAVEL PUBLISHING
EMERYVILLE, CALIFORNIA

JAMES C. SIMMONS
AVALON TRAVEL PUBLISHING
EMERYVILLE, CALIFORNIA

AVALON
TRAVEL
publishing

BECAUSE TRAVEL MATTERS.

AVALON TRAVEL PUBLISHING knows that travel is more than coming and going—travel is taking part in new experiences, new ideas, and a new outlook. Our goal is to bring you complete and up-to-date information to help you make informed travel decisions.

AVALON TRAVEL GUIDES feature a combination of practicality and spirit, offering a unique traveler-to-traveler perspective perfect for an afternoon hike, around-the-world journey, or anything in between.

WWW.TRAVELMATTERS.COM

Avalon Travel Publishing guides are available
at your favorite book or travel store.

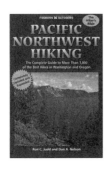

MOON HANDBOOKS

provide comprehensive coverage of a region's arts, history, land, people, and social issues in addition to detailed practical listings for accommodations, food, outdoor recreation, and entertainment. Moon Handbooks allow complete immersion in a region's culture—ideal for travelers who want to combine sightseeing with insight for an extraordinary travel experience in destinations throughout North America, Hawaii, Latin America, the Caribbean, Asia, and the Pacific.

WWW.MOON.COM

Rick Steves shows you where to travel
and how to travel—all while getting the most value for your dollar. His Back Door travel philosophy is about making friends, having fun, and avoiding tourist rip-offs.

Rick's been traveling to Europe for more than 25 years and is the author of 22 guidebooks, which have sold more than a million copies. He also hosts the award-winning public television series *Travels in Europe with Rick Steves*.

WWW.RICKSTEVES.COM

ROAD TRIP USA

Getting there is half the fun, and Road Trip USA guides are your ticket to driving adventure. Taking you off the interstates and onto less-traveled, two-lane highways, each guide is filled with fascinating trivia, historical information, photographs, facts about regional writers, and details on where to sleep and eat—all contributing to your exploration of the American road.

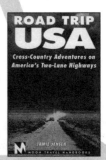

"Books so full of the pleasures of the American road, you can smell the upholstery."
~ BBC radio

WWW.ROADTRIPUSA.COM

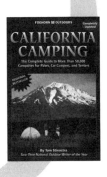
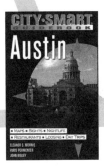

www.travelmatters.com

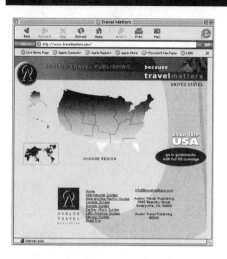

User-friendly, informative, and fun:

Because travel *matters*.

Visit our newly launched web site and explore the variety of titles and travel information available online, featuring an interactive *Road Trip USA* exhibit.

also check out:

www.ricksteves.com

The Rick Steves web site is bursting with information to boost your travel I.Q. and liven up your European adventure.

www.foghorn.com

Visit the Foghorn Outdoors web site for more information on the premier source of U.S. outdoor recreation guides.

www.moon.com

The Moon Handbooks web site offers interesting information and practical advice that ensure an extraordinary travel experience.